	a	*i*	*u*	*e*	*o*
ky	キャ kya		キュ kyu		キョ kyo
sh	シャ sha		シュ shu	シェ she	ショ sho
ch	チャ cha		チュ chu	チェ che	チョ cho
ny	ニャ nya		ニュ nyu		ニョ nyo
hy	ヒャ hya		ヒュ hyu		ヒョ hyo
my	ミャ mya		ミュ myu		ミョ myo
ry	リャ rya		リュ ryu		リョ ryo
gy	ギャ gya		ギュ gyu		ギョ gyo
j	ジャ ja		ジュ ju	ジェ je	ジョ jo
by	ビャ bya		ビュ byu		ビョ byo
py	ピャ pya		ピュ pyu		ピョ pyo

	a	*i*	*u*	*e*	*o*
w		ウィ wi		ウェ we	ウォ wo
kw	クァ kwa	クィ kwi		クェ kwe	クォ kwo
ts	ツァ tsa	ツィ tsi		ツェ tse	ツォ tso
t		ティ ti	テュ tyu		
f	ファ fa	フィ fi	フュ fyu	フェ fe	フォ fo
d		ディ di	デュ dyu		
v	ヴァ va	ヴィ vi	ヴ vu	ヴェ ve	ヴォ vo

Other less frequently used *katakana* combinations include: イェ (*ye*), グァ (*gwa*), トゥ (*tu*), ドゥ (*du*), ヴュ (*vyu*).

GENKI

AN INTEGRATED COURSE IN ELEMENTARY JAPANESE
THIRD EDITION

初級日本語［げんき］

げんき

［第3版］ II

坂野永理・池田庸子・大野裕・品川恭子・渡嘉敷恭子
Eri Banno / Yoko Ikeda / Yutaka Ohno / Chikako Shinagawa / Kyoko Tokashiki

the japan times PUBLISHING

初級日本語 げんき II　GENKI: An Integrated Course in Elementary Japanese II

1999 年 10 月 20 日　初版発行
2011 年 10 月 20 日　第 2 版発行
2020 年 10 月 5 日　第 3 版発行
2021 年 1 月 20 日　第 3 刷発行

JASRAC 出 2005393-002
著　者：坂野永理・池田庸子・大野裕・品川恭子・渡嘉敷恭子
発行者：伊藤秀樹
発行所：株式会社 ジャパンタイムズ出版
　　　　〒 102-0082 東京都千代田区一番町 2-2　一番町第二 TG ビル 2F
　　　　電話 (050)3646-9500（出版営業部）
ISBN978-4-7890-1732-9
本書の無断複製は著作権法上の例外を除き禁じられています。

First edition: October 1999
Second edition: October 2011
Third edition: October 2020
3rd printing: January 2021

Illustrations: Noriko Udagawa and Reiko Maruyama
Photos: Imagenavi, Pixta, and Photolibrary
English translations and copyreading: EXIM International, Inc.
Narrators: Miho Nagahori, Kosuke Katayama, Toshitada Kitagawa, Miharu Muto, and Rachel Walzer
Recordings: The English Language Education Council, Inc.
Typesetting: guild
Cover art and editorial design: Nakayama Design Office (Gin-o Nakayama and Akihito Kaneko)
Printing: Nikkei Printing Inc.

Published by The Japan Times Publishing, Ltd.
2F Ichibancho Daini TG Bldg., 2-2 Ichibancho, Chiyoda-ku, Tokyo 102-0082, Japan
Phone: 050-3646-9500

Website: https://jtpublishing.co.jp/
Genki-Online: https://genki3.japantimes.co.jp/

ISBN978-4-7890-1732-9

Printed in Japan

はじめに
● ●

　本書は『初級日本語げんき』の改訂第3版です。『げんき』は長年、世界中の日本語学習者に愛用されてきました。

　『げんき』は関西外国語大学で教えていた同僚の私たちが、教師にとっても学習者にとっても使いやすく、楽しく日本語を学べる教科書を目指して作ったものです。テキストのほか、ワークブック、音声教材、教師用指導書など必要な教材が揃っています。そして、豊富なイラストで楽しく練習しながら、基本から応用へと無理なく日本語能力が身に付く教材になっています。また、『げんき』では日本に留学しているメアリーとその仲間のストーリーが展開されます。彼女たちは多くの学習者に日本語学習の友達として愛されてきました。

　社会の変化、学習者の多様化に伴い、『げんき』も変化してきました。この改訂版では、語彙、練習などの改訂に加え、教科書の電子版や音声アプリを提供することにしました。また、登場人物の多様性にも留意しました。私たちが、初版から目指していた「学びやすさ」「教えやすさ」が、さらに改善できたと感じています。

　この改訂は『げんき』を使用してくださった多くの先生方や学習者の方々の貴重なご意見なしではかないませんでした。心より感謝いたします。また、本書のトレードマークとも言えるイラストを描いてくださった宇田川のり子さん、愛らしいメアリーさんの声をご担当の永堀美穂さん、ジャパンタイムズ出版の皆様、そして、初版以来ずっと労を注いでくださったジャパンタイムズ出版の関戸千明さんに、著者一同心より感謝いたします。さらに新しくなった『げんき』で、いっそう楽しく日本語を学んでいただけることを心から願っています。

2020年9月　著者一同

Preface

This book is the third edition of *GENKI: An Integrated Course in Elementary Japanese*, which has long been a favorite textbook for Japanese-language learners around the world.

We were inspired to create *GENKI* during our days as language instructors at Kansai Gaidai University. Our idea was to conceive a textbook that not only would be easy to use for both teachers and students, but also would make learning Japanese fun. We also developed workbooks, audio material, a teacher's manual, and other resources for making the most of the textbook lessons.

By offering many fun illustrations and other user-friendly features, *GENKI* provides a stress-free approach for learners to advance their Japanese skills from the basics to applied communication. To help learners more closely identify with the material presented, *GENKI* is framed as the story of Mary, an international student living in Japan, and her friends and acquaintances. For many learners, these characters have come to be bosom buddies on their Japanese language journey.

Over the years, *GENKI* has evolved to stay in step with the changing times and the diversification of learners. The third edition continues this evolution with enhancements such as revisions to vocabulary and practices, and with the addition of an e-book version and an audio app. Also, the cast of characters has been made more diverse. We believe that these changes have brought *GENKI* closer to our original goal by making it even easier to study and teach.

This new edition was made possible by the valuable feedback provided by many teachers and learners who have used *GENKI*. We are also very grateful to Noriko Udagawa, whose illustrations have become a trademark feature of this series, Miho Nagahori, who provided the adorable voice of Mary, and The Japan Times Publishing's Chiaki Sekido, who has tirelessly edited *GENKI* from day one. We hope that this edition and its new enhancements will make studying Japanese more fun than ever before!

The Authors
September 2020

初級日本語 [げんき] II

もくじ

| 会話・文法編 | Conversation and Grammar |
| かい わ　ぶん ぼう へん | |

読み書き編 よみかきへん Reading and Writing

Introduction

I What's *GENKI*?

GENKI: An Integrated Course in Elementary Japanese is a study resource for people who are starting to learn Japanese. The book is intended mainly for use in university courses, but is also effective for high school students and adults who are beginning to learn Japanese either at school or on their own. It is designed to comprehensively build communication competencies across all four skill areas—listening, speaking, reading, and writing. Emphasis has been placed on balancing accuracy, fluency, and complexity so that students using the material will not end up speaking accurately yet in a stilted manner, or fluently but employing only simple grammatical structures.

GENKI consists of 23 lessons, divided into two volumes of textbooks and workbooks. Vol. 1 contains Lessons 1–12, and Vol. 2 covers Lessons 13–23. The audio material of the textbooks and workbooks can be downloaded and played on mobile devices by using an app called OTO Navi. Information on how to acquire this app can be found on the last page of this book.

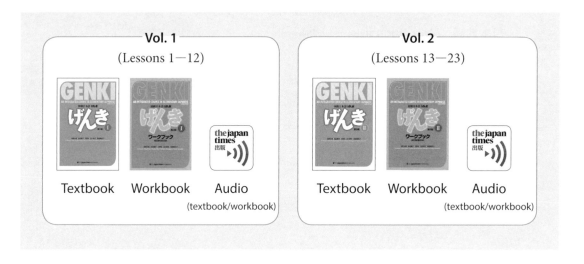

Completion of Vol. 1 should place you at a skill level on par with JLPT N5 or CEFR A1. Vol. 2 is intended to further raise your abilities to N4 or A2.

II Textbook Structure

Each textbook volume is divided into two main sections: Conversation and Grammar, and Reading and Writing.

> **Conversation and Grammar:**
> Develops speaking and listening skills while building grammar knowledge and vocabulary.
> **Reading and Writing:**
> Cultivates reading and writing skills, including mastery of *hiragana*, *katakana*, and kanji.

Textbook 2 presents Lessons 13–23 in both of those sections. The overall structure of Textbook 2 is as follows.

GENKI Textbook Vol. 2   ♪ Audio files available

Conversation and Grammar	Lessons 13-23	Lesson Goals (In this lesson, we will...) **Dialogue** ♪ **Vocabulary** (50-60 words per lesson) ♪ **Grammar** **Practice** ♪
		(Additional Information/Tasks) ● Culture Notes ● Useful Expressions ● Let's Find Out (Research topics)
Reading and Writing	Lessons 13-23	Kanji List (14-16 kanji per lesson) Kanji Practice / Reading Practice ♪ / Writing Practice
Appendix	Grammar Index Vocabulary Index 1 & 2 (J-E / E-J) Map of Japan Numbers Conjugation Chart	

III How to Use *GENKI*

1. Conversation and Grammar / Reading and Writing

As noted earlier, this textbook is divided into two main sections: Conversation and Grammar, and Reading and Writing. For each lesson, first go through the lesson in the Conversation and Grammar section, and then proceed to the corresponding lesson in the Reading and Writing section. However, if you do not need to work on reading and writing, you can study the Conversation and Grammar section on a stand-alone basis.

2. Orthography

The Conversation and Grammar section is written in a natural mix of *hiragana*, *katakana* and kanji in a way normally seen in the newspapers and books. The readings of all kanji are given in *hiragana* so that this section can be studied by those who do not need to learn kanji. The Reading and Writing section does not provide readings in *hiragana* for kanji already studied.

3. Using the Conversation and Grammar section

● Dialogue

The dialogues contain the lesson's new learning targets. Learn them after studying the vocabulary and grammar items presented in the lesson.

❶ Every lesson begins with a preview of the skills it will teach.

❷ Each dialogue has two audio recordings. The first is recorded as a normal conversation, and the second adds a pause after each sentence for practice.

● Vocabulary

This is a list of the words and expressions that appear in the dialogues and practices. A good way to learn them is to repeatedly go over a handful at a time.

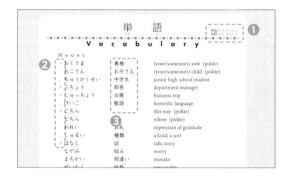

❶ There are two audio recordings of the vocabulary and English translations. The first presents each Japanese entry followed by its English equivalent, and the second is in the opposite order. Use the recordings to help you learn the words with your ears.

❷ Words that appear in the dialogues are marked with an asterisk.

❸ There is no need to memorize the kanji listed.

● Grammar / Expression Notes

The Grammar section explains the grammar items presented in the lesson. The Expression Notes at the end provide commentary on expressions and words not included among the grammar points.

● Practice

The Practice section contains exercises dealing with the points covered in the Grammar section. The workbook also provides practices for the grammar points covered in the lesson. First do the practices in the textbook, and then check your mastery by doing the ones in the workbook.

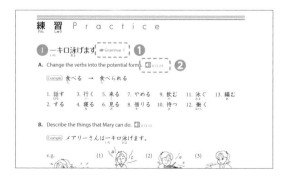

❶ The serial number of the corresponding grammar item is listed next to each practice's heading. Be sure to read the grammar explanation before doing the practice.

❷ Exercises marked with a speaker icon 🔊 have audio recordings of the cues and responses. Listen to the recording as you practice.

● Additional Information

Some lessons include the following extra content.

> **Useful Expressions:** Lists of words and expressions associated with a particular topic.
>
> **Culture Notes:** Commentary on Japanese culture, lifestyles, etc.
>
> **Let's Find Out:** Tasks that require you look up certain information on Japan.

Useful Expressions	Culture Notes	Let's Find Out
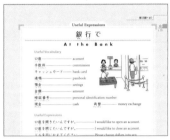		

4. Using the Reading and Writing section

● Kanji List

Each lesson presents a table of kanji at the beginning. Try learning the characters by repeatedly going over a few at a time. Readings and words that are shaded should be memorized.

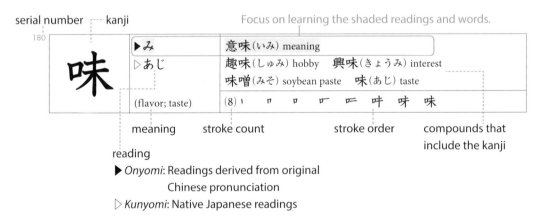

serial number ⋯⋯ kanji

Focus on learning the shaded readings and words.

180 味

▶ み	意味 (いみ) meaning
▷ あじ	趣味 (しゅみ) hobby　興味 (きょうみ) interest 味噌 (みそ) soybean paste　味 (あじ) taste
(flavor; taste)	(8) 丨　⼝　⼝　⼝⁻　⼝⁼　咊　味　味

meaning　stroke count　　　　stroke order　　compounds that include the kanji

reading

▶ *Onyomi*: Readings derived from original Chinese pronunciation

▷ *Kunyomi*: Native Japanese readings

The workbook's Reading and Writing section includes kanji practice sheets.

146	物	物	物	物					
147	鳥	鳥	鳥	鳥					
148									

● Kanji Practice（漢字の練習）

Kanji Practice A presents new kanji compounds. New readings of kanji that have been previously introduced are shown in bold face. Kanji Practice B lists kanji words that are to be reviewed, which will appear in the main text of that lesson.

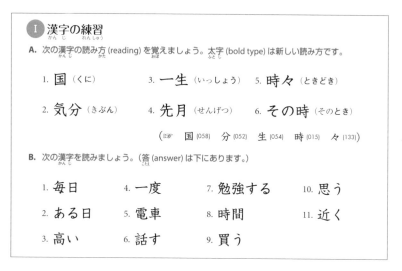

● Reading Practice

The reading practices assume that you have learned the grammar points and vocabulary presented in the corresponding lesson in the Conversation and Grammar section.

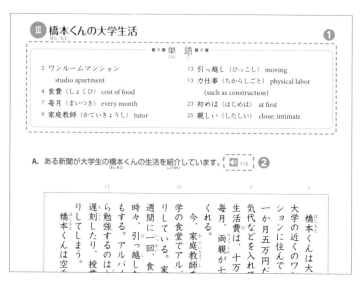

❶English translations are provided for words not yet covered.

❷An audio recording is available for each reading.

● Writing Practice（書く練習）

Write about the topic provided using the expressions and kanji you have learned.

> Ⅳ 書く練習
> れんしゅう
>
> **A.** あなたのおもしろい経験を書きましょう。
> けいけん
>
> **B.** 日本や他の (other) 国・町に行って、何にびっくりしましたか。経験について書きましょ
> ほか けいけん
> う。その後、グループで話しましょう。

5. Appendix

● Grammar Index

This index lists the Grammar entries of all lessons, as well as grammatical items from Expression Notes, Useful Expressions, and Culture Notes.

● Vocabulary Index (J-E / E-J)

The vocabulary entries presented in this textbook are listed in Vocabulary Index 1 (a Japanese-English index in *a-i-u-e-o* order) and Vocabulary Index 2 (an English-Japanese index in alphabetical order).

● Map of Japan / Numbers / Conjugation Chart

For your reference, the appendix also includes a map of Japan with a list of all prefectures, a table of Japanese numbers/counters that shows changes in pronunciation, and a chart of verb conjugations.

Fonts Used in This Book

The Japanese text in this book is mainly set in the Textbook font, which closely resembles handwriting. Note that there are many different fonts used in Japan (a few examples are shown below), and that the shape of a particular character can vary depending on the font used. For example, certain fonts depict the two strokes of さ as a single stroke.

Example								
	Textbook font	さ	う	り	ふ	心	道	入
	Mincho font	さ	う	り	ふ	心	道	入
	Gothic font	さ	う	り	ふ	心	道	入
	Handwriting	さ	う	り	ふ	心	道	入

Ⓥ Other *GENKI* Resources

● GENKI-Online (https://genki3.japantimes.co.jp/)

GENKI-Online is a website providing additional *GENKI* materials for both teachers and learners.

● GENKI Apps

The following apps are also available to assist your study of *GENKI*.

GENKI Vocab for 3rd Ed. (iOS/Android)

Digital vocabulary flashcards that help you learn all the words and expressions studied in *GENKI* I and II.

GENKI Kanji for 3rd Ed. (iOS/Android)

Digital flashcards that aid your study of the readings and shapes of 317 kanji covered by *GENKI* I and II. The cards feature around 1,100 kanji words, plus illustrations that help you memorize kanji shapes.

GENKI Conjugation Cards (iOS/Android)

An app for mastering the conjugation of verbs and adjectives. Audio recordings, example sentences, and illustrations help you to efficiently learn 28 conjugation patterns.

Note: The apps for the 3rd edition will be subsequently released, starting in October 2020. See GENKI-Online or The Japan Times Publishing website for updates.

Main Characters in This Book

登場人物紹介
とう じょう じん ぶつ しょう かい

メアリー

たけし

[友だちと先生]
  とも　　せんせい

ジョン

ソラ

ゆい

ロバート

山下先生
やましたせんせい

ナオミ

カルロス

ヤスミン

ウデイ

健
けん

[ホストファミリー]

お母さん
かあ

お父さん
とう

まな

会話・文法編
かい　わ　ぶん　ぼう　へん
Conversation and Grammar

L E S S O N 13

第13課

アルバイト探し Looking for a Part-time Job

In this lesson, we will...

- ● Say what we can or cannot do
- ● Give several reasons
- ● Express first impressions
- ● Talk about part-time job experience

会 話 D i a l o g u e

I John calls the restaurant Little Asia. 🔊 K13-01/02

1 店　長： はい、「リトル・アジア」です。

2 ジョン： 私、ジョン・ワンと申します。アルバイト募集の広告を見たんですが。

3 店　長： そうですか。じゃあ、会って、話しましょうか。今日店に来られますか。

4 ジョン： 今日はちょっと行けないんですが、あしたなら行けると思います。

5 店　長： そうですか。今日はだめですか。じゃあ、あしたの一時ごろはどうで

6 　　　　 すか。

7 ジョン： 一時ですね。わかりました。

II At the restaurant. 🔊 K13-03/04

1 店　長： ワンさんはどうしてこのアルバイトに興味があるんですか。

2 ジョン： おもしろそうですから。いろいろな人に会えるし、日本語も使えるし。

3 店　長： 日本で働いたことがありますか。

4 ジョン： はい。コンビニのアルバイトならしたことがあります。

5 店　長： あしたから始められますか。

6 ジョン： はい。よろしくお願いします。

7 店　長： がんばってください。

Ⅲ Professor Yamashita comes to Little Asia. 🔊 K13-05/06

1 ジョン： 　　いらっしゃいませ。あ、山下先生。

2 山下先生： 　ジョンさん。ここでアルバイトをしているんですか。

3 ジョン： 　　ええ。一週間に三日働いています。

4 山下先生： 　そうですか。どれがおいしいですか。

5 ジョン： 　　このカレーが一番人気がありますよ。

6 山下先生： 　おいしそうですね。

7 　　　　　　　じゃあ、食べてみます。

Ⅰ

Manager: Hello, this is Little Asia.

John: My name is John Wang. I saw your part-time wanted ad.

Manager: I see. Well, shall we meet and have a talk? Can you come to the restaurant today?

John: I cannot come today, but if it's tomorrow, I think I can come.

Manager: I see. Today is no good . . . All right. How about one o'clock tomorrow?

John: One o'clock. Okay, I've got it.

Ⅱ

Manager: Mr. Wang, why are you interested in this job?

John: It seems interesting. I can meet various people, and I can use Japanese . . .

Manager: Have you worked in Japan before?

John: Yes. I've worked part-time at a convenient store.

Manager: Can you start tomorrow?

John: Yes. I'll do my best.

Manager: Good luck.

Ⅲ

John: Welcome. Oh, Professor Yamashita.

Prof. Yamashita: John. Do you work here?

John: Yes. I work three days a week.

Prof. Yamashita: I see. Which one is good?

John: This curry is the most popular one.

Prof. Yamashita: It looks good. Well, I will try it.

単語
たんご

🔊 K13-07 (J-E)
K13-08 (E-J)

V o c a b u l a r y

N o u n s

おとな	大人	adult
べんごし	弁護士	lawyer
* わたくし	私	I (formal)
* カレー		curry
こうちゃ	紅茶	black tea
きもの	着物	kimono; Japanese traditional dress
セーター		sweater
がっき	楽器	musical instrument
からて	空手	karate
ゴルフ		golf
バイク		motorcycle
ぞう	象	elephant
からだ	体	body
がいこくご	外国語	foreign language
ことば	言葉	language
ぶんぽう	文法	grammar
アプリ		application
アパート		apartment; smaller apartment building
マンション		larger apartment building; condominium
くうこう	空港	airport
* みせ	店	shop; store
ぶっか	物価	consumer prices
* こうこく	広告	advertisement
* ぼしゅう	募集	recruitment
やくそく	約束	promise; appointment

い - a d j e c t i v e s

うれしい		glad
かなしい	悲しい	sad
きびしい	厳しい	strict
きぶんがわるい	気分が悪い	to feel sick

＊Words that appear in the dialogue

会
L13

からい	辛い	hot and spicy; salty
すごい		incredible; awesome
ちかい	近い	close; near

な-adjectives
* いろいろ（な）		various; different kinds of
しあわせ（な）	幸せ	happy (lasting happiness)
* だめ（な）		no good

U-verbs
あむ	編む	to knit （〜を）
* がんばる	頑張る	to do one's best; to try hard
なく	泣く	to cry
みがく	磨く	to brush (teeth); to polish （〜を）
やくそくをまもる	約束を守る	to keep a promise

Irregular Verb
| かんどうする | 感動する | to be moved/touched (by . . .) （〜に） |

Adverbs and Other Expressions
〜かい	〜回	. . . times
〜キロ		. . . kilometers; . . . kilograms
ぜんぶ	全部	all
* 〜ともうします	〜と申します	my name is . . .
とくに	特に	especially

Numbers (used to count days)
いちにち	一日	one day
ふつか	二日	two days
* みっか	三日	three days
よっか	四日	four days
いつか	五日	five days
むいか	六日	six days
なのか	七日	seven days
ようか	八日	eight days
ここのか	九日	nine days
とおか	十日	ten days

文法 Grammar
ぶん ぼう

1 Potential Verbs

We use the potential verb to say that someone "can" or "has the ability to" do something, or that something is "possible."

私 は日本語が話せます。
わたし にほんご はな
I can speak Japanese.

私 は泳げないんです。
わたし およ
(The truth is) I cannot swim.

雨 が降ったので、海 に行けませんでした。
あめ ふ うみ い
We could not go to the beach, because it rained.

We make potential verbs using the rules listed below:

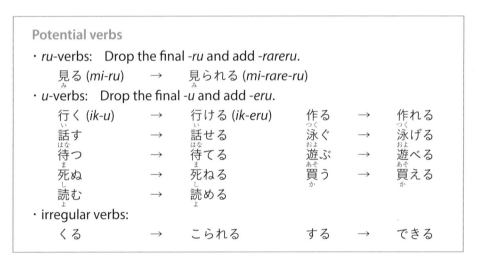

Potential verbs

· *ru*-verbs: Drop the final *-ru* and add *-rareru*.

　　　見る (*mi-ru*)　　　　→　　　　見られる (*mi-rare-ru*)
　　　み　　　　　　　　　　　　　　み

· *u*-verbs: Drop the final *-u* and add *-eru*.

行く (*ik-u*)	→	行ける (*ik-eru*)	作る	→	作れる
話す	→	話せる	泳ぐ	→	泳げる
待つ	→	待てる	遊ぶ	→	遊べる
死ぬ	→	死ねる	買う	→	買える
読む	→	読める			

· irregular verbs:

　　　くる　　　　　　→　　　　こられる　　　　する　　　→　　　できる

You can think of the *u*-verb conjugation in terms of a *hiragana* table:

	行 い	話 はな	待 ま	死 し	読 よ	作 つく	泳 およ	遊 あそ	買 か	
negative	か	さ	た	な	ま	ら	が	ば	わ	〜ない
stem	き	し	ち	に	み	り	ぎ	び	い	〜ます
affirmative	く	す	つ	ぬ	む	る	ぐ	ぶ	う	= Dictionary form
potential	け	せ	て	ね	め	れ	げ	べ	え	〜る

会

L13

The potential verbs for *ru*-verbs are longer than those for *u*-verbs. (Compare 見られる for 見る, and 乗れる for 乗る.) There actually are shorter, alternative potential verbs for *ru*-verbs and the irregular verb くる, which use the suffix *-reru*, instead of *-rareru*. These *ra*-less forms were once considered substandard, but are now used without hesitation by most speakers.[1]

With and without *ra*			potential forms	*ra*-less potential forms
ru-verbs:	出る	→	出られる	出れる
	見る	→	見られる	見れる
irregular verbs:	くる	→	こられる	これる

Potential verbs themselves conjugate as regular *ru*-verbs. The table below summarizes the conjugation pattern of potential verbs.

Conjugation of potential verbs				
e.g. 書ける	short forms		long forms	
	affirmative	negative	affirmative	negative
[Present]	書ける	書けない	書けます	書けません
[Past]	書けた	書けなかった	書けました	書けませんでした
[*Te*-form]	書けて			

Those verbs that take the particle を can take either を or が when they are turned into the potential, as in the first sentence above. できる, the potential counterpart of the verb する, is somewhat special, and takes が almost all the time. All particles other than を remain the same when the verb is turned into the potential.

Particles in potential sentences
· verbs with を:
漢字を読む → 漢字が読める or 漢字を読める
· する—できる:
仕事をする → 仕事ができる (仕事をできる is much less commonly used.)
· verbs with particles other than を:
山に登る → 山に登れる (No particle change involved.)

---

[1] The *ra*-less forms are still not sanctioned by school grammar. Grammar and spelling checker apps suggest rewrites for these *ra*-less forms.

You can also express the idea of "can do" using a more complex construction: verb dictionary form ＋ことができる.[2]

　　メアリーさんはギターを弾くことができます。　　(Compare: ギターが弾けます)
　　　　　　　　　　ひ
　　Mary can play the guitar.

　　このアパートでは犬を飼うことができません。　　(Compare: 犬が飼えません)
　　　　　　　　いぬ　か
　　You cannot keep dogs in this apartment.

2 ～し

As we learned in Lesson 9, to give the reason for something, we can use the conjunction から.

　　日本語はおもしろいから、日本語の授業が大好きです。
　　にほんご　　　　　　　　にほんご　じゅぎょう　だいす
　　I really like my Japanese class, because Japanese is interesting.

When you want to mention not just one but two (or more) reasons, you can use し in place of から. し usually follows a predicate in the short form.[3]

> (reason₁) し、(reason₂) し、(situation)。

　　日本語はおもしろいし、先生はいいし、私は日本語の授業が大好きです。
　　にほんご　　　　　　　　せんせい　　　　　わたし　にほんご　じゅぎょう　だいす
　　I really like my Japanese class, because Japanese is interesting, and our teacher is good.

　　Ａ：国に帰りたいですか。
　　　　くに　かえ
　　　　Do you want to go back home?

　　Ｂ：いいえ、日本の生活は楽しいし、いい友だちがいるし、帰りたくないです。
　　　　　　にほん　せいかつ　たの　　　　　　とも　　　　　　かえ
　　　　No. Life here in Japan is good, and I have good friends here, so I don't want to go back.

When you use just one し clause, you imply that it is not the only reason for the situation.

　　物価が安いし、この町の生活は楽です。
　　ぶっか　やす　　　　　まち　せいかつ　らく
　　Life in this city is easygoing. Things are inexpensive, for one thing.

---

[2] When you have an を-taking verb in the ことができる construction, you keep the original particle を, unlike with the potential verbs.

[3] In the very polite speech style, し can also follow the long forms.
　　私は来年も日本語を勉強します。日本が好きですし、日本語はおもしろいですし。
　　わたし　らいねん　にほんご　べんきょう　　　にほん　す　　　　にほんご
　　I will study Japanese next year, too. I like Japan, and what is more, the Japanese language is interesting.

You can also add the し clauses in a separate sentence, providing reasons for the situation just mentioned.

山下先生はいい先生です。教えるのが上手だし、親切だし。
やましたせんせい　せんせい　　　　おし　　　　じょうず　　　しんせつ
Professor Yamashita is a great teacher. He is good at teaching, and he is kind.

Note that you find だ in the present tense with な-adjectives and nouns, but not with い-adjectives.

い-adjectives:	おもしろいし	（×おもしろいだし）
な-adjectives:	好きだし	（×好きし）
noun＋です:	学生だし	（×学生し）

3 ～そうです (It looks like . . .)

We add そうです to い- and な-adjective bases to say that something "seemingly" has those properties.[4] When we say ～そうです, we are guessing what something is like on the basis of our impressions.

このりんごはおいしそうです。	*This apple looks delicious.*
あしたは天気がよさそうです。	*It looks like the weather will be fine tomorrow.*
メアリーさんは元気そうでした。	*Mary looks like she was doing well.*

To form ～そうです sentences with い-adjectives, you drop the final い; with な-adjectives, you just drop な. The only exception is the い-adjective いい, which changes to よさ before そう.

い-adjectives:	おいしい	→	おいしそうです
(exception)	いい	→	よさそうです
な-adjectives:	元気（な）	→	元気そうです

---

[4] You can also use そうです with a verb stem to describe your impression or guess.
このセーターは家で洗えそうです。 (With 洗える, the potential form of 洗う.)
It looks like this sweater is washable at home.
The impression you express may be an event about to happen.
雨が降りそうです。 *It looks like it will rain.*

You can use そうです with negative adjectives, too. The negative ending ない is changed to なさ before そう.[5]

この本は難しく<u>なさそう</u>です。
This book does not look difficult.

ソラさんはテニスが上手じゃ<u>なさそう</u>です。
It does not look like Sora is good at tennis.

You can use the adjective ＋ そう combination to qualify a noun. そう is a な-adjective, thus we say そうな before a noun.

暖か<u>そうな</u>セーターを着ています。
She is wearing a warm-looking sweater.

In many そうです sentences, the guesswork is done on the basis of visual impressions. It is wrong, however, to assume that そう is linked only to the visual medium. Rather, we use そうです *when we lack conclusive evidence.* (For example, we say an apple is おいしそう *before* we have had the chance to taste it. Once we have tasted it, we can conclude whether it really is おいしい.) With an adjective for which visual evidence is crucial, such as きれいな, we do not use そう and say ✕ きれいそうです for something looking pretty; if we can see it, we already have enough evidence to conclude that it is pretty.

4 ～てみる

You can use the *te*-form of a verb plus the helping verb みる to express the idea of "doing something tentatively," or "trying something." You are not sure what the outcome of your action will be, but you dare to do it and see what effect it might have.

漢字がわからなかったので、日本人の友だちに聞いてみました。
I did not know the kanji, so I tried asking a Japanese friend of mine.

Ａ：この本、おもしろかったですよ。   *This book was interesting.*

Ｂ：じゃあ、読んでみます。   *Okay, I will take a look at it.*

みる comes from the verb 見る, and conjugates as a regular *ru*-verb. Unlike the main verb 見る, however, ～てみる is always written in *hiragana*.

---

[5] Another option is to use the negative of そうです instead of negating the adjective, as in:
この本は難し<u>そうじゃないです</u>。
ソラさんはテニスが上手<u>そうじゃないです</u>。

5 なら

You can say "X (noun) なら Y (predicate)" when you think that the predicate Y applies *only to* X and is not more generally valid. The main ideas of a なら sentence, in other words, are contrast (as in Situation 1) and limitation (as in Situation 2).

Situation 1

A：ブラジルに行ったことがありますか。

Have you ever been to Brazil?

B：チリなら行ったことがありますが、ブラジルは行ったことがありません。[6]

I've been to Chile, but never to Brazil. (If the question were about Chile, yes, but Brazil, no.)

Situation 2

A：日本語が読めますか。

Can you read Japanese?

B：ひらがななら読めます。

If it is (written) in hiragana, yes.

なら introduces a sentence that says something "positive" about the item that is contrasted. In the first situation above, なら puts Chile in a positive light, and in contrast with Brazil, which the question was originally about. In the second situation, a smaller part, namely *hiragana*, is brought up and contrasted with a larger area, namely, the language as a whole.

6 一週間に三回

You can describe the frequency of events over a period of time by using the following framework.

(period) に (frequency)	(frequency) *per* (period)

Q：一週間に何回髪を洗いますか。　　　*How many times a week do you shampoo?*

A：私は一週間に三回髪を洗います。　　*I shampoo three times a week.*

---

[6] You can optionally keep the particle に before なら in this example and say チリになら. Particles such as に, で, and から may, but do not have to, intervene between the noun and なら, while は, が, and を never go with なら.

一日に三時間ぐらいゲームをします。

いちにち　　さんじかん

I play games for about three hours a day.

一か月に三日か四日、アルバイトをします。

いっ　げつ　みっか　よっか

I work part-time three or four days a month.

表現ノート
ひょう　げん

ギターを弾く ▶ Different verbs are used to express the playing of different musical instruments.
ひ

For stringed and keyboard instruments:

ギターを弾く ひ	*to play the guitar*
ピアノを弾く ひ	*to play the piano*

For wind instruments:

サックスを吹く ふ	*to play the saxophone*

For percussion instruments:

ドラムをたたく	*to play the drum*

When referring to musical instruments in general, やる and できる (for potential) are usually used.

何か楽器ができますか。 なに　がっき	*Can you play any instruments?*
何か楽器をやりますか。 なに　がっき	*Do you play any instruments?*

楽しく/上手に ▶ Both い-adjectives and な-adjectives can modify verbs as ad-
たの　じょうず
verbs. With い-adjectives, the final い is dropped and く is added. With な-adjectives, に is added.

日本語のクラスは楽しいです。 にほんご　たの	*The Japanese class is fun.*
毎日日本語を楽しく勉強しています。 まいにちにほんご　たの　べんきょう	*I enjoy studying Japanese every day.*
ロバートさんは料理が上手です。 りょうり　じょうず	*Robert is good at cooking.*
ロバートさんは上手に料理ができます。 じょうず　りょうり	*Robert cooks well.*

練 習 P r a c t i c e
れん しゅう

I 一キロ泳げます 👉Grammar 1
いち およ

A. Change the verbs into the potential forms. 🔊 K13-09

Example 食べる → 食べられる
た　　　　　　た

1. 話す　　3. 行く　　5. 来る　　7. やめる　　9. 飲む　　11. 泳ぐ　　13. 編む
　はな　　　　い　　　　く　　　　　　　　　　の　　　　　およ　　　　　あ
2. する　　4. 寝る　　6. 見る　　8. 借りる　　10. 待つ　　12. 働く
　　　　　　ね　　　　み　　　　か　　　　　　　ま　　　　　はたら

B. Describe the things that Mary can do. 🔊 K13-10

Example メアリーさんは一キロ泳げます。
　　　　　　　　　　　いち　　およ

e.g.

1 km

(1)

Japanese song

(2)

バイオリン (violin)

(3)

(4)

(5)

(6)

(7)

(8)

sweater

(9)

many kanji

(10)

early in the morning

(11)

hot bath

C. Pair Work—Ask if your partner can do the above.

Example A：一キロ泳げますか。
          いち   およ

          B：はい、泳げます。／いいえ、泳げません。
                およ   およ

D. Pair Work—You meet a person on a blind date. To get to know them, ask if they can do the following things and take notes. Add your own questions. After asking the questions, decide if you want to go on a date with them again.

Questions	Your partner's information		
speak foreign languages?	Yes / No	(what language?)	
drive a car?	Yes / No	(good?)	
cook?	Yes / No	(what dish?)	
play tennis?	Yes / No	(good?)	

E. Pair Work—Ask if your partner could do the following things as a child. Expand your conversation.

Example 泳ぐ
       およ
  → A：子供の時、泳げましたか。
         こども とき およ
      B：はい、泳げました。
            およ
      A：どのぐらい泳げましたか。
              およ
      B：100メートルぐらいです。
      A：すごいですね。今も100メートル泳げますか。
               いま   およ
      B：たぶん泳げると思います。
           およ   おも

1. 自転車に乗る
  じてんしゃ の
2. 辛い料理を食べる
  から りょうり た
3. サッカーをする

4. ピアノを弾く
        ひ
5. 外国語を話す
  がいこくご はな
6. 夜一人でトイレに行く
  よる ひとり   い

F. Answer the questions using the potential verb in the negative.  K13-11

Example Q：着物を買いましたか。(too expensive)
A：いいえ、高すぎて買えませんでした。

1. スリランカ (Sri Lanka) のカレーを食べましたか。(too spicy)
2. 宿題をしましたか。(too difficult)
3. 温泉に入りましたか。(too hot)
4. きのう出かけましたか。(too busy)
5. 漢字を全部覚えましたか。(too many)
6. 海で泳ぎましたか。(too cold)

G. Group Activity—"What Is It?" Game

The class is divided into two or more groups. The instructor shows the name of a place to the representative of each group. The rest of the group members ask their representative whether one can do certain things there and guess the place. The representative can answer the questions only with はい or いいえ. The first group to guess correctly gets a point. Change representatives and repeat.

Example

図 書 館
（と　し ょ　か ん）

Sample Questions:
そこで食べられますか。　→　いいえ。
本が読めますか。　→　はい。
図書館ですか。　→　そうです。

Ⅱ　物価が高いし、人がたくさんいるし　☞Grammar 2

A. Answer the questions using 〜し〜し. Examine the ideas in the cues and decide whether you want to answer in the affirmative or in the negative.  K13-12

Example Q：日本に住みたいですか。
A：（物価が高いです。人がたくさんいます。）
→　物価が高いし、人がたくさんいるし、住みたくないです。

1. 今週は忙しいですか。

   （試験があります。宿題がたくさんあります。）

2. 新しいアパートはいいですか。

   （空港に近いです。便利です。）

3. 経済の授業を取りますか。

   （先生は厳しいです。長いレポートを書かなきゃいけません。）

4. 旅行は楽しかったですか。

   （食べ物がおいしくなかったです。言葉がわかりませんでした。）

5. 今晩、パーティーに行きますか。

   （ちょっと気分が悪いです。きのうもパーティーに行きました。）

6. 日本語の新聞が読めますか。

   （漢字が読めません。文法がわかりません。）

7. 一人で旅行ができますか。

   （日本語が話せます。もう大人です。）

8. 田中さんが好きですか。

   （うそをつきます。約束を守りません。）

B. Answer the following questions and add reasons for your answer.

Example Q：日本の生活は楽しいですか。

A：はい、楽しいです。友だちがたくさんいるし、みんなは親切だし。

1. このごろ忙しいですか。
2. 今、幸せですか。
3. 来学期も日本語の授業を取りますか。
4. 日本に住みたいですか。
5. 日本語の授業は大変ですか。

Ⅲ おいしそうです ☛Grammar 3

A. Describe the following pictures using 〜そう.  K13-13

Example このすしはおいしそうです。

e.g. すし　　(1) カレー　　(2) ケーキ

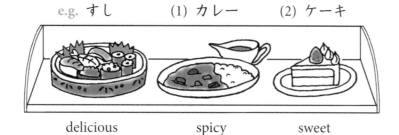

delicious　　spicy　　sweet

(3) 家
いえ　　(4) アパート　　(5) マンション

old　　new　　convenient

(6) 先生
せんせい　　(7) 学生
がくせい　　(8) おじいさん　　(9) おばあさん

strict　　sleepy　　energetic　　mean

(10) 子供
こども　　(11) 男の人
おとこ ひと　　(12) 弁護士
べんごし　　(13) やくざ (yakuza)

sad　　lonely　　smart　　scary

B. Look at the pictures in A and make sentences as in the example. K13-14

Example すし　→　おいしそうなすしです。

C. Pair Work—Talk about the picture taken at a party using 〜そう.

Example A：おいしそうな料理ですね。
B：そうですね。
A：この人はうれしそうですね。
B：そうですね。

D. Pair Work—Comment on your partner's belongings using 〜そうな.

Example A：おいしそうなお弁当ですね。
B：ええ、このお弁当、おいしいですよ。コンビニで買ったんです。
A：そうですか。どこのコンビニですか。
B：大学の前のコンビニです。安くておいしいですよ。

E. Pair Work—B acts out the following situations and A makes a guess. Continue the conversation like the example below.

Example おなかが痛い
→ A：おなかが痛そうですね。どうしたんですか。
B：食べすぎたんです。
A：そうですか。薬を飲んだほうがいいですよ。

1. うれしい　　2. 悲しい　　3. 眠い　　4. 忙しい　　5. 気分が悪い

Ⅳ 着(き)てみます 👉Grammar 4

A. Respond to the following sentences using 〜てみる. 🔊 K13-15

(Example) A：この服(ふく)はすてきですよ。

B：じゃあ、着(き)てみます。

1. 経済(けいざい)の授業(じゅぎょう)はおもしろかったですよ。
2. あの映画(えいが)を見(み)て泣(な)きました。
3. この本(ほん)は感動(かんどう)しました。
4. 豆腐(とうふ) (tofu) は体(からだ)にいいですよ。

5. 東京(とうきょう)はおもしろかったですよ。
6. あの歌手(かしゅ)の歌(うた)はいいですよ。
7. このアプリは便利(べんり)ですよ。

B. Pair Work—You are at a shopping center. Ask the store attendants whether you can try out the following, using appropriate verbs.

(Example)

Customer: すみません。使(つか)ってみてもいいですか。

Store attendant: どうぞ、使(つか)ってみてください。

(1)　　　　　　(2)　　　(3)　　　　　(4)　　　　　　(5)

C. Talk about what you want to try in the following places.

(Example) インド (India)

→　A：インドに行(い)ったことがありますか。

B：いいえ。ありません。でも、行(い)ってみたいです。

A：そうですか。インドで何(なに)がしたいですか。

B：インドで象(ぞう)を見(み)たり、ヨガ (yoga) を習(なら)ったりしてみたいです。

1. ケニア (Kenya)
2. 東京(とうきょう)
3. タイ (Thailand)
4. ブラジル (Brazil)
5. チベット (Tibet)
6. (your own)

Ⅴ 紅茶なら飲みました ☛Grammar 5

A. Answer the questions as in the example. 🔊 K13-16

Example Q：ロバートさんは今朝、コーヒーを飲みましたか。

A：(◯ tea　× coffee)

→ 紅茶なら飲みましたが、コーヒーは飲みませんでした。

1. ロバートさんはバイクに乗れますか。　　　(◯ bicycle　× motorbike)
2. ロバートさんはニュージーランドに行ったことがありますか。

(◯ Australia　× New Zealand)
3. ロバートさんはゴルフをしますか。　　　(◯ soccer　× golf)
4. カルロスさんは日本の経済に興味がありますか。

(◯ history　× economics)
5. カルロスさんは彼女がいますか。　　(◯ friend　× girlfriend)
6. カルロスさんは土曜日に出かけられますか。　(◯ Sunday　× Saturday)

B. Answer the following questions, and continue the conversation. Use 〜なら whenever possible.

Example A：スポーツをよく見ますか。

B：ええ、野球なら見ます。　　　｜　B：いいえ、見ません。でも、

A：そうですか。　　　　　　　　｜　　　運動するのは好きです。

どのチーム (team) が好きですか。｜

1. 外国語ができますか。
2. アルバイトをしたことがありますか。
3. 日本の料理が作れますか。
4. 有名人に会ったことがありますか。
5. 楽器ができますか。
6. 外国に行ったことがありますか。

会
L13

Ⅵ 一日に二回食べます 👉Grammar 6
いち にち　　に かい た

A. Look at the following pictures and make sentences as in the example. 🔊 K13-17

Example 一日に二回食べます。
いちにち　　に かい た

e.g. twice a day

(1) three times a day

(2) seven hours a day

(3) three hours a day

(4) once a week

(5) twice a week

(6) three days a week

part-time job

(7) five days a week

school

(8) once a month

B. Pair Work—Look at the pictures in A and ask your partner the questions using the patterns below.

Example

Ａ：Ｂさんは一日に何回食べますか。
　　　　　　　いちにち　なんかい た

Ｂ：そうですね。たいてい一日に二回食べます。朝ご飯は食べません。
　　　　　　　　　　　　　　　　　いちにち　に かい た　　　あさ　はん　た

C. Class Activity—Ask two people how often they do the following things. Add your own questions.

[Example] 美容院に行く
　　　　　びよういん い
　　→　　A：Bさんはよく美容院に行きますか。
　　　　　　　　　　　　びよういん い
　　　　　B：一か月に一回ぐらい行きます。
　　　　　　　いっ げつ いっかい い

Questions	(　　　　　)さん	(　　　　　)さん
スーパーに行く		
料理する		
運動する		
ゲームをする		

Ⅶ　まとめの練習
　　　　　れんしゅう

A. Answer the following questions.

1. 子供の時に何ができましたか。何ができませんでしたか。
　　こども とき なに　　　　　　　　　　　なに
2. 百円で何が買えますか。
　　ひゃくえん なに か
3. どこに行ってみたいですか。どうしてですか。
　　　　　い
4. 子供の時、何がしてみたかったですか。
　　こども とき なに
5. 今、何がしてみたいですか。
　　いま なに
6. 一日に何時間ぐらい勉強しますか。
　　いちにち なん じ かん　　　べんきょう
7. 甘い物が好きですか。特に何が好きですか。
　　あま もの す　　　　　とく なに す
8. 一か月にいくらぐらい使いますか。
　　いっ げつ　　　　　つか

B. Pair Work—Talk about part-time jobs.

1. アルバイトをしたことがありますか。
2. いつしましたか。
3. どんなアルバイトでしたか。
4. 一週間に何日働きましたか。
　　いっしゅうかん　なんにちはたら
5. 一時間にいくらもらいましたか。
　　いち じ かん
6. どんなアルバイトがしてみたいですか。どうしてですか。

C. Role Play—One of you is the manager of one of the following organizations, and the other is a student who is looking for a job.

(a) Call the organization and make an appointment for a job interview, as in Dialogue Ⅰ.

(b) Then, discuss experiences and qualifications, etc., as in Dialogue Ⅱ.

> 小山日本語学校　　リトル・アジア (restaurant)　　アピホテル
> こ やま に ほん ご がっこう
>
> げんきスポーツクラブ　　ハロー子供英語学校
> 　　　　　　　　　　　　こ ども えい ご がっこう

Let's Find Out 調べてみよう
しら

どこに行きたい？
い

Your group is going on a trip, and you have to decide on the destination. Each person is responsible for making a slide presentation for the place of their choice. Do some research to find out (1) what its attractions are, (2) what you can do there, and (3) other appealing features. Listen to the presentation from each member of your group and discuss where your group should go.

Example

> 　私は横浜を紹介します。横浜でいろいろなことができます。
> わたし よこはま しょうかい 　　　　よこはま
> 　横浜には中華街があるので、おいしい中華料理が食べられます。
> よこはま ちゅう か がい 　　　　　　　　　　ちゅう か りょう り 　た
> 　それから「カップヌードルミュージアム」があります。そこでは好
> 　　　　　　　　　　　　　　　　　　　　　　　　　　　　　　　す
> きなもので、私だけのカップヌードルが作れます。
> 　　　　わたし
> 　横浜マリンタワーの上から海や横浜の町が見られます。特に夜はき
> よこはま 　　　　　うえ 　うみ よこはま まち み 　　　とく よる
> れいで、いい写真が撮れます。
> しゃしん と

中華街　Chinatown　　カップヌードル　Cup Noodles
ちゅう か がい
横浜マリンタワー　Yokohama Marine Tower
よこはま

Culture Notes

元号と干支 Names of Years
げんごう えと

元号
げんごう

Japanese people use two systems of reference for years. One is the Gregorian calendar year, and the other is 元号, Japanese imperial eras that, since the Meiji era, have coincided with the emperors' tenures. Under the 元号 system, the year 2020, for instance, was 令和 ２年, the second year of the Reiwa era (Emperor Naruhito's tenure).

The five most recent 元号 are: 明治 (1868–1912), 大正 (1912–1926), 昭和 (1926–1989), 平成 (1989–2019), and 令和 (2019–). Japanese people remember Meiji as the era of modernization, Taisho as the time the movement toward democracy was born, Showa as a period of war and economic growth, and Heisei as an era marked by recession and big earthquakes.

干支
えと

Japanese people associate their birth years with the 12 animals in the East Asian zodiac, which is referred to as 干支 and 十二支. The table below lists the animals in the zodiac, and the years they are associated with. People born in 2000, for example, are 辰年生まれ.

Eto		Animal		Years of birth			
子	ne = nezumi	rat		1984	1996	2008	2020
丑	ushi	ox		1985	1997	2009	2021
寅	tora	tiger		1986	1998	2010	2022
卯	u = usagi	rabbit		1987	1999	2011	2023
辰	tatsu	dragon		1988	2000	2012	2024
巳	mi = hebi	snake		1989	2001	2013	2025
午	uma	horse		1990	2002	2014	2026
未	hitsuji	sheep		1991	2003	2015	2027
申	saru	monkey		1992	2004	2016	2028
酉	tori	chicken		1993	2005	2017	2029
戌	inu	dog		1994	2006	2018	2030
亥	i = inoshishi	boar		1995	2007	2019	2031

Useful Expressions

銀 行 で
ぎん こう

A t   t h e   B a n k

Useful Vocabulary

口座 —————————— account
こう ざ

手数料 —————————— commission
て すうりょう

キャッシュカード —————— bank card

通帳 ————————— passbook
つうちょう

預金 ————————— savings
よ きん

金額 ————————— amount
きんがく

暗証番号 ——————————— personal identification number
あんしょうばんごう

現金 ——————————— cash
げんきん

両替 ————— money exchange
りょうがえ

Useful Expressions

口座を開きたいんですが。————— I would like to open an account.
こう ざ ひら

口座を閉じたいんですが。————— I would like to close an account.
こう ざ と

ドルを円にかえてください。———— Please change dollars into yen.
えん

口座にお金を振り込みたいんですが。
こう ざ かね ふ こ

——————————— I would like to deposit money into an account.

一万円札を千円札十枚に両替できますか。
いちまんえんさつ せんえんさつじゅうまい りょうがえ

——————————— Can you change a 10,000-yen bill into ten

1,000-yen bills?

お金をおろします。—————————— I will withdraw money.
かね

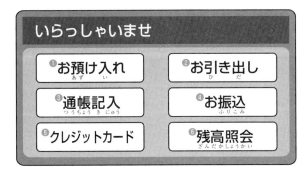

いらっしゃいませ

❶お預け入れ　　❷お引き出し
あず い　　　　　ひ だ

❸通帳記入　　　❹お振込
つうちょう き にゅう　　ふりこみ

❺クレジットカード　❻残高照会
ざんだかしょうかい

ATM

❶ deposit
❷ withdrawal
❸ passbook update
❹ bank transfer
❺ credit card
❻ balance inquiry

第14課

L E S S O N 14

バレンタインデー Valentine's Day

In this lesson, we will...

🖉 Express what we want
🖉 Talk about uncertain things

🖉 Give and receive presents
🖉 Talk about Valentine's Day and special days

会 話 D i a l o g u e
(かい)(わ)

Ⅰ A month before Valentine's Day. 🔊 K14-01/02

1 メアリー：　バレンタインデーのプレゼントは何がいいと思いますか。
　　　　　　　　　　　　　　　　　　　　　(なに)　　　　(おも)

2 ゆ い：　そうですね。たけしさんはいつも同じセーターを着ているから、
　　　　　　　　　　　　　　　　　　　　　(おな)　　　　　(き)

3 　　　　　　セーターをあげたらどうですか。

4 メアリー：　それはいいかもしれませんね。

Ⅱ On Valentine's Day. 🔊 K14-03/04

1 メアリー：　たけしくん、はい、これ。

2 たけし：　えっ、ぼくに？　どうもありがとう。開けてもいい？
　　　　　　　　　　　　　　　　　　　　　　　　　(あ)

3 メアリー：　うん。

4 たけし：　わあ、いいね、このセーター。こんなのがほしかったんだ。

5 　　　　　　メアリーが編んだの？
　　　　　　　　　(あ)

6 メアリー：　うん、小さいかもしれないから着てみて。
　　　　　　　　　(ちい)　　　　　　　　　(き)

7 たけし：　ちょうどいいよ。ありがとう。

Ⅲ The next day. 🔊 K14-05/06

1 ジョン： 暖かそうなセーターですね。

2 たけし： これ、メアリーがくれたんです。

3 ジョン： よく似合っていますよ。ぼくも彼女がほしいなあ。ロバートさんは

4 チョコレートを十個ももらったんですよ。

5 たけし： へえ、すごいですね。ジョンさんは？

6 ジョン： ぼくは一個しかもらえませんでした。大家さんから。さびしいなあ。

7 たけし： でも、ロバートさんはホワイトデーが大変ですよ。

8 ジョン： ホワイトデー？

9 たけし： ええ、男の人は三月十四日にお返しをしなきゃいけないんですよ。

Ⅰ

Mary: What do you think is good for a Valentine's present?

Yui: Well, Takeshi always wears the same sweater, so why don't you give him a sweater?

Mary: That might be a good idea.

Ⅱ

Mary: Takeshi, this is for you.

Takeshi: For me? Thank you. May I open it?

Mary: Yes.

Takeshi: Wow, this is a nice sweater! I've wanted one like this. Did you knit it, Mary?

Mary: Yes. It may be small, so please try it on.

Takeshi: It fits perfectly. Thank you.

Ⅲ

John: Your sweater looks warm.

Takeshi: Mary gave me this.

John: It looks good on you. I want a girlfriend, too. You know, Robert got as many as ten chocolates.

Takeshi: Hah, that's incredible. How about you, John?

John: I only got one. From my landlady. How sad.

Takeshi: But Robert will probably have a tough day on White Day.

John: White Day?

Takeshi: Yes, men have to return the favor on March 14.

単語
たんご

Vocabulary

Nouns

おくさん	奥さん	(your/someone's) wife
ごしゅじん	ご主人	(your/someone's) husband
パートナー		partner
おじさん		uncle; middle-aged man
おばさん		aunt; middle-aged woman
りょうしん	両親	parents
* おおやさん	大家さん	landlord; landlady
みなさん	皆さん	everyone; all of you
* チョコレート		chocolate
みかん		mandarin orange
トレーナー		sweatshirt
シャツ		shirt
ネクタイ		necktie
マフラー		winter scarf
ゆびわ	指輪	ring
えんぴつ	鉛筆	pencil
ぬいぐるみ		stuffed animal (e.g., teddy bear)
まんが	漫画	comic book
けしょうひん	化粧品	cosmetics
ラジオ		radio
おさら	お皿	plate; dish
* おかえし	お返し	return (as a token of gratitude)
りれきしょ	履歴書	résumé
クリスマス		Christmas
* バレンタインデー		Valentine's Day
* ホワイトデー		"White Day" (yet another gift-giving day)

い-adjective

* ほしい	欲しい	to want (*thing* が)

＊ Words that appear in the dialogue

な-adjectives

おしゃれ（な）	fashionable; stylish
けち（な）	stingy; cheap

U-verbs

おくる	送る	to send （*person* に *thing* を）
* におう	似合う	to look good (on somebody)（*thing* が）

Ru-verbs

あきらめる		to give up （〜を）
* あげる		to give (to others)
		（*person* に *thing* を）
* くれる		to give (me) （*person* に *thing* を）
できる		to come into existence; to be made
		（〜が）

Irregular Verbs

そうだんする	相談する	to consult （*person* に）
ちゅういする	注意する	to give warning （*person* に）;
		to watch out （〜に）
プロポーズする		to propose marriage （*person* に）

Adverbs and Other Expressions

* 〜くん	〜君	Mr./Ms. . . . (casual)
〜たち		[makes a noun plural]
わたしたち	私たち	we
* こんな〜		. . . like this; this kind of . . .
きゅうに	急に	suddenly
* ちょうど		exactly
よく		well
さあ		I am not sure . . .
どうしたらいい		what should one do

Counters

* 〜こ	〜個	[generic counter for smaller items]
〜さつ	〜冊	[counter for bound volumes]
〜だい	〜台	[counter for equipment]
〜ひき	〜匹	[counter for smaller animals]
〜ほん	〜本	[counter for long objects]

文法 Grammar
ぶん ぽう

1 ほしい

ほしい means "(I) want (something)." ほしい follows the い-adjective conjugation pattern. The object of desire is usually followed by the particle が. In negative sentences, the particle は is also used.

いい成績がほしいです。
せいせき
I want a good grade.

子供の時、ポケモンのゲームがほしかったです。
こども　とき
When I was young, I wanted a Pokémon game.

Q：プレゼントがほしい？　　　　　*Do you want a present?*

A：ううん、ほしくない。　　　　　*No, I don't.*

(私は) X が　ほしい　　　　　*I want X.*
わたし

ほしい is like たい (I want to do . . .), which we studied in Lesson 11, and its use is mostly limited to the first person, the speaker.[1] So, we use ほしい to say "I want this" but not for "Mary wants that." To talk about somebody else's wishes or desires, you either quote that person's expression of desire, or you describe it as your guess.

ヤスミンさんは新しいスマホがほしいと言っています。
あたら　　　　　　　　　　　　　　い
Yasmin says she wants a new phone.

亜美さんはぬいぐるみがほしくないでしょう。
あ　み
Ami probably doesn't want a stuffed animal.

Or you can replace ほしい with the derived verb ほしがる, which indicates that you can tell by the way the person acts that they want something. ほしがる is like たがる in the first example below, which replaces たい (see Lesson 11). ほしがる conjugates as an *u*-verb and is usually used in the form ほしがっている. Unlike ほしい, the particle after the object of desire is を.

---

[1] Among the words we have learned so far, かなしい (sad), うれしい (glad), and いたい (painful) are similarly limited to first-person descriptions.

ななみさんは英語を習いたがっています。　　＜ 習いたい
(I understand that) Nanami wants to study English.

L14

カルロスさんは友だちをほしがっています。　　＜ ほしい
(I understand that) Carlos wants a friend.

Because the core meaning of ほしい is "desire to possess," when you can use a verb + たい instead of ほしい, you should use the verb. For example,

昼ご飯が食べたい。　　(*not* 昼ご飯がほしい)
旅行に行きたい。　　(*not* 旅行がほしい)

2 〜かもしれません

かもしれません means that something is a "possibility." You can use it when you think that something *may be* the case. When you say かもしれません, you are less sure about the state of affairs than when you say でしょう. There are stylistic variants of かもしれません: in casual speech, you say かもしれない or just かも.

> short form ＋ かもしれません　　　*Maybe . . .*

You can add かもしれません to the short forms of predicates, in the affirmative and in the negative, in the present as well as the past tense.

あしたは雨が降るかもしれません。
It may rain tomorrow.

田中さんより、鈴木さんのほうが背が高いかもしれない。
Suzuki is perhaps taller than Tanaka.

あしたは天気がよくないかも。
The weather may not be good tomorrow.

ロバートさんは、子供の時、いじわるだったかもしれません。
Robert may have been a bully when he was a kid.

When the last part of a sentence is a noun or a な-adjective in the present tense, you put かもしれません directly after that noun or な-adjective. In other words, だ is dropped in such sentences.

ウデイさんはインド人だ。　→　ウデイさんはインド人かもしれません。

Uday is an Indian.　　　　　　*Uday may be an Indian.*

山下先生は犬がきらいだ。　→　山下先生は犬がきらいかもしれません。

Professor Yamashita doesn't like dogs.　*Professor Yamashita may not like dogs.*

3 あげる / くれる / もらう

Japanese has two verbs for giving: くれる and あげる. The choice between the pair depends on the direction of the transaction. Imagine a set of concentric spheres of relative psychological distances, with me at the center, you next to me, and all the others on the edge. When a thing moves *toward* the center, the verb we use is くれる. Otherwise, when a thing moves *away* from the center or when a thing stays *away* from the center, the transaction is described in terms of あげる.

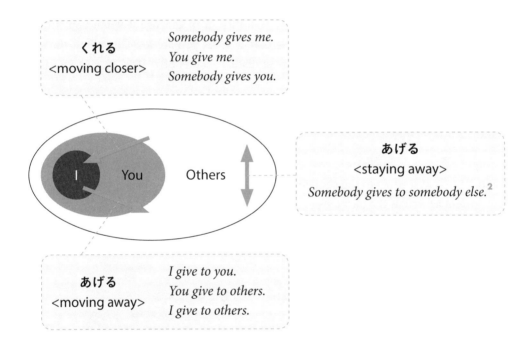

With both あげる and くれる, the giver is the subject of the sentence, and is accompanied by the particle は or が. The recipient is accompanied by the particle に.

---

[2] If a transaction takes place between others but you think you yourself have benefited because somebody very close to you received something, くれる is also possible. In the example below, you identify yourself more closely with your family than with somebody you have never met. Hence くれる.

大統領が妹に手紙をくれました。　*The President gave my little sister a letter.*

私 はその女の人に花をあげます。
_{わたし} _{おんな} _{ひと} _{はな}
I will give the woman flowers.

その女の人は男の人に時計をあげました。
_{おんな} _{ひと} _{おとこ} _{ひと} _{とけい}
The woman gave the man a watch.

両親が（私に）新しい車をくれるかもしれません。
_{りょうしん} _{わたし} _{あたら} _{くるま}
My parents may give me a new car.

そのプレゼント、だれがくれたんですか。
Who gave you that present?

(giver) は / が (recipient) に	あげる くれる	(giver) *gives to* (recipient)

Transactions that are described with the verb くれる can also be described in terms of "receiving" or もらう. With もらう, it is the recipient that is the subject of the sentence, and the giver is accompanied by the particle に or から. Compare the もらう and くれる sentences below, which describe the same event.[3]

(recipient) は / が (giver) に / から もらう	(recipient) *receives from* (giver)

私は 姉に／姉から マフラーをもらいました。
_{わたし} _{あね} _{あね}
I received a winter scarf from my big sister.

姉が私にマフラーをくれました。
_{あね} _{わたし}
My big sister gave me a winter scarf.

---

[3] もらう implies that you feel closer to the recipient than to the giver. Thus もらう is not appropriate when the transaction is outbound.

×（あなたは）私から手紙をもらいましたか。　　*Did you receive a letter from me?*
_{わたし} _て _{がみ}
You can use もらう for third-party transactions if you can assume the perspective of the recipient.

妹 は大統領に手紙をもらいました。　　*My little sister received a letter from the President.*
_{いもうと} _{だいとうりょう} _{て がみ}

4 〜たらどうですか

たらどうですか after a verb conveys advice or recommendation. The initial た in たらどうですか stands for the same ending as in the past tense short form of a verb in the affirmative. In casual speech, たらどうですか may be shortened to たらどう or たら.

verb (short, past) ＋ らどうですか	*why don't you . . .*

薬を飲んだらどうですか。　　　*How about taking some medicine?*

もっと勉強したらどう。　　　*Why don't you study harder?*

たらどうですか may sometimes have a disapproving tone, expressing criticism of the person for not having performed the action already. It is, therefore, safer to avoid using it unless you were asked for advice.

Also, the pattern is not to be used for extending invitations. If, for example, you want to tell your friend to come visit, you do not want to use たらどうですか, but should use ませんか.

うちに来ませんか。　　　Compare: ×うちに来たらどうですか。

Why don't you come to my place?

5 Number ＋も / Number ＋しか ＋ Negative

Let's recall the basic structure for expressing numbers in Japanese.

noun $\begin{Bmatrix} が \\ を \end{Bmatrix}$ ＋ number

私のうちには猫が三匹います。

There are three cats in our house.

傘を二本買いました。

We bought two umbrellas.

You can add も to the number word when you want to say "as many as."

私の母は猫を三匹も飼っています。

My mother owns three, count them, three cats.

きのうのパーティーには<ruby>学生<rt>がくせい</rt></ruby>が<ruby>二十人<rt>に じゅうにん</rt></ruby>も<ruby>来<rt>き</rt></ruby>ました。

As many as twenty students showed up at the party yesterday.

You can add しか to the number word, *and* turn the predicate into the negative when you want to say "as few as" or "only."

<ruby>私<rt>わたし</rt></ruby>は<ruby>日本語<rt>に ほん ご</rt></ruby>の<ruby>本<rt>ほん</rt></ruby>を<ruby>一冊<rt>いっさつ</rt></ruby>しか<ruby>持<rt>も</rt></ruby>っていません。

I have only one Japanese book.

この<ruby>会社<rt>かいしゃ</rt></ruby>にはパソコンが<ruby>二台<rt>に だい</rt></ruby>しかありません。

There are only two computers in this company.

number ＋ も	*as many as*
number ＋ しか ない	*as few as*

Expression Notes ②

表現ノート
ひょう げん

The use of short forms in casual speech ▶ The dialogues in this lesson contain many examples of short forms as they are used in casual spoken Japanese. Let's examine some of the lines from the Dialogue section.

<ruby>開<rt>あ</rt></ruby>けてもいい？　This is a question that simply asks for a yes or a no. These types of questions hardly ever have the question particle か at the end. The rising intonation alone marks them as questions.

わあ and へえ　You say わあ when you find something exciting. It is like the English "wow!" We saw this interjection of enthusiasm in Lesson 5. You say へえ when you hear something amusing, hard to believe, or mildly surprising: "Oh, is that right?"

こんなのがほしかったんだ。　んだ is the explanation modality, the short form counterpart of んです. Female speakers have the choice between the gender-neutral んだ and the more feminine の in closing an explanation sentence.

メアリーが編んだの？　Many question sentences in casual spoken Japanese end in の, which is the short form counterpart of the explanation modality ん です. As are questions ending in んですか, most の questions are fishing for detailed explanations as a response. They are gender-neutral.

着てみて。　The *te*-form of a verb is used as a request. More politely, you of course would want to say 〜てください.

なあ ▶ なあ at the end of a sentence, after a short form predicate, indicates exclamation of admiration, frustration, or some such strong emotion. なあ is mostly used when you are talking to yourself.

日本語の先生はやさしいなあ。	*Wow, isn't my Japanese professor nice!*
いい教科書だなあ。	*Whoa, this is a great textbook!*
おなかがすいたなあ。	*Gee, am I hungry!*
あの人はけちだなあ。	*Darn, isn't that guy cheap!*

できる ▶ できる has a number of different meanings depending on the context.

"can do/be good at/do well"

日本語ができます。	*I am capable in Japanese.*
彼はスキーができません。	*He can't ski.*
テストであまりできませんでした。	*I didn't do well on the exam.*

"be completed/finished"

晩ご飯ができましたよ。	*Dinner is ready.*
宿題はできましたか。	*Is your homework done yet?*

"appear/come into existence/be made"

新しい店ができました。	*A new store has opened.*
友だちがたくさんできました。	*I have made many friends.*

〜からです ▶ 〜からです means "it's because . . ." and answers a "why" question. The part that precedes から is in the short form.

A：どうして日本語を勉強しているんですか。
　Why are you studying Japanese?

B：日本のアニメが好きだからです。
　It's because I like Japanese anime.

練習 Practice
れん　しゅう

会
L14

I チョコレートがほしいです ☛Grammar 1

A. You are looking at an award gift catalog. Say whether you want or do not want each of the items below as in the example. K14-09

Example チョコレートがほしいです。／チョコレートがほしくないです。

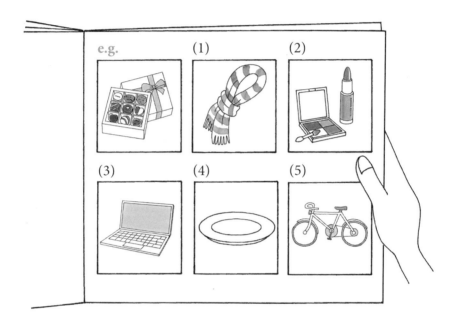

B. Say whether you wanted or did not want each of the items below when you were a child. K14-10

Example

子供の時、まんががほしかったです。
こ ども とき
子供の時、まんががほしくなかったです。
こ ども とき

(1)   (2)   (3)   (4)   (5)

C. Group Work—Discuss what you wanted when you were a child. Keep your conversation going by listing more items, asking for more details, and so forth.

(Example) A：子供の時、何がほしかったですか。

B：まんががほしかったです。

C：私もです。どんなまんががほしかったですか。

(Continue the conversation.)

D. Pair Work—Ask your partner which of the two items in the list they want more of and why.

(Example) 車／パソコン

→　A：車とパソコンと、どちらがほしいですか。

B：車よりパソコンのほうがほしいです。

A：どうしてですか。

B：車が運転できないからです。

1. 歌舞伎のチケット／相撲 (Sumo wrestling) のチケット
2. 小さい家／大きいマンション
3. おしゃれな友だち／頭がいい友だち
4. 猫／犬
5. 時間／お金

E. Class Activity—Ask four people when their birthdays are and what they want on their birthdays.

名前	誕生日はいつですか	何がほしいですか

Based on the findings, make a short dialogue by filling in the underlined parts.

Example

A : もうすぐ、メアリーさんの誕生日ですよ。

B : そうですか。じゃあ、何かプレゼントを買いましょうか。
　　何がいいと思いますか。

A : そうですね。キティちゃん (Hello Kitty) のぬいぐるみはどうですか。
　　メアリーさんはぬいぐるみがほしいと言っていましたから。
　　　　　　　　　　　　　　　　　（をほしがっています。）

B : いいですね。そうしましょう。

Ⅱ ギターが弾けるかもしれません ☞Grammar 2

A. Your friend asks you about Takeshi. Answer the questions using 〜かもしれません both in the affirmative and in the negative. 🔊 K14-11

Example

Q : たけしさんはギターが弾けますか。

A : さあ……。弾けるかもしれません。でも、弾けないかもしれません。

1. あした忙しいですか。
2. 料理が上手ですか。
3. けちですか。
4. 政治に興味がありますか。
5. 空手ができますか。
6. 英語が話せますか。
7. メアリーさんに指輪をあげましたか。

B. Complete the following sentences.

1. あしたの天気は_____かもしれません。
2. 今週の週末、私は_____かもしれません。
3. 私たちの日本語の先生は_____かもしれません。
4. 私のとなりの人は、きのう_____かもしれません。
5. 今学期の後、私は_____かもしれません。

C. Pair Work—Ask your partner what they think they will be doing in ten years.

Example 日本語を勉強していますか。
　　→　Ａ：十年後、日本語を勉強していますか。
　　　　Ｂ：日本語を勉強しているかもしれません。／
　　　　　　たぶん、日本語を勉強していると思います。

1. どこに住んでいますか。
2. 結婚していますか。
3. 奥さん／ご主人／パートナーは
   どんな人ですか。
4. 子供がいますか。
5. 仕事は何ですか。
6. お金持ちですか。
7. 週末よく何をしますか。

D. Pair Work—Make a dialogue with your partner by filling out the blanks as in the example.

Example Ａ：今度の週末、うちに来ない？
　　　　Ｂ：今度の週末はちょっと……。
　　　　　　アルバイトがあるかもしれないから。
　　　　Ａ：そうか。じゃあ、また今度。

Ａ：今度の週末、_____ない？
Ｂ：今度の週末はちょっと……。
　　_____かもしれないから。
Ａ：そうか。じゃあ、また今度。

Ⅲ 友だちにチョコレートをあげました 🖝Grammar 3
とも

A. You have just come back from a trip with a lot of souvenirs. Look at the picture and say what you will give to the following people. 🔊 K14-12

会
L14

Example 父にお酒をあげます。
ちち さけ

I

B. Pair Work—Ask what your partner would give the following people on their birthdays. When you answer, give reasons, too.

Example A：お父さんの誕生日に何をあげるつもりですか。
とう たんじょう び なに
B：料理の本をあげるつもりです。父は料理をするのが好きですか
りょう り ほん ちち りょう り す
ら。

1. お母さん
かあ
2. おばさん
3. おじさん
4. 友だち
とも
5. 兄弟
きょうだい
6. 彼／彼女／パートナー
かれ かのじょ

C. On your birthday, you have got a lot of presents. Look at the pictures and make sentences using くれる／もらう. 🔊 K14-13

[Example] 彼女がマフラーをくれました。／彼女にマフラーをもらいました。
かのじょ　　　　　　　　　　　　　　　　　　　　かのじょ

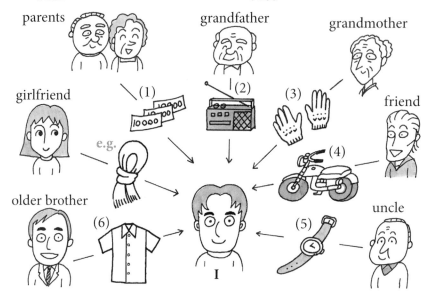

D. Describe who gave what to whom using あげる／くれる／もらう. 🔊 K14-14

[Example] ヤスミンさんはカルロスさんにトレーナーをあげました。
　　　　　カルロスさんはヤスミンさんにトレーナーをもらいました。

E. Pair Work—One student looks at picture A below, and the other looks at picture B on p. 67. Ask and answer questions to find out who gave what to whom in order to complete the picture below.

Example A：たけしさんはメアリーさんに何をあげましたか。／

メアリーさんはたけしさんに何をもらいましたか。

B：花をあげました／もらいました。

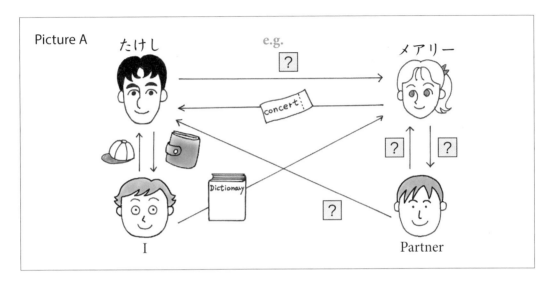

F. Answer the following questions.

1. 去年の誕生日に何をもらいましたか。
2. 家族の誕生日に何をあげましたか。
3. 友だちの誕生日に何をあげたいですか。
4. バレンタインデーに何かあげたことがありますか。何をあげましたか。
5. バレンタインデーに何かもらったことがありますか。何をもらいましたか。
6. あなたの国ではお正月に何かあげますか。だれがだれにあげますか。
7. 一番うれしかったプレゼントは何ですか。だれにもらいましたか。
8. 一番うれしくなかったプレゼントは何ですか。だれにもらいましたか。

Ⅳ 新聞を見たらどうですか ☛Grammar 4
しん ぶん み

A. Give advice to the people below. 🔊 K14-15

[Example] メアリー／check newspaper → 新聞を見たらどうですか。
　　　　　　　　　　　　　　　　　　　　しんぶん　み

日本で仕事がしたいんです。
に ほん　　し ごと

メアリー

e.g. check newspaper
1. consult with the teacher
2. send résumé to companies

彼女がほしいです。
かのじょ
でも、できないんです。

ジョン

3. go to a party
4. join a club (サークルに入る)
　　　　　　　　　　　　　はい
5. give up

彼女と結婚したいんです。
かのじょ　けっこん

けん

6. propose marriage
7. give her a ring
8. meet her parents

B. Pair Work—Give your partner some suggestions on the following comments using 〜たらどうですか.

[Example] A：急におなかが痛くなったんです。
　　　　　　きゅう　　　　　　いた
　　　　　　B：病院に行ったらどうですか。
　　　　　　　　びょういん　い

1. おいしいケーキが食べたいんです。
　　　　　　　　　　　　た
2. 安い着物がほしいんです。
　　やす　き もの
3. ちょっと太ったんです。
　　　　　　　ふと
4. このごろ疲れているんです。
　　　　　　　つか
5. 勉強が大きらいなんです。
　　べんきょう　だい

6. よく寝られないんです。
　　　　　ね
7. 友だちができないんです。
　　とも
8. お金がないんです。
　　かね
9. 彼／彼女／パートナーがけちで、
　　かれ　かのじょ
　　何もくれないんです。
　　なに

C. Group Work—You have a problem. Ask your classmates for advice.

Example A：アパートに住んでいるんですが、となりの人が夜遅くギターを
弾くんです。どうしたらいいですか。
B：となりの人に注意したらどうですか。
A：うーん。こわそうな人なので、ちょっと……。
C：じゃあ、大家さんに相談したらどうですか。
A：そうですね。そうします。

Ⅴ 四時間も勉強しました ☞Grammar 5

A. Describe the picture using counters. 🔊 K14-16

Example fish → 魚が五匹います。

1. cat
2. flower
3. necktie
4. book
5. radio
6. shirt
7. magazine
8. pencil
9. mandarin orange
10. plate

B. Describe the following pictures using 〜も or 〜しか. 🔊 K14-17

Example 勉強しました
→ メアリーさんは四時間も勉強しました。
ジョンさんは三十分しか勉強しませんでした。

e.g. 勉強しました

4 hours　　　　30 minutes

	(1) 食べました た	(2) 読みました よ	(3) 持っています も	(4) 飲みました の	(5) 寝ます ね
メアリー			|30		 11 hours
ジョン		|6			 5 hours

C. Pair Work—Ask your partner the following questions. Respond to the answers using 〜しか or 〜も when appropriate.

Example まんがを何冊持っていますか。
なんさつ も

  →   Ａ：まんがを何冊持っていますか。
                なんさつ も
            Ｂ：一冊持っています。
              いっさつ も
            Ａ：えっ、一冊しか持っていないんですか。
              いっさつ も
            Ｂ：ええ、興味がありませんから。
              きょう み

  →   Ａ：まんがを何冊持っていますか。
                なんさつ も
            Ｂ：百冊ぐらい持っています。
              ひゃくさつ も
            Ａ：えっ、百冊も持っているんですか。
              ひゃくさつ も
            Ｂ：日本のまんがが大好きですから。
              に ほん   だい す

1. 今いくら持っていますか。
  いま   も
2. きのう何時間勉強しましたか。
      なん じ かんべんきょう
3. 一か月に映画を何本ぐらい見ますか。
  いっ げつ えい が なんぼん   み
4. 今学期、授業をいくつ取っていますか。
  こんがっ き じゅぎょう   と
5. 今学期、授業を何回サボりましたか。
  こんがっ き じゅぎょう なんかい
6. 将来、子供が何人ほしいですか。
  しょうらい こ ども なんにん
7. セーターを何枚持っていますか。
        なんまい も
8. 週末、何時間ぐらいゲームをしましたか。
  しゅうまつ なん じ かん

Ⅵ まとめの練習
<small>れんしゅう</small>

A. Choose one of the special days celebrated in your country and talk about it.

Example みなさんの国には「先生の日」がありますか。私の国では、五月十五
<small>くに</small>　　　<small>せんせい</small>　<small>ひ</small>　　　　　　　　<small>わたし</small>　<small>くに</small>　　　　　<small>ご がつじゅう ご</small>
日は「先生の日」です。学生は先生に花やカードをあげます。
<small>にち</small>　<small>せんせい</small>　<small>ひ</small>　　　　<small>がくせい</small>　<small>せんせい</small>　<small>はな</small>

B. Class Activity—Show and Tell
Bring something that you have received from someone and talk about it.

Example これは指輪です。誕生日に母がくれました。将来、私の子供にあげた
<small>ゆび わ</small>　　　<small>たんじょう び</small>　<small>はは</small>　　　　　　　<small>しょうらい</small>　<small>わたし</small>　<small>こ ども</small>
いです。

C. Role Play—Using actual items, engage in short conversations about giving and receiving things. Use Dialogue Ⅱ as a model.

Pair Work Ⅲ E. (p. 63)

Example A：たけしさんはメアリーさんに何をあげましたか。／
<small>なに</small>
　　　　メアリーさんはたけしさんに何をもらいましたか。
<small>なに</small>
　　　B：花をあげました／もらいました。
<small>はな</small>

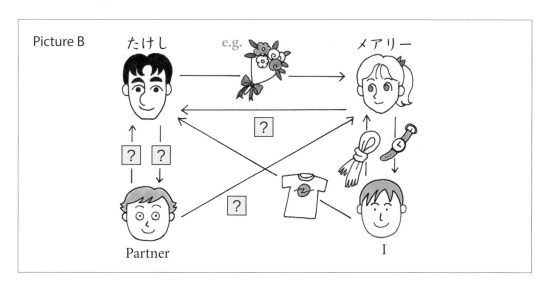

Culture Notes

日本の年中行事 Annual Events in Japan
（にほん）（ねんちゅうぎょうじ）

節分 (Bean-throwing Festival)──二月三日
（せつぶん）　　　　　　　　　　　　　　（にがつみっか）

節分 is a festival held on February 3, one day before the start
（せつぶん）
of spring, according to the old Japanese lunar calendar. People
hold a ceremony called 豆まき (bean-throwing) at shrines,
（まめ）
temples, and their homes to chase away evil spirits at the start
of spring.

ひな祭り (Doll Festival)──三月三日
（まつ）　　　　　　　　　　　（さんがつみっか）

On the day of ひな祭り, families with young daughters display ひ
（まつ）
な人形 (*hina* dolls) inside the home to express their wish for their
（にんぎょう）
girls' health and happiness. The dolls represent the emperor, em-
press, attendants, and musicians in traditional court dress of the
Heian period (794–1185).

こどもの日 (Children's Day)──五月五日
（ひ）　　　　　　　　　　　　　　　（ごがついつか）

This festival was originally for boys but was renamed for both
sexes since the aforementioned Girls' Day is not a public holiday. Families with young sons wish for the healthy growth and
happiness of their boys by flying 鯉のぼり (carp streamers) and
（こい）
displaying decorations of samurai helmets and armor. Both
carp and armor are symbols of strength and success.

七夕 (Tanabata Festival)──七月七日
（たなばた）　　　　　　　　　　　（しちがつなのか）

七夕 is based on a Chinese legend in which 彦星 (the star Altair)
（たなばた）　　　　　　　　　　　　　　　　　　　　（ひこぼし）
and 織姫 (the star Vega) are two lovers who are separated by the
（おりひめ）
Milky Way and can meet over it only once a year on this day (see
読み書き編, Lesson 12). People write their wishes on 短冊 (paper
（よ）（か）（へん）　　　　　　　　　　　　　　　　　　（たんざく）
strips) and hang them on bamboo branches.

お盆 (Obon Festival)──八月十五日ごろ
（ぼん）　　　　　　　　　　　　（はちがつじゅうごにち）

お盆 is a Buddhist event held on three days around August
（ぼん）
15 (or July 15 in some regions). Many people believe that the
spirits of deceased ancestors come home during this period.
Around お盆, outdoor dance events called 盆踊り(*Bon* Dance)
（ぼん）　　　　　　　　　　　　　　　　　（ぼんおど）
are held, and many take summer vacations to return to their
hometown to see their family.

Useful Expressions

数え方
かぞ　　かた

Counters

	こ（個） small items	さつ（冊） bound volumes	ひき（匹） small animals	ほん（本） long objects	だい（台） equipment	まい（枚） flat objects
1	いっこ	いっさつ	いっぴき	いっぽん	いちだい	いちまい
2	にこ	にさつ	にひき	にほん	にだい	にまい
3	さんこ	さんさつ	さんびき	さんぼん	さんだい	さんまい
4	よんこ	よんさつ	よんひき	よんほん	よんだい	よんまい
5	ごこ	ごさつ	ごひき	ごほん	ごだい	ごまい
6	ろっこ	ろくさつ	ろっぴき	ろっぽん	ろくだい	ろくまい
7	ななこ	ななさつ	ななひき	ななほん	ななだい	ななまい
8	はっこ	はっさつ	はっぴき	はっぽん	はちだい	はちまい
9	きゅうこ	きゅうさつ	きゅうひき	きゅうほん	きゅうだい	きゅうまい
10	じゅっこ	じゅっさつ	じゅっぴき	じゅっぽん	じゅうだい	じゅうまい
How many	なんこ／いくつ	なんさつ	なんびき	なんぼん	なんだい	なんまい
e.g.	candy tomato eraser	book magazine dictionary	cat dog snake	pencil umbrella movie bottle	computer TV car bicycle	paper plate T-shirt

Notes:

1. The pronunciation of numbers 1, 6, 8, and 10 changes before the counters こ, さつ, ひき, and ほん, except for ろくさつ.

2. The initial sound of the counters ひき and ほん changes to ぴき and ぽん after numbers 1, 6, 8, and 10, and to びき and ぼん after number 3 and なん, respectively.

3. じゅっ in じゅっこ, じゅっさつ, じゅっぴき, and じゅっぽん is also pronounced じっ.

第15課

長野旅行 A Trip to Nagano
なが　の　りょ　こう

In this lesson, we will..

- Suggest doing something together
- Make preparations
- Describe people or things in detail
- Make plans for the trip with friends

会 話 D i a l o g u e
かい　わ

Ⅰ Before the vacation. 🔊 K15-01/02

1 メアリー： たけしくん、今度の休み、予定ある？
　　　　　　　　　　　こん ど　　やす　　　　よ てい

2 たけし： うぅん。別に。どうして？
　　　　　　　　　べつ

3 メアリー： ゆいさんの長野のうちに行こうと思ってるんだけど、一緒に行かな
　　　　　　　　　　　　なが の　　　　　　い　　　　おも　　　　　　　　　　　　いっしょ　　い

4 　　　　　　い？

5 たけし： いいの？

6 メアリー： うん。ゆいさんが、「たけしくんも誘って」と言ってたから。
　　　　　　　　　　　　　　　　　　　　　　　　　　さそ　　　　い

7 たけし： じゃあ、行く。電車の時間、調べておくよ。
　　　　　　　　　　　い　　でんしゃ　 じ かん　 しら

8 メアリー： ありがとう。じゃあ、私、ゆいさんに電話しておく。
　　　　　　　　　　　　　　　　　　わたし　　　　　　　　　でん わ

Ⅱ At Nagano Station. 🔊 K15-03/04

1 たけし： 早く着いたから、ちょっと観光しない？
　　　　　　はや　つ　　　　　　　　　　かんこう

2 メアリー： うん。どこに行く？
　　　　　　　　　　　　　　い

3 たけし： 善光寺はどう？ 有名なお寺だよ。
　　　　　　ぜんこう じ　　　　　　ゆうめい　　てら

4 メアリー： いいね。昼ご飯は何にする？
　　　　　　　　　　ひる　はん　なん

5 たけし： 長野はそばがおいしいから、
　　　　　　なが の

6 　　　　　　そばを食べようよ。
　　　　　　　　　　　た

Ⅲ At the Travel Information Office. 🔊 K15-05/06

1 たけし： すみません、善光寺に行くバスはどれですか。
　　　　　　　　　　　　　　　ぜんこう じ　い

2 案内所の人：善光寺なら、十一番のバスですよ。
　 あんないじょ　ひと　ぜんこう じ　　　　じゅういちばん

3 たけし：　　ありがとうございます。この地図、もらってもいいですか。

4 案内所の人：ええ、どうぞ。それから、これ、美術館の割引券ですが、よかった
5 　　　　　　らどうぞ。

6 メアリー：　この美術館、あした行く予定なんです。どうもありがとうございます。

7 案内所の人：気をつけて。

「白馬の森 (Forest with a White Horse)」
東山魁夷 /1972 年
長野県信濃美術館 東山魁夷館蔵

Ⅰ

Mary: Takeshi, do you have any plans for the holiday?

Takeshi: Not really. Why?

Mary: I am thinking of going to Yui's home in Nagano. Do you want to go?

Takeshi: Is it okay?

Mary: Yes, Yui told me to invite you.

Takeshi: Then, I will go. I will check the train schedule.

Mary: Thanks. I will call Yui.

Ⅱ

Takeshi: Since we got here early, do you want to do a little sightseeing?

Mary: Yes. Where shall we go?

Takeshi: How about Zenkoji Temple? It's a famous temple.

Mary: Sounds good. What shall we eat for lunch?

Takeshi: *Soba* noodles in Nagano are delicious, so let's eat *soba*.

Ⅲ

Takeshi: Excuse me, which bus goes to Zenkoji Temple?

Information agent: For Zenkoji, it's bus number 11.

Takeshi: Thank you very much. Can I have this map?

Information agent: Yes. And these are discount tickets for the art museum. Please take them, if
you like.

Mary: We are planning to go to this museum tomorrow. Thank you very much.

Information agent: Have a safe trip.

単語
たんご

K15-07 (J-E)
K15-08 (E-J)

V o c a b u l a r y

N o u n s

がいこくじん	外国人	foreigner
* そば		*soba*; Japanese buckwheat noodles
え	絵	painting; picture; drawing
* ちず	地図	map
じしょ	辞書	dictionary
かぐ	家具	furniture
でんち	電池	battery
ジャケット		jacket
ペット		pet
* わりびきけん	割引券	discount coupon
インターネット		internet （more colloquially, ネット）
じしん	地震	earthquake
ほけん	保険	insurance
ぜいきん	税金	tax
きょうしつ	教室	classroom
たてもの	建物	building
プール		swimming pool
えいがかん	映画館	movie theater
りょかん	旅館	Japanese inn
にわ	庭	garden
ボランティア		volunteer
かつどう	活動	activity
けいけん	経験	experience
しゅうかん	習慣	custom
しめきり	締め切り	deadline
* よてい	予定	schedule; plan
そつぎょうしき	卒業式	graduation ceremony
けっこんしき	結婚式	wedding

U - v e r b s

うる	売る	to sell （～を）
おろす	下ろす	to withdraw (money) （～を）

＊Words that appear in the dialogue

かく	描く	to draw; to paint（～を）
さがす	探す	to look for（～を）
* さそう	誘う	to invite（～を）
しゃべる		to chat
つきあう	付き合う	(1) to date (someone)（*person* と）
		(2) to keep company（*purpose* に）
* つく	着く	to arrive（*place* に）
ほけんにはいる	保険に入る	to buy insurance

Ru-verbs

* きをつける	気をつける	to be cautious/careful（～に）
* しらべる	調べる	to look into (a matter)（*matter* を）
みえる	見える	to be visible（～が）

Irregular Verbs

* する		to decide on (an item)（*item* に）
* かんこうする	観光する	to do sightseeing
よやくする	予約する	to reserve（～を）
さんかする	参加する	to participate（～に）
そつぎょうする	卒業する	to graduate (from . . .)（*school* を）
はっぴょうする	発表する	to make a presentation; to make public

Adverbs and Other Expressions

* ～けど		. . . , but; . . . , so
～め	～目	-th
いちにちめ	一日目	first day
いちにちじゅう	一日中	all day long
さいきん	最近	recently
もういちど	もう一度	one more time
たのしみです	楽しみです	cannot wait; to look forward to it

会
L15

文 法 _{ぶん ぽう} G r a m m a r

1 Volitional Form

The volitional form of a verb is a more casual equivalent of ましょう. You can use it to suggest a plan to a close friend, for example.

> A：あしたは授業がないから、今晩どこかに行こう。
> _{じゅぎょう} _{こんばん} _い
>
> *We won't have any classes tomorrow. Let's go somewhere this evening.*
>
> B：いいね。そうしよう。
>
> *Sounds good. Let's do so.*

You can make the volitional forms using the rules listed below:

Volitional form

・ *ru*-verbs:　Drop the final *-ru* and add *-yoo*.

　　見る (*mi-ru*) →　見よう (*mi-yoo*)
　　み　　　　　　　　み

・ *u*-verbs:　Drop the final *-u* and add *-oo*.

行く (*ik-u*)	→	行こう (*ik-oo*)	作る → 作ろう	
い		い	つく　　つく	
話す	→	話そう	泳ぐ → 泳ごう	
はな		はな	およ　　およ	
待つ	→	待とう	遊ぶ → 遊ぼう	
ま		ま	あそ　　あそ	
死ぬ	→	死のう	買う → 買おう	
し		し	か　　　か	
読む	→	読もう		
よ		よ		

・ irregular verbs:

　　くる　　　　→　こよう　　　　　　　　する　→　しよう

Think of the *u*-verb conjugation in terms of a *hiragana* chart.

	行 _い	話 _{はな}	待 _ま	死 _し	読 _よ	作 _{つく}	泳 _{およ}	遊 _{あそ}	買 _か	
negative	か	さ	た	な	ま	ら	が	ば	わ	～ない
stem	き	し	ち	に	み	り	ぎ	び	い	～ます
affirmative	く	す	つ	ぬ	む	る	ぐ	ぶ	う	= Dictionary form
potential	け	せ	て	ね	め	れ	げ	べ	え	～る
volitional	こ	そ	と	の	も	ろ	ご	ぼ	お	～う

You can use the volitional plus the question particle か to ask for an opinion in your offer or suggestion.

A：手伝おうか。 *Shall I lend you a hand?*
B：ううん。大丈夫。 *No, I'm doing okay.*
A：今度、いつ会おうか。 *When shall we meet again?*
B：来週の土曜日はどう？ *How about Saturday next week?*

2 Volitional Form ＋ と思っています

We use the volitional form ＋ と思っています to talk about our resolutions.

毎日三時間日本語を勉強しようと思っています。
I've decided to/I'm going to study Japanese for three hours every day.

You can also use the volitional ＋ と思います, which suggests that the decision to perform the activity is being made *on the spot* at the time of speaking. と思っています, in contrast, tends to suggest that you have *already decided* to do something.

Situation 1

Q：十万円あげましょう。何に使いますか。
I will give you 100,000 yen. What will you use it for?

A：旅行に行こうと思います。
I will go on a trip. (decision made on the spot)

Situation 2

Q：両親から十万円もらったんですか。何に使うんですか。
You got 100,000 yen from your parents? What are you going to use it for?

A：旅行に行こうと思っています。
I am going to go on a trip. (decision already made)

Note that verbs in volitional forms and verbs in the present tense convey different ideas when they are used with と思います or と思っています. When you use volitionals, you are talking about your intention. When you use the present tense, you are talking about your prediction.

日本の会社で働こうと思います。
I will/intend to work for a Japanese company.

日本の会社で働くと思います。
I think they/I will be working for a Japanese company.

3 〜ておく

The *te*-form of a verb plus the helping verb おく describes an action performed *in preparation for something*.

あした試験があるので、今晩勉強しておきます。
しけん　　　　　　　　こんばんべんきょう
Since there will be an exam tomorrow, I will study (for it) tonight.

友だちが来るから、部屋を掃除しておかなきゃいけません。
とも　　　く　　　　　へ　や　そうじ
I have to clean the room, because my friends are coming.

> 〜ておく　　　　*do something in preparation*

ておく is often shortened to とく in speech.

ホテルを予約しとくね。
よやく
I will make a hotel reservation in advance.

4 Using Sentences to Qualify Nouns

In the phrase おもしろい本, the い-adjective おもしろい qualifies the noun 本 and tells us what kind of book it is. You can also use sentences to qualify nouns. The sentences that are used as qualifiers of nouns are shown in the boxes below.

1.	きのう買った	本	the book	that I bought yesterday
2.	彼がくれた	本	the book	my boyfriend gave me
3.	つくえの上にある	本	the book	that is on the table
4.	日本で買えない	本	the book	that you can't buy in Japan

Qualifier sentences in these examples tell us what kind of book we are talking about, just like adjectives. The verbs used in such qualifier sentences are in their short forms, either in the present (as in examples 3 and 4) or the past tense (1 and 2), and either in the affirmative (1-3) or in the negative (4). When the subject of the verb—that is to say, the person performing the activity—appears inside a qualifier sentence, as in example 2 above, it is accompanied by the particle が, and not は.

A "qualifier sentence + noun" combination is just like one big noun phrase. You can put it anywhere in a sentence that has a noun.

これは <u>去年の誕生日に彼女がくれた</u> 本です。　　(cf. これは本です。)
This is a book that my girlfriend gave me on my birthday last year.

父が <u>村上春樹が書いた</u> 本をくれました。　　(cf. 父が本をくれました。)
My father gave me a book that Haruki Murakami wrote.

<u>私が一番感動した</u> 映画は「生きる」です。　　(cf. 映画は「生きる」です。)
The movie I was touched by the most is "To Live," a 1952 film directed by Akira Kuosawa.

会
L15

Culture Notes

日本の宿 Japanese Accommodations

There are different types of accommodations in Japan, such as ホテル (hotels), 旅館 (Japanese-style inns), and ゲストハウス (guest houses).

ホテル in Japan offer Western-style facilities. There are also inexpensive hotels called "ビジネスホテル," which have only small rooms but suffice for those who just need a good night's rest.

旅館, which offer Japanese-style rooms with a 畳 floor, let you experience the uniqueness of Japan—the architecture, lifestyle, traditions, and culture. Guests change into a 浴衣 (Japanese cotton robe) and sleep on a 布団 mattress. Most 旅館 have gender-separated communal baths, which are sometimes fed by an 温泉 (hot spring). Some even have a smaller bath that can be reserved for private use. A stay includes dinner and breakfast. Usually both meals are Japanese style and feature regional and seasonal specialties.

ゲストハウス offers cheaper options. You usually stay in dormitory-style shared rooms or small private rooms (Japanese or Western style). You can meet the owner, staff, and other guests in the common area. Some houses offer a bit of Japanese culture such as origami and cooking.

表現ノート
ひょう　げん

The use of short forms in casual speech ▶ Let's examine some more examples of short forms used in casual spoken Japanese in the Dialogue.

今度の休み、予定ある？　The verb ある calls for the particle が, as in 予定が
こんど　やす　　よてい
ある. The particles は, が, and を are frequently dropped in casual speech. Note also that this sentence is a yes/no question, and the particle か is dropped. (The question particle か is retained in special cases only, such as the pattern "the volitional ＋ か (*Shall we . . . ?*)")

思ってるんだけど　思ってる is the contraction of 思っている, where the
おも　　　　　　　おも　　　　　　　　　　　　　　　　　おも
vowel い of the helping verb いる is dropped. Such contractions do occur in the long form (です and ます) speech patterns, too, but are more frequent in casual speech with short forms.

言ってたから。　言ってた is the contraction of 言っていた, and another ex-
い　　　　　　　い　　　　　　　　　　　　　　　　い
ample of the vowel い in the helping verb ている dropping out.

有名なお寺だよ。　だ is systematically dropped at the end of a sentence, but it
ゆうめい　　てら
is retained when followed by よ or ね.

> A：今日、何曜日？
> きょう　なんようび
> B：水曜日。／水曜日だよ。
> すいようび　　すいようび

〜けど and 〜が ▶ You can use けど and が not only in the sense of "but" (con-trasting two situations), but also to present the background to what you are about to say. In the Dialogue, 一緒に行かない？ alone would be too abrupt, and
いっしょ　い
Takeshi would wonder what Mary is talking about. Mary could have used two separate sentences, as in ゆいさんの長野のうちに行こうと思ってるんだ。一
ながの　　　　　い　　　おも
緒に行かない？ By inserting けど, Mary indicates that she still has something to
しょ　い
say at the end of the first sentence.

Short present ＋予定です ▶ You can add 予定です to a verb in the present tense
よてい　　　　　　　　　　　　　　　　　　よてい
short form when you want to say that something is scheduled to take place.

> 私は今度の週末に韓国に行く予定です。
> わたし　こんど　しゅうまつ　かんこく　い　よてい
> *I am scheduled to go to Korea this coming weekend.*
> 兄は九月に結婚する予定です。
> あに　くがつ　けっこん　よてい
> *My big brother is scheduled to get married this September.*

You can also use 予定です with verbs in the negative.

> あしたは学校に来ない予定です。
> *I am not planning to come to school tomorrow.*

見える/見られる ▶ 見える is different from 見られる, the regular potential form of 見る. 見える means "something or someone is spontaneously visible"; 見られる, on the other hand, means that the subject of the sentence can see something or someone actively rather than passively.

> 部屋の窓から海が見えます。
> *I can see the ocean from the window of the room.*
> どこであの映画が見られますか。
> *Where can I see that movie?*

The difference between 聞こえる and 聞ける is the same. 聞こえる means "something is spontaneously audible." On the other hand, 聞ける, the potential form of 聞く, means that the subject of the sentence can hear the sound actively.

> 今朝、鳥の声が聞こえました。
> *This morning, I heard the voices of the birds.*
> インターネットで日本のラジオ番組が聞けます。
> *We can listen to Japanese radio programs on the internet.*

〜目 ▶ The suffix 目 turns a number into a reference to a position in a series, like *first*, *second*, *third*, and *fourth*.

	first	second	third
〜人目	一人目 (first person)	二人目 (second person)	三人目 (third person)
〜枚目	一枚目 (first sheet)	二枚目 (second sheet)	三枚目 (third sheet)
〜年目	一年目 (first year)	二年目 (second year)	三年目 (third year)
〜日目	一日目 (first day)	二日目 (second day)	三日目 (third day)

練習 Practice
れん しゅう

Ⅰ コーヒーを飲もうか ☞Grammar 1
の

A. Change the verbs into the volitional forms. 🔊 K15-09

〔Example〕 行く → 行こう
い   い

1. 食べる
   た
2. 誘う
   さそ
3. 借りる
   か

4. 読む
   よ
5. 来る
   く
6. 待つ
   ま

7. 入る
   はい
8. 急ぐ
   いそ
9. 話す
   はな

10. 見る
    み
11. 書く
    か
12. 予約する
    よ やく

B. Pair Work—Suggest your plans to your partner using informal speech. 🔊 K15-10

〔Example〕 Ａ：カフェでコーヒーを飲もう（か）。
                            の
         Ｂ：うん、そうしよう。／うーん、ちょっと……。

e.g.

drink coffee at a cafe

(1)

play soccer

(2)

see a movie in town

(3)

take pictures at school

(4)

swim in a pool

(5)

buy hamburgers at
McDonald's

(6)

(7)

(8)

eat boxed lunches in a classroom　　climb a mountain　　have a barbecue at a park

C. Pair Work—You and your partner are going on a trip together for four days. Gather information, decide where you are going, and discuss what you are going to do each day. Think of as many activities as possible.

(Example) A：どこに行こうか。
B：九州に行こう。
A：うん。じゃあ、九州で何をしようか。
B：いい温泉があるから、温泉に入ろう。

1. どこに行きますか。 _____
2. 何をしますか。　一日目 _____
　　　　　　　　二日目 _____
　　　　　　　　三日目 _____
　　　　　　　　四日目 _____

D. Let's sing the song 幸せなら手をたたこう. 🔊 K15-11

♪　幸せなら手をたたこう　　幸せなら手をたたこう
　幸せなら態度で示そうよ　ほら、みんなで手をたたこう

＊手をたたく (clap your hands)　態度 (attitude)　示す (show)

What do you suggest doing when you are happy?
Change the underlined parts into other verbs using the volitional forms.

(Example) 握手をする (shake hands)　→　握手をしよう
ウインクする (wink)　→　ウインクしよう

Ⅱ 運動しようと思っています  Grammar 2
うんどう　　　　　　　おも

A. Describe what each person is planning to do. 🔊 K15-12

Example メアリー (have various experiences in Japan)

→ メアリーさんは日本でいろいろな経験をしようと思っています。
　　　　　　　　　　にほん　　　　　　　　　けいけん　　　　　　　おも

1. ナオミ　　　(do physical exercise)
2. 山下先生　　(go on a diet)
   やましたせんせい
3. カルロス　　(quit smoking)
4. ヤスミン　　(make lots of Japanese friends)
5. ロバート　　(practice Japanese all day)
6. ソラ　　　　(look into Japanese customs)
7. ウデイ　　　(look for a job in Japan)
8. ジョン　　　(participate in volunteer activity（ボランティア活動）)
　　　　　　　　　　　　　　　　　　　　　　　　　　かつどう

B. Ask three classmates what they are going to do this weekend and fill in the chart.

Example A：週末何をしようと思っていますか。
　　　　　　しゅうまつなに　　　　　　おも
　　　　　B：キャンプをしようと思っています。
　　　　　　　　　　　　　　　　　おも
　　　　　A：いいですね。だれと行くんですか。
　　　　　　　　　　　　　　　　い
　　　　　B：けんさんと行こうと思っています。
　　　　　　　　　　　　い　　　おも

名前 なまえ	何を なに	どこで	だれと

C. Pair Work—Practice the following dialogue with your partner. Then substitute the boxed part with the other occasions listed below and complete the rest of the underlined parts accordingly.

Dialogue:

A：もうすぐ、二十一歳の誕生日ですね。

B：ええ、うちでパーティーをしようと思っています。

A：そうですか。それは、いいですね。

会
L15

冬休み _{ふゆやす}	夏休み _{なつやす}	試験 _{しけん}	レポートの締め切り _{し き}
卒業式 _{そつぎょうしき}	お正月 _{しょうがつ}	先生の結婚式 _{せんせい けっこんしき}	日本語のクラスの発表 _{に ほん ご はっぴょう}

Ⅲ お金を借りておきます　☞Grammar 3
_{かね か}

A. A famous psychic said that there will be a big earthquake next week. Say what the people below will do in advance. 🔊 K15-13

> 来週、大きい地震があります。
> _{らいしゅう おお じしん}

(Example) ゆい（電池を買う）
_{てん ち か}

　　→　ゆいさんは電池を買っておきます。
　　　　　　　　_{てん ち か}

1. メアリー　　（水と食べ物を買う）
_{みず た もの か}
2. ヤスミン　　（お金をおろす）
_{かね}
3. ロバート　　（お金を借りる）
_{かね か}
4. 山下先生　　（うちを売る）
_{やましたせんせい}　　　_う
5. ソラ　　　　（保険に入る）
_{ほ けん はい}
6. けん　　　　（大きい家具を捨てる）
_{おお か ぐ す}
7. たけし　　　（たくさん食べる）
_た
8. 私　　　　　（　　　　　　　　　　　　　　）
_{わたし}

B. What do you need to do to prepare for the following situations? Make as many sentences as possible using 〜おく.

Example 週末、旅行します。
しゅうまつ　　りょこう

> インターネットで旅館を予約しておきます。
> りょかん　　よやく
> おしゃれなカフェを調べておきます。
> しら
> ガイドブック (guidebook) を買っておきます。
> か

1. 来週ハワイに行きます。
   らいしゅう　　　　い
2. 両親が来ます。
   りょうしん　き
3. デートをします。
4. パーティーをします。
5. 来週、日本語で発表します。
   らいしゅう　にほんご　はっぴょう

C. Pair Work—Talk with your partner about what you would need to do in preparation for the following events.

Example 土曜日にパーティーをする
どようび
→　Ａ：土曜日にパーティーをしようか。
　　　どようび
Ｂ：いいね。食べ物や飲み物を買っておかなきゃいけないね。
　　　た　もの　の　もの　か
Ａ：そうだね。それから、部屋を掃除しておいたほうがいいよ。
　　　へや　そうじ
Ｂ：じゃあ、私／ぼくは部屋を掃除しておく。
　　　わたし　　　　へや　そうじ
Ａ：じゃあ、私／ぼくは飲み物を買っておく。
　　　わたし　　　　の　もの　か
Ｂ：楽しみだね。
　　　たの
Ａ：うん。楽しみ。
　　　たの

1. 今度の休みに旅行する
   こんど　やす　　りょこう
2. 週末にキャンプをする
   しゅうまつ
3. (your own)

Ⅳ 韓国に住んでいる友だち　☞Grammar 4
かんこく　　す　　　　とも

A. These are photos you posted on social media. Explain them, using noun phrases. 🔊 K15-14

Example 韓国に住んでいる友だち
かんこく　　す　　　　とも

e.g. a friend who lives in Korea

(1) a friend who can speak Spanish

(2) a watch I got from my girlfriend

(3) a friend who went to China last year

(4) a bag I use every day

(5) a cafe I sometimes go to

(6) a temple I saw last week

(7) a T-shirt I bought in Hawaii

(8) the house I live in now

会
L15

B. You are a collector of items associated with world-famous figures. Show your collection to your guest. 🔊 K15-15

Example これはブルース・リーが使ったヌンチャクです。
つか

e.g.

a nunchaku Bruce Lee used

(1)

a picture Picasso painted
（ピカソ）

(2)

a piano Beethoven played
（ベートーベン）

(3)
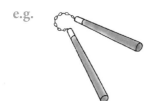
a jacket Elvis Presley wore
（エルビス・プレスリー）

(4)

a car Batman rode
（バットマン）

(5)

a letter Gandhi wrote
（ガンジー）

(6) 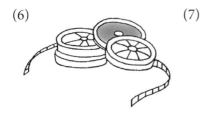 (7)  (8)

a movie Kurosawa made a dictionary Napoleon used a hat Chaplin wore
          （ナポレオン）   （チャップリン）

C. Talk about something you have, as in the example.

Example A：これは父にもらった時計です。
     　ちち   とけい
   B：いい時計ですね。
     　とけい

D. Combine the following two sentences into one sentence. The underlined words will be modified. 🔊 K15-16

Example <u>コーヒー</u>を飲んでみました。
       の
   ┗━━ （田中さんにもらいました）
     　たなか
  → 田中さんにもらった<u>コーヒー</u>を飲んでみました。
    たなか   の

1. <u>料理</u>はおいしくないです。
 りょうり
 ┗━━ （妹が作りました）
   いもうと　つく

2. <u>人</u>と結婚したくないです。
 ひと　けっこん
 ┗━━ （料理ができません）
   りょうり

3. <u>外国人</u>を探しています。
 がいこくじん　さが
 ┗━━ （日本の習慣についてよく知っています）
   にほん　しゅうかん   　し

4. <u>人</u>にもう一度会いたいです。
 ひと いちど あ
 ┗━━ （去年の夏に会いました）
   きょねん　なつ　あ

5. <u>人</u>とルームメイトになりたくないです。
 ひと
 ┗━━ （よくしゃべります）

6. <u>会社</u>はこの建物の中にあります。
 かいしゃ たてもの　なか
 ┗━━ （おじさんが働いています）
     はたら

7. 冬休みに旅館に泊まろうと思っています。
　　ふゆやす　　りょかん　と　　　おも
　　　　　↑――（温泉があります）
　　　　　　　　　　おんせん

8. 留学に興味があるんですが、学生を知っていますか。
　　りゅうがく　きょうみ　　　　　　がくせい　し
　　　　　　　　　　　　　↑――（アメリカに留学したことがあります）
　　　　　　　　　　　　　　　　　　　　　　りゅうがく

E. Pair Work—Ask your partner the following questions. Later, report your findings to the class, as in the example.

Example　What did you buy lately?

　　　→　A：最近何を買いましたか。
　　　　　　　さいきんなに　か
　　　　　B：辞書です。
　　　　　　　じしょ
　　　　　A：Bさんが最近買った物は辞書です。
　　　　　　　　　　　さいきん か　　もの　じしょ

1. What movie did you see recently?

2. What gift have you received lately?

3. Which celebrity do you want to meet?

4. What country have you been to?

5. What kind of music did you listen to when you were in high school?

6. (your own)

F. Pair Work—Ask which of the three alternatives your partner likes the most.

Example　A：どのケーキが食べたいですか。
　　　　　　　　　　　　　　た
　　　　　B：先生が作ったケーキが食べたいです。
　　　　　　　せんせい　つく　　　　　　た

(a)　　　　　　　　　　　(b)　　　　　　　　　　　(c)

Mary gave me

I bought yesterday

my teacher made

1. どのレストランに行きましょうか。

(a)

we went last week to

(b)

our friend is working
part-time at

(c)

we have never been to

2. どの人と付き合いたいですか。

(a)

graduated from
the University of Tokyo

(b)

has a Porsche（ポルシェ）

(c)

can play the piano

3. どんな町に住みたいですか。

(a)

there are movie theaters

(b)

there are nice restaurants

(c)

tax is not high

4. どんな家に住みたいですか。

(a)

there is a swimming pool

(b)

garden is spacious

(c)

with an ocean view
（海が見える）

5. ルームメイトを探しています。どの人がいいですか。

(a)

likes cooking

(b)

doesn't smoke

(c)

has pets

V まとめの練習

A. Pair Work—Guessing Game
Write down what you do often in Column Ⅰ. Write down what you think your partner does often in Column Ⅱ. Ask each other to find out if you have guessed right. If you have guessed your partner's answers correctly, you score a point. You win the game if you have scored higher than your partner.

Example A：よく食べる物は、ハンバーガーですか。
B：はい、そうです。／いいえ、私がよく食べる物は、そばです。

	I. I do often:	**II.** I think my partner does often:	Was I correct?
よく食べる物			
よく行く所			
よく作る料理			
よく聞く音楽			
よく見るドラマ (drama)			
よく飲む飲み物			
よくするゲーム			

B. Class Activity—Find someone who . . .

1. 来週、発表があります。 _____ さん
2. ボランティア活動をしています。 _____ さん
3. 旅館に泊まったことがあります。 _____ さん
4. 週末、一日中寝ます。 _____ さん
5. 週末、大学に行かなきゃいけません。 _____ さん
6. 来年も日本語を勉強しようと思っています。 _____ さん
7. アルバイトを探しています。 _____ さん

Later, report to the class, as in the example.

[Example] 来週、発表がある人は_____さんです。

C. Tell the class about your New Year's resolution (新年の抱負).

[Example] 去年は遊びすぎたから、今年は、もっと勉強しようと思っています。
それから、韓国語を習いたいです。

D. Pair Work—Suppose you and your partner have just arrived at your travel destination. (You choose the place.) Using Dialogue Ⅱ as a model, decide to do something together with your partner. Use informal speech.

Useful Expressions

ホテルで

At the Hotel

Useful Vocabulary

〜泊(はく) —— . . . nights

（何泊(なんばく)／一泊(いっぱく)／二泊(にはく)／三泊(さんぱく)／四泊(よんぱく)……）

朝食付き(ちょうしょくつき) —— with breakfast

一泊二食付き(いっぱくにしょくつき) —— one night with two meals

チェックイン（する） —— checking in

チェックアウト（する） —— checking out

シングル —— single room	フロント —— receptionist; front desk
ダブル —— double room	禁煙(きんえん) —— non-smoking
ツイン —— twin room	喫煙(きつえん) —— smoking
〜名(めい) —— . . . person(s)	大浴場(だいよくじょう) —— large spa

Useful Expressions

予約(よやく)した○○です。チェックインお願(ねが)いします。

—— I have a reservation under the name of XX. Could you check me in, please?

○○で払(はら)えますか。—— Can I pay by XX?

アメリカドルを日本円(にほんえん)に両替(りょうがえ)できますか。

—— Can you change US dollars to Japanese yen?

タクシーを呼(よ)んでもらえますか。—— Would you call a taxi for us?

近(ちか)くにおすすめのレストランがありますか。

—— Are there any restaurants you recommend near here?

二時(にじ)まで荷物(にもつ)を預(あず)かってもらえますか。

—— Could you keep my luggage until 2 o'clock?

第16課

LESSON 16

忘れ物 Lost and Found
わす もの

In this lesson, we will...

◉ Talk about doing a favor   ◉ Apologize
◉ Express our hopes and wishes   ◉ Describe lost items

会 話 Dialogue
かい わ

Ⅰ At Professor Yamashita's office. 🔊 K16-01/02

1 ジョン： 失礼します。先生、今日授業に来られなくてすみませんでした。
   しつれい せんせい きょう じゅぎょう こ

2 山下先生： どうしたんですか。
   やましたせんせい

3 ジョン： 実は、朝寝坊して、電車に乗り遅れたんです。すみません。
   じつ あさねぼう てんしゃ の おく

4 山下先生： もう三回目ですよ。もっと早く寝たらどうですか。
   やましたせんせい さんかいめ はや ね

5 ジョン： はい。あのう、先生、宿題をあしたまで待っていただけませんか。
   せんせい しゅくだい ま

6 宿題を入れたファイルがないんです。
   しゅくだい い

7 山下先生： 困りましたね。見つかるといいですね。
   やましたせんせい こま み

Ⅱ At the station. 🔊 K16-03/04

1 ジョン： すみません。ファイルをなくしたんですが。

2 駅 員： どんなファイルですか。
   えき いん

3 ジョン： 青くてこのぐらいの大きさです。電車を降りる時、忘れたと思うんで
   あお おお てんしゃ お とき わす おも

4 すが。

5 駅 員： ええと……ちょっと待ってください。電話して聞いてみます。
   えき いん ま てんわ き

Ⅲ At school the next day. 🔊 K16-05/06

1 山下先生：　ジョンさん、ファイルはありましたか。

2 ジョン：　　はい、駅員さんが探してくれたんです。

3 山下先生：　よかったですね。

4 ジョン：　　これ、宿題です。遅くなってすみませんでした。

5 山下先生：　いいえ。よくできていますね。

6 ジョン：　　ええ、駅員さんに宿題を手伝ってもらいましたから。

Ⅰ

John: Excuse me. Professor Yamashita, I'm sorry that I couldn't come to class today.

Prof. Yamashita: What happened?

John: Well, I got up late and I missed the train. I'm sorry.

Prof. Yamashita: This is the third time. Why don't you go to bed earlier?

John: Yes . . . um, Professor Yamashita, as for the homework, could you please wait till tomorrow? I cannot find the folder I put my homework in.

Prof. Yamashita: That's a problem. I hope you find it.

Ⅱ

John: Excuse me, I have lost my folder.

Station attendant: What is it like?

John: It's blue and about this size. I think I left it when I got off the train.

Station attendant: Well . . . Please wait a minute. I will call and ask.

Ⅲ

Prof. Yamashita: John, did you find the folder?

John: Yes, a station attendant found it for me.

Prof. Yamashita: Good.

John: This is the homework. I'm sorry it's late.

Prof. Yamashita: That's okay. It's well done.

John: Yes, that's because the station attendant helped me.

単語
たん ご

🔊 K16-07 (J-E)
K16-08 (E-J)

V o c a b u l a r y

N o u n s

* えきいん（さん）	駅員（さん）	station attendant
おや	親	parent
しんせき	親せき	relatives
ごみ		garbage
さとう	砂糖	sugar
* ファイル		(file) folder; portfolio; file
* おおきさ	大きさ	size
みち	道	way; road; directions
きまつしけん	期末試験	final examination
けんきゅう	研究	research
だいがくいん	大学院	graduate school
しょうがくきん	奨学金	scholarship
すいせんじょう	推薦状	letter of recommendation
たいふう	台風	typhoon
ぶんか	文化	culture
へんじ	返事	reply
ひ	日	day

い - a d j e c t i v e

きたない	汚い	dirty

U - v e r b s

おこす	起こす	to wake (someone) up （〜を）
おごる		to treat (someone) to a meal （*person* に *meal* を）
わらう	笑う	to laugh
おちこむ	落ち込む	to get depressed
* こまる	困る	to have difficulty
だす	出す	to take (something) out; to hand in (something) （〜を）
なおす	直す	to correct; to fix （〜を）
* みつかる	見つかる	to be found （〜が）
やくす	訳す	to translate （*source* を *target* に）

＊Words that appear in the dialogue

かす	貸す	to lend (*person* に *thing* を)
つれていく	連れていく	to take (someone) to (a place) (*person* を *place* に)
みちにまよう	道に迷う	to become lost; to lose one's way
むかえにいく	迎えに行く	to go to pick up (*place* まで/に *person* を)

Ru-verbs

あつめる	集める	to collect (〜を)
*いれる	入れる	to put (something) in (*thing* を *place* に)
みせる	見せる	to show (*person* に *thing* を)
*のりおくれる	乗り遅れる	to miss (a train, bus, etc.) (〜に)
アイロンをかける		to iron (clothes) (〜に)

Irregular Verbs

*あさねぼうする	朝寝坊する	to oversleep
あんないする	案内する	to show (someone) around (*place* を)
せつめいする	説明する	to explain
むかえにくる	迎えに来る	to come to pick up (*place* まで/に *person* を)

Adverbs and Other Expressions

きょうじゅうに	今日中に	by the end of today
じゅぎょうちゅうに	授業中に	in class; during the class
このあいだ	この間	the other day
これから		from now on
*このぐらい		about this much (＝これぐらい/このくらい/これくらい)
じぶんで	自分で	(do something) by oneself
ほかの	他の	other
*ええと		well . . . ; let me see . . .
じつは	実は	actually; in fact
〜いがい	〜以外	other than . . .
ごめん		I'm sorry. (casual)
*しつれいします	失礼します	Excuse me.; Sorry to interrupt you.

文法 ぶん ぽう G r a m m a r

1 ～てあげる / てくれる / てもらう

We learned in Lesson 14 that the verbs あげる, くれる, and もらう describe transactions of things. Here we will learn the use of these words as helping verbs. When these verbs follow the *te*-form of a verb, they describe the giving and receiving of services.

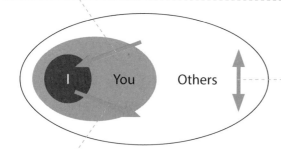

te-form **+ くれる**
<for me or somebody close to me>

Somebody does something for me.
You do something for me.
Somebody does something for you.

te-form **+ あげる**
<for somebody other than me>
Somebody does something for somebody else.

te-form **+ あげる**
<for somebody other than me>
I do something for you.
You do something for others.
I do something for others.

We use the *te*-form **+ あげる** when we do something for the sake of others, or somebody does something for somebody else. The addition of the helping verb あげる does not change the basic meaning of the sentences, but puts focus on the fact that the actions were performed "on demand" or "as a favor."[1]

私は妹にお金を貸してあげました。
I (generously) lent my sister money (to help her out of her destitute conditions).

cf. 私は妹にお金を貸しました。 [an objective statement]

---

[1] Note that in あげる sentences the nouns referring to the beneficiaries are accompanied by whatever particle the main verb calls for. 貸す goes with the particle に, while 連れていく goes with を. These particles are retained in the あげる sentences.

When you want to add the idea of "doing somebody a favor" to a verb which does not have the place for the beneficiary, you can use ～のために.

私はゆいさんのために買い物に行きました。　cf. 私は買い物に行きました。
I went shopping for Yui.

ななみさんはヤスミンさんを駅（えき）に連れていって<u>あげました</u>。

Nanami (kindly) took Yasmin to the station (because she would be lost if left all by herself).

cf. ななみさんはヤスミンさんを駅（えき）に連れていきました。 [an objective statement]

We use くれる when somebody does something for us.[2]

友（とも）だちが宿題（しゅくだい）を手伝（てつだ）って<u>くれます</u>。

A friend helps me with my homework (for which I am grateful).

親（しん）せきがりんごを送（おく）って<u>くれました</u>。

A relative sent me apples. (I should be so lucky.)

We use the *te*-form ＋ もらう to say that we get, persuade, or arrange for, somebody to do something for us. In other words, we "receive" somebody's favor. The person performing the action for us is accompanied by the particle に.[3]

私（わたし）は友（とも）だちに宿題（しゅくだい）を手伝（てつだ）って<u>もらいました</u>。

I got a friend of mine to help me with my homework.

Compare the last sentence with the くれる version below. They describe more or less the same event, but the subjects are different. In もらう sentences, the subject is the beneficiary. In くれる sentences, the subject is the benefactor.

友（とも）だちが宿題（しゅくだい）を手伝（てつだ）って<u>くれました</u>。

A friend of mine helped me with my homework.

---

[2] The beneficiary is almost always understood to be the speaker in くれる sentences. Therefore it usually does not figure grammatically. If you have to explicitly state who received the benefit, you can follow the same strategies employed in あげる sentences. That is, if the main verb has the place for the person receiving the benefit, keep the particle that goes with it. The verb 連れていく calls for を, while 教える calls for に, for example.

ななみさんが<u>私（わたし）を</u>駅（えき）に連れていって<u>くれました</u>。　(Compare: <u>私（わたし）を</u>駅（えき）に連（つ）れていく)
Nanami took me to the station.

たけしさんが<u>私（わたし）に</u>漢字（かんじ）を教（おし）えて<u>くれました</u>。　(Compare: <u>私（わたし）に</u>漢字（かんじ）を教（おし）える)
Takeshi taught me that kanji.

If the main verb does not have the place for the person, use 〜のために. 掃除（そうじ）する is one such verb.

けんさんが<u>私（わたし）のために</u>部屋（へや）を掃除（そうじ）して<u>くれました</u>。
Ken cleaned the room for me.

[3] Sometimes, a もらう sentence simply acknowledges a person's goodwill in doing something for us. For example, you can say the following, even if you had not actively asked for any assistance. (The sentence is of course okay with the "get somebody to do" reading.)

私（わたし）は知（し）らない人（ひと）に漢字（かんじ）を読（よ）んで<u>もらいました</u>。
I am glad that a stranger read the kanji for me.

2 〜ていただけませんか

We will learn three new ways to make a request. They differ in the degrees of politeness shown to the person you are asking.

〜て	いただけませんか	(polite)
	くれませんか	
	くれない？	(casual)

We use the *te*-form of a verb ＋ いただけませんか to make a polite request.[4] This is more appropriate than ください when you request a favor from a nonpeer such as your professor or your boss or from a stranger.

手伝っていただけませんか。
てつだ
Would you lend me a hand?

The *te*-form ＋ くれませんか is a request which is roughly equal in the degree of politeness to ください. くれませんか of course comes from the verb くれる. This is probably the form most appropriate in the host-family context.

ちょっと待ってくれませんか。
ま
Will you wait for a second?

You can use the *te*-form ＋ くれない, or the *te*-form by itself, to ask for a favor in a very casual way. This is good for speaking with members of your peer group.

それ取ってくれない？　or　それ取って。
と　　　　　　　　　　　　と
Pick that thing up (and pass it to me), will you?

---

[4] いただけませんか comes from いただける, the potential verb, which in turn comes from いただく, "to receive (something or a favor) from somebody higher up." We will come back to this verb in Lesson 20. We also have くださいませんか, which comes from the verb くださる, "somebody higher up gives me (something or a favor)." ください is historically a truncation of くださいませんか.

The variants of the いただけませんか pattern are listed in what is felt by most native speakers to be the order of decreasing politeness. In addition to these, each verb can be used in the affirmative as well as in the negative.

〜ていただけませんか	（いただける, the potential verb for いただく）
〜てくださいませんか	（くださる）
〜てもらえませんか	（もらえる, the potential verb for もらう）
〜てくれませんか	（くれる）
〜てもらえない？	（もらえる, in the short form）
〜てくれない？	（くれる, in the short form）

3 〜といい

You can use the present tense short form + といいですね (polite) or といいね (casual) to say that you hope something nice happens. When you say といいですね or といいね, you are wishing for the good luck of somebody other than yourself.

いいアルバイトが見つかるといいですね。 *I hope you find a good part-time job.*

雨が降らないといいね。 *I hope it doesn't rain.*

To say what you hope for, for your own good, you can use といいんですが (polite) or といいんだけど (casual). These endings show the speaker's attitude is more tentative and make the sentence sound more modest.[5]

試験がやさしいといいんですが。 *I am hoping that the exam is easy.*

八時の電車に乗れるといいんだけど。 *I hope I can catch the eight o'clock train.*

| (short, present) と | いいですね / いいね | *I hope . . . (for you/them)* |
| | いいんですが / いいんだけど | *I hope . . . (for myself)* |

Note that all these といい sentences mean that you are hoping that something nice *happens*. This means that these patterns cannot be used in cases where you hope *to do* something nice, which is under your control. In such cases, you can usually turn the verb into the potential form.

大学に行けるといいんですが。 Compare: ✕ 大学に行くといいんですが。
I am hoping to go to college. = I am hoping that I can go to college.

4 〜時

We use the word 時 to describe *when* something happens or happened.

sentence A 時、	sentence B。	*When A, B.*
↑	↑	
time reference	main event	

---

[5] If I hope that *you* do something *for me*, that is, if I want to make an indirect request, we use てくれる before といいんですが, as in:

ソラさんが来てくれるといいんですが。 *Sora, I hope you will come.*

Sentence A always ends with a short form, either in the present tense or the past tense. You can decide which tense to use in A by doing a simple thought experiment. Place yourself at the time the main event B takes place, and imagine how you would describe the event in A. If A is current or yet to happen, use the present tense in A. If A has already taken place, use the past tense.[6]

The present tense in A

If, at the time the main event B takes place, A is current or is still "in the future," use the present tense in A.

チベットに行く時、ビザを取ります。
When I go to Tibet [=A], I will get a visa [=B].

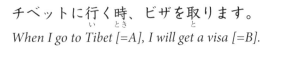

going to Tibet

A: ————————————|————————— チベットに行く時

B: ————————|——————————————— ビザを取ります。

getting a visa

チベットに行きます。

Note that as long as the event A occurs after the event B, the clause A gets the present tense (行く), irrespective of the tense in clause B (取ります or 取りました). In the example below, the whole sequence of events has been shifted to the past: at the time you applied for the visa (=B), the departure (=A) was yet to be realized. The temporal order between the two events is exactly the same as in the example above, hence the present tense of 行く. Note especially that we use the present tense in A, even if the two events took place in the past.

チベットに行く時、ビザを取りました。
When I was going to Tibet [=A], I got a visa [=B].

Observe more examples of this tense combination.

寝る時、電気を消します。
When I go to sleep, I turn off the light.
(You turn off the light [=B], and then go to bed [=A].)

出かける時、ドアにかぎをかけました。
When I went out, I locked the door.
(You locked the door [=B], and then went out [=A].)

---

[6] The grammar of the 時 temporal clauses in reality has more twists and quirks than are shown here, but this should be a good enough start.

Clause A also gets the present tense when the state of A holds true when the event of B takes place.[7]

さびしい時、友だちに電話します。
I call up friends when I am lonely.

さびしいです。

A: ————————————— さびしい時
feeling lonely

B: ————————————— 友だちに電話します。
make phone calls

Note that な-adjectives take な, and nouns take の before 時.

寒い時、頭が痛くなります。
I get a headache when it's cold.

元気な時、公園を走ります。
I jog in the park when I feel fit.

犬が病気の時、病院に連れていきました。
I took the dog to a vet when it was sick.

The past tense in A

If, at the time of main event B, A is already "in the past," use the past tense in A. Note that we use the past tense even when the two events are yet to take place; it is the order of the two that matters. In the example below, you will have already arrived in China (=A) at the time you buy tea (=B).

---

[7] If A is a verbal idea (action) and describes an ongoing event during which B takes or took place, the verb in A is in the ている form. In the example below, the phone call event (=B) occurs in the middle of TV viewing (=A).

テレビを見ている時、友だちから電話がありました。
A phone call came when I was watching TV.

テレビを見ています。

watching TV

A: ————————————— テレビを見ている時

B: ————————————— 友だちから電話がありました。
phone call

Note in this connection that it is wrong to use the following sentence pattern, because 行っている does not describe an ongoing event but is a description of the result of "going," that is, being in a faraway place after going (see Lesson 7).

×沖縄に行っている時、飛行機に乗りました。
(Should be: 沖縄に行く時、飛行機に乗りました。)
I went by plane when I was going to Okinawa.

中国に行った時、ウーロン茶を買います。
I will buy oolong tea when I go to China.

中国に行った時、ウーロン茶を買いました。
I bought oolong tea when I went to China.

中国に来ました

```
                    going to China
A: ─────────────┼─────────────── 中国に行った時
                                 ちゅうごく  い  とき
B: ─────────────┼─────────────── ウーロン茶を買います／買いました。
            buying oolong tea      ちゃ   か        か
```

疲れた時、ゆっくりお風呂に入ります。
When I have gotten tired, I take a long bath.
(You get tired [=A], and then take a bath [=B].)

財布を忘れた時、友だちにお金を借りました。
When I had forgotten to bring my wallet, I borrowed money from a friend.
(You found out about the wallet [=A] and then decided to borrow money [=B].)

5 ～てすみませんでした

You use the *te*-form of a verb to describe the things you have done that you want to apologize for.

汚い言葉を使ってすみませんでした。　　　　　*I'm sorry for using foul language.*

デートの約束を忘れてごめん。　　　　　　　　*Sorry that I stood you up.*

～て	すみませんでした (polite) ごめん (casual)	*Sorry for doing . . .*

When you want to apologize for something you have failed to do, you use ～なくて, the short, negative *te*-form of a verb. (To derive the form, first turn the verb into the short, negative ～ない, and then replace the last い with くて.)[8]

宿題を持ってこなくてすみませんでした。
I'm sorry for not bringing the homework.

もっと早く言わなくてごめん。
Sorry that I did not tell you earlier.

Expression Notes

表現ノート
ひょう　げん

④

このぐらいの大きさです ▶ You can turn an い-adjective into a noun by replacing the last い with さ. Thus from 大きい you can get 大きさ (size). Other examples include やさしさ (kindness) and さびしさ (loneliness). Some な-adjectives
can likewise be turned into nouns by replacing な with さ, as in 便利さ (convenience).
べん り

おごる ▶ おごる is mainly used among friends. ごちそうする is a polite alternative for おごる. Use ごちそうする instead when the person who will treat, or
treated, you to a meal is a superior, such as a teacher or a business associate. ごち
そうする refers to "invite for a meal" as well as "pay for a meal."

週末友だちを呼んで晩ご飯をごちそうしました。
しゅうまつとも　　　よ　　　ばん　はん

I invited friends for dinner this weekend.

Culture Notes

贈り物の習慣 Gift-giving in Japan
おく　もの　しゅう かん

Gift-giving is an important part of Japanese culture. In July/August and December, people
give お中元 and お歳暮 gifts to their relatives, parents, friends, business clients and so on.
ちゅうげん　　　せい ぼ
Japanese department stores offer a wide variety of お中元/お歳暮 items during the season.
ちゅうげん　　せい ぼ
The most common gifts are food such as sweets, fruits, and drinks. On
average, the gifts cost somewhere between 3,000–5,000 yen.

　Another type of gift is お土産 (souvenirs). When Japanese people
みやげ
travel, they purchase local food products or small items to give to
their friends, family, and co-workers.

　When visiting someone's house, Japanese people often take 手土産
て みやげ
(lit., hand souvenir), such as sweets or fruits. If you are invited to a
Japanese home, it is a good idea to take some 手土産 with you.
て みやげ

お中元 items at a
ちゅうげん
department store

写真提供：共同通信社

---

[8] The past tense version すみませんでした implies that you have made a clean break from the mistake that you
made, while the present tense すみません is good if you consider that the problem still persists. You can use ご
めん for both cases.

遅刻してすみませんでした。　　*Sorry for being late for class.* [After the class]
ち こく
遅刻してすみません。　　　　　*Sorry for being late for class.* [As you arrive at the classroom]
ち こく

練習 P r a c t i c e
れん　しゅう

Ⅰ 晩ご飯を作ってあげました ☞Grammar 1
ばん　はん　つく

A. Your friend is sick, and you did the following for your friend. Say what you did with 〜てあげる. 🔊 K16-09

Example cook dinner → 晩ご飯を作ってあげました。
ばん　はん　つく

1. be with them
2. help with their homework
3. correct their paper
4. buy flowers
5. take them to the hospital
6. do laundry
7. clean their room
8. lend them your notebook
9. send an e-mail to their teacher
10. do dishes

B. Pair Work—Your partner needs help. Say what you would do for your partner in each situation using 〜てあげる.

Example A：友だちがいなくてさびしいんです。
とも
B：そうですか。私の友だちを紹介してあげましょうか。
わたし　とも　しょうかい
A：ありがとうございます。

1. 天ぷらが食べたいけど、作れないんです。
てん　た　つく
2. 海に行きたいけど、車がないんです。
うみ　い　くるま
3. 今日中に宿題をしなきゃいけないんです。
きょう じゅう　しゅくだい
4. お金がないので、昼ご飯が食べられないんです。
かね　ひる　はん　た
5. 部屋が汚いんです。
へ　や　きたな
6. バスに乗り遅れたんです。
の　おく
7. 美術館に行きたいけど、道がわからないんです。
び じゅつかん　い　みち
8. 日本語のクラス以外で日本語を話したいんです。
に ほん ご　い がい　に ほん ご　はな

C. The following are what your host family, your friend, and a stranger did for you. State them with 〜てくれる and 〜てもらう. 🔊 K16-10/11

[Example] ホストファミリーがご飯を作ってくれました。
ホストファミリーにご飯を作ってもらいました。

ホストファミリー

友だち

知らない人

e.g. ご飯を作る	5. コーヒーをおごる	9. 案内する
1. 部屋を掃除する	6. 京都に連れていく	10. 道を教える
2. 洗濯する	7. セーターを編む	11. 荷物を持つ
3. アイロンをかける	8. 家族の写真を見せる	12. 千円貸す
4. 迎えに来る		

D. Describe what the following people did for you using 〜てくれる／〜てもらう.

1. 母／父　　2. 兄弟　　3. 親せき　　4. 友だち　　5. 同じクラスの人

E. You visited a Japanese family last weekend. Describe what they did for you and what you did for them using 〜てくれる／〜てあげる／〜てもらう. 🔊 K16-12

お父さん

お母さん

ひな

[Example] お母さんが晩ご飯を作ってくれました。
お母さんに晩ご飯を作ってもらいました。

F. *Omiai* Game—You are at an *Omiai* Party. Ask three people if they are willing to do the following after they get married. Add your own question. After the interview, tell the class who you want to see again and why.

＊*Omiai* (お見合い) is a meeting between potential mates for a marriage.
　　　　　　　　　み　あ

[Example] do laundry

→　A：洗濯してくれますか。
　　　　せんたく
　　B：はい、もちろんしてあげます。／

　　　　いいえ、自分でしてください。
　　　　　　　じぶん

(After the interview)

→　私はたけしさんと付き合いたいです。たけしさんは日本料理を
　　わたし　　　　　　　　つ　あ　　　　　　　　　　　　　　　　　　に　ほんりょう　り
　　作ってくれますから。
　　つく

	name ( )	name ( )	name ( )
cook			
clean the house			
wake me up			
do dishes			
take out the garbage			
buy presents			
iron			

G. Answer the following questions.

1. 今度の母の日／父の日に何をしてあげようと思いますか。
　こんど　はは　ひ　ちち　ひ　なに　　　　　　　　　おも

2. 子供の時、家族は何をしてくれましたか。
　こども　とき　かぞく　なに

3. 彼／彼女／パートナーに何をしてもらいたいですか。
　かれ　かのじょ　　　　　　　なに

4. 家族に何をしてもらいたいですか。
　かぞく　なに

5. 友だちが落ち込んでいます。何をしてあげますか。
　とも　　お　こ　　　　　　なに

6. 病気の時、友だちに何をしてもらいたいですか。
　びょうき　とき　とも　　　なに

Ⅱ ゆっくり話していただけませんか ☛Grammar 2
　　　　　はな

A. Ask these people the following favors, as in the example. 🔊 K16-13

(Example) ゆっくり話す
　　　　　　　　はな

→　（友だち）ゆっくり話してくれない？
　　とも　　　　はな

（ホストファミリー）ゆっくり話してくれませんか。
　　　　　　　　　　　はな

（先生）ゆっくり話していただけませんか。
　せんせい　　はな

友だち
とも

ホストファミリー

先生
せんせい

1. 自転車を貸す じ てん しゃ か	
2. 本を返す ほん かえ	
3. 友だちを紹介する とも しょうかい	
4. ノートを見せる み	

5. 六時に起こす ろく じ お
6. 駅に迎えに来る えき むか く
7. お弁当を作る べんとう つく
8. 宿題を手伝う しゅくだい て つだ

9. 文法を説明する ぶんぽう せつめい
10. 推薦状を書く すいせんじょう か
11. 英語に訳す えい ご やく
12. 作文を直す さくぶん なお

B. Pair Work—Make requests in the following situations, using the appropriate speech style (〜くれない／くれませんか／いただけませんか). Expand the conversation.

Example You want to go somewhere. (to your boyfriend/girlfriend/partner)

→　Ａ：ドライブに連れていってくれない？
　　　　　　　　　　　　つ
　　Ｂ：いいよ。どこに行きたい？
　　　　　　　　　　い
　　Ａ：海に行きたい。
　　　　うみ　い

1. You are broke. (to your host mother)
2. You need one more day to finish the homework. (to your teacher)
3. You are expecting a guest, and you need help around the house. (to your child)
4. You love your host father's tempura. (to your host father)
5. You want to meet more people. (to your friend)
6. You want to have the letter that you wrote corrected. (to your boss)

Ⅲ よくなるといいですね ☞Grammar 3

A. Read each person's situation, and express what you hope for them. 🔊 K16-14

Example

かぜをひいたんです。

You get well soon.
→ 早くよくなるといいですね。
　 はや

ロバート

あしたから旅行に行くんです。
りょこう　い

1. It is good weather.
2. It is not cold.
3. It is fun.

会
L16

ヤスミン

大学院で日本の文化について研究したいんです。
だいがくいん　にほん　ぶんか　けんきゅう

4. You can get into a graduate school.
5. You can get a scholarship.
6. You can do good research.

ジョン

宿題を忘れたんです。
しゅくだい　わす

7. Your teacher does not collect the homework.
8. Your teacher does not come to class.
9. A typhoon comes and there is no class today.

B. You are in the following situations. Explain your situation and say what you hope for.

Example　You want to live in Japan.

→　日本に住みたいんです。仕事が見つかるといいんですが。
にほん　す　しごと　み

Talking about your current situation:

1. You have a test tomorrow.
2. You are going to climb a mountain next week.
3. You are starting a new part-time job.
4. (your own)

Talking about your future plans:

5. You want to get married.
6. You intend to graduate next year.
7. You will study abroad.
8. (your own)

C. Pair Work—One of you is in the following situations. Change the underlined parts and make a short dialogue for each situation expressing what you hope for. A starts each conversation.

Example B is going to Disneyland this weekend.

→　A：どうしたの。<u>うれしそうだね</u>。
　　B：<u>週末、ディズニーランドに行く</u>んだ。
　　　　_{しゅうまつ}　　　　　　　　　　　_い
　　A：そう。<u>天気がいい</u>といいね。(I hope for you.)
　　　　　　_{てんき}
　　B：うん。<u>ミッキーと写真が撮れる</u>といいんだけど。
　　　　　　　　　　_{しゃしん}　_と
　　　　　　　　　　　　　　　　　　　　　　(I hope for myself.)

1. B is going to go skiing this weekend.
2. B has a final exam tomorrow.
3. B is going to have a date for the first time.

4. B lost their wallet.
5. B has caught a cold.
6. (your own)

Ⅳ かぜをひいた時、病院に行きます 👉Grammar 4
　　　　　　　_{とき}　_{びょういん}　_い

A. Describe each situation using 〜時. 🔊 K16-15
　　　　　　　　　　　　　　　　_{とき}

Example

食べすぎました。
_た

コーヒーを飲みます。
　　　　　　_の

→　食べすぎた時、
　　_た　　_{とき}
　　薬を飲みます。
　　_{くすり}　_の

→　コーヒーを飲む時、
　　　　　　　_の　_{とき}
　　砂糖を入れます。
　　_{さとう}　_い

(1)
眠いです。
_{ねむ}

(2)
わかりません。

(3)
日本語で手紙を書きました。
_{にほんご}　_{てがみ}　_か

(4)

ホームシックです。

(5)

友だちの家に行きます。

(6)
ひまです。

会
L16

(7)

おいしいピザが
食べたいです。

(8)
朝寝坊しました。

タクシー

B. Connect the sentences using 〜時. Pay attention to the tense before 時. 🔊 K16-16

(Example) 道に迷う／親切そうな人に道を聞く
→ 道に迷った時、親切そうな人に道を聞きます。

1. 友だちが来る／私の町を案内する
2. さびしい／友だちに電話する
3. 電車に乗る／切符を買う
4. 写真を撮る／「チーズ」と言う
5. ひまだ／料理をする

6. ディズニーランドに行く／
ミッキーのぬいぐるみを買った
7. 友だちが病気だ／一緒にいてあげる
8. かぜをひく／病院に行く

C. Pair Work—Ask each other the following questions. Answer them with 〜時.

(Example) A：どんな時、薬を飲みますか。
B：頭が痛い時、薬を飲みます。

1. どんな時、学校をサボりますか。
2. どんな時、親に電話しますか。
3. どんな時、うれしくなりますか。
4. どんな時、緊張しますか。
5. どんな時、泣きましたか。
6. どんな時、感動しましたか。

D. Complete the following sentences.

1. ＿＿＿＿＿＿＿＿＿＿＿＿＿＿＿＿＿＿時（とき）、笑（わら）ってはいけません。

2. ＿＿＿＿＿＿＿＿＿＿＿＿＿＿＿＿時（とき）、友（とも）だちに相談（そうだん）します。

3. さびしい時（とき）、＿＿＿＿＿＿＿＿＿＿＿＿＿＿＿＿＿＿＿。

4. 初（はじ）めて日本語（にほんご）を習（なら）った時（とき）、＿＿＿＿＿＿＿＿＿＿＿＿＿。

5. 友（とも）だちが＿＿＿＿＿＿＿＿時（とき）、＿＿＿＿＿＿＿＿てあげます。

Ⅴ 来（こ）られなくてすみませんでした　☛Grammar 5

A. Make sentences apologizing for the following things using 〜てすみませんでした／〜てごめん. 🔊 K16-17

Example)
授業（じゅぎょう）に来（こ）られない　→　授業（じゅぎょう）に来（こ）られなくてすみませんでした。
夜遅（よるおそ）く電話（でんわ）する　→　夜遅（よるおそ）く電話（でんわ）してごめん。

(to your professor)

1. 授業中（じゅぎょうちゅう）に話（はな）す
2. 授業中（じゅぎょうちゅう）に寝（ね）る
3. 遅刻（ちこく）する
4. 教科書（きょうかしょ）を持（も）ってこない

(to your friend)

5. 返事（へんじ）が遅（おそ）くなる
6. 約束（やくそく）を守（まも）らない
7. パーティーに行（い）かない
8. 迎（むか）えに行（い）けない

B. Make sentences to apologize for the following things and add excuses. Use 〜てすみませんでした or 〜てごめん depending on whom you are talking to.

Example) You came late to the class. (to your professor)

→　A：先生（せんせい）、遅（おそ）くなってすみませんでした。
　　B：どうしたんですか。
　　A：きのうの夜遅（よるおそ）くレポートを書（か）いていて、朝寝坊（あさねぼう）したんです。
　　B：そうですか。これから気（き）をつけてください。

1. You couldn't come to the class. (to your professor)
2. You woke your roommate up. (to your roommate)
3. You forgot your friend's birthday. (to your friend)
4. You laughed at your friend. (to your friend)
5. You told a lie. (to your host father)

Ⅵ まとめの練習
れんしゅう

A. Share your good experience of someone helping you or doing something for you. Use
〜てくれる／〜てもらう.

[Example] この間、京都にお寺を見に行った時、道に迷ったんです。
あいだ きょうと てら み い とき みち まよ
　　　　私が道を聞いた人はとても親切で、お寺に連れていってくれました。
わたし みち き ひと しんせつ てら つ
　　　　そして、ほかのお寺も案内してくれました。とてもうれしかったです。
てら あんない

会

L16

B. Role Play—Make a skit based on the following situations.

1. You were absent from class yesterday. Apologize to your teacher and explain why you
   were absent.

2. You forgot your date. Apologize to them. Then tell them that you are too busy to have
   a date this week, and ask them to wait till next week.

Let's Find Out 調べてみよう
しら

日本のお土産
に ほん みやげ

You are in Japan and planning to buy souvenirs—for yourself or for a friend/family.
Find something that is uniquely Japanese. Show pictures of the item you have
chosen and tell the class what it is. Optionally, class may vote on the best gift.

[Example]

これは風呂敷 (wrapping cloth) です。
ふ ろ しき
昔はかばんがなかったので、この中に
むかし なか
いろいろな物を入れて、持っていきました。
もの い も
今はきれいな風呂敷がたくさんあります。
いま ふ ろ しき
風呂敷はかわいいバッグ (bag) にもなります。
ふ ろ しき
テーブルクロス (table cloth) にもなります。
とても便利だと思います。
べん り おも

第17課

ぐちとうわさ話 Grumble and Gossip
ばなし

In this lesson, we will ....

◉ Tell what we hear from others
◉ Talk about hypothetical situations

◉ Point out similarities
◉ Grumble about our situations

会 話 D i a l o g u e
かい わ

Ⅰ Sora and Takeshi have just run into each other at the station. 🔊 K17-01/02

1 ソラ： たけしさん、久しぶりですね。旅行会社に就職したそうですね。
　　　　　　　ひさ　　　　　　　りょこうがいしゃ　しゅうしょく

2 　　　　　おめでとうございます。

3 たけし： ありがとうございます。

4 ソラ： もう仕事に慣れましたか。
　　　　　　　しごと　な

5 たけし： ええ。でも学生の時に比べてすごく忙しくなりました。自分の時間が
　　　　　　　　　　　がくせい　とき　くら　　　　　いそが　　　　　　　　　じぶん　じかん

6 　　　　　ぜんぜんないんです。

7 ソラ： 大変ですね。私の友だちの会社は休みが多くて、残業をしなくてもい
　　　　　たいへん　　　わたし　とも　　　かいしゃ　やす　　おお　　　ざんぎょう

8 　　　　　いそうですよ。

9 たけし： うらやましいなあ。ぼくの会社は休みも少ないし、給料も安いし、
　　　　　　　　　　　　　　かいしゃ　やす　　すく　　　きゅうりょう　やす

10 　　　　　最悪です。
　　　　　さいあく

11 ソラ： 会社に入る前にどうしてもっと調べなかったんですか。
　　　　　かいしゃ　はい　まえ　　　　　　　　しら

12 たけし： 旅行会社に入ったら、旅行ができると思ったんです。
　　　　　りょこうがいしゃ　はい　　　　　りょこう　　　　　　おも

Ⅱ Ken and Sora are talking. 🔊 K17-03/04

1 ソラ： 今朝、駅でたけしさんに会ったよ。
　　　　　けさ　えき　　　　　　　あ

2 けん： たけしさんが卒業してからぜんぜん会ってないけど、元気だった？
　　　　　　　　　　そつぎょう　　　　　　　あ　　　　　　げんき

3 ソラ： ずいぶん疲れているみたい。毎晩四、五時間しか寝ていないそうだよ。
　　　　　つか　　　　　　　まいばんし　ごじかん　　ね

4 けん： やっぱりサラリーマンは大変だよね。
　　　　　　　　　　　　　　たいへん

5 ソラ： それに、忙しすぎてメアリーとデートする時間もないって。
　　　　　　　いそが　　　　　　　　　　　　じかん

6 けん：　そうか。ぼくだったら、仕事より彼女を選ぶけど。あの二人、大丈夫か
　　　　　　　　　　しごと　　　かのじょ　えら　　　　　　　　　　　　　ふたり　　　だいじょうぶ
7 　　　　　なあ。

Ⅰ

Sora: Takeshi, long time no see. I've heard you got a job at a travel agency. Congratulations!

Takeshi: Thank you.

Sora: Have you gotten used to the job yet?

Takeshi: Yes. But compared to my college days, I have become very busy. I don't have any time for myself.

Sora: That's tough. At my friend's company, there are many holidays, and they don't have to work overtime, I heard.

Takeshi: I'm envious. At my company, there are few holidays and the salary is low . . . It can't get worse.

Sora: Why didn't you check more before you entered the company?

Takeshi: I thought that I could travel around when I got in a travel agency.

Ⅱ

Sora: I happened to meet Takeshi at the station this morning.

Ken: I haven't seen him since he graduated. How was he?

Sora: He looked very tired. He said he sleeps only four or five hours every night.

Ken: Office workers in Japan have a hard time, after all.

Sora: Besides that, he said he doesn't have time to go out with Mary.

Ken: I see. If I were him, I would choose the girlfriend over the job. I hope they'll be okay.

単 語
たん　　ご

🔊 K17-05 (J-E)
K17-06 (E-J)

■■■■ V o c a b u l a r y ■■■■

N o u n s

あかちゃん	赤ちゃん	baby
おきゃくさん	お客さん	guest; visitor; client; customer
しゅしょう	首相	prime minister
* サラリーマン		salaryman; office worker
* きゅうりょう	給料	salary
* ざんぎょう	残業	overtime work
パンダ		panda
コンタクト（レンズ）		contact lenses
ひげ		beard
ブーツ		boots
かぎ	鍵	lock; key
たからくじ	宝くじ	lottery
かみ	紙	paper
スプーン		spoon
おゆ	お湯	hot water
でんしレンジ	電子レンジ	microwave oven
ヒーター		heater
ニュース		news
かじ	火事	fire
* りょこうがいしゃ	旅行会社	travel agency
ショッピングモール		shopping mall
りょう	寮	dormitory
ちがい	違い	difference
ひみつ	秘密	secret
じゅんび	準備	preparation
* じぶん	自分	oneself

い - a d j e c t i v e s

あぶない	危ない	dangerous
* うらやましい		envious
* すくない	少ない	a little; a few
つごうがわるい	都合が悪い	inconvenient; to have a scheduling conflict
つよい	強い	strong

* Words that appear in the dialogue

な-adjective

* さいあく（な）	最悪	the worst

U-verbs

* えらぶ	選ぶ	to choose; to select （〜を）
おゆをわかす	お湯を沸かす	to boil water
かみをとかす	髪をとかす	to comb one's hair
ひげをそる		to shave one's beard
ぬぐ	脱ぐ	to take off (clothes) （〜を）
こむ	混む	to get crowded （〜が）
たからくじにあたる	宝くじに当たる	to win a lottery

Ru-verbs

いれる		to make tea, coffee, etc. （〜を）
うまれる	生まれる	to be born （〜が）
かぎをかける	鍵をかける	to lock （〜に）
たりる	足りる	to be sufficient; to be enough （〜が）
* なれる	慣れる	to get used to . . . （〜に）

Irregular Verbs

おいのりする	お祈りする	to pray （〜に）
けしょうする	化粧する	to put makeup on
* しゅうしょくする	就職する	to get a full-time job (at . . .) (company に)
りこんする	離婚する	to get a divorce (person と)
する		to wear small items (necktie, watch, etc.) （〜を）

Adverbs and Other Expressions

* ずいぶん		very
たとえば	例えば	for example
* 〜にくらべて	〜に比べて	compared with . . .
〜によると		according to . . .
* まえ	前	before . . .
* やっぱり		after all
* 〜かな（あ）		I wonder . . . (casual)
* そうか		I see. (casual)
* おめでとうございます		Congratulations!

会
L17

文法 Grammar
ぶん ぽう

1 ～そうです (I hear)

In Lesson 13, we discussed the sentence-final expression そうです, which means "seemingly." Here we will study another sentence-final そうです, which presents a "hearsay report." The two そうです differ not only in their semantics, but also in the forms of predicates they are attached to.

You can add the そうです of a report to a sentence ending in the short form.[1]

If you heard someone say:		You can report it as:
「日本語の授業は楽しいです。」 にほんご じゅぎょう たの *"Our Japanese class is fun."*	→	日本語の授業は楽しいそうです。 にほんご じゅぎょう たの *I've heard that their Japanese class is fun.*
「先生はとても親切です。」 せんせい しんせつ *"Our professor is very kind."*	→	先生はとても親切だそうです。 せんせい しんせつ *I've heard that their professor is very kind.*
「今日は授業がありませんでした。」 きょう じゅぎょう *"We did not have a class today."*	→	その日は授業がなかったそうです。 ひ じゅぎょう *I've heard that they didn't have a class that day.*

When we use そうです, the reported speech retains the tense and the polarity of the original utterance. We simply turn the predicates into their short forms. (Thus です after a な-adjective or a noun changes to だ, while です after an い-adjective is left out.) Compare the paradigms of the two そうです.

～そうです			*I hear that . . .*	*It looks like . . .*
· verbs:	話す はな	→	話すそうです はな	—[2]
· い-adjectives:	さびしい	→	さびしいそうです	さびしそうです
· な-adjectives:	好きだ す	→	好きだそうです す	好きそうです す
· noun ＋です:	学生だ がくせい	→	学生だそうです がくせい	—

---

[1] The そうです of report is robustly invariant. The only forms commonly used are そうです and the more casual そうだ. We do not use the negative そうじゃないです, and the past tense version そうでした.

[2] See the footnote on そうです in Lesson 13.

To specify the information source, you can preface a sentence with the phrase 〜によると, as in トムさんによると (according to Tom), 新聞によると (according to the newspaper report), and 天気予報によると (according to the weather forecast).

天気予報によると、台風が来るそうです。
According to the weather forecast, a typhoon is approaching.

2 〜って

In informal speech, you can add って at the end of a sentence, instead of そうです, to quote what you have heard. って is the informal variant of the quotation particle と and follows the short forms in much the same way as と言っていました and そうです.[3]

Thus, when your friend Mary says,

「今日は忙しいです。あした、試験があるんです。」

you can report it as:

メアリーさん、今日は忙しい<u>って</u>。あした、試験があるんだ<u>って</u>。
Mary says she's busy today. She says she has an exam tomorrow.

You can also use って in place of the quotation particle と before verbs like 言う.

ロバートさんは何<u>て</u>言ってた?[4]　　　　　*What did Robert say?*

チョコレートを食べすぎた<u>って</u>言ってた。　*He said he ate too much chocolate.*

3 〜たら

たら is one of the several words in Japanese that refer to conditional (*if*) dependence.[5] When we say "A たら B," we mean that the event, action, or situation in B is realized if and when the condition in A is met.

日本に行ったら、着物を買います。
I will buy kimono if and when I go to Japan.

---

[3] って and と can also follow the long forms, and indeed sentence final particles like か, ね, and よ, if your intent is to quote verbatim, preserving the style and tone of the original utterance.

[4] って changes to て after ん.

[5] We learned one use of this word in Lesson 14: たらどうですか used in recommending an activity to the listener. たらどうですか literally translates as "how is it if."

The initial た in たら comes from the short form past tense endings of predicates.

～たら	short form (aff.) short form (neg.)		～たら (if . . .)
・verbs:	読む 読まない	→ →	読んだら 読まなかったら
・い-adjectives:	やさしい やさしくない	→ →	やさしかったら やさしくなかったら
・な-adjectives:	静かだ 静かじゃない	→ →	静かだったら 静かじゃなかったら
・noun ＋です:	休みだ 休みじゃない	→ →	休みだったら 休みじゃなかったら

Sometimes, the clause before たら describes a *possible* condition and the clause after it the consequence which *then* follows. Whether or not the condition is actually met is largely an open issue with this set of sentences.

山下先生に会ったら、そのことを聞こうと思います。
I will ask about it, if I see Professor Yamashita.

日本人だったら、この言葉を知っているでしょう。
If somebody is a Japanese person, then they will probably know this word.

天気がよくなかったら、キャンプに行きません。
We will not go camping, if the weather is not good.

Note that when you say "A たら B," you cannot express a sequence of events in which B occurs before A; B can only take place at the time A comes true or later. You cannot therefore use たら to describe an "if" sentence like the following. ("B" = this weekend, which comes before "A" = next week.)

× 来週試験があったら、今度の週末は勉強したほうがいいですよ。
   It will be better for you to study this weekend, if you have an exam next week.

Sometimes, the たら clause describes a very *probable* condition, and the second clause describes the event that will take place *as soon as* the situation is realized. With this type of sentence, たら simply arranges future events and activities in a temporal sequence.

宿題が終わったら、遊びに行きましょう。
<ruby>宿<rt>しゅく</rt></ruby><ruby>題<rt>だい</rt></ruby>が<ruby>終<rt>お</rt></ruby>わったら、<ruby>遊<rt>あそ</rt></ruby>びに<ruby>行<rt>い</rt></ruby>きましょう。
Let's go out and have some fun once we are done with the homework.

Note that the very same sentences could be interpreted in this way or in the way shown earlier. The difference lies not in the sentences themselves, but in the different ways the real world could possibly be. With the last example above, if you think that you can finish your homework in due course, the sentence means that you want to go out *when* it is done. If you are not sure whether you can finish your homework, the sentence describes what you will do *if* it gets finished.[6]

Finally, the たら clause can describe a condition that is unreal and contrary to fact. With this type of sentence, you express a purely hypothetical condition and its probable result.

<ruby>私<rt>わたし</rt></ruby>が<ruby>猫<rt>ねこ</rt></ruby>だったら、<ruby>一日中<rt>いちにちじゅう</rt></ruby><ruby>寝<rt>ね</rt></ruby>ているでしょう。
If I were a cat, I would be asleep all day long.

<ruby>百万円<rt>ひゃくまんえん</rt></ruby>あったら、<ruby>車<rt>くるま</rt></ruby>を<ruby>買<rt>か</rt></ruby>うんですけど。
If I had a million yen, I would buy a car.

4 ～なくてもいいです

To describe what you *do not need to* do, take a negative sentence in the short form, drop the final い of ない, and add くてもいいです. なくて is the negative *te*-form, which we studied in Grammar 5 in Lesson 16.[7]

<ruby>靴<rt>くつ</rt></ruby>を<ruby>脱<rt>ぬ</rt></ruby>がなくてもいいです。
You do not need to take off your shoes.

プレゼントは<ruby>高<rt>たか</rt></ruby>くなくてもいいです。
The present does not need to be anything expensive.

~ない → ～なくてもいいです *does not need to . . .*

---

[6] Throughout the uses of the たら conditional clauses discussed here, one thing remains constant: A たら B can only describe a conditional dependency that holds *naturally* between A and B. You cannot describe with たら an "if" dependency of the "B even if A" type, where B holds *in spite of* A. We will learn about "even if" sentences in Lesson 23.

× あなたが<ruby>結婚<rt>けっこん</rt></ruby>したかっ<u>たら</u>、<ruby>私<rt>わたし</rt></ruby>は<ruby>結婚<rt>けっこん</rt></ruby>しません。
I will not marry you even if you want to.

[7] You can omit も in なくてもいい and say なくていい, which makes it slightly more casual.

5 ～みたいです

みたいです follows a noun and expresses the idea that something or somebody *resembles* the thing or the person described by the noun. The resemblance noted is usually in terms of external characteristics, but not necessarily so.[8]

私の父はカーネルおじさんみたいです。
My dad looks/acts like Colonel Sanders, the KFC founder.

(Has a portly figure? Has a white goatee? Stands on the street 24/7?)

みたいです can also follow a verb[9] and expresses the idea that something "appears to be the case." It can follow the short form of the present tense and the past tense, both in the affirmative and in the negative.

雨が降ったみたいですね。
It looks like it has rained, doesn't it?

あの人はおなかがすいているみたいです。
It looks like that person is hungry.

あの人はきのうの夜寝なかったみたいです。
It looks like that person did not sleep last night.

noun/verb ＋ みたいです	*It looks like . . .*

6 ～前に / ～てから

You can use the present tense short form and 前に to describe the event *before* which something happens.

verb A (short, present) ＋ 前に　verb B	*B before A.*

ジーンズを買う前に、はいてみます。
I try on jeans before I buy them.

---

[8] You can use みたいです about yourself, when you are not clear about the situation you are in.
　　財布を忘れたみたいです。　　*It looks like I have left my wallet at home.*
[9] みたいです can in fact follow adjectives too, but it is far more common to use そうです with adjectives. See Lesson 13 for the adjective base ＋ そうです construction.

日本に来る前に、一学期日本語を勉強しました。
_{に ほん く まえ いちがっ き に ほん ご べんきょう}
I studied Japanese for one semester before I came to Japan.

The verb that precedes 前に is always in the present tense, whether the tense of the overall sentence is in the present tense (as in the first example above) or in the past tense (as in the second).

To describe an event after which another thing happens, you can use the *te*-form of a verb ＋ から.[10]

---

verb A ＋ てから　verb B　　　*A, and then B. / B after A.*

勉強してから、遊びに行きました。
_{べんきょう あそ い}
I studied and then went out.

けんさんが来てから、食べましょう。
_{き た}
Why don't we (start) eat(ing) after Ken has arrived?

表現ノート
_{ひょう げん}

Expression Notes **5**

サラリーマンは大変だよね_{たいへん}▶You can add よね to a statement if both you and the person you are speaking to know about the situation equally well. Compare よ, ね, and よね in the following examples.

サラリーマンは大変だよ。_{たいへん} "You may not know this because you're still a student, but working for a company is tough." (Said by an office worker to a student, for example.)

サラリーマンは大変だね。_{たいへん} "I see that you are very tired. Working for a company is tough, I guess." (Said by a student to an office worker.)

サラリーマンは大変だよね。_{たいへん} "Working for a company is tough, isn't it?" (Typically, a comment made between students or office workers.)

---

[10] An "A てから B" sentence can also describe the state of B that has held true since event A.
猫が死んでから、とてもさびしいです。_{ねこ し}　　*I have been feeling very lonely since my cat died.*

日本人のジェスチャー Japanese Gestures
に ほん じん

We use language to communicate with people. However, we send and receive more messages through nonverbal communication than we do with words. Nonverbal communication includes gestures, facial expressions, eye contact, posture, touching, and even the way you dress.

The use of gestures varies around the world. Here are some examples of gestures that Japanese people use.

Come here.

Sorry.

I / me

OK!

No good.

Not me. / I don't understand.

I don't know.

V-sign in photos

練習 Practice

れん しゅう

I 就職したそうです ☞Grammar 1

しゅうしょく

A. Read Takeshi's and Naomi's social media posts and report them using 〜そうです.

🔊 K17-07

Example 就職しました。 → （たけしさんは）就職したそうです。
しゅうしょく しゅうしょく

会 L17

 たけし

10月25日

e.g. 就職しました！
しゅうしょく
1. 今、サラリーマンです。
いま
2. 仕事はすごく大変です。
しごと たいへん
3. 寝る時間がありません。
ね じかん
4. 彼女に会えません。
かのじょ あ

 ナオミ

10月19日

5. 横浜に行きました。
よこはま い
6. 中華街は混んでいました。
ちゅうかがい こ
7. ラーメンを食べました。
た
8. ラーメンはおいしかったです。
9. おみやげは買いませんでした。
か

* 中華街 (Chinatown)
ちゅうかがい

B. Pair Work—You have heard the following news. Tell your partner and discuss it.

Example 長野で大きい地震がありました。
ながの おお じしん
→ A：ニュースによると、長野で大きい地震が
ながの おお じしん
あったそうですよ。
B：そうなんですか。死んだ人がいるんですか。
し ひと

1. 山下先生の家で火事がありました。
やましたせんせい いえ かじ
2. 動物園でパンダの赤ちゃんが生まれました。
どうぶつえん あか う
3. 首相がやめました。
しゅしょう
4. ショッピングモールができます。
5. (your own)

C. Pair Work—One person chooses one of the following topics and talks about it. The other takes notes about what the person says and reports it to the class using 〜そうです.

1. 先週の週末
   せんしゅう　　しゅうまつ
2. 家族
   か ぞく
3. 休みの予定
   やす　　 よ てい

Ⅱ 土曜日は都合が悪いって ☞Grammar 2
   ど ようび 　 つ ごう 　 わる

A. Report on what Mary and Robert said using 〜って. 🔊 K17-08

Example メアリー／Saturday is inconvenient for me.

→ Q：メアリーさんは何て言ってた？
　　　　　　　　　　なん い
A：土曜日は都合が悪いって。
　　ど ようび 　 つ ごう 　 わる

メアリー

e.g. Saturday is inconvenient for me.
1. I have to give a presentation.
2. Tom and Mai are dating.
3. I slept only three hours last night.

ロバート

4. Mr. Tanaka got divorced.
5. I quit my part-time job.
6. I have to go back to England in June.
7. Japan is not dangerous.

B. Pair Work—Make a dialogue with your partner by filling out the blanks as in the example.

Example A：知ってる？ ジョンさん、宝くじに当たったって。
　　　　　 し　　　　　　　　　　　　たから　　 あ
B：えっ、そうなの？
A：うん、百万円もらえるって。
　　　 ひゃくまんえん
B：いいなあ。

```
┌─────────────────────────────────────────────────┐
│  A：知ってる？ ＿＿＿＿＿＿＿＿＿＿＿＿＿＿＿って。 │
│     し                                            │
│  B：えっ、そうなの？                              │
│                                                   │
│  A：うん、＿＿＿＿＿＿＿＿＿＿＿＿＿＿＿＿＿って。  │
│                                                   │
│  B：＿＿＿＿＿＿＿＿＿＿＿＿＿＿＿。                │
└─────────────────────────────────────────────────┘
```

Ⅲ お金がたくさんあったら、うれしいです　☞Grammar 3
　　　 かね

A. Make sentences with 〜たら、うれしいです using the cues. 🔊 K17-09

[Example] お金がたくさんある　→　お金がたくさんあったら、うれしいです。
　　　　　 かね　　　　　　　　　　　かね

1. 友だちがたくさんできる　　　　6. プレゼントをもらう
　 とも
2. 成績がいい　　　　　　　　　　7. 物価が安い
　 せいせき　　　　　　　　　　　 ぶっか　やす
3. 日本に行ける　　　　　　　　　8. 雨が降らない
　 に ほん　い　　　　　　　　　　 あめ　ふ
4. 学校が休みだ　　　　　　　　　9. 弁護士になれる
　 がっこう　やす　　　　　　　　　べん ご し
5. 宿題がない　　　　　　　　　 10. 先生がやさしい
　 しゅくだい　　　　　　　　　　　 せんせい

B. Change cues 1 through 8 into たら clauses, choose the appropriate phrases to follow them from a through i, and make sentences. 🔊 K17-10

[Example] 卒業したら、旅行会社に就職するつもりです。
　　　　　 そつぎょう　　りょこうがいしゃ　しゅうしょく

e.g. 卒業する　　　　・　　　　　・a. 掃除します。
　　 そつぎょう　　　　　　　　　　 そう じ
1. 太る　　　　　　・　　　　　・b. どこにも行けません。
　 ふと　　　　　　　　　　　　　　　　　　 い
2. 動物園に行く　　・　　　　　・c. 買おうと思っています。
　 どうぶつえん　い　　　　　　　　か　　　おも
3. 宿題が終わらない・　　　　　・d. 旅行会社に就職するつもりです。
　 しゅくだい　お　　　　　　　　 りょこうがいしゃ　しゅうしょく
4. 寒い　　　　　　・　　　　　・e. ダイエットをしなきゃいけません。
　 さむ
5. 安い電子レンジがある・　　　・f. 薬を買いに行ってあげます。
　 やす　でんし　　　　　　　　　　 くすり　か　　い
6. 友だちが病気だ　・　　　　　・g. パンダが見られます。
　 とも　　びょうき　　　　　　　　　　　　 み
7. 部屋がきれいじゃない・　　　・h. お茶をいれてください。
　 へ や　　　　　　　　　　　　　　 ちゃ
8. お客さんが来る　・　　　　　・i. ヒーターをつけたほうがいいですよ。
　 きゃく　　く

C. Pair Work—Talk about what you would do if you experienced in the following situations.

[Example] 首相だ　→　Ａ：首相だったら、どうしますか。
しゅしょう

Ｂ：私が首相だったら、税金を安くします。
わたし　しゅしょう　　　　　ぜいきん　やす

1. 宝くじに当たる
たから　　あ

2. タイムマシン (time machine) がある

3. 日本語の先生だ
にほんご　せんせい

4. ドラえもんの「どこでもドア」が使える
つか

(The door that takes you wherever you want to go. See p. 296.)

5. (your own)

D. Group Work—In a small group, talk about what you would/want to do in the following situations. Use casual style.

[Example] 試験が終わる
しけん　お

→　Ａ：試験が終わったら何がしたい？
しけん　お　　　なに

Ｂ：家で一日中ごろごろしたい。Ｃさんは？
いえ　いちにちじゅう

Ｃ：私は友だちとカラオケに行きたい。
わたし　とも　　　　　　　　い

1. 週末いい天気だ　　　　　　　　3. 大学を卒業する
しゅうまつ　てんき　　　　　　　　だいがく　そつぎょう

2. 日本に行く／国に帰る　　　　　4. (your own)
にほん　い　　くに　かえ

Ⅳ 勉強しなくてもいいです　☛Grammar 4
べんきょう

A. Carlos doesn't have to do the following things. Make sentences using 〜なくてもいい. 🔊 K17-11

[Example] need not study　→　カルロスさんは勉強しなくてもいいです。
べんきょう

On Saturday:

1. need not memorize vocabulary

2. need not practice kanji

3. need not speak Japanese

4. need not get up early in the morning

5. need not go to school

At his homestay:

6. need not wash dishes

7. need not do laundry

8. need not cook

9. need not clean his own room

10. need not come home early

B. Pair Work—Tell your partner what you have to do this week and ask if they have to do it. You may choose from the following.

Example prepare for a presentation

→　Ａ：今週、発表の準備をしなきゃいけません。Ｂさんは？
　　　　こんしゅう　はっぴょう　じゅん び
　　Ｂ：私はしなくてもいいです。
　　　　わたし
　　Ａ：いいですね。

memorize new kanji	write a paper
do homework	go shopping
return books to the library	pay the rent（家賃）
	や ちん
read a book	buy a present
study for exam（試験の勉強をする）	work part-time
し けん　べんきょう	
go on a diet	practice the piano
make a hotel reservation	withdraw money

C. Pair Work—You and your friend are doing research on companies. Student A has looked into SOMY and Student B has looked into Nantendo (B's memo is on p. 134). The things you must do are checked. Look at the memo and exchange the information using 〜なきゃいけませんか. After getting all the information, discuss which company would be better.

Example Ａ：ナンテンドーでは土曜日に働かなきゃいけませんか。
　　　　　　　　　　　ど ようび　はたら
　　　　Ｂ：いいえ、働かなくてもいいです。ソミーはどうですか。
　　　　　　　　はたら

Student A

SOMY		Nantendo
✓	work on Saturdays	
✓	be able to use a computer	
	quit at the age of 60	
✓	work until late hours	
	live in a dormitory	
	wear a tie	
¥250,000	salary	

Ⅴ スーパーマンみたいですね ☞Grammar 5

A. Describe what the following things/people are like with 〜みたいですね。 🔊 K17-12

Example スーパーマンみたいですね。

e.g. 友だちは強いんです。   (1) のり (seaweed) です。   (2) 耳かき (earpick) です。

スーパーマン

紙

スプーン

(3) イタリアです。   (4) パンダです。   (5) 友だちはよく寝るんです。

ブーツ

ぬいぐるみ

猫

(6) 友だちは秘密が
たくさんあるんです。

バットマン

(7) おじさんは
かわいいんです。

マリオ

B. Describe the following pictures with a verb ＋ みたいです.

Example 出かけるみたいです。
　　　　 て

e.g. 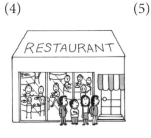　　(1)　　(2)　　(3)

L17

(4)　　(5)　　(6)　　(7)

C. Pair Work—Ask your partner the following questions about the picture. When you answer, use ～みたいです.

Example　Ａ：この人は男の人ですか。
　　　　　　　ひと　おとこ　ひと
　　　　　Ｂ：ええ、男の人みたいです。／
　　　　　　　　　　おとこ　ひと
　　　　　　　いいえ、男の人じゃないみたいです。
　　　　　　　　　　　おとこ　ひと

1. この人は学生ですか。
　　 ひと　がくせい
2. 結婚していますか。
　　 けっこん
3. 今日は休みですか。
　　 きょう　やす
4. 今、雨が降っていますか。
　　 いま　あめ　ふ
5. この人はテニスをしますか。
　　 ひと
6. たばこを吸いますか。
　　　　　す
7. よく掃除しますか。
　　　　 そうじ
8. 料理ができますか。
　　 りょうり
9. ギターが弾けますか。
　　　　　ひ
10. 今、何をしていますか。
　　 いま　なに

D. Pair Work—Make a dialogue, as in the example.

(Example) It seems like you (=B) caught a cold.

   →   A：どうしたの？

          B：かぜをひいたみたい。

          A：そう。早くよくなるといいね。お大事に。

          B：ありがとう。

1. It seems like you lost your wallet.
2. You cannot find your homework. It seems like you forgot your homework at home.
3. You are driving a car. It seems like you got lost.
4. You are interested in (one of your classmates). But it looks like they are dating someone.

Ⅵ　電話してから、友だちの家に行きます ☞Grammar 6

A. Look at the following pictures and make sentences using 〜てから. 🔊 K17-13

(Example) 電話してから、友だちの家に行きます。

e.g.

(4)　(5)

(6)　(7)

B. Look at the pictures above and make sentences using 〜前に. 🔊 K17-14
　　　　　　　　　　　　　　　　　　　　　　　　まえ

(Example) 友だちの家に行く前に、電話します。
　　　　とも　　いえ　い　まえ　　てんわ

C. Pair Work—Ask your partner the following questions.

1. 学校に来る前に、何をしますか。
　がっこう　く　まえ　なに

2. 就職する前に、何をしなければいけませんか。
　しゅうしょく　まえ　なに

3. 結婚する前に、何がしたいですか。
　けっこん　まえ　なに

4. きのううちへ帰ってから、何をしましたか。
　　　　　　かえ　　　なに

5. 今日授業が終わってから、何をするつもりですか。
　きょうじゅぎょう　お　　　　なに

Ⅶ まとめの練習
れんしゅう

A. Suppose you have just run into one of your classmates ten years from now. Exchange gossip about your mutual friends/your teachers, using ～そうです or ～って. You can make up your own story. But be nice!

Expressions you may want to use:

久しぶり ひさ	うらやましい	信じられない しん	最悪 さいあく
就職する しゅうしょく	結婚／離婚する けっこん　りこん	すごい	秘密 ひ みつ

B. Talk about the things you have or don't have to do in Japan, comparing them to similar situations in your country.

Example 日本とカナダ (Canada) の間にはいろいろな違いがあります。例えば、
にほん　　　　　　　　あいだ　　　　　　　　　　ちが　　　　　　　　たと
日本ではうちの中で靴を脱がなければいけません。でも、カナダでは
にほん　　　　なか　くつ　ぬ
脱がなくてもいいです。
ぬ

Pair Work Ⅳ C. (p. 129)

Example Ａ：ナンテンドーでは土曜日に働かなきゃいけませんか。
どようび　はたら
Ｂ：いいえ、働かなくてもいいです。ソミーはどうですか。
はたら

Student B

Nantendo		SOMY
	work on Saturdays	
	be able to use a computer	
	quit at the age of 60	
✓	work until late hours	
✓	live in a dormitory	
✓	wear a tie	
¥220,000	salary	

Useful Expressions

美容院／ヘアサロンで
びょういん
At the Hair Salon

Useful Expressions

カットをお願いします。
ねが
──────── I would like to have my hair cut.

あまり短くしないでください。
みじか
──────── Please don't make it too short.

そらないでください。──────── Please don't shave me.

３センチぐらい切ってください。──── Please cut off about 3 centimeters.
き

後ろをそろえてください。──────── Please cut the back all the same length.
うし

赤にそめてください。──────── Please dye my hair red.
あか

ボブ・マーリーみたいな髪形にしたいんですが。
かみがた
──────── I want my hair to be like Bob Marley's. (showing a picture)

会
L17

Useful Vocabulary

メニュー	
シャンプー (Shampoo)	¥1,500
カット (Cut)	¥4,000
ブロー (Blow-dry)	¥1,500
パーマ (Perm)	¥8,000~
カラー (Hair coloring)	¥5,000~
セット (Set)	¥4,000

髪形──────hairstyle
かみがた
切る──────to cut
き
そる──────to shave
刈る──────to crop
か
そめる──────to dye
そろえる──to make hair even; to trim
パーマをかける
──────to have one's hair permed
すく──────to thin out (hair)

分け目　前髪
わ　め　まえがみ

横
よこ

後ろ
うし

第18課

ジョンさんのアルバイト John's Part-time Job

In this lesson, we will ....

- Describe the states of things
- Talk about failures
- Express our regret
- Talk with the manager at a workplace

会 話 Dialogue
かい わ

I At Little Asia restaurant. 🔊 K18-01/02

1 店　長：　ジョン、今日は森田くん、かぜで来られないそうだ。夕方になると忙
てん ちょう　　　　　　きょう　もりた　　　　　　こ　　　　　　　　ゆうがた　　　　　　いそが

2 　　　　　しくなるから、頼むよ。
　　　　　　　　　　　　　たの

3 ジョン：　はい。がんばります。

4 店　長：　まず、冷蔵庫に野菜が入っているから、出しておいて。
てん ちょう　　　　　れいぞうこ　やさい　はい　　　　　　　　だ

5 　　　　　それから、外の電気はついている？
　　　　　　　　　　そと　でんき

6 ジョン：　いいえ、ついていません。

7 　　　　　つけましょうか。

8 店　長：　うん。そこのスイッチを押すとつくよ。
てん ちょう　　　　　　　　　　　　　お

9 ジョン：　はい。

Ⅱ A customer calls John. 🔊 K18-03/04

1 客：　　すみません。しょうゆを落としちゃったんです。ごめんなさい。
きゃく　　　　　　　　　　　　　お

2 ジョン：　いいえ、大丈夫です。あっ、スカートが汚れてしまいましたね。
　　　　　　　　だいじょうぶ　　　　　　　　　　よご

3 客：　　本当だ。どうしよう。
きゃく　　ほんとう

4 ジョン：　今すぐ、タオルを持ってきます。
　　　　　いま　　　　　　も

Ⅲ After closing time. 🔊 K18-05/06

1	店長 _{てんちょう}：	今日_{きょう}はジョンのおかげで、助_{たす}かったよ。
2	ジョン：	いいえ。でも本当_{ほんとう}に忙_{いそが}しかったですね。
3	店長 _{てんちょう}：	あしたは学校_{がっこう}があるんだろう。アルバイトをしながら学校_{がっこう}に行_いくのは
4		大変_{たいへん}だね。
5	ジョン：	ええ、時々_{ときどき}、遅刻_{ちこく}しちゃうんですよ。
6	店長 _{てんちょう}：	ぼくも学生_{がくせい}の時_{とき}はよく授業_{じゅぎょう}をサボったよ。もっと勉強_{べんきょう}すればよかった
7		なあ。後_{あと}はぼくが片付_{かたづ}けるから。
8	ジョン：	すみません。じゃあ、お先_{さき}に失礼_{しつれい}します。お疲_{つか}れさまでした。
9	店長 _{てんちょう}：	お疲_{つか}れさま。

会
L18

Ⅰ

Manager: John, Mr. Morita said he has a cold and is not able to come today. In the evening it will get busy, so I am counting on you.

John: Sure, I will do my best.

Manager: First of all, vegetables are in the refrigerator, so take them out. Then, is the outside light on?

John: No, it isn't. Shall I turn it on?

Manager: Yes. If you press the button there, the light will turn on.

John: Yes.

Ⅱ

Customer: Excuse me. I dropped the soy sauce. I'm sorry.

John: Please don't worry. Oh, your skirt has become dirty, hasn't it?

Customer: Oh, no! What should I do?

John: I will bring a towel right away.

Ⅲ

Manager: You were so helpful today.

John: Don't mention it. But, it was such a busy day.

Manager: You have school tomorrow, right? It's tough to go to school while holding a part-time job, isn't it?

John: Yes. I'm late for classes sometimes.

Manager: When I was a student, I often cut classes. I should have studied more. Well, I'll finish tidying up the rest (so you can leave now).

John: Thank you. Excuse me for leaving early. Good-bye.

Manager: Thank you. Bye.

単語

<ruby>単<rt>たん</rt></ruby> <ruby>語<rt>ご</rt></ruby>

🔊 K18-07 (J-E)
K18-08 (E-J)

V o c a b u l a r y

N o u n s

カーテン		curtain
ソファ		sofa
* れいぞうこ	冷蔵庫	refrigerator
* スイッチ		switch
* しょうゆ	しょう油	soy sauce
スープ		soup
バナナ		banana
ポップコーン		popcorn
シャンプー		shampoo
ろうそく		candle
* タオル		towel
* スカート		skirt
にっき	日記	diary
けいたい（でんわ）	携帯（電話）	cell phone
さくら	桜	cherry blossom
むし	虫	insect
やちん	家賃	rent
* そと	外	outside
* あと	後	the rest
* ゆうがた	夕方	evening

い - a d j e c t i v e s

あかるい	明るい	bright
くらい	暗い	dark
はずかしい	恥ずかしい	embarrassing; to feel embarrassed

な - a d j e c t i v e s

たいせつ（な）	大切	precious; important
ふあん（な）	不安	anxious; worried
むり（な）	無理	impossible

U - v e r b s

あく	開く	(something) opens （〜が）
しまる	閉まる	(something) closes （〜が）

* Words that appear in the dialogue

あやまる	謝る	to apologize（*person* に）
* おす	押す	to press; to push（〜を）
* おとす	落とす	to drop (something)（〜を）
おゆがわく	お湯が沸く	water boils
ころぶ	転ぶ	to fall down
こわす	壊す	to break (something)（〜を）
さく	咲く	to bloom（〜が）
* たすかる	助かる	to be saved; to be helped
* たのむ	頼む	to ask (a favor)（*person* に〜を）
* つく		(something) turns on（〜が）
よごす	汚す	to make dirty（〜を）

Ru-verbs

おちる	落ちる	(something) drops（〜が）
* かたづける	片付ける	to tidy up（〜を）
かんがえる	考える	to think (about); to consider
きえる	消える	(something) goes off（〜が）
こわれる	壊れる	(something) breaks（〜が）
* よごれる	汚れる	to become dirty（〜が）

Irregular Verb

ちゅうもんする	注文する	to place an order（〜を）

Adverbs and Other Expressions

* いますぐ	今すぐ	right away
〜までに		by (time/date)
* ほんとうに	本当に	really
* まず		first of all
* おかげで		thanks to . . .（〜の）
* どうしよう		What should I/we do?
* 〜（ん）だろう		short form of 〜（ん）でしょう
* おさきにしつれい します	お先に失礼 します	See you. (lit., I'm leaving ahead of you.)
* おつかれさま （でした）	お疲れ様 （でした）	You must be tired after working so hard. (greeting between friends and coworkers)

文法 Grammar
ぶん ぼう

1 Transitivity Pairs

Some verbs describe situations in which people act on things. For example, I open the door, you turn on the TV, and they break the computer. Such verbs are called "transitive verbs." Some other verbs describe changes that things or people undergo. For example, the door opens, the TV goes on, and the computer breaks down. These verbs are called "intransitive verbs."

While most verbs are loners and do not have a counterpart of the opposite transitivity, some important verbs come in pairs.

	Transitive		Intransitive
開ける あ	open something	開く あ	something opens
閉める し	close something	閉まる し	something closes
入れる い	put something in	入る はい	something goes inside
出す だ	take something out	出る で	something goes out
つける	turn something on	つく	something goes on
消す け	turn something off; extinguish something	消える き	something goes off
壊す こわ	break something	壊れる こわ	something breaks
汚す よご	make something dirty	汚れる よご	something becomes dirty
落とす お	drop something	落ちる お	something drops
沸かす わ	boil water	沸く わ	water boils

Transitive verbs call for both the subject (agent) and the object (the thing that is acted upon). Intransitive verbs call only for the subject (the thing or the person that goes through the change).

たけしさんが電気をつけました。
てん き
Takeshi turned the light on.

電気がつきました。
てん き
The light came on.

たけしさんがお湯を沸かしました。
ゆ わ
Takeshi boiled the water.

お湯が沸きました。
ゆ わ
The water boiled.

2 Paired Intransitive Verbs + ている

Transitive verbs describe activities, while intransitive verbs describe changes. They behave differently when they are followed by the helping verb ている. Let us first recall that activity verbs (話す, for example) + ている refer to actions in progress, while change verbs (結婚する, for example) + ている refer to the states resulting from the change, as we learned in Lesson 7.

ソラさんは今、友だちと話しています。　(activity, action in progress)
Sora is talking with a friend right now.

山下先生は結婚しています。　(change, result state)
Professor Yamashita is married.

Similarly, when followed by ている, transitive verbs refer to actions in progress, while intransitive verbs refer to states that hold true after the change takes place.

Transitive (action in progress):

ウデイさんは窓を開けています。
Uday is opening the windows.

ともさんは電気を消しています。
Tomo is turning the light off.

ゴジラが町を壊しています。
Godzilla is destroying the city.

Intransitive (result of a change):

窓が開いています。
The windows are open.

電気は消えています。
The light is off.

このパソコンは壊れています。
This computer is broken.

3 〜てしまう

The *te*-form of a verb + しまう has two meanings, which at first might appear rather incongruous. In the first instance, しまう indicates that one "carries out with determination" a plan described by the verb. It typically involves bringing something to a culmination. You, in other words, do something completely, or finish doing something, or have something done.

本を読んでしまいました。
I read the book completely. / I finished reading the book.

The second meaning of しまう is "lack of premeditation or control over how things turn out." This often comes with *the sense of regret*; something regrettable happens, or you do something which you did not intend to.[1]

---

[1] Since しまう goes with the verbal *te*-form, which is affirmative, it only gives us sentences meaning that something regrettable does or did happen. In other words, we cannot express negated ideas with しまう such as "regrettably, X did not take place" or "unfortunately, I did not do X."

電車の中にかばんを忘れてしまいました。
I inadvertently left my bag on the train.

宿題を忘れたので、先生は怒ってしまいました。
To my horror, my professor got angry because I had forgotten my homework.

> ～てしまう ＝ 1. *finish doing*
> 2. *regrettably*

Both nuanced meanings focus on the discrepancy between what we intend and what the world is like when it is left on its own. A しまう sentence may be ambiguous between the two meanings. How a given しまう sentence should be interpreted depends on the assumptions the speaker has when uttering it. For example, the "finished reading" sentence above can be read as meaning "regrettably" just as easily if you read the book although you had not planned to, or knowing that it was wrong but unable to resist the temptation.

In speech, ～てしまう and ～でしまう are often contracted to ～ちゃう and ～じゃう, respectively.

宿題をなくしちゃった。　　　　　*I lost my homework!*

食べてしまいました	→	食べちゃいました
食べてしまった	→	食べちゃった
飲んでしまいました	→	飲んじゃいました
飲んでしまった	→	飲んじゃった

4 ～と

The present tense short form of a predicate ＋ と means *whenever* the situation described by the predicate holds true, another thing happens. In most と sentences, the first clause describes the cause, and the second the effect.

私はその人と話すと元気になる。
Whenever I talk with that person, I feel uplifted.

道が混んでいると時間がかかる。
Whenever the streets are crowded, it takes longer to get there.

> <u>clause A</u>　と　<u>clause B</u>。　*Whenever A happens, B happens, too.*
> (short, present)

Sometimes, a と sentence describes a cause-effect relationship between specific events.

メアリーさんが国に帰るとさびしくなります。
If Mary goes back home, we will be sad and lonely.

While the clause that comes before と is always in the present tense, the second clause can be in the present or in the past tense.

私は子供の時、冬になるとかぜをひきました。
When I was young, whenever winter arrived, I caught a cold.

The event described by the second clause must follow the event described in the first half of the sentence. Thus it is wrong to say:

× 私はその人と話すとカフェに行きます。
Whenever I talk with that person, we go to a cafe.

If you want an adjective idea in the second clause, it is usually expressed as a change. It is very common therefore to find in the second clause an い-adjective base ＋ くなる, and a な-adjective base ＋ になる (see Lesson 10 for adjective ＋ なる).

秋になると木が赤くなります。
Whenever fall arrives, trees turn red.

夜になると町が静かになります。
Whenever night comes, the town becomes quiet.

5 ～ながら

You can connect two verbs with ながら to say that the two actions are performed at the same time. ながら follows a verb stem. The second verb, which goes after ながら, can be in any form.

私はいつも音楽を聞きながら日本語を勉強します。
I always study Japanese while listening to music.

たけしさんは歌を歌いながら洗濯しています。
Takeshi is doing laundry singing a song.

会
L18

アルバイトをしながら学校に行くのは大変です。

It is not easy to go to school while holding a part-time job.

V₁ (stem) ＋ ながら、V₂	*while V₁-ing, V₂*

Note that the two verbs that flank ながら must be two actions performed by the same person. ながら, in other words, cannot describe an action performed while another person does something.

× メアリーが買い物しながら、たけしは部屋を掃除します。
　　While Mary does shopping, Takeshi cleans the room.

　Compare: メアリーが買い物する時、たけしは部屋を掃除します。

6 ～ばよかったです

ばよかったです means *I wish I had done* or *I should have done* something. You can use it to describe an alternative course of action you, to your great regret, did not take.

Affirmative:	～ばよかった	*I wish I had done . . .*
Negative:	～なければよかった	*I wish I had not done . . .*

あの時、「愛している」と言えばよかったです。
I wish I had told her that I loved her.

彼女と別れなければよかったです。
I should not have broken up with her.

All verbs can regularly be turned into a ばよかったです sentence with no exception or irregularity. You form the ば-form on the basis of the present tense short forms.

> **ば-form**
> ・Verbs in the affirmative:　Drop the final *-u* and add *-eba*.
>
> | | | |
> |---|---|---|
> | 食べる (*tabe-ru*) | → | 食べれば (*tabe-r-eba*) |
> | 行く (*ik-u*) | → | 行けば (*ik-eba*) |
> | 待つ | → | 待てば |
> | 買う | → | 買えば |
> | する | → | すれば |
> | くる | → | くれば |

> ・Verbs in the negative:　Drop the final い and add ければ.
>
> | | | |
> |---|---|---|
> | 食べない | → | 食べなければ |
> | 行かない | → | 行かなければ |
> | 待たない | → | 待たなければ |
> | 買わない | → | 買わなければ |
> | しない | → | しなければ |
> | こない | → | こなければ |

We will learn about the ば-forms used in broader contexts in Lesson 22.

L18

E x p r e s s i o n N o t e s

表現ノート
ひょう　　げん

おかげ ▶ "Nounのおかげ（で）" is used to express gratitude for something or to someone when things turn out as desired.

> 友だちが書いてくれた地図のおかげで道に迷わなかった。
> *Thanks to the map my friend drew, I didn't get lost.*

> 先生：卒業おめでとう。　　　　*Congratulations on your graduation.*
> 学生：先生のおかげです。　　　*I owe it to you, Professor.*

The expression おかげさまで (lit., Thanks to you) is the proper response when asked 元気ですか.

> A：元気ですか。　　　　　　*How are you?*
> B：ええ、おかげさまで。　　*I'm fine, thanks to you.*

おかげさまで is also used to show appreciation for the addressee's help/support/concern.

> A：仕事に慣れましたか。
> 　　*Have you gotten used to the job?*
> B：ええ、おかげさまで、だいぶ慣れました。
> 　　*Yes, I have gotten used to it mostly. Thank you for your concern.*

練 習　P r a c t i c e
れん　しゅう

I　ドアを開けます/ドアが開きます　☛Grammar 1
　　　　　あ　　　　　　　　　あ

A. Describe the pictures using transitive and intransitive verbs. 🔊 K18-09

Example (a) ドアを開けます。　　(b) ドアが開きます。
　　　　　　　　あ　　　　　　　　　　　　あ

e.g.

(a)　　　　　　(b)

1.

(a)　　　　　　(b)

2.

(a)　　　　　　(b)

3.

(a)　　　　　　(b)

4.

(a)　　　　　　(b)

5.

(a)　　　　　　(b)

6.

(a)　　　　　　(b)

7.

(a)　　　　　　(b)

8.

(a)    (b)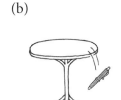

9.

(a)    (b)

B. Answer the following questions.

1. 寝る時、窓を閉めますか。
2. 寝る時、電気／エアコンを消しますか。
3. 朝、窓を開けますか。
4. 今朝、かばんの中に何を入れましたか。
5. いつまでに宿題を出さなければいけませんか。
6. 子供の時、大切なおもちゃを壊したことがありますか。
7. 好きな服を汚したことがありますか。
8. どんな時、お湯を沸かしますか。
9. 携帯を落としたことがありますか。

Ⅱ 窓が開いています ☞Grammar 2

A. Describe the condition using ～ている. 🔊 K18-10

Example) 窓が開いています。

e.g. 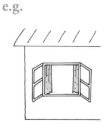   (1)    (2)    (3)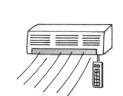

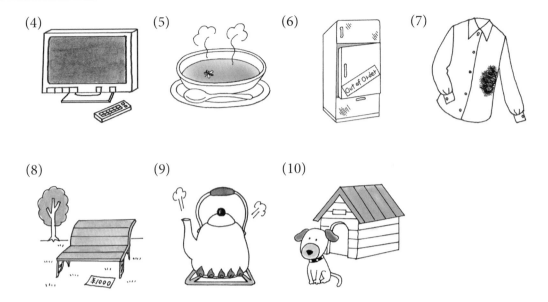

(4)　(5)　(6)　(7)

(8)　(9)　(10)

B. Pair Work—One person looks at picture A below and the other looks at picture B (p. 158). The two pictures look similar but are not identical. Find out the difference by asking each other questions.

[Example]　A：冷蔵庫にりんごが入っていますか。
　　　　　　　　れいぞうこ　　　　　　　　　　　はい

　　　　　　B：はい。一つ入っています。
　　　　　　　　　ひと　はい

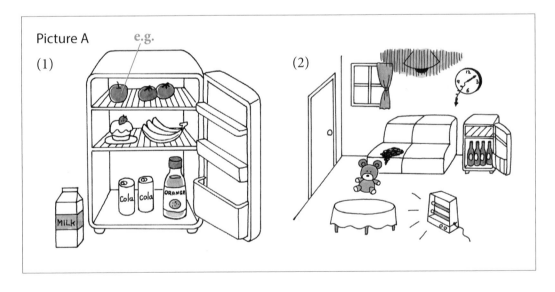

Picture A　　　　e.g.

(1)　　　　　　　　　　(2)

C. Pair Work—You and your partner are working part-time at Little Asia. The manager is sick, and you need to take care of the restaurant for the day. Look at the picture and discuss what needs to be done to open the place for business.

Example
A：エアコンがついていませんね。

B：そうですね。じゃあ、私がつけますよ。

A：すみません。お願いします。

III 新しい単語を覚えてしまいました 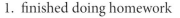 ☞Grammar 3

A. You finished doing the following things. Express what you did with ～てしまう. 🔊 K18-11

Example finished memorizing words → もう新しい単語を覚えてしまいました。

1. finished doing homework
2. finished writing a paper
3. finished reading a book
4. finished preparing for the presentation
5. finished tidying up the room
6. finished doing the laundry

B. The following things happened and you regret them. Express them with 〜てしまう. 🔊 K18-12

(Example) お金があまりないんですが、(bought a lot)
　　　　→　お金があまりないんですが、たくさん買ってしまいました。

1. 友だちにパソコンを借りたんですが、(broke it)
2. 給料をもらったんですが、(spent all)
3. 急いでいたので、(fell down)
4. きのう寒かったので、(caught a cold)
5. きのうあまり寝なかったので、(slept in class)
6. ゆみさんが好きだったんですが、(Yumi got married)
7. 今日までに家賃を払わなきゃいけなかったんですが、(forgot it)
8. 朝寝坊したので、(missed a train)

C. You stayed at your friend's apartment while they were away. Now your friend is back; make an apology using 〜ちゃう／じゃう for what you have done in the apartment.

(Example) A：ごめん。
　　　　　B：どうしたの？
　　　　　A：実は冷蔵庫の食べ物を全部食べちゃった。
　　　　　B：えっ！

e.g.

(1)  friend's shampoo

(2) friend's diary

(3) friend's magazine

(4)

(5)

(6)

D. Pair Work—You did the following things. Explain the situations to your partner in informal speech. Continue the conversation.

(Example) You borrowed a camera from your friend but broke it.

→ A：友だちにカメラを借りたんだけど、壊しちゃった。
B：えっ。今すぐ謝ったほうがいいよ。
A：そうだね。そうするよ。

1. You borrowed a book from your friend but lost it.

2. You received a scholarship but you bought a car with that money.

3. You told a lie to your friend.

4. You had a fight with your friend.

5. You didn't want to go to class, so you cut class.

6. You overslept and came late for class.

L18

Ⅳ 秋になると涼しくなります ☞Grammar 4

A. Change the cues in 1 through 6 into と clauses and choose the correct phrase on the right to complete each sentence. 🔊 K18-13

(Example) 秋になると涼しくなります。

e.g. 秋になります ・	・ a. 日本語が上手になりません。
1. 電気をつけます ・	・ b. 目が疲れます。
2. 窓を開けます ・	・ c. 明るくなります。
3. 日本語を話しません ・	・ d. 桜が咲きます。
4. 友だちから返事が来ません ・	・ e. 涼しくなります。
5. 暗い所で本を読みます ・	・ f. 不安になります。
6. 春になります ・	・ g. 虫が入ります。

B. Pair Work—Give advice to your partner who has the following problems using 〜と.

Example A：疲れているんです。
B：甘い物を食べると元気になりますよ。

1. A：友だちがいないんです。
   B：＿＿＿＿＿＿＿＿＿＿＿＿＿＿と友だちができますよ。

2. A：かぜをひいたんです。
   B：＿＿＿＿＿＿＿＿＿＿＿＿＿＿とよくなりますよ。

3. A：太りたいんです。
   B：＿＿＿＿＿＿＿＿＿＿＿＿＿＿と太りますよ。

4. A：寝られないんです。
   B：＿＿＿＿＿＿＿＿＿＿＿＿＿＿と寝られますよ。

5. A：(your problem)＿＿＿＿＿＿＿＿＿＿＿＿＿＿＿＿＿＿んです。
   B：＿＿＿＿＿＿＿＿＿＿＿と＿＿＿＿＿＿＿＿＿＿＿＿よ。

C. Pair Work—Talk with your partner using the cues below. Expand your conversation.

Example ＿＿＿＿＿＿と顔が赤くなる
→ A：私は、恥ずかしいと顔が赤くなるんです。
B：そうですか。ぼくは、お酒を飲むと顔が赤くなるんです。
A：どれぐらい飲むと顔が赤くなるんですか。

1. ＿＿＿＿＿＿＿＿＿＿＿＿＿＿＿＿＿＿＿と気分が悪くなる
2. ＿＿＿＿＿＿＿＿＿＿＿＿＿＿＿＿＿＿＿とうれしくなる
3. ＿＿＿＿＿＿＿＿＿＿＿＿＿＿＿＿＿＿＿と悲しくなる
4. ＿＿＿＿＿＿＿＿＿＿＿＿＿＿＿＿＿＿＿と元気になる
5. ＿＿＿＿＿＿＿＿＿＿＿＿＿＿＿＿＿＿＿と疲れる
6. ＿＿＿＿＿＿＿＿＿＿＿＿＿＿＿＿＿＿＿と緊張する
7. ＿＿＿＿＿＿＿＿＿＿＿＿＿＿＿＿＿＿＿と踊りたくなる

V 携帯を見ながら朝ご飯を食べます ☞Grammar 5
けい たい み あさ はん た

A. The pictures below show what Yui does. Describe them using 〜ながら. 🔊 K18-14

(Example) 携帯を見ながら朝ご飯を食べます。/朝ご飯を食べながら携帯を見ます。
けいたい み あさ はん た あさ はん た けいたい み

B. Pair Work—Ask your partner the following questions.

1. ご飯を食べながら、何をしますか。
はん た なに
2. 何をしながら、勉強しますか。
なに べんきょう
3. シャワーを浴びながら、何をしますか。
あ なに
4. 音楽を聞きながら、何をしますか。
おんがく き なに
5. 何をしながら、考えますか。
なに かんが

C. Class Activity—Let's play charades. The teacher gives a sentence card to each student. One of the students mimes the sentence. All other students guess what the person is doing and raise their hands when they recognize the action. The person that gets the most points is the winner.

(Example) 歩きながら、アイスクリームを食べています。
ある た

D. Talk about the following, using 〜ながら.

1. two things you often do at the same time when you are busy

    (Example) 忙しい時、食べながら勉強します。

2. two things it is better not to do at the same time

    (Example) 歩きながらメールをしないほうがいいです。

3. two things you like to do at the same time

    (Example) 音楽を聞きながら運転するのが好きです。

4. two things you cannot do at the same time

    (Example) 自転車に乗りながらそばを食べられません。

Ⅵ **もっと勉強すればよかったです** ☞Grammar 6

A. Change the following verbs into ば-forms. 🔊 K18-15

(Example) 行く　→　行けば

1. 読む	4. 話す	7. 遊ぶ	10. 食べない	13. しない
2. 来る	5. する	8. 起きる	11. 聞かない	
3. 見る	6. 使う	9. 来ない	12. 使わない	

B. The following pictures are what happened to you as a result of action you took or didn't take (marked with ✕). Express your regret using 〜ばよかったです. 🔊 K18-16

(Example) 傘を持ってくればよかったです。

e.g.   (1)

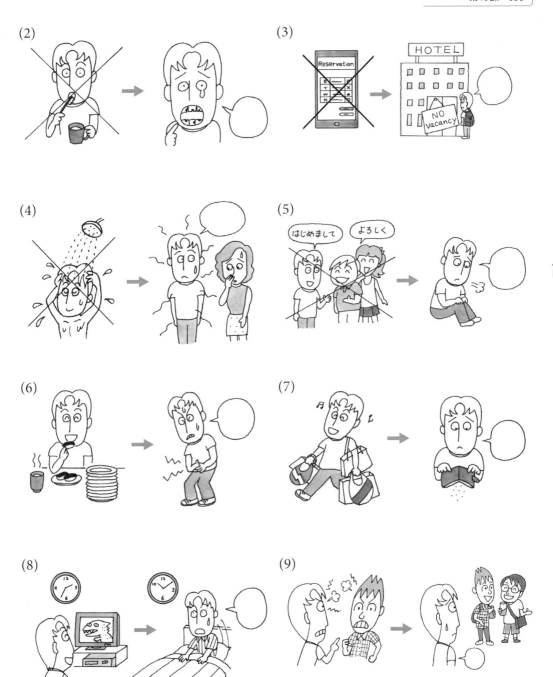

C. Pair Work—You are unhappy. Explain your situation and express your regret using 〜ば よかった. Expand the conversation.

Example You did terribly on your test.

→ 　A：テストが最悪だったんです。
　　　　　もっと勉強すればよかったです。
　　　　B：どれぐらい勉強したんですか。
　　　　A：テストの前に30分ぐらい。
　　　　B：それは少なすぎますよ。

1. You were late for class.

2. You went to a restaurant but it was closed for a holiday.

3. You sold your bicycle, but you will move to a new apartment and need a bicycle.

4. Your college life is boring.

5. You ordered a hamburger but it didn't taste good.

6. You ate too much and you are not feeling well.

7. You have just started a job. You have too much work.

8. You broke up with your boyfriend/girlfriend. You can't help thinking about them.

D. Pair Work—Express your regret using 〜ばよかった, then expand the conversation.

Example きのう

→ 　A：きのう、買い物しなければよかった。
　　　　B：どうして？
　　　　A：買いすぎて、お金がぜんぜんないんだ。
　　　　　千円、貸してくれない？
　　　　B：私もお金ないから、無理。ごめんね。

1. 先週
　せんしゅう

2. 子供の時
　こども　とき

3. 高校の時
　こうこう　とき

4. (your own)

Ⅶ まとめの練習
（れんしゅう）

A. You are an owner of a restaurant. Look at the picture Ⅱ-C (p. 149) and tell your employee what they should do. Use Dialogue Ⅰ as a model.

B. Pair Work—Tell each other a story of a failure or a sad experience, which happened contrary to your wishes.

(Example)　Ａ：今朝、起きられなくて、授業に遅れてしまったんです。
　　　　　　　（けさ）　（お）　　　　　　　　　（じゅぎょう）（おく）

　　　　　　Ｂ：きのう何時に寝たんですか。
　　　　　　　　　　（なんじ）　（ね）

　　　　　　Ａ：二時です。
　　　　　　　　（にじ）

　　　　　　Ｂ：もっと早く寝ればよかったですね。
　　　　　　　　　　　（はや）（ね）

C. Yui talks about the seasonal changes in Nagano, Japan. Reading the passage as a model, talk about the seasonal changes in your hometown or a place of your choice.

長野では、４月になると、桜が咲きます。６月から７月は
（なが の）　　（がつ）　　　（さくら）（さ）　　　　（がつ）　　（がつ）
梅雨 (rainy season) です。梅雨が終わると暑くなります。
（つゆ）　　　　　　　　　（つゆ）（お）　　（あつ）
気温は35度ぐらいになります。秋は紅葉 (autumn leaves) が
（き おん）　（ど）　　　　　　　　（あき）（こうよう）
きれいです。冬になると、雪がたくさん降ります。
　　　　　　（ふゆ）　　　　　（ゆき）　　　　　（ふ）

Seasonal Changes in Nagano, Japan

３月	４月	５月	６月	７月	８月	９月	10月	11月	12月	１月	２月

Expressions you may want to use:

梅雨 (rainy season in East Asia)　　蒸し暑い (hot and humid)
（つゆ）　　　　　　　　　　　　　　（む）（あつ）
紅葉 (autumn leaves/colors)　　台風／ハリケーン (typhoon/hurricane)
（こうよう）　　　　　　　　　　（たいふう）
竜巻 (tornado)　　雨季 (rainy season)　　乾季 (dry season)
（たつまき）　　　（う き）　　　　　　　（かんき）

D. Pair Work—Ask your partner the following questions.

1. あしたまでに何をしなければいけませんか。
2. 卒業までに何をしようと思っていますか。
3. 大学の食堂は何時から何時まで開いていますか。
4. 図書館は何曜日に閉まっていますか。
5. あなたの冷蔵庫の中に何が入っていますか。
6. お酒を飲みすぎるとどうなりますか。

Pair Work Ⅱ B. (p. 148)

〔Example〕　Ａ：冷蔵庫にりんごが入っていますか。
　　　　　　　Ｂ：はい。一つ入っています。

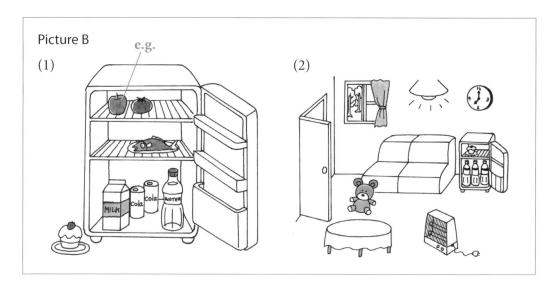

Culture Notes

すし Sushi

Sushi is probably the best-known Japanese dish. Some of you might think all sushi is made with raw fish, but actually quite a few types are made with cooked items. There are also some vegetarian choices, such as かっぱ巻き (cucumber roll) and いなりずし (a pouch of fried tofu filled with sushi rice). Rice for sushi is vinegared rice, and sushi is generally dipped in しょうゆ (soy sauce) before being eaten.

すしの種類 (Types of sushi)

にぎりずし

Pressed sushi rice topped with a piece of fish/shellfish, roe, etc., and seasoned with わさび (green horseradish).

Popular sushi toppings		
まぐろ tuna	とろ fatty tuna	えび shrimp
いか squid	あなご saltwater eel	うなぎ freshwater eel
たこ octopus	はまち yellowtail	サーモン salmon
うに sea urchin	いくら salmon roe	たい snapper

巻きずし

Rice with various ingredients inserted, rolled up in Japanese seaweed. In most 巻きずし, the のり (seaweed) is on the outside, but in some the rice is placed on the outside.

手巻きずし

Very similar to 巻きずし except that it is rolled into a cone shape by hand. It is easy to make at home. Everyone picks their favorite ingredients to make their own hand-rolled sushi.

ちらしずし

Various ingredients scattered artfully over a bed of sushi rice in a box.

回転ずし (Conveyor belt sushi)

回転ずし is sushi served at a restaurant where the plates are placed on a rotating conveyor belt that moves past every seat. Customers pick the items they want. Items of the same price are placed on the same type of plate, so the bill is based on the number and type of plates taken. Conveyor belt sushi is rather inexpensive compared to traditional sushi restaurants. They have lots of fishless options on the menu such as fried chicken, salad and desserts. In many 回転ずし places, you can order via a tablet with the multilingual menu on the table.

会
L18

第19課

L E S S O N 19

出迎え Meeting the Boss
で　むか

In this lesson, we will ....

🔵 Show our respect   🔵 Talk about things we are glad that we did

🔵 Express gratitude   🔵 Talk politely with bosses

会 話 D i a l o g u e
かい　わ

I Takeshi came to the airport to pick up the department manager, who went to America on business. 🔊 K19-01/02

1 たけし： 部長、出張お疲れさまでした。
　　　　　ぶちょう　しゅっちょう　つか

2 部　長： 木村くん、迎えに来てくれてありがとう。本当はシアトルを一時に
　　ぶ　ちょう　きむら　　むか　き　　　　　　　　　　ほんとう　　　　　　　いちじ

3　　　　　 出るはずだったんだけど、遅れちゃってね。
　　　　　 て　　　　　　　　　　　おく

4 たけし： じゃあ、お疲れになったでしょう。
　　　　　　　　　つか

5 部　長： 大丈夫だけど、ちょっとおなかがすいてるんだ。
　　ぶ　ちょう　だいじょうぶ

6 たけし： じゃあ、何か召し上がってから、お帰りになりますか。
　　　　　　　　なに　め　あ　　　　　　　　　かえ

7 部　長： うん。そうしようか。
　　ぶ　ちょう

II At a restaurant. 🔊 K19-03/04

1 店　員： いらっしゃいませ。何名様ですか。
　てん　いん　　　　　　　　　　なんめいさま

2 たけし： 二人です。
　　　　　ふたり

3 店　員： 少々お待ちください。
　てん　いん　しょうしょう　ま

　　　　　　　　　　　　＊　　　　　　　　＊　　　　　　　　＊

4 店　員： こちらへどうぞ。お決まりになりましたらお呼びください。
　てん　いん　　　　　　　　　　き　　　　　　　　　　　よ

Ⅲ In front of the department manager's house. 🔊 K19-05/06

1 部長： うちまで送ってくれてありがとう。

2 たけし： いいえ。今日はごちそうしてくださってありがとうございました。

3 部長： ゆっくり話ができてよかったよ。ちょっとうちに寄らない？

4 たけし： いえ、もう遅いし、奥様もお休みになっているでしょうから。

5 部長： この時間ならまだ起きているはずだよ。

6 たけし： でも、今日は遠慮しておきます。奥様によろしくお伝えください。

Ⅰ

Takeshi: Boss, welcome back. You must be tired after the business trip.

Department manager: Thank you for coming here to pick me up, Mr. Kimura. Originally, I was supposed to leave Seattle at one o'clock, but it ran late.

Takeshi: You must be tired then.

Department manager: No, I'm fine, but I'm a little hungry.

Takeshi: Then would you like to eat something before going home?

Department manager: That sounds good to me.

Ⅱ

Waitress: Welcome. How many?

Takeshi: Two.

Waitress: Just a moment, please.

   *   *   *

Waitress: This way, please. When you decide, please call me.

Ⅲ

Department manager: Thank you for giving me a ride home.

Takeshi: Not at all. Thank you very much for paying for the dinner.

Department manager: It was nice to have a good talk with you. Would you like to come inside?

Takeshi: That's okay. It's late, and your wife is probably sleeping.

Department manager: No, she must still be awake at this time.

Takeshi: But I'd rather not today. Please give her my regards.

単語

<ruby>単<rt>たん</rt></ruby> <ruby>語<rt>ご</rt></ruby>

🔊 K19-07 (J-E)
K19-08 (E-J)

Vocabulary

Nouns

* おくさま	奥様	(your/someone's) wife (polite)
おこさん	お子さん	(your/someone's) child (polite)
ちゅうがくせい	中学生	junior high school student
* ぶちょう	部長	department manager
* しゅっちょう	出張	business trip
けいご	敬語	honorific language
* こちら		this way (polite)
どちら		where (polite)
おれい	お礼	expression of gratitude
しゅるい	種類	a kind; a sort
* はなし	話	talk; story
なやみ	悩み	worry
まちがい	間違い	mistake
せいかく	性格	personality
なまけもの	怠け者	lazy person
はずかしがりや	恥ずかしがり屋	shy person

い-adjective

なかがいい	仲がいい	be on good/close terms; to get along well

な-adjective

まじめ（な）		serious; sober; diligent

U-verbs

いらっしゃる		honorific expression for いく, くる, and いる
* めしあがる	召し上がる	honorific expression for たべる and のむ
くださる	下さる	honorific expression for くれる
なさる		honorific expression for する
* おやすみになる	お休みになる	honorific expression for ねる
ごらんになる	ご覧になる	honorific expression for みる
おっしゃる		honorific expression for いう
〜ていらっしゃる		honorific expression for 〜ている

＊Words that appear in the dialogue

* おくる	送る	to walk/drive (someone) (*person* を *place* まで)
おこる	怒る	to get angry
* きまる	決まる	to be decided（〜が）
しりあう	知り合う	to get acquainted with（〜と）
* よぶ	呼ぶ	to call (one's name)（〜を）; to invite（*person* を *event* に）
ひっこす	引っ越す	to move (to another place to live)（〜に）
* よる	寄る	to stop by（*place* に）

Ru-verbs

* おくれる	遅れる	to become late（〜に）
かける		to sit down（seat に）
もてる		to be popular (in terms of romantic interest)（*people* に）
はれる	晴れる	to become sunny

Irregular Verbs

* ごちそうする		to treat/invite (someone) to a meal（*person* に *meal* を）
* えんりょする	遠慮する	to hold back for the time being; to refrain from
しょうたいする	招待する	to invite someone (to an event/a place)（*person* を *event/place* に）
* はなしをする	話をする	to have a talk

Adverbs and Other Expressions

おととい		the day before yesterday
まいあさ	毎朝	every morning
それで		then; therefore
なぜ		why（＝どうして）
* ほんとうは	本当は	in fact; originally
* まだ		still
* しょうしょう	少々	a few seconds
* 〜めいさま	〜名様	party of . . . people
ようこそ		Welcome.
* よろしくおつたえ ください	よろしくお伝え ください	Please give my best regards (to . . .).（〜に）

文 法 G r a m m a r
ぶん　ぼう

1 Honorific Verbs

We use special verbs to describe the actions of people whom you respect. These special verbs are called honorific verbs, because they bestow honor on, or exalt, the person performing the activity.

	Honorific verbs	Irregular conjugations
いる 行く¹ い 来る く	いらっしゃる	いらっしゃ<u>い</u>ます
食べる た 飲む の	召し上がる め　あ	
くれる	くださる	くださ<u>い</u>ます
する²	なさる	なさ<u>い</u>ます
寝る ね 見る み	お休みになる やす ご覧になる らん	
言う い	おっしゃる	おっしゃ<u>い</u>ます
～ている	～ていらっしゃる	～ていらっしゃ<u>い</u>ます

All the honorific verbs listed above are *u*-verbs, but some of them have irregular conjugations. The long forms of いらっしゃる, おっしゃる, なさる, くださる, and ～ていらっしゃる end with います, instead of the expected ります.

When we use an honorific verb instead of a normal verb, we will have sentences which mean that somebody graciously does something. Thus, we never use these verbs to describe our own actions. Instead, we use them when we talk about what is done by (1) somebody higher up in the social hierarchy, or (2) somebody whom you do not know very well, especially when addressing them directly.

先生は今日学校に<u>いらっしゃいません</u>。　cf. 行きません／来ません／いません
せんせい　きょう　がっこう　　　　　　　　　　　　　　い　　　　　　　　　き

The professor will (graciously) not go to/come to/be at the school.　　　(three-way ambiguous)

---

¹ This replacement by the special verb いらっしゃる also applies to compound verbs like 持っていく and 連れ
も　　　　　　　　つ
てくる.

社長はお子さんを会社に連れていらっしゃいました。
しゃちょう　こ　　　かいしゃ　つ
The president has brought her child to the office.

² This replacement applies to all compound verbs like 勉強する as well as the main verb する.
べんきょう

何を召し上がりますか。
What will you (graciously) eat/drink?

cf. 食べますか／飲みますか

田中さんのお母さんがこの本をくださいました。
Ms. Tanaka's mother (graciously) gave me this book.

cf. くれました

心配なさらないでください。
Please don't (graciously) worry.

cf. 心配しないでください

先生は十時ごろお休みになるそうです。
I hear that the professor (graciously) goes to bed around 10.

cf. 寝るそうです

社長はニュースをご覧になっています。
The president is (graciously) watching the news.

cf. 見ています

For the activities for which we lack special honorific verbs, we add the respect factor as follows:

(1) Using ていらっしゃいます instead of ています, if the sentence has the helping verb ている.

先生は電話で話していらっしゃいます。　　（＜話しています）
The professor is (graciously) talking on the phone.

部長は疲れていらっしゃるみたいです。　　（＜疲れているみたいです）
It appears that the department manager is (graciously) tired.

(2) Flanking a verb stem with お and になる.[3]

> お ＋ verb stem ＋ になる

先生はもうお帰りになりました。　　（＜帰りました）
The professor has already (graciously) gone home.

---

[3] As the examples show, you can turn most combinations of a verb and a post-predicate expression into the honorific style by simply turning the verb into the honorific form. Post-predicate expressions, such as ことがあります and ください, remain unchanged. This rule also applies to expressions like てもいい and てはいけない, and to the potential verbs. It is, however, not considered in good taste to talk about what an "honorable" person can or cannot do, and may or must not do.

ている is exceptional in being a post-predicate that regularly undergoes the honorific style shift. Special honorific verbs generally take priority over ていらっしゃる, as seen in the ご覧になっています example above, but forms like 見ていらっしゃいます are also considered acceptable.

この雑誌をお読みになったことがありますか。　　（＜読んだことがありますか）
Have you ever (graciously) read this magazine?

どうぞお使いになってください。　　　　　　　　（＜使ってください）
Please (graciously) use it.

2 Giving Respectful Advice

You may hear the form "お ＋ verb stem ＋ ください" in public service announcements and in the speech of store attendants.

> お＋ verb stem ＋ ください

切符をお取りください。　　*Please take a ticket.*　　　　　　　　（＜取る）

説明をお読みください。　　*Please read the instruction.*　　　　　（＜読む）

Although such sentences end with ください, it is better to consider that they are (courteously phrased) commands, rather than requests. When somebody tells you お～ください, you are being encouraged to perform the actions *for your own good*. Thus if I want somebody to pass the salt *for me* it is wrong to say:

×　塩をお取りください。
Please take the salt (and pass it to me).

You should say instead:　塩を取っていただけませんか。

With most する compound verbs, for example, the prefix ご is used instead of お. Note also the examples with special honorific verbs below.

ご注意ください。　　　　*Please watch out.*　　　　　（＜注意する）

ご覧ください。　　　　　*Please look.*　　　　　　　（＜ご覧になる ＜見る）

お召し上がりください。　*Please help yourself.*　　　（＜召し上がる ＜食べる）

お休みください。　　　　*Please have a good rest.*　　（＜お休みになる ＜寝る）

3 〜てくれてありがとう

When you want to express gratitude to someone for a specific action, you can use the *te*-form ＋ くれてありがとう.[4]

手伝ってくれてありがとう。　　*Thank you for helping me out.*

If you are thanking someone who needs to be talked to with the honorific language, such as when you and the person are not close or when the person ranks higher than you in any of the social hierarchies, you should say "*te*-form ＋ くださってありがとうございました."[5]

推薦状を書いてくださってありがとうございました。
Thank you for writing a letter of recommendation for me.

verb *te*-form ＋	くれてありがとう　(casual) くださってありがとうございました (polite)	*Thank you for doing . . .*

会
L19

4 〜てよかったです

Te-form ＋ よかった means "I'm glad that such and such is/was the case." If you want to mention something in the negative in the part before よかった, you can use the negative *te*-form なくて.

〜てよかったです	*I am glad that I did . . . / . . . was the case*
〜なくてよかったです	*I am glad that I didn't . . . / . . . was not the case*

日本語を勉強してよかったです。
I'm glad that I have studied Japanese.

メアリーさんが元気になってよかったです。
I'm glad that Mary got well.

約束の時間に遅れなくてよかったです。
I'm glad that I was not late for the appointment.

---

[4] You can use this pattern to say "thank you for being such-and-such a person," by using でいる instead of です.
　　いい友だちでいてくれてありがとう。　　*Thank you for being a good friend.*

[5] To show appreciation for an ongoing act of kindness, use the present tense ありがとうございます.
　　いつも親切に教えてくださってありがとうございます。　　*Thank you for your kind instructions.*

5 ～はずです

You can say something is "supposed to be the case," by adding はずです to a sentence ending in the short form.

今日は日曜日だから、銀行は閉まっているはずです。
きょう　　にちようび　　　　　　　　ぎんこう　し
Banks must be closed, because today is a Sunday.

レポートの締め切りはあしたじゃないはずです。[6]
　　　　　し　き
I believe that the paper is not due tomorrow.

A はずです sentence is a statement about what you believe is true or likely, though you lack conclusive evidence. It is used when situations surrounding the case and/or our common sense point naturally to such a belief. はずです cannot be used in a situation in which you are "supposed" to do something because of duty, responsibility, or law.

You can turn はずです into the past tense to describe something that was supposed to have been the case but actually turned out otherwise. The part that precedes はずでした is in the present tense.

先週電話をもらうはずでしたが、電話がありませんでした。
せんしゅうてん わ　　　　　　　　　　　　　てん わ
I was supposed to receive a phone call last week, but I didn't.

You can use はずです with adjectives, nouns, and verbs.

short form ＋はずです		*It is supposed to be the case . . .*
・verbs:	来るはずです	
	く	
・い-adjectives:	おもしろいはずです	
・な-adjectives:	元気なはずです	
	げん き	
・nouns:	日本人のはずです	
	に ほんじん	

---

[6] You see in this example that predicates in the negative can come before はずです. You may also hear another type of negative, はずがありません and はずがない, which means that something is inconceivable.
　彼がうそをつくはずがありません。　　　*I cannot imagine that he would tell a lie.*
　かれ

表現ノート
ひょう　げん

Honorific forms of nouns and adjectives ▶ Some nouns and adjectives are made into honorific forms by adding the prefixes お or ご. お is usually used with words that originated in Japanese and ご with words borrowed from Chinese.

お～：	お名前	お仕事	お好き	お元気	おたばこ	お忙しい
	な まえ	し ごと	す	げん き		いそが

ご～：	ご両親	ご兄弟	ご病気	ご主人	ご親切
	りょうしん	きょうだい	びょう き	しゅ じん	しんせつ

Some other words are replaced by special vocabulary items.

家	→	お宅		どこ	→	どちら
いえ		たく				
子供	→	お子さん		どうですか	→	いかがですか
こ ども		こ				
だれ	→	どなた／どちら様				
			さま			

These words and expressions cannot be used when you refer to yourself, your family, or the group you belong to.

A：ご両親はお元気ですか。　　　　*How are your parents?*
　　りょうしん　　げん き
B：はい。おかげさまで元気です。　*Thanks to you, they are fine.*
　　　　　　　　　　　　げん き
　　　　　（×お元気です）
　　　　　　　　　げん き

たら in polite speech ▶ We learned that the conditional たら is based on the past tense short forms. In honorific speech, たら also follows the long form.

お決まりになりましたらお呼びください。　　cf. 決まったら呼んで
　き　　　　　　　　　　　　よ　　　　　　　　　　　き　　　　　よ
Please let us know when you are ready to order.　　　　　ください。

それで/そして/それから ▶ These "and" words are used in different meanings.

それで　"and therefore" (to introduce the consequence of what comes before it)

電車が来ませんでした。それで、遅刻しました。
てんしゃ　き　　　　　　　　　　　ち こく
Trains didn't come. Therefore, I was late for class.

そして　"and in addition" (to say something notable)

ソラさんは韓国語と英語が話せます。そして、日本語も話せます。
　　　　　かんこく ご　えい ご　はな　　　　　　　　　に ほん ご　はな
Sora speaks Korean and English. And believe it or not, Japanese, too.

それから　"and then" (to add an item that comes later in time or in the order
　　　　　of importance)

京都と奈良に行きました。それから、大阪にも行きました。
きょう と　な ら　い　　　　　　　　　おおさか　　い
I went to Kyoto and Nara. And then I also went to Osaka.

会
L19

練習 P r a c t i c e
れん しゅう

Ⅰ コーヒーを召し上がります ☞Grammar 1
め あ

A. Change the following verbs into honorific expressions.

(a) Special honorific verbs 🔊 K19-09

[Example] 行く → いらっしゃる
い

1. 食べる　　3. いる　　5. 寝る　　7. 見る　　9. 住んでいる　　11. くれる
　　た　　　　　　　　　　　ね　　　　み　　　　　す
2. 言う　　　4. する　　6. 来る　　8. 飲む　　10. 結婚している
　　い　　　　　　　　く　　　　の　　　　けっこん

(b) お～になる 🔊 K19-10

[Example] 歌う → お歌いになる
うた　　　うた

1. わかる　　　3. 読む　　　5. 座る　　　7. 乗る　　　9. 待つ
　　　　　　　　よ　　　　すわ　　　　の　　　　ま
2. 調べる　　　4. 聞く　　　6. 立つ　　　8. 入る　　　10. 似合う
　　しら　　　　き　　　　た　　　　はい　　　　に あ

B. Describe what Professor Yamashita does in a day using honorific expressions. 🔊 K19-11

[Example] 山下先生はコーヒーを召し上がります。
やましたせんせい　　　　　　め あ

e.g. 　(1) 　(2) 　(3)

(4) 　(5) 　(6) 　(7)

(8)　　　　　　(9)　　　　　　(10)

C. Change the following questions into honorific expressions. 🔊 K19-12

(Example) よく写真を撮りますか。　→　よく写真をお撮りになりますか。

1. お名前は何と言いますか。
2. どちらに住んでいますか。
3. どんな音楽をよく聞きますか。
4. 車を持っていますか。
5. ご兄弟／お子さんがいますか。
6. 週末、よく何をしますか。
7. 週末、どちらへよく行きますか。
8. 今朝、何を食べましたか。
9. 外国に行ったことがありますか。
10. どんな外国語を話しますか。

11. 最近、映画を見ましたか。
12. 毎日、何時ごろ寝ますか。
13. 日本の歌を知っていますか。
14. ペットを飼っていますか。
15. どんなスポーツをしますか。
16. お酒を飲みますか。
17. 結婚していますか。
18. 有名人に会ったことがありますか。
19. なぜ日本語を勉強しているんですか。

会
L19

D. Pair Work—Ask your partner the questions above made with honorific expressions. Make sure that you don't use honorific forms when you answer.

(Example) Q：よく写真をお撮りになりますか。
　　　　　A：はい、よく撮ります。

E. Role Play—Act the role of a reporter asking questions using honorific expressions and a Japanese celebrity who answers them.

(Example) Reporter：初めまして。ＬＡタイムズのジョンソンと申します。
　　　　　　　　　～さんは、いつロサンゼルスにいらっしゃいましたか。
　　　　　Celebrity：きのう来ました。……

Ⅱ お待ちください ☞Grammar 2

ま

Match the following expressions with the pictures. Put answers in the (   ). 🔊 K19-13

(1)   (   )

(2)   (   )

(3)   (   )

(4)   (   )

(5)   (   )

(6)   (   )

(7)   (   )

(8)   (   )

(9)   (   )

a. お待ちください。
   ま

b. ご覧ください。
   らん

c. お入りください。
   はい

d. ご注意ください。
   ちゅう い

e. お召し上がりください。
   め あ

f. おかけください。

g. お使いください。
   つか

h. お書きください。
   か

i. おたばこはご遠慮ください。
   えんりょ

III 悩みを聞いてくれてありがとう ☞Grammar 3
なや き

A. Express your appreciation to the following people using 〜てくれてありがとう／〜てくださってありがとうございました. 🔊 K19-14

Example 悩みを聞く
なや き

to your friend　→　悩みを聞いてくれてありがとう。
　　　　　　　　　なや き

to your teacher　→　悩みを聞いてくださってありがとうございました。
　　　　　　　　　なや き

Your friend

Your teacher

1. ノートを見せる
　　　　み

2. うちまで送る
　　　　おく

3. 宿題を手伝う
　しゅくだい てつだ

4. 部屋を片付ける
　へや かたづ

5. 昼ご飯をおごる
　ひる はん

6. 推薦状を書く
　すいせんじょう か

7. 宿題の間違いを直す
　しゅくだい まちが なお

8. パーティーに招待する
　　　　　しょうたい

9. 日本の文化を教える
　にほん ぶんか おし

10. 辞書を貸す
　じしょ か

B. Role Play—In pairs, act the role of the following, expressing your appreciation to each other as much as possible.

Example Husband and Wife

　→　Husband : おいしい料理を作ってくれてありがとう。
　　　　　　　　　　　りょうり つく

　　　Wife :　　犬を散歩に連れていってくれてありがとう。
　　　　　　　　いぬ さんぽ つ

1. Classmates

2. Boss and Secretary

3. Roommates/Housemates

4. Boyfriend/Girlfriend/Partner

5. Family

会
L19

C. Tell the class who you want to express your gratitude to, and what you want to say to them, as in the example.

Example 私はホストファミリーのお母さんにお礼が言いたいです。お母さんは
毎朝起こしてくれました。おかげで日本語の授業に遅刻しませんでし
た。「毎朝起こしてくれてありがとう」と言いたいです。

Ⅳ 日本に留学してよかったです 👉Grammar 4

A. Express that you are glad you did/didn't do the things below using 〜てよかった.

🔊 K19-15

Example 日本に留学する → 日本に留学してよかったです。

1. この大学を選ぶ
2. 日本語の勉強をやめない
3. いろいろな人と知り合える
4. 敬語を習う
5. サークルに入る
6. ボランティア活動に参加する

7. 寮に引っ越す
8. 授業をサボらない

B. Pair Work—Talk about the things you are glad you did/didn't do. Expand the conversation as in the example.

Example おととい

→ A：おととい、秋葉原でゲームを買いました。秋葉原に行って
よかったです。

B：どうしてですか。

A：ほかの店より安いし、いろいろな種類のゲームがあるし。

B：それで、何を買ったんですか。

1. きのう
2. 先週
3. 去年
4. 大学に入ってから
5. 子供の時

Ⅴ 頭がいいはずです ☞Grammar 5
あたま

A. Read the information about Mr. Ishida and Ms. Tani and answer the questions using
〜はず. K19-16

[Example] Q：石田さんは頭がいいですか。
いしだ　　　あたま
A：ええ。東京大学を卒業したから、頭がいいはずです。
とうきょうだいがく　そつぎょう　　　　　あたま

石田さん
いしだ

> graduated from the University of Tokyo
> lives in a big house
> vegetarian（ベジタリアン）
> good personality
> works at a TV station（テレビ局）
> きょく

谷さん
たに

> diligent student
> studied in China for one year
> tennis club member
> lives alone

1. 石田さんはお金持ちですか。
いしだ　　　かねも
2. 石田さんは肉を食べますか。
いしだ　　にく　た
3. 石田さんは女の人にもてますか。
いしだ　　おんな　ひと
4. 石田さんは有名人に会ったことがありますか。
いしだ　　ゆうめいじん　あ
5. 谷さんはよく授業をサボりますか。
たに　　　　じゅぎょう
6. 谷さんは中国語が話せますか。
たに　　ちゅうごくご　はな
7. 谷さんはテニスが上手ですか。
たに　　　　　じょうず
8. 谷さんは自分で洗濯や掃除をしますか。
たに　　じぶん　せんたく　そうじ

B. Complete the sentences using 〜はず.

1. まいさんは性格_{せいかく}がいいから、_____。

2. たくやくんはまだ中学生_{ちゅうがくせい}だから、_____。

3. けんさんは怠_{なま}け者_{もの}だから、_____。

4. れいさんは恥_はずかしがり屋_やだから、_____。

5. たけしさんとメアリーさんは仲_{なか}がいいから、_____。

6. ソラさんはまじめだから、_____。

C. Takeshi worked overtime and finally got a day off to go out with Mary. However, things turned out differently from what he had expected. Talk about (a) what he had expected and (b) what really happened as in the example. 🔊 K19-17

Example お父_{とう}さんが車_{くるま}を貸_かしてくれるはずでしたが、
車_{くるま}でゴルフに行_いってしまいました。

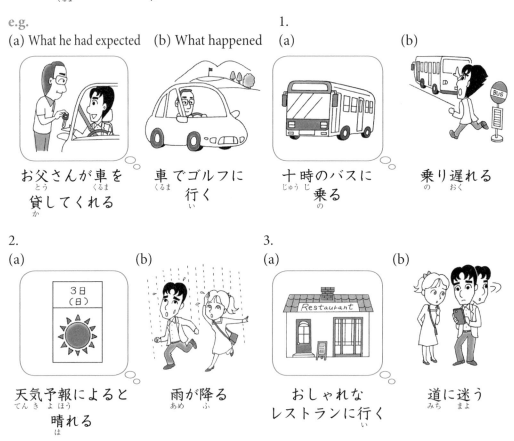

e.g.
(a) What he had expected　(b) What happened

お父_{とう}さんが車_{くるま}を
貸_かしてくれる

車_{くるま}でゴルフに
行_いく

1.
(a)　(b)

十時_{じゅうじ}のバスに
乗_のる

乗_のり遅_{おく}れる

2.
(a)　(b)

3日
（日）

天気予報_{てんきよほう}によると
晴_はれる

雨_{あめ}が降_ふる

3.
(a)　(b)

Restaurant

おしゃれな
レストランに行_いく

道_{みち}に迷_{まよ}う

4.   5.

(a)   (b)   (a)   (b)

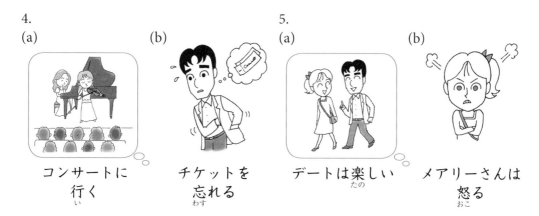

コンサートに　　　チケットを　　　デートは楽しい　　　メアリーさんは
行く　　　　　　　忘れる　　　　　　　　　　　　　　　怒る

D. Pair Work—Talk about a thing that turned out differently as in the example.

> Example　きのう引っ越す
>
> →　A：きのう引っ越すはずだったけど……
> 　　B：どうしたの。
> 　　A：車が借りられなかったんだ。
> 　　B：車があるから、手伝ってあげるよ。
> 　　A：ありがとう。助かる。

1. きのうまでにレポートが終わる　　　3. 友だちにおごってあげる
2. 親が来る　　　　　　　　　　　　　4. (your own)

Ⅵ まとめの練習

A. Class Activity—You are at a formal party. Let's practice talking elegantly. Use honorific expressions to ask questions and find someone who . . .

1. plays golf   _____

2. reads many books   _____

3. has an older brother   _____

4. often watches Japanese dramas（ドラマ）_____

5. has been to Hokkaido   _____

6. drinks coffee every day   _____

7. goes to bed by 11:00 p.m.   _____

8. (your own)   _____

会
L19

B. Role Play—Make a skit based on the following situations.

1. You have participated in a weekend homestay in Japan. You had a great time because of your host family. Now you are leaving their home. Express your appreciation to them.

2. Studying Japanese was hard for you. You thought about quitting many times during the semester, but you were able to get by because of your teacher's help. Visit your teacher's office and express your appreciation.

C. Reflect on your past semester/year and talk about the things you are glad that you did or didn't do and about the things you wish you had (not) done. Use 〜(なく)てよかった and 〜(なけれ)ばよかった.

Example 日本語の授業を取ってよかったです。クラスはおもしろかったし、友だちもできたし。でも、あまり勉強しなかったので、もっと勉強すればよかったと思います。

Culture Notes

訪問のしかた Visiting Someone's House
ほう もん

Here are some examples of expressions used when you visit someone's house.

1.  The guest arrives at the entrance of the house.
   Guest: こんにちは。吉田です。
   よし だ
   Hello. It's Yoshida.

2.  The host comes to the entrance.
   Host: よくいらっしゃいました。どうぞ、おあがりください。
   Welcome. Please come in.

   The guest goes inside.
   Guest: おじゃまします。*
   I'm sorry to intrude on you.

   *At the entrance, take off your shoes and place them neatly together facing the doorway.

3.  The guest gives a gift (usually food).
   Guest: これ、みなさんで召し上がってください。
   め あ
   I hope you enjoy it with your family.

   Host: どうもすみません。
   Thank you very much.

4.  The guest senses that the host is going to serve tea.
   Guest: どうぞ、おかまいなく。すぐ失礼しますから。
   しつれい
   Please don't bother. I will excuse myself soon.

5.  The guest leaves the house.
   Guest: おじゃましました。*
   I'm sorry to have intruded on you.

   Host: また、いらっしゃってください。
   Please come again.

*おじゃまします is used only when you visit someone's residence; when visiting a professor's office, for example, use 失礼します instead. Likewise, おじゃましました is used when leaving someone's house, while 失礼しました is
しつれい
used when leaving a professor's office.
しつれい

第20課

メアリーさんの買い物 Mary Goes Shopping
かもの

In this lesson, we will...

- Speak modestly about ourselves
- Express what is difficult or easy to do
- Return and exchange merchandise
- Ask for directions

会 話 D i a l o g u e
かい わ

I At an electric appliance store. 🔊 K20-01/02

1 メアリー： すみません。この間 このヘッドホンを買ったんですが、音が聞こえ
あいだ   か   おと き

2   ないんです。

3 店 員： 少々、お待ちください。今、係の者を呼んで参ります。
てん いん しょうしょう ま   いま かかり もの よ   まい

4 田 中： お待たせいたしました。田中と申します。ヘッドホンを見せていた
た なか   たなか もう   み

5   だけますか。……壊れているみたいですね。失礼いたしました。よ
こわ   しつれい

6   ろしかったら、交換いたしますが。
こうかん

7 メアリー： じゃあ、お願いします。
ねが

*   *   *

8 田 中： 申し訳ございません。今、同じ物がございませんので、二、三週間
た なか もう わけ   いま おな もの   に さんしゅうかん

9   待っていただけませんか。
ま

10 メアリー： それは、ちょっと……。もうすぐ国に帰るので、できれば返品した
くに かえ   へんぴん

11   いんですが。

12 田 中： かしこまりました。まことに申し訳ございませんでした。
た なか   もう わけ

II On a street. 🔊 K20-03/04

1 メアリー： すみません。にしき屋という店がどこにあるか教えていただけませ
や   みせ   おし

2   んか。地図を見ているんですが、わかりにくいんです。
ちず み

3 おじいさん：扇子の店ですね。次の角を左に曲がったら見えますよ。扇子を買い
せんす みせ   つぎ かど ひだり ま   み   せんす か

4   に行くんですか。
い

5 メアリー：　ええ。おみやげに扇子を買おうと思っているんです。
6 おじいさん：いいおみやげになりますよ。あっ、雨ですね。傘を持っていますか。
7 メアリー：　いいえ。急いでいたから、傘を持たないで、来ちゃったんです。
8 おじいさん：じゃあ、一緒に店まで行きましょう。
9 メアリー：　どうもすみません。荷物が重そうですね。
10 　　　　　　お持ちします。
11 おじいさん：ありがとう。

(I)

Mary: Excuse me. I bought these headphones the other day, but I can't hear anything.

Shop assistant: Please wait a moment. I will call the person in charge.

Tanaka: I'm sorry to have kept you waiting. My name is Tanaka. Could I see your headphones?
. . . They seem to be broken. I'm sorry. If you like, we will exchange them.

Mary: Please.

*　　　*　　　*

Tanaka: I'm very sorry. We don't have the same type now, so could you wait for a couple of weeks?

Mary: Well . . . I'm going back to my country soon. If possible, I want to return them.

Tanaka: Certainly. I'm really sorry.

(II)

Mary: Excuse me. Could you please tell me where the shop called "Nishikiya" is? I've been looking at this map, but I can't make it out.

Old man: It's a fan store, isn't it? You can see it when you turn left at the next corner. Are you going to buy fans?

Mary: Yes. I'm thinking of buying some as souvenirs.

Old man: They'll make good souvenirs. Oh, it's starting to rain. Do you have an umbrella?

Mary: No. I was in a hurry, so I left without one.

Old man: Then let's go to the store together.

Mary: Thank you so much. Your bag looks heavy. I'll carry it.

Old man: Thank you.

単語
<ruby>単<rt>たん</rt></ruby> <ruby>語<rt>ご</rt></ruby>

K20-05 (J-E)
K20-06 (E-J)

Vocabulary

Nouns

アニメ		animation
しょうせつ	小説	novel
しゅみ	趣味	hobby; pastime
つき	月	moon
うちゅうじん	宇宙人	space alien
* せんす	扇子	(hand) fan
スニーカー		sneakers
* ヘッドホン		headphones
おにぎり		rice ball
どうぶつ	動物	animal
あちら		that way (polite)
* かかりのもの	係の者	our person in charge
おたく	お宅	(someone's) home/house
* 〜や	〜屋	. . . shop
してん	支店	branch office
ドイツ		Germany
しんごう	信号	traffic light
* かど	角	corner
じ	字	letter; character
* おと	音	sound

い-adjectives

* おもい	重い	heavy; serious (illness)
かるい	軽い	light

な-adjective

ふしぎ（な）	不思議	mysterious

U-verbs

おる		extra-modest expression for いる
* まいる	参る	extra-modest expression for いく and くる
* もうす	申す	extra-modest expression for いう
* いたす	致す	extra-modest expression for する

＊Words that appear in the dialogue

いただく	頂く	extra-modest expression for たべる and のむ
* ござる		extra-modest expression for ある
〜ておる		extra-modest expression for 〜ている
〜でござる		extra-modest expression for です
* いただく	頂く	humble expression for もらう
うかがう	伺う	(1) to humbly visit（place に）
		(2) to humbly ask（person に）
* まがる	曲がる	to turn (right/left)（corner を direction に）
もどる	戻る	to return; to come back（〜に）

Ru-verbs

さしあげる	差し上げる	humble expression for あげる
* きこえる	聞こえる	to be audible（〜が）
つたえる	伝える	to convey message（person に）
* またせる	待たせる	to keep (someone) waiting（〜を）
つづける	続ける	to continue（〜を）

Irregular Verbs

* こうかんする	交換する	to exchange（X と Y を）
* へんぴんする	返品する	to return (merchandise)（〜を）
せいかつする	生活する	to lead a life

Adverbs and Other Expressions

〜かい	〜階	. . . th floor
いっかい	一階	first floor
〜みたいな X		X like . . .
また		again
では		well then (polite)
* できれば		if possible
* まことに	誠に	really (very polite)
* よろしかったら		if it is okay (polite)
* かしこまりました		Certainly.
* しつれいしました	失礼しました	I'm very sorry.
* もうしわけありません	申し訳ありません	You have my apologies. (polite)

文法 Grammar
ぶん ぽう

1 Extra-modest Expressions

In the last lesson, we learned the special expressions to be used when we want to show respect to another person. Here we will learn to *talk modestly of our own actions*. We use the verbs below when we want to sound modest and respectful in our speech, to show an extra amount of deference to the listener. These verbs are almost always used in long forms, because the purpose of using them is to be polite to the person you are talking to. Having one of these verbs is like ending a sentence with words like *sir* or *ma'am*.

Extra-modest expressions		
いる	おります	（おる）
行く 来る	参ります まい	（参る） まい
言う する	申します もう いたします	（申す） もう （いたす）
食べる 飲む	いただきます	（いただく）
ある	ございます	（ござる）
〜ている	〜ております	（〜ておる）
〜です	〜でございます	（〜でござる）

You can use these verbs instead of the normal ones on very formal occasions, for example, when you introduce yourself at a job interview. (They are typically used with the more stilted first-person word 私, rather than the normal 私.)
わたくし   わたし

私は来年も日本に<u>おります</u>。   cf. います
わたくし らいねん に ほん
I will be in Japan next year, too, sir/ma'am.

私は今年の六月に大学を卒業<u>いたしました</u>。   cf. 卒業しました
わたくし ことし ろくがつ だいがく そつぎょう   そつぎょう
I graduated from college this June, sir/ma'am.

私は一年間日本語を勉強<u>しております</u>。   cf. 勉強しています
わたくし いちねんかん に ほん ご べんきょう   べんきょう
I have been studying Japanese for a year.

私は木村たけしと<u>申します</u>。   cf. 言います
わたくし き むら もう   い
My name is Takeshi Kimura.

You can also use these expressions to talk modestly about your own family or about the company you work for. Extra-modest expressions are frequently used by people in business when they talk to customers. Thus you hear many extra-modest sentences like the examples below in public service announcements (as in the first example), and in the speech of shop clerks (as in the second).

電車が参ります。   cf. 来ます
A train is pulling in.

お手洗いは二階でございます。   cf. です
The bathroom is on the second floor.

ございます and でございます are very stylized and you rarely hear them outside formal business-related situations.

Because the effect of the extra-modest expressions is to put the subject in a modest light, you cannot use them to describe the actions performed by the person you are talking to or by somebody who is not in your group. Therefore, it is wrong to say:

× 先生はあした学校に参りますか。
Are you coming to school tomorrow, Professor?

2 Humble Expressions

When you do something out of respect for somebody, you can sometimes describe your action using a verb in the humble pattern "お ＋ verb stem ＋ する." (Not all verbs are used this way, so you may want to use only the ones you have actually heard used.) You can speak of "humbly" meeting, lending to, or borrowing from someone, for example.

お ＋ verb stem ＋ する   *I (humbly) do . . .*

私はきのう社長のご主人にお会いしました。
I (humbly) met husband of the company president yesterday.

私は先生に本をお貸しするつもりです。
I intend to (humbly) lend my professor a book.

私は先生に辞書をお借りしました。
I borrowed a dictionary from my professor (and feel very obliged).

Note that this "お＋stem＋する" pattern demotes the actor (*I humbly do something*) while the "お＋stem＋になる" pattern that we examined in Lesson 19 promotes the actor (*Somebody graciously does something*). They look similar because they share "お＋stem," but semantically they are polar opposites.

する する compound verbs do not follow this pattern. Instead they simply have the prefix ご or お, such as ご紹介する, ご案内する, ご説明する, and お電話する.

外国人に人気がある店をご紹介しましょう。
Let us tell you about a shop that is popular among foreigners.

きのうお電話した田中です。
This is Tanaka. I called yesterday.

もらう／あげる もらう and あげる have special replacement verbs:

もらう → いただく	私は先生にこの本をいただきました。 *I (humbly) received this book from my professor.*	
	私は先生に漢字を教えていただきました。 *I (humbly) had my professor teach me kanji.*	
あげる → さしあげる[1]	私は先生に花をさしあげます。 *I will (humbly) give my professor flowers.*	

うかがう うかがう is a verb with which you can portray yourself as humble in the actions of visiting and asking questions:

私は部長のお宅にうかがいました。
I (humbly) visited my department manager's house.

私は先生にテストについてうかがいました。
I (humbly) asked my professor about the exam.

---

[1] We do not endorse the use of さしあげる with the *te*-form of a verb in the sense of "humbly doing something for somebody," because many people object to this type of sentence. They argue that the idea that you are doing a service for somebody is ultimately an insolent belief and that trying to talk humbly about it is a rather unconvincing facade. Such speakers prefer instead to use the "お ＋ stem ＋ する" pattern.

Instead of: 私は先生に地図を見せてさしあげました。
Use: 私は先生に地図をお見せしました。   *I (humbly) showed a map to my professor.*

The subject in every example above is "I," and "I" humbly performs the action in deference to the person underlined.[2] The difference between this pattern and the extra-modest expressions that we studied earlier lies here: the extra-modest expressions show respect to the listeners you are talking to, while the humble pattern shows respect to someone that appears in the event you are describing. This of course does not preclude the possibility of you humbly performing an action for the person you are talking to.[3] For example,

（私はあなたを）駅までお送りします。
I will (humbly) walk you to the station.

Let us summarize the three types of "respect language" we have learned in this and the preceding lesson. The up arrow and the down arrow indicate the person whose profile is raised or lowered, respectively, by the use of the respect element in the sentence.

1. **Honorific expressions** exalt the subject of the sentence.

   先生が↑いらっしゃいました／お帰りになりました。
   My professor has (graciously) arrived/left.

2. **Extra-modest expressions** talk modestly of what you do.

   私は↓メアリー・ハートと申します。(person listening to you ↑)
   My name is Mary Hart.

3. **Humble expressions** demote the subject and raise the profile of another person.

   私は↓先生に↑本をお返ししました。
   I (humbly) returned the book to my professor.

---

[2] You can also talk about one of "your people," such as a family member or a coworker, humbly performing an action in deference to somebody outside the group.

　　父はお客さんにお茶をおいれしました。　　*My father (humbly) served the guest tea.*

[3] Sometimes we can use a humble expression to describe a situation where we do something for the person we are talking to, meaning "for you," "instead of you," and "saving you trouble."

　　テレビをおつけしましょう。　　*Let me (humbly) turn on the TV (for you).*

3 〜ないで

If you do something without doing something else, the action not performed can be expressed with 〜ない (the short negative present) plus で. Note that the present tense form 〜ない is used for both present and past actions.

> verb (short, negative) ＋ で   *without doing X*

きのうの夜は、寝ないで、勉強しました。
Last night, I studied without getting any sleep.

辞書を使わないで、新聞を読みます。
I read newspapers without using dictionaries.

4 ▶ Questions within Larger Sentences

You can include a question as a part of a longer sentence and express ideas such as "I don't know when the test is" and "I don't remember whether Mary came to the party."

Embedded question clauses are shown in the boxes in the examples below. Embedded questions are in short forms. Note (1) that the clause ends with the question particle か when it contains a question word like だれ and なに, as in the first two examples, and (2) that it ends with かどうか when it does not contain such a question word, as in the third example.[4]

山下先生は きのう何を食べたか 覚えていません。
Professor Yamashita does not remember what he ate yesterday.

メアリーさんがどこに住んでいるか 知っていますか。
Do you know where Mary lives?

週末、 旅行に行くかどうか 決めましょう。
Let's decide whether we will go on a trip this weekend.

> Question-word question か
> Yes/no question かどうか   わかりません / 知っています / etc.

---

[4] Many people use か instead of かどうか in their speech for questions of this second type as well.

The present tense short form だ which is used with a な-adjective or a noun at the end of the clause is usually dropped.[5]

だれが一番上手だ か わかりません。
いちばんじょう ず
I don't know who is the best.

あの人が学生だ かどうか わかりません。
ひと　　がくせい
I don't know if that person is a student.

We often use the particle が with the subject of an embedded sentence where は is expected. Thus, for the embedded question corresponding to the direct question たけし さんはだれが好きです か, we say:

私 はたけし さんがだれが好きか知っています。
わたし　　　　　　　　　　　　　す　　　し
I know who Takeshi is in love with.

5 Name という Item

When you want to talk about a person or a thing that goes by a certain name, but if you believe the person you are talking to is not familiar with it, you can use the following pattern.

(name) という (item)	(item) *called* "(name)"

ポチという犬 （を飼っていました。）
いぬ　　　か
(I used to have) a dog called "Pochi."

「花」 という 歌 （を知っていますか。）
はな　　　　うた　　し
(Do you know) a song called "Hana"?

---

[5] Explanatory んです sentences can also be embedded. When a んですか question is embedded, だ (the short form of です) is dropped, and ん is changed to の.
Direct question:　　　どうしてメアリーさんは来なかったんですか。
Embedded question:　　どうしてメアリーさんが来なかったのかわかりません。

6 ～やすい／～にくい

You can describe that something is easy to do by adding the adjective-forming suffix やすい to the verb stem. A verb stem ＋ やすい conjugates like an い-adjective.[6]

使う　　→　　使いやすい　　　　　この電子レンジは使いやすいです。
This microwave oven is easy to use.

読む　　→　　読みやすい　　　　　この本は読みやすかったです。
This book was easy to read.

To express that something is hard to do, you can use the い-adjective-forming suffix にくい with the verb stem.

食べる　→　　食べにくい　　　　　骨が多いので、魚は食べにくいです。
Fish are hard to eat, because they have many bones.

| verb stem + | やすい | *easy to do* |
| | にくい | *hard to do* |

Sometimes, the subject of a ～やすい／にくい sentence is a place (where it is easy/difficult to do something), a tool (that is easy/difficult to use for some purpose), and so forth.

この町はとても住みやすいです。
This town is quite livable.

この靴は歩きにくいです。
These shoes are not comfortable to walk in.

～やすい and ～にくい tend to focus on the psychological ease or difficulty of doing something when you use them with verbs describing actions. It is therefore odd to use やすい or にくい when the difficulty is defined in terms of a physical or statistical *success rate*. Thus compare:

漢字は覚えにくい。
Kanji are hard to memorize.　（＝I have kanji anxieties）

漢字を覚えるのは難しい。
It is hard to memorize kanji.　（＝too complicated, too many）

---

[6] Note that やすい as a separate word means "cheap" and not "easy." "Easy" is やさしい.

練習 Practice
れん しゅう

I 田中と申します ☛Grammar 1
た なか もう

A. Change the following words into extra-modest expressions. 🔊 K20-07

Example 行く → 参ります
い　　　　　　　まい

1. 食べる 2. 言う 3. 来る 4. する 5. いる 6. ある 7. 飲む 8. あちらだ
た　　　　い　　　　く　　　　　　　　　　　　　　　　　　　の

B. Match the following sentences with the pictures. Put answers in the (　　). 🔊 K20-08

(1) (　　)　　(2) (　　)　　(3) (　　)

(4) (　　)　　(5) (　　)　　(6) (　　)

---

a. あちらが東京スカイツリー (Tokyo Skytree) でございます。
　　　　とうきょう

b. 電車が参ります。
　　てんしゃ まい

c. 田中と申します。よろしくお願いいたします。
　　た なか もう　　　　　　　　　　ねが

d. 父は今出かけております。
　　ちち いまで

e. いただきます。

f. お手洗いは二階にございます。
　　て あら　　　に かい

C. Pair Work—You are at a formal reception and make small talk with someone you have just met. Use honorific expressions to ask questions, and extra-modest expressions to answer them. 🔊 K20-09

Example Q：お名前は何と言いますか。　→　お名前は何とおっしゃいますか。
　　　　　　　　　なまえ　なん　い　　　　　　　　　　　　　　なまえ　なん
　　　　A：田中と言います。　　　　　　→　田中と申します。
　　　　　　たなか　い　　　　　　　　　　　　　たなか　もう

1. Q：いつ日本に来ましたか。　　　　　A：先月来ました。
　　　　　　にほん　き　　　　　　　　　　　　せんげつき
2. Q：どちらに住んでいますか。　　　　A：名古屋に住んでいます。
　　　　　　す　　　　　　　　　　　　　　なごや　す
3. Q：お酒をよく飲みますか。　　　　　A：少し飲みます。
　　　　さけ　の　　　　　　　　　　　　　すこ　の
4. Q：ご兄弟がいますか。　　　　　　　A：兄が一人います。
　　　　きょうだい　　　　　　　　　　　あに　ひとり
5. Q：何かスポーツをしますか。　　　　A：はい、サッカーをします。
　　　　なに
6. Q：毎日何時間日本語を勉強しますか。　A：二時間ぐらい勉強します。
　　　　まいにちなんじかんにほんご　べんきょう　　　にじかん　べんきょう
7. Q：毎日何時ごろ晩ご飯を食べますか。　A：七時ごろ食べます。
　　　　まいにちなんじ　ばんはん　た　　　　しちじ　た
8. Q：週末はどこかへ行きましたか。　　A：はい、美術館へ行きました。
　　　　しゅうまつ　い　　　　　　　　　びじゅつかん　い
9. Q：日本文学に興味がありますか。　　A：はい、あります。
　　　　にほんぶんがく　きょうみ

Now ask and answer on your own.

D. Below on the left is Mr. Taylor's speech of self-introduction at an informal party. Rephrase the speech for a very formal reception by filling in the blanks with extra-modest expressions. 🔊 K20-10

ビル・テイラーと言います。
　　　　　　　い
トマス銀行から来ました。
　　ぎんこう　き
横浜支店で働いています。
よこはましてん　はたら
どうぞよろしくお願いします。
　　　　　　　ねが

ビル・テイラーと＿＿＿＿＿＿＿＿＿。
トマス銀行から＿＿＿＿＿＿＿＿＿＿。
　　ぎんこう
横浜支店で働いて＿＿＿＿＿＿＿＿＿。
よこはましてん　はたら
どうぞよろしくお願い＿＿＿＿＿＿＿。
　　　　　　　ねが

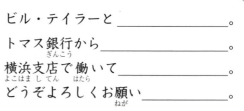

Now make your own formal speech supposing you were representing a company.

E. Pair Work—Telephone Conversation

Mr. Smith calls Ms. Sekido's company, The Japan Times Publishing. Her coworker answers the phone. Change the underlined parts and practice the dialogue with your partner. 🔊 K20-11

岡本： はい。<u>ジャパンタイムズ出版</u>でございます。

スミス： <u>スミス</u>と申しますが、<u>関戸さん</u>はいらっしゃいますか。

岡本： 申し訳ありません。<u>関戸は今日休んでおります</u>が。

スミス： そうですか。では、<u>スミスから電話があった</u>と伝えていただけませんか。

岡本： <u>スミス</u>さんですね。かしこまりました。

スミス： 失礼いたします。

Ⅱ お持ちします ☛Grammar 2

A. Change the verbs into humble expressions. 🔊 K20-12

(Example) 会う → お会いする

1. 借りる
2. 返す
3. 送る
4. 持つ
5. 取る
6. 話す
7. 読む
8. 貸す
9. もらう
10. あげる
11. 紹介する
12. 案内する

B. Look at the pictures and politely offer your help. 🔊 K20-13

(Example) お持ちしましょうか。

e.g.
(1)
取れない
(2)

(3) 駅まで
行くんです

(4) 書けない

(5) 一緒に
撮ろうよ

(6)

(7) 病院の電話番号
わかる？

C. Pair Work—Play the role of a guest and a host in a business situation. The guest seems to be in situations 1-5. The host offers to do the things listed in the box.

(Example) The guest's bag looks heavy.

→ Host： 荷物をお持ちしましょうか。

Guest：えっ、いいんですか。重いですよ。

Host： はい、大丈夫です。

1. The guest looks sleepy.

2. It seems the guest wants to look around the company.

3. It seems the guest wants to be introduced to the company president.

4. It seems the guest likes a T-shirt with the company logo.（会社の Ｔ シャツ）

5. The guest is going back to the hotel.

---

e.g. 荷物を持つ　　案内する　　車で送る

紹介する　　あげる　　コーヒーをいれる

D. Change the underlined parts into honorific, humble, or extra-modest expressions.

1. たけし：部長、何か^(a)飲みますか。

   部　長：うん。

   たけし：では、お茶を^(b)いれますね。

2. たけし：部長、もうこの本を^(a)読みましたか。

   部　長：うん、読んだよ。

   たけし：では、^(b)借りてもいいですか。

   来週、^(c)返します。

3. たけし：部長、荷物が重そうですね。^(a)持ちます。

   部　長：ありがとう。

   たけし：どちらに^(b)行くんですか。

   部　長：駅まで行くんだ。

   たけし：では、車で^(c)送ります。

4. たけし：アジアトラベルの木村と^(a)言います。

   山田部長に^(b)会いたいんですが。

   受　付：^(c)申し訳ありません。山田は今、

   出張で東京に行っ^(d)ています。

   たけし：そうですか。いつ^(e)戻りますか。

   受　付：あしたの夕方に戻ると思います。

   たけし：そうですか。では、またあした

   うかがいます。

Ⅲ ひげをそらないで、会社に行きました Grammar 3
かいしゃ い

A. Describe the pictures using 〜ないで. 🔊 K20-14

e.g.

(Example) たけしさんはひげをそらないで、会社に行きました。
かいしゃ い

1. たけしさんは会社に行きました。
かいしゃ い

　(a) 　(b) 　(c)

2. メアリーさんは寝ました。
ね

　(a) 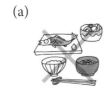　(b) 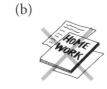　(c)

3. ジョンさんは出かけました。
て

　(a) 　(b) 　(c)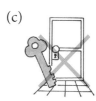

B. Complete the following sentences.

1. _____ないで、空港に行ってしまいました。
くうこう い

2. _____ないで、ジーンズを買ってしまいました。
か

3. _____ないで、部長のお宅にうかがってしまいました。
ぶちょう たく

4. 忙しかったので、_____ないで、寝ました。
いそが　　　　　　　　　　　　　　　　　　　　　　　　　　ね

5. お金がないので、_____ないで、生活しています。
かね　　　　　　　　　　　　　　　　　　　　　　　　　　せいかつ

6. 宿題は難しかったけど、_____ないで、やりました。
しゅくだい　むずか

IV アメリカ人かどうかわかりません 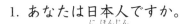 ☞Grammar 4

A. You have been involved in a car accident and have lost all your memory. (For some reason you can speak Japanese.) You are at the hospital and your doctor will ask you the questions below. Answer them using 〜か（どうか）わかりません。 🔊 K20-15

Example　Q：名前は何ですか。
　　　　　A：さあ、何かわかりません。
　　　　　Q：あなたはアメリカ人ですか。
　　　　　A：さあ、アメリカ人かどうかわかりません。

1. あなたは日本人ですか。
2. 学生ですか。
3. 結婚していますか。
4. 子供がいますか。
5. 字が書けますか。
6. 何歳ですか。

7. 仕事は何をしていますか。
8. どこに住んでいますか。
9. 今日何を食べましたか。
10. きのう何をしましたか。
11. どうやってここに来ましたか。

会
L20

B. Pair Work—Ask the following questions about your classmates or somebody that you both know. Continue the conversation.

Example

Do you know if [NAME] has a romantic partner?

→　A：カルロスさんを知っていますね？
　　B：はい。
　　A：付き合っている人がいるかどうか知っていますか。
　　B：さあ……。時々、女の人と一緒にいますよ。
　　　　でも、彼女じゃないと思います。
　　A：そうですか。じゃあ、今度、映画に誘ってみます。

Do you know . . .

1. if they like karaoke
2. if they are interested in animation
3. how old they are
4. which floor in the dormitory they live

5. what their hobbies are
6. what kind of music they like
7. what they will do this weekend

C. Pair Work—Ask your partner the following questions.

(Example) Ａ：先週の土曜日に何をしましたか。
　　　　　Ｂ：さあ、何をしたか覚えていません。／映画を見に行きました。

1. 一年後も日本語の勉強を続けていますか。
2. 五年後、何をしていますか。
3. きのうの夜、夢を見ましたか。どんな夢を見ましたか。
4. メアリーさんとたけしさんは結婚しますか。
5. 宇宙人がいると思いますか。
6. 将来、人が月に住めると思いますか。

Ⅴ　ローソンというコンビニ　☞Grammar 5

A. Describe the pictures using 〜という。　🔊 K20-16

(Example)　ローソンというコンビニ

e.g.

(1)

(2)

(3)

(4)

(5)

(6)

(7)

(8)

B. Pair Work—Talk about the following topics, using 〜という as in the example.

Example animation

→ 　Ａ：「となりのトトロ」というアニメを知っていますか。

　　Ｂ：いいえ、どんなアニメですか。

　　Ａ：二人の女の子がトトロという不思議な動物に会う話です。
　　　　日本語もやさしいし、絵もきれいだし、おもしろいですよ。

　　Ｂ：そうですか。見てみたいです。

1. person	4. shop	7. (your own)
2. restaurant	5. movie	
3. book	6. singer	

C. Pair Work—What is your favorite restaurant/store? Exchange information about your favorite restaurant or store with your partner. Include (1) name of the place, (2) location, and (3) your recommendation.

Example 私の好きな店は、「つじた」というラーメンの店です。駅の前にあります。しょうゆラーメンと唐揚げ (fried chicken) がとてもおいしいです。人気があるので、いつも混んでいます。時々、一時間も待ちます。でも、ここで食べると幸せになります。

Ⅵ 覚えやすいです 👉Grammar 6

A. Make sentences using やすい and にくい. 🔊 K20-17

Example 川という漢字は覚えやすいですが、髪という漢字は覚えにくいです。

e.g. 覚える　　　　　　　　　　　　　(1) 食べる

川という漢字　　　髪という漢字　　　　ハンバーガー　　　魚

(2) 歩く
　　ある

げた (wooden clogs)　　スニーカー

(3) 持つ
　　も

メアリーさんの　　たけしさんの
　かばん　　　　　　かばん

(4) わかる

ソラさんの話　　けんさんの話
　　　はなし　　　　　　はなし

(5) 使う
　　つか

紙の辞書　　スマホの辞書
かみ　じしょ　　　　　じしょ

(6) 運転する
　　うんてん

せまい道　　　広い道
　　みち　　　ひろ　みち

(7) 読む
　　よ

お元気
ですか？

お元気
ですか？

ソラさんの字　　ロバートさんの字
　　　　　じ　　　　　　　　じ

B. Class Activity—Show something to the class. Introduce it and talk about it using 〜やすい／にくい.

(Example)

これは誕生日に母にもらったかばんです。軽くて、とても持ちやすいです。
　　　たんじょうび　はは　　　　　　　　　　かる　　　　　　　　　も
これはぼくの水筒 (water bottle) です。大きくて重いので、使いにくいです。
　　　　　　すいとう　　　　　　　　　おお　　　おも　　　　　つか
でも、たくさん水が入ります。
　　　　　　　みず　はい

C. Pair Work—Ask your partner the following questions and expand the conversation.

Example どんな人が話しやすいと思いますか。
　ひと　はな　　　　　　おも

→ 　A：どんな人が話しやすいと思いますか。
　　　　ひと　はな　　　　　　おも

　　　B：そうですね。ソラさんみたいな人が話しやすいです。
　　　　　　　　　　　　　　　　　　ひと　はな

　　　A：どうしてですか。

　　　B：ソラさんはやさしいし、話を聞いてくれるし。
　　　　　　　　　　　　　　　　はなし　き

　　　　　Aさんはどんな人が話しやすいと思いますか。
　　　　　　　　　　ひと　はな　　　　　　おも

1. どんな車が運転しやすいと思いますか。
　　　　くるま　うんてん　　　　　おも

2. どんな町が住みやすいと思いますか。
　　　　まち　す　　　　おも

3. どんな会社が働きにくいと思いますか。
　　　　かいしゃ　はたら　　　　おも

Ⅶ まとめの練習
　　　　　れんしゅう

会
L20

A. Class Activity—Suppose you are at a very formal party. Walk around the reception hall (classroom) and make acquaintance with VIPs (classmates). Ask questions and fill in the table below. Add your own questions.

	VIP 1	VIP 2	VIP 3
name?			
live where?			
do what for a living?			
play what sport?			
drink what?			
have brothers & sisters?			

B. Pair Work—One of you looks at picture A and the other looks at picture B (p. 204). Ask each other questions about how to get to the following places from "HERE" on the map. When you are asked, answer the question as in the example.

Example 店「にしきや」
みせ

→ A：にしきやという店がどこにあるか教えていただけませんか。
みせ

B：三つ目の信号を右に曲がったら左に見えますよ。
みっ め しんごう みぎ ま ひだり み

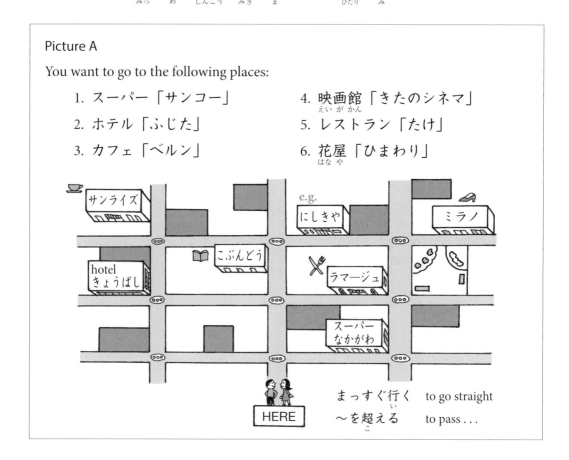

Picture A

You want to go to the following places:

1. スーパー「サンコー」   4. 映画館「きたのシネマ」
えい が かん

2. ホテル「ふじた」   5. レストラン「たけ」

3. カフェ「ベルン」   6. 花屋「ひまわり」
はな や

サンライズ

e.g.

にしきや

ミラノ

こぶんどう

hotel
きょうばし

ラマージュ

スーパー
なかがわ

まっすぐ行く   to go straight
い

HERE   ～を超える   to pass . . .
こ

C. Role Play—One of you is working at a shop, and the other is a customer. Using Dialogue Ⅰ as a model, make conversations about the following situations.

1. The customer bought a shirt for their father, but it was too small. The customer wants to exchange it for a bigger one.

2. The customer bought a bag and wants to return it with some reason.

調べてみよう
しら

日本の文化
に ほん　ぶん か

After 20 lessons in Japanese, you are now a Japan expert. Let's take a deep look at Japan.

Choose one Japanese item you are interested in. It can be from traditional culture (such as *kendo* and kimono), a person/thing in popular culture (such as cosplay and anime), food (ramen, for example), or a place. Do some research and present your findings in class. Your presentation should include the following:

1. Why you chose the topic
2. A brief explanation
3. Demonstration or visual aids (video clips, pictures, etc.)

会
L20

(Example)　花見
　　　　　はな み

私 は子供の時、日本の桜の写真を見て
わたし　こ ども　とき　に ほん　さくら　しゃしん　み
感動したので、日本のお花見の文化について
かんどう　　　　　　に ほん　　はな み　　ぶん か
調べてみようと思いました。
しら　　　　　　　おも
三月から四月に日本では桜が咲きます。
さんがつ　　し がつ　に ほん　　さくら　さ
友だちや家族、一緒に仕事をしている人と、
とも　　　か ぞく　いっしょ　し ごと　　　　　　ひと
桜 の花を見に行きます。これがお花見です。
さくら　はな　み　い　　　　　　　　　　はな み
桜 を見ながら、お弁当を食べたり、歌を歌った
さくら　み　　　　　　べんとう　た　　　　うた　うた
りします。東京なら、上野公園が有名です。
　　　　とうきょう　　　うえ の こうえん　ゆうめい

Pair Work Ⅶ B. (p. 202)

Example 店「にしきや」

→ A：にしきやという店がどこにあるか教えていただけませんか。

B：三つ目の信号を右に曲がったら左に見えますよ。

Picture B

You want to go to the following places:

1. スーパー「なかがわ」　　4. 本屋「こぶんどう」

2. ホテル「きょうばし」　　5. レストラン「ラマージュ」

3. カフェ「サンライズ」　　6. 靴屋「ミラノ」

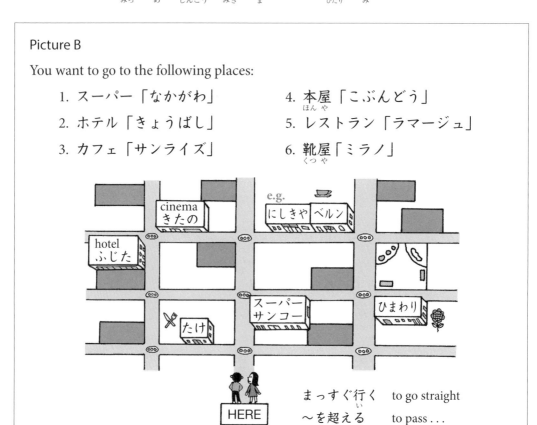

まっすぐ行く　　to go straight

〜を超える　　to pass . . .

Culture Notes

日本のポップカルチャー Japanese Pop Culture
にほん

Some of you may have grown up watching セーラームーン (Sailor Moon), collecting ポケモン (Pokemon), or playing ドラゴンクエスト (Dragon Quest). Japanese pop culture—manga, anime, video games, music, fashion, and more—is attracting attention worldwide. Here is a quick introduction to some forms of this culture.

秋葉原 (Akihabara)
あきはばら

Located in central Tokyo, Akihabara has long been known as a major shopping area for electronic appliances and computer goods. It has a reputation as a hangout for オタク*. There are many shops for games, anime character figures, and other pop-culture merchandise. You can also enjoy live pop idol shows at theaters and cafes.

*オタク: People with a passionate, or even obsessive, interest in anime, manga, computers, etc.

会
L20

まんが (Manga)

Manga, or Japanese comics, are not just for children—many titles are targeted at grownups as well. They deal with a broad range of subjects, covering basically everything found in films and literature. They also form an important part of the Japanese publishing industry;『ワンピース』(ONE PIECE), for example, has sold over 470 million volumes as of 2020.

©尾田栄一郎／集英社

アニメ (Anime)

Like manga, anime (Japanese animation) has developed distinctive styles of character design, story-telling, and other features of animation. Countless anime TV shows and films have been produced since 1963, the year when Osamu Tezuka created the first animated Japanese TV show,『鉄腕アトム』
てつわん
(Astro Boy).

©手塚プロダクション

コスプレ (Cosplay)

Cosplay means "costume play." Cosplayers wear the costume of characters from manga, anime, games, and so on. Cosplay events are now held all over the world.

©ビリビリ／新華社／共同通信イメージズ

第21課

LESSON 21

どろぼう Burglar

In this lesson, we will......

- Talk about bad experiences
- Check if things have been prepared
- Tell somebody what we wish them to do
- Report incidents to police

会 話 Dialogue
かい わ

I John runs into his landlady's house. 🔊 K21-01/02

1 ジョン： 大家さん、大変です。どろぼうに入られました。
おおや たいへん はい

2 大 家： えっ。何かとられたんですか。
おお や なに

3 ジョン： パソコンとスマホと……バイトでためたお金もないです。
かね

4 大 家： とにかく、警察に連絡したほうがいいですよ。
おお や けいさつ れんらく

II A police officer comes to John's apartment. 🔊 K21-03/04

1 警 察： かぎはかけてあったんですか。
けい さつ

2 ジョン： さあ……きのうの夜は飲んで帰ってきたから、かぎをかけたかどうか
よる の かえ

3 よく覚えていないんです。
おぼ

4 警 察： じゃあ、何時ごろ帰ってきたか覚えていますか。
けい さつ なんじ かえ おぼ

5 ジョン： 終電だったから……たぶん、一時半ごろです。
しゅうでん いちじはん

6 警 察： どろぼうは、その後入ったんですね。
けい さつ あとはい

7 ジョン： ええ。朝、部屋がめちゃくちゃだった
あさ へや

8 ので、びっくりしたんです。

9 警 察： 寝ている間にどろぼうに入られて、
けい さつ ね あいだ はい

10 気がつかなかったんですか。
き

11 ジョン： はい……。

III A few days later. 🔊 K21-05/06

₁ 大家：ジョンさん、留守の間に警察から電話がありましたよ。犯人が捕まっ
_{おお や}　　　　　　　　_{る す}　_{あいだ}　_{けいさつ}　　　　_{でん わ}　　　　　　　　　　_{はんにん}　_{つか}

₂ 　　　　たので、警察に来てほしいそうです。
　　　　　　_{けいさつ}　_き

₃ ジョン：ありがとうございます。よかった。

₄ 大家：それから、かぎを新しくしましたから、どうぞ。本当に大変でしたね。
_{おお や}　　　　　　　　　　_{あたら}　　　　　　　　　　　　　　_{ほんとう}　_{たいへん}

₅ ジョン：ええ。でも、そのおかげで、いいこともありました。みんないろいろ

₆ 　　　　な物をくれたり、おごってくれたりしたんです。
　　　　　　_{もの}

₇ 大家：ジョンさんは、いい友だちがたくさんいて、幸せですね。
_{おお や}　　　　　　　　　　　　_{とも}　　　　　　　　　_{しあわ}

I

John: Ms. "Landlady"! I'm in trouble. I had my room broken into.

Landlady: Oh! Has something been taken?

John: My computer, smartphone, and . . . the money that I've saved from my part-time job has gone.

Landlady: Anyway, you should call the police.

II

Police: Was the door locked?

John: Let me think . . . I don't remember whether I locked it or not since I had been drinking (alcohol) before coming home last night.

Police: Well, do you remember about what time you returned home?

John: I took the last train, so maybe around one-thirty.

Police: The burglar broke in after that, right?

John: Yes. I was surprised that the room was such a mess in the morning.

Police: Your room was broken into while you were sleeping, and you didn't notice it?

John: Yeah. That's right.

III

Landlady: John, there was a phone call when you were out. They said that they want you to come to the police station because the burglar has been arrested.

John: Thank you. I'm glad.

Landlady: Oh, I changed the lock. Here's the key. You really had a hard time, didn't you?

John: Yes, but because of that, many good things have happened to me as well. Everyone gave me various things, treated me to meals, and so on.

Landlady: John, you're lucky because you have many good friends.

単語
たん　　ご

K21-07 (J-E)
K21-08 (E-J)

V o c a b u l a r y

N o u n s

ちかん		groper; pervert
* どろぼう	泥棒	thief; burglar
* はんにん	犯人	criminal
どうりょう	同僚	colleague
かいぎ	会議	business meeting; conference
スピーチ		speech
か	蚊	mosquito
ガソリン		gasoline
ポスター		poster
もんく	文句	complaint
* るす	留守	absence; not at home
* けいさつ	警察	police; police station
せいふ	政府	government
じゅぎょうりょう	授業料	tuition
こうじょう	工場	factory
かんきょう	環境	environment
* しゅうでん	終電	last train (of the day)
* こと	事	things; matters
むかし	昔	old days; past

い - a d j e c t i v e s

とおい	遠い	far (away)
ひどい		awful

な - a d j e c t i v e s

あんぜん（な）	安全	safe
* めちゃくちゃ（な）		messy; disorganized
へん（な）	変	strange; unusual

U - v e r b s

おく	置く	to put; to lay; to place (place に object を)
つつむ	包む	to wrap; to cover （〜を）
はる	貼る	to post; to stick (place に object を)

＊Words that appear in the dialogue

やく	焼く	to bake; to burn; to grill （〜を）
やる		to give (to pets, plants, younger siblings, etc.) （〜を）
ける		to kick （〜を）
なぐる	殴る	to strike; to hit; to punch （〜を）
ふむ	踏む	to step on （〜を）
さす	刺す	to bite （〜を）
ぬすむ	盗む	to steal; to rob （〜を）
さわる	触る	to touch （〜に/を）
* つかまる	捕まる	to be arrested; to be caught （〜が）
* きがつく	気が付く	to notice （〜に）
ふる		to turn down (somebody); to reject; to jilt （〜を）
もんくをいう	文句を言う	to complain

Ru-verbs

いじめる		to bully （〜を）
ほめる		to praise; to say nice things （〜を）
きがえる	着替える	to change clothes
しんじる	信じる	to believe （〜を）
* ためる		to save money （〜を）
まちがえる	間違える	to make a mistake （〜を）
みつける	見つける	to find （〜を）
くらべる	比べる	to compare （X と Y を）

Irregular Verbs

ばかにする		to insult; to make a fool of . . . （〜を）
* びっくりする		to be surprised （〜に）
ひるねをする	昼寝をする	to take a nap
* れんらくする	連絡する	to contact (*person*に)

Adverbs and Other Expressions

ごぜんちゅう	午前中	in the morning
* 〜ころ		time of . . . ; when . . .
すこし	少し	a little
* とにかく		anyhow; anyway

文法 ぶん ぼう G r a m m a r

1 Passive Sentences

When you are inconvenienced by something somebody else has done, you can express your dissatisfaction using a passive sentence. Suppose, for example, that you were bothered by your friend's unauthorized use of your car. Compare (a) the objective description of the event and (b) the passive version, which makes clear how you feel about it:

(a) 友だちが 車を 使いました。 *A friend of mine used my car.*

(b) 私は 友だちに 車を 使われました。 *I had my car used by a friend of mine (and I am mad/sad about it).*

As you can see from the above example, the basic makeup of a passive sentence is like the following examples.

Passive sentence

私は 友だちに 車を使われました。
(victim) は (villain) に (evil act)

I had my car used by a friend.

· The victim is affected by an event. Marked with the particle は or が.
· The villain performs an action which causes the suffering. Marked with に.
· The evil act is described with the passive form of a verb.

Let us first examine what the passive form of a verb looks like.

Passive form
· *ru*-verbs: Drop the final -*ru* and add -*rare-ru*.
    食べる → 食べられる
· *u*-verbs: Drop the final -*u* and add -*are-ru*.

行く → 行かれる	死ぬ → 死なれる	泳ぐ → 泳がれる
話す → 話される	読む → 読まれる	遊ぶ → 遊ばれる
待つ → 待たれる	取る → 取られる	買う → 買われる [1]

· irregular verbs:
    くる → こられる   する → される

---

[1] With the verbs that end with the *hiragana* う, we see a "*w*" intervening, just as in the negative short forms.

You may have noticed that the passive forms of *ru*-verbs and the irregular くる are the same as the potential verbs (see Lesson 13), but the passive form of an *u*-verb looks different from the potential verb: for the verb 読む, the passive is 読まれる, while the potential is 読める.

Passive forms of verbs themselves conjugate as regular *ru*-verbs.

Conjugation of passive form

e.g. **読まれる**

	short forms		long forms	
	affirmative	negative	affirmative	negative
[Present]	読まれる	読まれない	読まれます	読まれません
[Past]	読まれた	読まれなかった	読まれました	読まれませんでした
[*Te*-form]	読まれて			

Let us now turn to the ways in which these forms are used in sentences. In most passive sentences, the "victim" has been unfavorably affected by the "villain's" act. They may be unfavorably affected in various ways, such as being angry, embarrassed, sad, or hurt.[2]

私は となりの人に たばこを吸われました。
I was annoyed with the person sitting next to me for smoking.

たけしさんは メアリーさんに よく笑われます。
Takeshi is often laughed at by Mary.

山下先生は だれかに パスワードを盗まれたそうです。
I hear that Professor Yamashita had his password stolen by someone.

Compare the inadvertent/unfavorable focus of a passive sentence with the intended/favorable focus of a てもらう sentence (see Lesson 16).

子供の時 姉に 日記を 読まれました。
I was annoyed with my big sister for reading my diary when I was a kid.

子供の時 寝る前に 父に 本を 読んでもらいました。
I had my dad read a book for me before I went to sleep when I was a kid.

---

[2] Since the passive only applies to a verb, you cannot express your suffering from an adjectival situation. Thus you can say 私は雨に降られました (I was annoyed by the fact that it rained/I was rained on), because 降る is a verb, but you cannot use the passive to say something like "I was annoyed by the fact that the weather was bad," because 悪い (bad) is an adjective. You cannot express your suffering from somebody *failing* to do something either, because you cannot add the passive suffix to an already negated verb. Therefore you cannot use the passive to say things like "Professor Yamashita was annoyed because students did not come to his class."

Finally, we note that some passive sentences are not perceptibly unfavorable.

私は その人に デートに誘われました。
わたし　ひと　　　　　　　　さそ
I was asked out by that person for a date.

私は 兄に 友だちに紹介されました。
わたし　あに　とも　　　しょうかい
I was introduced by my big brother to a friend of his.

その人は みんなに 尊敬されています。
ひと　　　　　　　　そんけい
That person is looked up to by most everyone.

When someone says these, they probably do not mean that they were inconvenienced by how things have turned out. There are relatively few verbs that come out neutral in their meaning when they are turned into the passive form.[3]

2 ～てある

You can use the *te*-form of a verb ＋ the helping verb ある to characterize a situation that *has been brought about on purpose* by somebody who remains unnamed in the sentence.

～が　　verb ＋てある　　　　. . . *has been done on purpose*

寒いので、ヒーターがつけてあります。
さむ
The heater is on, because it is cold.
(＝ *The heater was turned on and has been kept that way.*)

テーブルの上に花が置いてあります。
うえ　はな　お
Flowers are on the table.
(＝ *Flowers were put on the table and they have remained there ever since.*)

---

[3] There is another type of passive sentence, with non-human subjects, which naturally lacks the implication that the inanimate, nonsentient subjects are inconvenienced. The passive sentences of this type are found more commonly in the written language than in the spoken language. The type of passive sentences we learn in this lesson is called "affective passive," while the other type presented in this footnote is called "direct passive."

ここに公園が作られます。　　　　　　　*A park will be built here.*
こうえん　つく
この絵はピカソによって描かれました。　*The picture was drawn by Picasso.*
え　　　　　　　　　　えが
その年、オリンピックは開かれませんでした。　*The Olympic Games were not held that year.*
とし　　　　　　　　　　ひら

As you can see in the second example above, the human agent of the actions in such sentences is followed by によって instead of に.

You can say 〜てあります if somebody, possibly yourself, performed an action on purpose earlier, which can be described in terms of 〜ておきました ("do something by way of preparation," see Lesson 15), and if the result of that action can still be observed at this moment. Note that 〜てあります describes a current state, hence the present tense.

レストランの予約がしてあります。　is the result of　予約をしておきました。
A restaurant reservation has been made.　　　　　　*(I) made a reservation in advance.*

パンが買ってあります。　　　　　is the result of　パンを買っておきました。
Bread has been bought (and is ready).　　　　　　*(I) bought bread (for future use).*

As you can see from the above examples, てある normally assigns the particle が (or は) to the noun, which is usually marked with を. てある almost exclusively goes with a transitive verb.

Compare also てある sentences with ている sentences that describe current states. ている goes with intransitive verbs, in contrast with てある.

窓が閉めてあります。　　　　　（閉める＝transitive）
The window has been kept closed.

窓が閉まっています。　　　　　（閉まる＝intransitive）
The window is closed.

These sentences describe the same situation: the window is closed. However, they differ in their connotations. With the transitive てある sentence, the current state of the window is the result of a human action; somebody closed it and kept it that way. With the intransitive ている sentence, there is no such clear implication of human intervention. The window is closed, but this may or may not be the result of somebody closing it.

3 〜間に

You can use the pattern "A 間に B" when a certain event B takes place *in the middle of* another event, A. Most often, event A is described with ている if the verb takes ている for an action in progress. The verb for A is in the present tense, even when clause A describes a situation in the past.

お風呂に入っている間に電話がありました。
There was a phone call while I was taking a bath.

きのうの夜、寝ている間に地震がありました。
There was an earthquake while I was asleep last night.

両親が日本にいる間に京都に連れていきたいです。　（×日本にいている間に）
I want to take my parents to Kyoto while they are in Japan.

> A（ている）間に B　　　*B takes place while A occurs.*

The "A" above can be a noun as well:

留守の間に友だちが来ました。
A friend came while I was out.

Event B must be of short duration and begin and end within the bounds of activity A. If B extends *throughout* the time when A occurs, we use 間 instead of 間に.

ルームメイトが買い物をしている間、私は本を読んで待ちました。
I waited, reading a book, while my roommate was shopping.

4 Adjective＋する

We learned in Lesson 10 how to say "become," as in 寒くなる (become cold/colder) and 上手になる (become good/better at doing X). Here we learn to use adjectives together with the irregular verb する, which in combination with adjectives means "to make."

冷たい	→ 冷たくする	*to make something cold / colder*
いい	→ よくする	*to make something better*
簡単な	→ 簡単にする	*to make something simple / simpler*

この間の試験は難しすぎたので、次の試験はやさしくしてください。
Please make the next exam easier, because the last one was too difficult.

みんなで世界をよくしましょう。
Let's join our forces and make the world a better place.

部屋をきれいにしました。
I cleaned the room. (lit., I made the room clean.)

Note also the following idiomatic use of this pattern:

静かにする　make it quiet　→　keep quiet　　　静かにしてください。
Please be quiet!

5 ～てほしい

When you want somebody to do something, you can describe your wish by using the *te*-form of a verb and the adjective ほしい. The person the wish is directed to is marked with the particle に.

私は 病気の友だちに 元気になってほしいです。
I want my sick friend to get well.

私は ルームメイトに 宿題を手伝ってほしかったです。
I wanted my roommate to help me with my homework.

> （私は）person に   verb *te*-form ほしい   *I want (person) to do . . .*

When you want to say you don't want them to do something, you can negate ほしい and say ～てほしくないです or negate the verb and say ～ないでほしいです.

私は お父さんに 昔の話をしてほしくないです。
I don't want my father to talk about the good old times.

私は 日本人の友だちに 英語で話さないでほしいです。
I don't want my Japanese friends to speak in English.

Let us now summarize the three words for "want":[4]

verb stem + たい (Lesson 11)	*I want to do . . .*
noun が ほしい (Lesson 14)	*I want something.*
verb *te*-form + ほしい (this lesson)	*I want somebody to do . . .*

私はベトナムに行きたいです。   *I want to go to Vietnam.*

私は歩きやすい靴がほしいです。   *I want comfortable shoes.*

私は 妹 に部屋を片付けてほしいです。   *I want my little sister to clean up her room.*

---

[4] These are all private predicates, and used only for the speaker's wishes. When you want to describe the emotions of people other than the speaker, the predicate needs to be changed as in the examples below (see Lessons 11 and 14 for details).

先生は 学生に たくさん勉強してほしいと言っています。
Our professors say they want their students to study a lot.

先生は 学生に たくさん勉強してほしがっています。
Our professors (are acting in a way that suggests that they) want their students to study a lot.

何時ごろ帰ってきたか▶帰ってくる is just like 帰る, except it implies in addition that you are speaking from the point of view of a person who is at the destination of the return trip. Similarly, if you say コンビニでお弁当を買ってきた, you will be saying either that you went out, bought food and came back to your apartment, or that you came home from work/school and on your way you dropped by at a convenience store.

バイトでためたお金もないです▶ないです is the alternative negative form of the verb ある. The standard negative form of ある is ありません, while the substandard alternative form is built up of the short form negative ない plus the politeness marker です.

More generally, you may hear the long form alternative negative verbs made up of short form negative plus です.

	standard	alternative
Present	見えません	見えないです
Past	見えませんでした	見えなかったです

練習 Practice
れん しゅう

I どろぼうにかばんをとられました ☞Grammar 1

A. Change the following verbs into the passive forms. 🔊 K21-09

Example　飲む　→　飲まれる
　　　　　の　　　　　の

1. 食べる
　　た
2. やめる
3. なくす
4. する

5. 捨てる
　　す
6. 壊す
　　こわ
7. 見る
　　み
8. 笑う
　　わら

9. うそをつく
10. 連れていく
　　　つ
11. ばかにする
12. たばこを吸う
　　　　　　す

13. 立つ
　　た
14. 来る
　　く
15. 怒る
　　おこ
16. 盗む
　　ぬす

B. Takeshi has been having a tough life. Describe what happened to him using passive forms. 🔊 K21-10

Example　たけしさんは　どろぼうに　かばんをとられました。

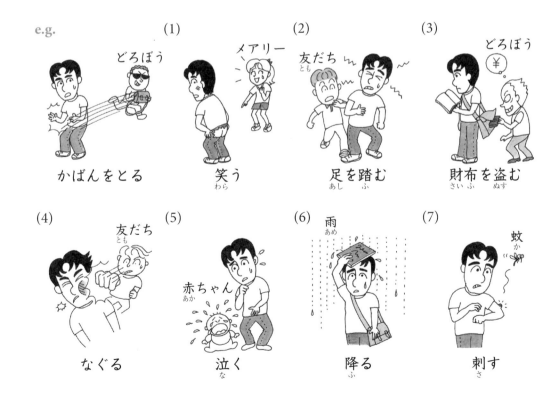

e.g.　どろぼう
かばんをとる

(1)　メアリー
笑う
わら

(2)　友だち
とも
足を踏む
あし　ふ

(3)　どろぼう（¥）
財布を盗む
さいふ　ぬす

(4)　友だち
とも
なぐる

(5)　赤ちゃん
あか
泣く
な

(6)　雨
あめ
降る
ふ

(7)　蚊
か
刺す
さ

(8)
あやか
ふる

(9)
ちかん
さわる

(10) 子供の時（こども とき）
友だち（とも）
いじめる

(11) 子供の時（こども とき）
おじさん
怒る（おこ）

C. Pair Work—Discuss your bad experiences. Ask your partner the following questions, using the passive forms.

(Example) 友（とも）だちが笑（わら）う

→ A：友（とも）だちに笑（わら）われたことがありますか。

B：はい、あります。この間（あいだ）、「かわいい」と「こわい」を

間違（まちが）えたんです。

1. 友（とも）だちがばかにする

2. 友（とも）だちがうそをつく

3. 先生（せんせい）が怒（おこ）る

4. 友（とも）だちが（あなたの）変な写真（へん しゃしん）を撮（と）る

5. だれかがなぐる

6. だれかが財布（さいふ）を盗（ぬす）む

7. きらいな人（ひと）がデートに誘（さそ）う

8. 付き合（つ あ）っている人（ひと）がふる

D. Pair Work—Your partner looks upset. Ask what the problem is. When you answer, use the passive form. Expand the conversation.

(Example) A stranger punched you.

→ A：どうしたんですか。

B：知（し）らない人（ひと）になぐられたんです。

A：それはひどいですね。警察（けいさつ）に行（い）ったほうがいいですよ。

B：大丈夫（だいじょうぶ）です。なぐられた後（あと）、私（わたし）もその人（ひと）をけりましたから。

1. Your roommate made the room dirty.

2. A burglar broke into your house.

3. A customer complained.

4. Your parent threw your precious thing away.

5. Your friends make fun of you all the time.

6. Your colleagues bully you.

Ⅱ 写真が置いてあります ☛Grammar 2
しゃしん　お

A. Describe the pictures with ～てある. 🔊 K21-11

Example 家族の写真が置いてあります。
かぞく　しゃしん　お

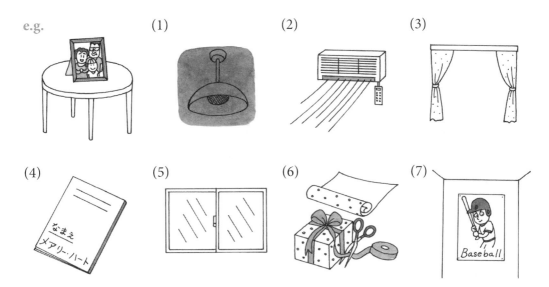

e.g.   (1)   (2)   (3)

(4)   (5)   (6)   (7)

会
L21

B. Pair Work—You work as a house-sitter for a Japanese couple. They left you a list of the things you are expected to do before they come home. When they come home, you have finished only half of the things. First, choose three things you have done from the list and mark them with ✓. Then start the conversation as in the example.

Example

(✔) Washing the car → A：車が洗ってありますか。
くるま　あら
B：はい、もう洗ってあります。
あら
A：どうもありがとう。

(   ) Washing the car → A：車が洗ってありますか。
くるま　あら
B：すみません、まだ洗ってありません。
あら
すぐ、します。
A：お願いします。
ねが

The things you are expected to do
(　　　) Cooking dinner
(　　　) Giving the cat water
(　　　) Doing laundry
(　　　) Doing shopping
(　　　) Putting the food in the refrigerator
(　　　) Cleaning the room

C. Pair Work—You and your friend have been making preparations for a party. Using the dialogue below as a model, go down the list of things to do, finding out what your partner has already done and dividing the remaining tasks between the two. Add your own question. B's list is on p. 226.

Example

Ａ：パーティーの準備をしなきゃいけませんね。スピーカー (speaker) が借りてありますか。

Ｂ：ええ、借りてあります。きのう、借りておきました。

Ａ：じゃあ、私は借りなくてもいいですね。

Ｂ：部屋が掃除してありますか。

Ａ：いいえ、まだしてありません。今日忙しいから、してくれませんか。

Ｂ：えっ！私がするんですか。

A's List

	Decide who will do it:
スピーカー (speaker) を借りる	
部屋を掃除する	
飲み物を買う	(I have done it.)
ケーキを焼く	
料理を作る	(I have done it.)
友だちに連絡する	
冷蔵庫にビールを入れる	

Ⅲ 社長が寝ている間に、起きます ☞Grammar 3
しゃちょう　　　ね　　　　　あいだ　　　　お

A. You are a chauffeur working for the president of a company. The following is the president's daily schedule. Describe your day as a chauffeur. 🔊 K21-12

(Example) 社長が寝ている間に、起きます。
しゃちょう　　ね　　　　　あいだ　　　　お

	the president		chauffeur
e.g.	still sleeping	7:00	← gets up
1.	changing his clothes	9:00	← puts gas in the car
2.	eating breakfast at the cafe	11:00	← buys a boxed lunch at a convenience store
3.	reading the newspaper	1:00	← eats the boxed lunch
4.	attending a meeting	3:00	← takes a nap
5.	going to see his factories	5:00	← talks to his friends on the phone
6.	drinking at a party	7:00	← drinks coffee in the car

B. Pair Work—You and your friend are on a trip together. The two of you are interested in totally different things. Using 間に, talk about what each of you will do in the morning, あいだ afternoon, and evening.

(Example)

Ａ：午前中、何をする？
　　ごぜんちゅう　なに

Ｂ：買い物したい。
　　か　もの

Ａ：じゃあ、Ａさんが買い物している間に、
　　　　　　　　　　か　もの　　　　　あいだ
　　私は美術館に行くね。
　　わたし　びじゅつかん　い
　　(Continue the conversation)

Examples of activities

- shopping
- go dancing
- do sightseeing
- climb a mountain

- stay at the hotel
- swim in the pool
- (your own)

C. Complete the following sentences.

1. 日本にいる間に＿＿＿＿＿＿＿＿＿＿＿＿＿＿＿＿＿＿＿＿＿たいです。
2. 両親が出かけている間に＿＿＿＿＿＿＿＿＿＿＿＿＿＿＿＿＿＿＿。
3. 赤ちゃんが寝ている間に＿＿＿＿＿＿＿＿＿＿＿＿＿＿＿＿＿＿＿。
4. 休みの間に＿＿＿＿＿＿＿＿＿＿＿＿＿＿＿＿＿つもりです。
5. 私が留守の間に＿＿＿＿＿＿＿＿＿＿＿＿＿＿＿ないでください。
6. ＿＿＿＿＿＿＿＿＿＿＿＿＿＿＿＿間にどろぼうに入られました。
7. ＿＿＿＿＿＿＿＿＿＿＿＿＿＿＿＿間に友だちから電話がありました。

Ⅳ 公園を多くします ☞Grammar 4

A. There will be an election for mayor soon. You are one of the candidates. Say your pledges below using 〜くします／〜にします. 🔊 K21-13

Example increase parks → 公園を多くします。

1. make the town cleaner
2. make the hospital new
3. make the town safer
4. make the environment better

5. make the tax lower（安い）
6. make school holidays longer
7. make the roads wider
8. make the town famous

B. Pair Work—Make a short dialogue for the following situations. Use 〜してください／〜していただけませんか.

Example Your teacher is so tough. He always gives you too much homework.

→ A：先生、すみませんが、もっと宿題を少なくしていただけませんか。多すぎて、ほかのクラスの勉強ができないんです。
B：わからない時は手伝ってあげます。がんばってください。

1. Your teacher is so tough. Her exams are always difficult.
2. Your host mother gave you too much rice.
3. Someone who lives next door is always noisy.
4. Your boss always makes a long speech. He will make a speech at your wedding.
5. You've found a nice item at the flea market but it is a little over your budget.

C. Role Play—One of you is a designer and the other is a director.

Designer: You drew the first draft shown in (1) below. Talk with the director and redraw the picture in the box next to (1).

Director: You think some changes are necessary. Give suggestions to the designer as in the example.

Switch roles for the other picture (2).

Example Picture (1)

→　Director：　目が小さいですね。もっと目を大きくしてください。

　　　Designer：　はい。少し大きくしました。もっと大きくしたほうが
　　　　　　　　　いいですか。

　　　Director：　それは大きすぎます。……

(1) First draft　　　Redraw here.　　(2) First draft　　　Redraw here.

　⇒　　　⇒

Words you may use:　手 (arm; hand)　耳 (ear)　鼻 (nose)
　　　　　　　　　　太い (thick)　　細い (thin)

Ⅴ 若いころの話をしてほしいです ☛Grammar 5

A. Say what you want the following people to do/not to do, using 〜てほしい. K21-14

Example　おばあさん／若いころの話をする
　　　→　おばあさんに若いころの話をしてほしいです。

1. 両親／私と兄を比べない
2. 友だち／日本語の勉強を続ける
3. 友だち／遠い所に行かない
4. 同僚／夢をあきらめない

5. 先生／もっと学生をほめる
6. 昔の彼氏／私を忘れる
7. 昔の彼女／幸せになる
8. 親／私を信じる

B. Say what you want your friend to do/not to do, using 〜てほしい.

Example Your friend likes cooking

→ 友だちは料理をするのが好きです。
だから時々晩ご飯を作ってほしいです。

Your friend lies all the time

→ 友だちはいつもうそをつきます。
だからうそをつかないでほしいです。

Your friend . . .

1. has a car
2. is good at Japanese
3. has many friends
4. always complains
5. is rich
6. has been to various foreign countries
7. always comes late
8. (your own)

C. Group Work—Discuss what you want the following people or organizations to do/not to do. Present your requests to the class.

Example あなたの大学

→ この大学の授業料は高すぎると思います。私たちは授業料を安くしてほしいです。授業料が安かったら、アルバイトをしなくてもいいです。もっと勉強ができます。

1. あなたの学校／大学　2. 先生　3. あなたの国の政府　4. (your own)

Ⅵ まとめの練習

A. Describe bad experience you had, using passive forms, e.g., when it happened/what happened/how you felt about it.

Example 先週、朝寝坊して、学校に行きました。急いでいたので、教室でころんでしまいました。みんなに笑われました。とても恥ずかしかったです。

B. Role Play—One of you is a police officer. The other was involved in the following incidents and is calling the police to explain the situation. (Refer to the vocabulary list below.)

(Example) A burglar broke into your room and took your ring last night.

→　Police：はい。警察です。

　　　Caller：もしもし。あのう、きのうの夜、どろぼうに入られて指輪を盗まれました。

　　　Police：何時ごろですか。

　　　Caller：アルバイトに行っている間に入られたので、八時から十一時までだと思います。

　　　Police：取られたのはどんな指輪ですか。

　　　Caller：ルビーの指輪です。誕生日に彼からもらったんです。
　　　　　　　(ruby)

1. You were punched by a man when you were walking on a street.
2. Your bicycle was stolen.
3. You were deceived by a salesperson (セールスの人), and money was taken.
4. You were followed by a man from the train station to your house.
5. Your wallet was taken while you were sleeping on a train.

会
L21

Vocabulary ——犯罪・事件 (Crimes and Accidents)

ごうとう (強盗)	robber	おそう (襲う)	to attack
さぎ (詐欺)	fraud	ける	to kick
さぎし (詐欺師)	a con man/woman	ころす (殺す)	to murder; to kill
ストーカー	stalker	する	to pick pocket
すり	pickpocket	だます	to deceive
ちかん	groper	あとをつける	to follow
ひったくり	purse-snatching	なぐる (殴る)	to punch; to strike; to hit
まんびき (万引き)	shoplifting	ぬすむ (盗む)	to steal
ゆうかい (誘拐)	kidnapping	ひく	(a car) runs over
こうつうじこ (交通事故)	traffic accident	ゆする	to blackmail; to threaten

Pair Work Ⅱ C. (p. 220)

Example

A：パーティーの準備をしなきゃいけませんね。スピーカー (speaker) が借りて

　　ありますか。

B：ええ、借りてあります。きのう、借りておきました。

A：じゃあ、私は借りなくてもいいですね。

B：部屋が掃除してありますか。

A：いいえ、まだしてありません。今日忙しいから、してくれませんか。

B：えっ！ 私がするんですか。

B's List

	Decide who will do it:
スピーカー (speaker) を借りる	(I have done it.)
部屋を掃除する	
飲み物を買う	
ケーキを焼く	(I have done it.)
料理を作る	
友だちに連絡する	
冷蔵庫にビールを入れる	(I have done it.)

Culture Notes

日本の宗教 Religion in Japan—Shinto and Buddhism
にほん しゅうきょう

Japan's two major religions are Shinto (神道) and Buddhism (仏教). Native to Japan, Shinto is based on the belief that everything has a spirit. Instead of defining an explicit set of tenets, Shinto advises people to live and act in a way that does not incur the wrath of the deities. Buddhism originated in India and was introduced to Japan in the 6th century. Both Shinto shrines (神社) and Buddhist temples (お寺) can be found all over Japan.

神社（厳島神社・広島）
じんじゃ いつくしまじんじゃ ひろしま

お寺（清水寺・京都）
てら きよみずでら きょうと

According to a survey, about 85% of Japanese believe either Shinto or Buddhism, or both. Other religions, such as Christianity and Islam, have very few Japanese adherents.

Shinto and Buddhism have coexisted harmoniously in Japan for many years. It is common for most people to engage in the rituals of both religions; wedding ceremonies are often conducted by Shinto priests, while funeral rites are generally performed by Buddhist monks. On New Year's, many Japanese go to a temple or shrine, with the choice of either mattering little to most of them.

会
L21

Tips for visiting temples and shrines

First, wash your hands and rinse your mouth at the purification fountain near the entrance. In front of the main hall, ring the bell (鈴), and throw offering coins (賽銭) into the offering box. Bow deeply (and if at a shrine, clap your hands twice), and pray with your palms clasped together. Finally, bow deeply again.

おみくじ

At temples and shrines, you will likely see folded paper attached to trees and small wooden plaques hung on racks. The paper is called おみくじ, and tells one's fortune. Some people believe that bad fortunes will go away and good fortunes will come true if the おみくじ is tied around a tree branch. The plaques are called 絵馬. People write wishes or prayers on the plaques and hang them on racks with the hope that the wish or prayer will come true.

絵馬
えま

第22課 LESSON 22

日本の教育 Education in Japan
にほん きょういく

In this lesson, we will..

- Talk about getting people to do things
- Instruct people to do things
- Ask for and give advice
- Express opinions on education

会 話 Dialogue
かい わ

I Mary's host mother and host sister Mana are talking. 🔊 K22-01/02

1 お母さん： まな、勉強しなさい。来週は期末試験があるのにぜんぜん勉強して
かあ べんきょう らいしゅう きまつしけん べんきょう
2 いないでしょ。

3 ま な： お母さん、私、もう十七なんだから、少しほっておいてよ。
かあ わたし じゅうなな すこ

4 お母さん： 今、がんばっておけば、いい大学に入れて、後で楽になるんだから。
かあ いま だいがく はい あと らく

5 ま な： 私、別にいい大学に行けなくてもいい。
わたし べつ だいがく い

6 お母さん： お父さんとお母さんはあなたをいい大学に行かせてあげたいの。お
かあ とう かあ だいがく い
7 母さんのうちは貧乏だったから、大学に行かせてくれなかったのよ。
かあ びんぼう だいがく い

8 ま な： わかった、わかった。その話、もう何度も聞いた。
はなし なんど き

II In Mary's room. 🔊 K22-03/04

1 ま な： メアリーも、高校の時、こんなふうだった？
こうこう とき

2 メアリー： そうねえ、やっぱり親はうるさかったけど、
おや

3 もう少し自由があったかな。
すこ じゆう

4 ま な： うちの親、ちょっと変だと思うでしょ。
おや へん おも

5 メアリー： そんなことないよ。ちょっと厳しいかもしれ
きび

6 ないけど、まなちゃんのことを心配している
しんぱい

7 んだよ。

III The next day Mary and Takeshi are on a date. 🔊 K22-05/06

₁ メアリー： うちのまなちゃん、高校生なのに忙しくて、ぜんぜん遊ぶ時間がな
₂ いみたい。
₃ たけし： 子供も大変だけど、親も大変だと思うよ。塾に行かせたり、英会話
₄ を習わせたり、お金がかかるだろうなあ。
₅ メアリー： たけしくんも子供の時、まなちゃんのように塾に行ってた？
₆ たけし： ぼくはずっと遊んでた。自分の子供にも、自由に遊ばせてあげたい
₇ なあ。
₈ メアリー： でも、日本で子供を育てるのは大変そうだね。

Ⓘ

Host mother: Mana, study! Even though you will have a final examination next week, you haven't studied at all, right?

Mana: Mom, I'm 17 years old. Leave me alone.

Host mother: If you do your best now, you'll be able to enter a good university, and life will be easier later.

Mana: It's okay not to be able to go to a good university.

Host mother: Your father and I want to let you go to a good university. My parents didn't let me go to college because my family was poor.

Mana: Okay, okay. I have heard that story many times.

Ⓘ I

Mana: Were you like me when you were in high school?

Mary: Let me think . . . My parents were strict, too, but I had a little more freedom, I guess.

Mana: Don't you think that my parents are a bit strange?

Mary: I don't think so. They might be a little strict, but they are concerned about you.

Ⓘ II

Mary: It seems that my host sister Mana is too busy to have time to play at all even though she is a high school student.

Takeshi: Children are having a hard time, but their parents are also suffering, I think. They spend a lot letting their children go to cram schools, learn English conversation, and so on.

Mary: Did you go to a cram school like Mana when you were a child?

Takeshi: I played all day. I want to let my children play freely.

Mary: But it seems that raising children in Japan is tough.

単語
たん　　ご

K22-07 (J-E)
K22-08 (E-J)

V o c a b u l a r y

N o u n s

かぜ	風	wind
き	木	tree
ボール		ball
さる	猿	monkey
めんきょ	免許	license
よしゅう	予習	preparation of a lesson
ふくしゅう	復習	review of a lesson
* じゅく	塾	cram school
* えいかいわ	英会話	English conversation
あいて	相手	partner; the other person
おじょうさん	お嬢さん	(someone's) daughter (polite)
かみさま	神様	God
せんぱい	先輩	senior member of a group
こうはい	後輩	junior member of a group
ぶか	部下	subordinate
うけつけ	受付	reception desk
しょるい	書類	document
プロジェクト		project
かじ	家事	housework
ヨーロッパ		Europe
ひとりぐらし	一人暮らし	living alone
* じゆう	自由	freedom
むだづかい	無駄遣い	waste (money)

い - a d j e c t i v e

* うるさい		noisy; annoying

な - a d j e c t i v e s

* しんぱい（な）	心配	worried about （〜が）
* びんぼう（な）	貧乏	poor
ぺらぺら（な）		fluent (language が)
* らく（な）	楽	easy; comfortable

＊Words that appear in the dialogue

U-verbs

かぜがふく	風が吹く	the wind blows
コピーをとる	コピーを取る	to make a photocopy
はこぶ	運ぶ	to carry（〜を）
ひろう	拾う	to pick up (something)（〜を）
* ほ（う）っておく	放っておく	to leave (someone/something) alone; to neglect（〜を）
まにあう	間に合う	to be in time（〜に）
かつ	勝つ	to win（〜に）

Ru-verbs

うける	受ける	to take (an examination)（〜を）
けいかくをたてる	計画を立てる	to make a plan
* そだてる	育てる	to raise; to bring up（〜を）
たすける	助ける	to help; to rescue（〜を）
まける	負ける	to lose (a match)（〜に）

Irregular Verbs

おねがいする	お願いする	to request help (*person* に〜を)
さんせいする	賛成する	to agree（〜に）
はんたいする	反対する	to oppose; to object to（〜に）
しっぱいする	失敗する	to fail; to be unsuccessful
てつやする	徹夜する	to stay up all night
ほんやくする	翻訳する	to translate (*source* と *target* に)

Adverbs and Other Expressions

* こんなふう		like this
* じゆうに	自由に	freely
* ずっと		for a long time; all the time
ぜったいに	絶対に	definitely
* なんども	何度も	many times
* もうすこし	もう少し	a little more
〜とか		. . . for example
* そんなこと（は）ない		I don't think so.
〜ちゃん		[suffix for names of children]
おおくの〜	多くの〜	many . . .

会
L22

文 法 G r a m m a r
ぶん ぽう

1 Causative Sentences

In this lesson, we learn yet another verb derivation called the "causative form." When you use the causative form of a verb, you can describe who *makes* someone do something, and who *lets* someone do something.

You can derive the causative form of a verb this way:

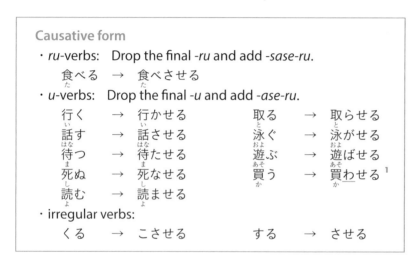

The basic structure of a causative sentence is like the following:

Causative sentence

先生は　　　　　学生に　　　　　会話を覚えさせました。
せんせい　　　　がくせい　　　　かいわ　おぼ
(director) は　　(cast) に　　　　(action)

The professor made the students memorize the dialogue.

· The director decides what is allowed and what is to be done. Marked with は or が.
· The cast performs the action. Usually goes with に.[2]
· The action is described with a causative form of a verb.

A causative verb can be interpreted either with the "*make* somebody do" reading or with the "*let* somebody do" reading. Thus you cannot tell simply from the sentences below in isolation whether they describe an authoritarian parent (forcing the children to eat what they do not want) or a doting parent (allowing the children to have what they want). Only our general knowledge about the parents' personalities, the children's attitudes (whether they are eager to eat vegetables/read books or not), and the linguistic context of the sentence solves the issue.

お父さんは 子供に 野菜を食べさせました。
The father made/let his child eat vegetables.

お母さんは 子供に 本を読ませました。
The mother made/let her child read the book.

2 Causative ＋ てあげる / てくれる / てもらう

If the helping verb てあげる, てくれる, or てもらう follows a causative verb, you can assume in almost all cases that it is a "let" causative (see Lesson 16 for those helping verbs).

先生は 私に 英語を話させてくれませんでした。
The professor did not allow me to speak in English.

私は 自分の子供に 好きなことをさせてあげるつもりです。
I think I will let my children do what they love.

You can use the causative ＋ てください to ask for permission to do something and to volunteer to do something.

私にこの仕事をやらせてください。
Please let me do this job.

会
L22

---

[1] With the verbs that end with the *hiragana* う, we see a "w" intervening, just as in the negative short forms and the passive forms.

[2] There are cases in which the cast gets を instead.

(1) When the caused action is a reflex, such as crying and laughing:

私は その子供を 泣かせてしまいました。
I accidentally made the child cry.
ジョーンズさんは おもしろい映画を作って みんなを 笑わせました。
Mr. Jones made funny movies and made everyone laugh.

(2) When the verb that is turned into the causative originally did not call for を:

In the first two examples below, the verbs 行く and 座る do not take the particle を, and therefore を is up for grabs for marking the cast in the causative sentences. In the last example, in contrast, 読む already calls for を, and therefore を is not available for marking the cast in the causative.

先生は 私を トイレに行かせました。　　*The professor made me go to the bathroom.*
その人は 私を そこに座らせました。　　*That person made me sit there.*
✕ 両親は 私を 本を読ませました。　　*My parents made me read books.*

> **Usage of causative verb**
> · (director) は (cast) に causative verb　　　(director) *makes/lets* (cast) *do . . .*
> · (director) は (cast) に causative verb ＋ てあげる/てくれる
> 　　　　　　　　　　　　　　　　　(director) *lets* (cast) *do . . .*
> · causative verb ＋ てください　　　　*please let me do . . .*

Verb Stem ＋ なさい

The verb stem ＋ なさい is a command. なさい has a strong implication that you are "talking down" to somebody, or that you think you are more mature, know better, and should be obeyed. なさい, therefore, is appropriate for parents to use toward their children. You also often see なさい in exam instructions.[3]

十時までに帰りなさい。	*Come home by 10 o'clock.*
かっこの中に単語を入れなさい。	*Fill in the blanks with a word.*
文句を言うのをやめなさい。	*Stop complaining.*

You see in the last example above that you can express the idea of the negative "don't do . . ." using a verb followed by のを and やめなさい, which comes from the verb やめる.

4 〜ば

"Clause A ば Clause B" is a conditional statement: "if A, then B." We have already seen an instance of this construction in Lesson 18, namely, the ば-form in the pattern ばよかった (I wish I had done . . .).

---

[3] Japanese verbs have another paradigm for commands called the "imperative" forms. As direct commands, imperative forms tend to sound very confrontational and aggressive. You probably hear them used often by anime characters or movie mobsters.

　Ru-verbs: Change the last *ru* to *ro*.　　e.g., やめる → やめろ　*Stop it!*
　　　　　　　　　　　　　　　　　　(Exception) くれる → くれ　*Give me that!*
　U-verbs: Change the last *u* to *e*.　　e.g., 死ぬ → 死ね　*Drop dead!*
　Irregular verbs:　する　→　しろ　e.g., 静かにしろ　*Be quiet!*
　　　　　　　　　くる　→　こい　e.g., 今すぐ来い　*Come here now!*

You can also turn a verb into the negative imperative by adding な to the dictionary form.
　e.g., あきらめる → あきらめるな　*Hang in there. Don't give up.*

Some established uses of imperatives are not confrontational. You may see 止まれ on traffic signs and road surface markings. You can also cheer someone on by saying がんばれ！

Let us first review the conjugation rule of the verb ば-form.[4]

ば -form

· Verbs in the affirmative:　Drop the final -u and add -eba.

食べる (tabe-ru)　→　食べれば (tabe-r-eba)

行く (ik-u) → 行けば (ik-eba)　待つ　→　待てば　　買う　→　買えば

する　→　すれば　　　くる　→　くれば

· Verbs in the negative:　Drop the final い and add ければ.

行かない　→　行かなければ

In an "A ば B" sentence, the "A" part describes the condition, *provided that* the consequence described in "B" will follow.

車があれば、いろいろな所に行けます。
If you have a car, you can go to various places.

かぎをかけておけば、どろぼうに入られません。
If you lock the doors and windows, you won't have your apartment broken into.

Student：	試験は難しいでしょうか。	*Will the exam be hard?*
Teacher：	単語を覚えれば、大丈夫ですよ。	*If you memorize the words, you should be good.*

You usually use the "A ば B" pattern when the condition "A" guarantees a *good result* in "B." Therefore, the sentence (i) below is natural, while the sentence (ii), though not impossible, sounds rather odd.[5]

(i)　　走れば、電車に間に合います。　　*If I run, I will be able to catch the train.*

(ii)　?? 歩けば、電車に遅れます。　　*If I walk, I will be late for the train.*

---

[4] We will focus on the verb ば-form in this lesson, but ば also goes with い-adjectives and negative predicates in general:

おもしろい　　　→　おもしろければ　　　　元気じゃない　→　元気じゃなければ
おもしろくない　→　おもしろくなければ　　　学生じゃない　→　学生じゃなければ

With な-adjectives and nouns in the affirmative, だ either becomes なら (see Lesson 13) or であれば:

静かだ　→　静かなら or 静かであれば　　　　先生だ　→　先生なら or 先生であれば

[5] You can express the idea in (ii) more appropriately with たら: 歩いたら、電車に遅れます. You may also note that (ii) is not totally ungrammatical. Embedded in a larger sentence that overtly cancels the "good result" implication, for example, (ii) improves significantly in acceptability:

歩けば電車に遅れるのはわかっていました。　　*I knew that I would be late for the train if I walked.*

Because of this "good result" implication, "A ば B" is often used to advise "A." Sometimes the part "B" contains vacuous generic expressions like 大丈夫です or いいんです.

この薬を飲めば大丈夫です。
You will be okay, if you take this medicine.

先生に聞けばいいんです。
All you have to do is ask the teacher. (If you ask, everything will be fine.)

5 〜のに

のに connects two facts, A and B, which hold in spite of the expectation that if A is the case, B is not to be the case. "A のに B," therefore means "A, but contrary to expectations, B, too" or "B, despite the fact A."

この会社はお金があるのに、給料は安いです。
This company is rich, but its workers' salaries are low.

八時間も勉強したのに、試験ができなかった。
I studied for eight hours, but I couldn't do well on the examination.

A (short form) のに B	*Despite the fact A, it is B.*

The predicate in part A is in the short form. When A ends with a な-adjective or with a noun + です, it appears as な, just like in the explanatory んです construction.

田中さんは親切なのに、山田さんは田中さんがきらいです。
Ms. Tanaka is nice, but Ms. Yamada does not like her.

大きい問題なのに、あの人はだれにも相談しません。
It is a big issue, but he does not consult with anybody.

Because のに connects two facts, you cannot have non-factual sentences, like requests or suggestions, in the B clause:

× この本は日本語が少し難しいのに、読んでください。
Compare: この本は日本語が少し難しいですが、読んでください。
Japanese in this book is a little difficult, but please read it.

× あまりおいしそうじゃないのに、ここで食べましょう。

Compare: あまりおいしそうじゃない<u>けど</u>、ここで食べましょう。

The food does not look very promising, but let's eat here.

6 〜のように / 〜のような

You use "Noun A のように" when you want to describe an action which is "done in the same way as A" or a characteristic which is "comparable to A."

メアリーさんは<u>魚のように</u>上手に泳げます。

Mary can swim very well, just like a fish.

アントニオさんは<u>孫悟空のように</u>強いです。

Antonio is strong like Goku, the martial arts hero of the Dragon Ball manga and anime series.

"Noun A のような Noun B" means "a B like/similar to A." When you say "A のような B," B has the same quality or appearance as A, or A is an example of B.[6]

私は<u>鎌倉のような</u>町が好きです。

I like towns like Kamakura.

Expression Notes 9

表現ノート
ひょう　げん

ちゃん ▶ ちゃん attached to a name is the diminutive version of さん and conveys affection. You can also replace さん with ちゃん in kinship terms to show endearment, for example, おねえちゃん and おじいちゃん.

---

[6] みたい, which we learned in Lesson 17, can be used in the same way as 〜のように + verb/adjective, and 〜のような + noun. Note that の does not come between the preceding noun and みたい.

たけしさんの犬はぬいぐるみ<u>みたい</u>にかわいいです。
Takeshi's dog is cute just like a teddy bear.

あの人はマザー・テレサ<u>みたいな</u>人です。
She is a person just like Mother Teresa.

練習 Practice
れん　しゅう

I 服を洗わせます ☞Grammar 1
　　ふく　　　あら

A. Change the following verbs into the causative forms. 🔊 K22-09

Example 食べる　→　食べさせる
　　　　た　　　　　　　た

1. やめる
2. 働く
　　はたら
3. 飲む
　　の
4. 持つ
　　も

5. あきらめる
6. 来る
　　く
7. 考える
　　かんが
8. 習う
　　なら

9. 取る
　　と
10. 拾う
　　ひろ
11. 帰る
　　かえ
12. 運ぶ
　　はこ

13. 持っていく
　　も
14. 練習する
　　れんしゅう

B. Make sentences using the causative forms.

(a) You are on the tennis team and make junior students do these things. 🔊 K22-10

Example 後輩に服を洗わせます。
　　　　こうはい　ふく　あら

e.g. 服を洗う
　　　ふく　あら

(1) お弁当を
　　　べんとう
買いに行く
か　　　い

(2) 荷物を運ぶ
　　　に もつ　はこ

(3) 部屋を片付ける
　　　へ や　かた づ

(4) 車を運転する
　　　くるま　うんてん

(5) ボールを拾う
　　　　　　ひろ

(6) 宿題をする
　　　しゅくだい

(b) You are the boss and make your subordinates do these things. 🔊 K22-11

Example 部下に書類を翻訳させます。

e.g. 書類を翻訳する (1) コピーを取る (2) お茶をいれる (3) 残業する

(4) 空港に迎えに来る (5) お客さんを案内する (6) 安いホテルを探す

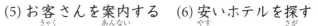

会
L22

C. Group Work—Talk about the following topics with your classmates.

Example A：あなたが先生だったら、学生に何をさせますか。
B：私が先生だったら、学生に毎日テストを受けさせます。
C：どうしてですか。
B：毎日テストがあると、学生がたくさん勉強するからです。
Aさんはどう思いますか。

1. あなたが日本語の先生だったら、学生に何をさせますか。
2. あなたが部長だったら、部下に何をさせますか。
3. あなたが先輩だったら、後輩に何をさせますか。
4. あなたが親だったら、自分の子供に何をさせますか。

D. Pair Work—You are executives in a company who are preparing for a conference. Look at the profiles of your subordinates and discuss who would be the best person to do the tasks.

Example A：だれに会社のホームページ (website) を作らせましょうか。

B：佐藤さんに作らせたらどうですか。コンピューターのことをよく知っていますから。

e.g. ホームページを作る　　　　　　　　　　　佐　藤

1. 町を案内する　　　　　　　　　　　＿＿＿＿＿＿＿＿
2. 翻訳する　　　　　　　　　　　　　＿＿＿＿＿＿＿＿
3. 受付に座る　　　　　　　　　　　　＿＿＿＿＿＿＿＿
4. お客さんを空港に迎えに行く　　　　＿＿＿＿＿＿＿＿
5. 部屋を掃除する　　　　　　　　　　＿＿＿＿＿＿＿＿
6. ポスターを描く　　　　　　　　　　＿＿＿＿＿＿＿＿

佐藤
knows a lot about computers

吉田
has a car

太田
remembers people's names well

川口
was a tour guide（ガイド）

加藤
fluent in English

木村
good at painting

渡辺
looks bored

Ⅱ 一人暮らしをさせてくれませんでした ☞Grammar 2
ひとりぐ

A. You wanted to do the following things. Your parents let you do some and didn't let you do others. Complete the sentences using 〜てくれる／〜てくれない. 🔊 K22-12

> [Example] 高校の時、一人暮らしをする（いいえ）
> こうこう　とき　ひとり　ぐ
>
> → 高校の時、両親は一人暮らしをさせてくれませんでした。
> こうこう　とき　りょうしん　ひとり　ぐ

1. 子供の時、夜遅くテレビを見る（いいえ）
こども　とき　よるおそ　み
2. 子供の時、友だちの家に泊まる（はい）
こども　とき　とも　いえ　と
3. 子供の時、ゲームをする（はい）
こども　とき
4. 子供の時、お菓子をたくさん食べる（いいえ）
こども　とき　かし　た
5. 子供の時、学校を休む（いいえ）
こども　とき　がっこう　やす
6. 高校の時、車の免許を取る（はい）
こうこう　とき　くるま　めんきょ　と
7. 高校の時、友だちと旅行する（いいえ）
こうこう　とき　とも　りょこう
8. 高校の時、アルバイトをする（はい）
こうこう　とき

B. Pair Work—Using the cues above, talk about the things your parents let you do/didn't let you do when you were a child and as a high school student.

会
L22

> [Example] 高校の時、一人暮らしをする
> こうこう　とき　ひとり　ぐ
>
> → Ａ：高校の時、両親は一人暮らしをさせてくれましたか。
> こうこう　とき　りょうしん　ひとり　ぐ
>
> 　Ｂ：いいえ、一人暮らしをさせてくれませんでした。私は一人暮
> ひとり　ぐ　わたし　ひとり　ぐ
>
> 　らしをしたかったんですけど。Ａさんは？

C. Pair Work—Talk about the following topics.

> [Example] Ａ：親になったら、子供に何をさせてあげますか。
> おや　こども　なに
>
> 　Ｂ：子供が楽器を習いたかったら、習わせてあげます。
> こども　がっき　なら　なら
>
> 　Ａ：どんな楽器ですか。
> がっき
>
> 　Ｂ：バイオリンとか、ピアノとか。

1. 親になったら、子供に何をさせてあげますか。
おや　こども　なに
2. 結婚したら、相手に何をさせてあげますか。
けっこん　あいて　なに
3. 社長になったら、部下に何をさせてあげますか。
しゃちょう　ぶか　なに

D. You have been working for a company, but your boss underestimates you. Volunteer to do the following activities using the causative ＋ てください. 🔊 K22-13

[Example] コピーを取る → 私にコピーを取らせてください。

1. 出張に行く
2. お客さんを案内する
3. 書類を翻訳する
4. その仕事をやる
5. 次のプロジェクトの計画を立てる
6. お嬢さんと結婚する

E. Pair Work—Make a short dialogue for the following situations. Use the causative ＋ てください.

[Example] Today is the birthday of your child. You want to leave the office early. Ask the boss.

→ Ａ：今日は早く帰らせてください。
Ｂ：どうしたの。
Ａ：今日は子供の誕生日なので、一緒に晩ご飯を食べる約束をしたんです。
Ｂ：そうか。じゃあ、いいよ。

1. You want to go abroad with your friend next month. You need a week off from the job. Ask the boss.
2. Your boss is looking for someone who can teach English to their child. You want the job.
3. You invited your *senpai* out for dinner. After the meal, offer to pay for dinner.
4. Your *senpai* is drunk, but he has to drive a car home.
5. You have been seeing someone for three months. They have just proposed marriage to you. You need time to think.

Ⅲ 掃除しなさい <small>そうじ</small> ☛Grammar 3

A. You are a parent. What would you say to your child in the following situations? 🔊 K22-14

<u>Example</u> Your child's room is always messy.　→　部屋を掃除しなさい。
<small>へ　や　　そう　じ</small>

1. Your child doesn't eat vegetables.
2. Your child doesn't study at all.
3. Your child stays up late.
4. Your child doesn't practice the piano.
5. Your child doesn't like to take a bath.
6. Your child doesn't play outside.
7. Your child doesn't come home right after school.

B. Pair Work—Make a short dialogue between a parent and their child, using 〜なさい。

<u>Example</u> Parent：ゆうた、起きなさい。
<small>　　　　　　　　　　お</small>
Child：　眠いよ。
<small>　　　　　ねむ</small>
Parent：早く起きなさい。もう八時だよ。学校に行かなきゃ。
<small>　　　　はや　お　　　　　　　　はち　じ　　　　がっこう　　い</small>
Child：　今日は日曜日だよ。
<small>　　　　きょう　　にちよう　び</small>

会
L22

Ⅳ 薬を飲めば、元気になります <small>くすり　の　　　　げん　き</small> ☛Grammar 4

A. Change phrases 1 through 6 into the ば-form and choose the correct phrase that follows from a through g. 🔊 K22-15

<u>Example</u> 薬を飲めば、元気になります。
<small>　　　　くすり　の　　　　げん　き</small>

e.g. 薬を飲む <small>くすり　の</small> ・　　　　　　　・a. 涼しくなります。<small>すず</small>
1. 風が吹く <small>かぜ　ふ</small> ・　　　　　　　・b. ほしいものが買えます。<small>か</small>
2. 試験がない <small>し　けん</small> ・　　　　　　　・c. 迎えに来てくれます。<small>むか　き</small>
3. 走る <small>はし</small> ・　　　　　　　・d. 元気になります。<small>げん　き</small>
4. 予習をする <small>よ　しゅう</small> ・　　　　　　　・e. 授業に間に合います。<small>じゅぎょう　ま　あ</small>
5. 友だちに電話する <small>とも　　　てん　わ</small> ・　　　　　　　・f. 授業がよくわかります。<small>じゅぎょう</small>
6. 無駄遣いしない <small>む　だ　づか</small> ・　　　　　　　・g. 遊びに行けます。<small>あそ　い</small>

B. Encourage the following people below using ～ば大丈夫ですよ. 🔊 K22-16

Example 復習すれば大丈夫ですよ。

e.g.

試験が心配なんです。

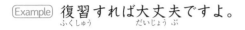

復習する

(1) 外国に行くけど、言葉がわからないんです。

ジェスチャーを使う
(gesture)

(2) レポートの締め切りに間に合わないんです。

先生に頼む

(3) 服を汚したんです。

早く洗う

(4) 歌手になりたいんです。

夢をあきらめない

(5) 仕事で失敗したんです。

今度がんばる

(6)

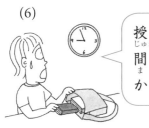

授業に
間に合わない
かもしれません。
(じゅぎょう)(ま あ)

朝ご飯を食べない
(あさ はん た)

(7)

絶対に
さくら大学に
入りたいんです。
(ぜったい)(だいがく)(はい)

神様にお願いする
(かみさま ねが)

C. Pair Work—Ask your partner the following questions.

Example A：どうすれば料理が上手になりますか。
(りょうり)(じょうず)
B：料理をたくさん作れば、上手になりますよ。
(りょうり)(つく)(じょうず)

1. どうすれば日本語が上手になりますか。
(にほんご)(じょうず)
2. どうすれば日本人の友だちができますか。
(にほんじん)(とも)
3. どうすれば日本で就職できますか。
(にほん)(しゅうしょく)
4. どうすれば有名になれますか。
(ゆうめい)
5. どうすればお金持ちになれますか。
(かね も)
6. どうすれば幸せになれますか。
(しあわ)

V 留学したことがないのに、日本語がぺらぺらです ☞Grammar 5
(りゅうがく)(にほんご)

A. Change the cues in 1 through 7 into のに clauses and choose the correct phrase that follows from the right column. K22-17

Example 日本に留学したことがないのに、日本語がぺらぺらです。
(にほん)(りゅうがく)(にほんご)

e.g. 日本に留学したことがありません・
(にほん)(りゅうがく)
1. かぎがかけてありました ・
2. いい天気です ・
(てんき)
3. きのうの夜早く寝ました ・
(よるはや ね)
4. この会社の仕事は楽です ・
(かいしゃ しごと らく)
5. ぜんぜん練習しませんでした ・
(れんしゅう)
6. あの二人は仲がよかったです ・
(ふたり なか)
7. 徹夜しました ・
(てつや)

・a. 眠くないです。
(ねむ)
・b. やめる人が多いです。
(ひと おお)
・c. 別れたそうです。
(わか)
・d. 日本語がぺらぺらです。
(にほんご)
・e. 試合に勝ちました。
(しあい か)
・f. どろぼうに入られました。
(はい)
・g. 朝寝坊してしまいました。
(あさねぼう)
・h. 家でごろごろしています。
(いえ)

B. Pair Work—Complain about the following situations. When you hear the complaint, give advice or encouragement.

Example You bought a camera last week. It has broken.

→　A：このカメラ、先週買ったのに、もう壊れてしまったんです。
　　B：店に持っていって、交換してもらったらどうですか。

1. You went to a baseball game. Your favorite team lost.
2. You studied a lot. You couldn't do well on the test.
3. You knitted a sweater for your boyfriend/girlfriend. They never wear it.
4. Your relatives came to see you. You were busy and couldn't take them anywhere.
5. Today is your birthday. Your friend forgot it.
6. You want to live by yourself. Your parents don't let you do so.
7. You are capable of doing various things. Your boss makes you photocopy and serve tea (and do other simple things).
8. You tidied up the room yesterday, but your roommate made it messy.

Ⅵ 魚のように泳げます 🖝 Grammar 6

A. You have just signed up to a Japanese social network app. Create an outrageous profile, using 〜のように. 🔊 K22-18

Example 私は魚のように泳げます。

e.g. 泳げる　魚

(1) 速く走れる　新幹線

(2) 歌が上手　オペラ (opera) 歌手

(3) かわいい　ぬいぐるみ

(4) 飛べる　鳥

(5) 木に登れる　猿

(6) まじめ　山下先生

B. Create your own impressive profile using 〜のように. Exaggerate your skills and abilities as in A.

C. Pair Work—Ask your partner the following questions. When you answer, use 〜のような as in the example.

(Example) A：どんな人になりたいですか。

B：父のような人になりたいです。

A：どうしてですか。

B：父は強くて、やさしいからです。

1. どんな人と結婚したいですか／付き合いたいですか。
2. どんな映画が好きですか。
3. どんな町に住みたいですか。

D. Group Work—Tell the others about a food, place, cultural practice, etc. that may be unfamiliar to them, using 〜のような＋noun.

(Example)

フィッシュアンドチップス (fish and chips) は日本の天ぷらのような料理です。
イギリス人はフィッシュアンドチップスが大好きで、多くの店で食べられます。

インドネシアのジョグジャカルタ (Yogyakarta) は京都のような古い町です。
お寺がたくさんあります。
古い建物もあります。

会
L22

Ⅶ まとめの練習
れんしゅう

A. Group Work—In a group, choose one topic on parenting from below and discuss it.

Example 親は子供に楽器を習わせたほうがいい
おや こども がっき なら
→ A：私は賛成です。子供の時に楽器を始めたら、上手になるから、
わたし さんせい こども とき がっき はじ じょうず
習わせたほうがいいと思います。
なら おも
B：私は反対です。習いたくないのに習わせたら、子供は音楽が
わたし はんたい なら なら こども おんがく
きらいになるかもしれません。
C：私は賛成です。いろいろなことをさせるのはいいことだと
わたし さんせい
思います。
おも

Topics:

1. 子供を塾に行かせたほうがいい
こども じゅく い
2. アルバイトをさせたほうがいい
3. 家事を手伝わせたほうがいい
かじ てつだ

4. 留学させたほうがいい
りゅうがく
5. 大学に行かせたほうがいい
だいがく い

B. Talk about things that you wanted to do but were not allowed to do when you were a child. How did you feel about it? How did you react?

Example 子供の時、ゲームをしたかったのに、両親はさせてくれませんでした。
こども とき りょうしん
友だちはみんなゲームを持っていたから、すごく悲しかったです。
とも も かな
それで、時々友だちのうちに行って、ゲームをしました。
ときどきとも い

C. Role Play—Using the first part of Dialogue Ⅰ as a model, act the role of a parent or a child.

Parent: Tell the child to do one of the things listed below using 〜なさい, and try to convince them to do it.

Child: Take a defiant attitude toward the parent.

practice the piano	go to bed	exercise	help cook
go to a cram school	eat vegetables	study (a foreign language)	

Culture Notes

日本の教育制度（2）Japan's Educational System (2)
にほん きょういくせいど

大学入試 (University entrance exams)
だいがくにゅうし

In general, those seeking to enter a Japanese university or college need to pass an entrance exam (大学入試). Most entrance
だいがくにゅうし
exams are held sometime from January through March. There are also alternative admission methods, such as admission by recommendation. When applying, students have to choose the department they wish to enter. Since getting into good schools is highly competitive, many students supplement their

Celebration for passing an exam

regular class work by attending a special preparation school (塾 or 予備校) or getting private
じゅく よびこう
tutoring (家庭教師). Those who fail an entrance examination have to wait a year to take it
かていきょうし
again. These students are called 一浪, and those who fail the exam twice are called 二浪.
いちろう にろう

大学生活 (College life)
だいがくせいかつ

Here are some of the keywords that represent college life.

- サークル：サークル is a group of students devoted to a particular hobby, interest, sport, social activity, and so forth. Some examples are 映画サークル, アニメサークル, アウトドア
えいが
サークル, and 写真サークル.
しゃしん

- ゼミ：ゼミ comes from the word "seminar." It is a class in which a small group of students studies an area of their major with a supervising professor. Students usually start taking ゼミ from their junior year.

- バイト (＝アルバイト)：Many students spend a lot of their time working at a part-time job, or バイト (see 読み書き編, Lesson 18). Common part-time jobs include tutoring, teaching
よ か へん
at preparation schools, and working at shops or restaurants.

- 就活：就活 is a short form of 就職活動, which means job hunting. Japa-
しゅうかつ しゅうかつ しゅうしょくかつどう
nese college students usually start to look for a job in their junior year.
During 就活, most students wear a dark-colored business suit, and some
しゅうかつ
with dyed hair restore their hair to its natural black.

写真提供：共同通信社

会
L22

第23課

別れ Good-bye
わか

In this lesson, we will..

● Complain about doing something undesirable   ● Reminisce about the past
● Make a resolution for a new phase of life   ● Say farewell

会 話 D i a l o g u e
かい わ

Ⅰ Mary and her host family at their last dinner together. 🔊 K23-01/02

1 お母さん： メアリーがいなくなるとさびしくなるね。
  かあ

2 メアリー： でも、来年大学を卒業したら、また日本に戻ってきますから。
  らいねんだいがく　そつぎょう　　　　　にほん　もど

3 お父さん、お母さん、本当にお世話になりました。
  とう　　かあ　　ほんとう　せわ

4 お父さん： 私たちもメアリーがいて、とても楽しかったよ。
  とう　　わたし　　　　　　　　　　たの

5 お母さん： 国に帰っても、私たちのことを忘れないでね。
  かあ　　くに　かえ　　わたし　　　　　わす

6 メアリー： もちろん。アメリカにも遊びに来てください。
  あそ　き

7 お父さん： じゃあ、この夏はアメリカに行くことにしよう。
  とう　　　　　　なつ　　　　　　い

8 お母さん： そうね。
  かあ

Ⅱ On the way to the airport. 🔊 K23-03/04

1 たけし： この一年、いろいろなことがあったね。
  いちねん

2 メアリー： そうそう。デートの時、よく待たされた。
  とき　　ま

3 たけし： ぼくが約束の場所を間違えて、後で、ものすごく怒られたり。
  やくそく　ばしょ　まちが　　あと　　　　　　　おこ

4 メアリー： たけしくんが作った料理を食べさせられて、おなかをこわしたり。
  つく　りょうり　た

5 たけし： 初めて一緒に踊った時、「盆踊りみたいだ」って笑われた。
  はじ　いっしょ　おど　とき　ぼんおど　　　　　　わら

6 メアリー： あの時は足を踏まれて、痛かった。
  とき　あし　ふ　　　いた

7 たけし： 考え方が違うから、けんかもよくしたね。でもみんないい思い出だ
  かんが　かた　ちが　　　　　　　　　　　　　　　　　おも　て

8 ね。

Ⅲ At the airport. 🔊 K23-05/06

1 たけし： じゃあ、元気でね。

2 メアリー： うん。たけしくんも。たけしくんに会えて本当によかった。

3 たけし： そんな悲しそうな顔しないで。

4 メアリー： わかってる。じゃあ、そろそろ行かなきゃ。

5 たけし： メアリーが卒業して日本に戻って
くるまで、待っているから。

Ⅰ

Host mother: We'll miss you when you're gone.

Mary: But I will come back to Japan after I graduate from college next year. Thank you for taking care of me, Father and Mother.

Host father: We had a great time with you, Mary.

Host mother: Don't forget us even though you are going back to your country.

Mary: Of course I won't. Please come to see me in the U.S.

Host father: Then let's visit the U.S. this summer.

Host mother: That sounds good.

Ⅱ

Takeshi: Many things happened in the past year.

Mary: You're right. You often made me wait when we had a date.

Takeshi: When I misunderstood where to meet, I was scolded badly later.

Mary: You made me eat that dish you cooked and I got a stomachache, and . . .

Takeshi: When we danced together for the first time, I was laughed at and you said it looked like I was doing the *Bon-odori*.

Mary: You stepped on my foot then and it hurt.

Takeshi: Because we think differently, we also fought a lot. But they are all good memories . . .

Ⅲ

Takeshi: Well, take care of yourself.

Mary: Okay. You, too. I'm really glad that I met you, Takeshi.

Takeshi: Don't look so sad.

Mary: I know, but . . . Well, I should go now.

Takeshi: I'll wait until you graduate and come back to Japan.

会
L23

単　語
たん　　ご
K23-07 (J-E)
K23-08 (E-J)

V o c a b u l a r y

N o u n s

くつした	靴下	socks
ふくろ	袋	sack; plastic/paper bag
ただ		free of charge
ゆうしょく	夕食	dinner
* ばしょ	場所	place
かいだん	階段	stairs
しょうがっこう	小学校	elementary school
めんせつ	面接	interview
けんこう	健康	health
りそう	理想	ideal
るすばん	留守番	looking after a house during someone's absence
メッセージ		message; text
きゅうこう	休講	class cancellation
かいがいりょこう	海外旅行	trip to a foreign country
* ぼんおどり	盆踊り	Bon dance (Japanese traditional dance)
* おもいで	思い出	memory
しゃかい	社会	society
けっか	結果	result
ちょうさ	調査	survey

い - a d j e c t i v e

まずい	(food is) terrible

な - a d j e c t i v e

かわいそう（な）	pitiful; feel sorry for; poor thing

U - v e r b s

あめがやむ	雨がやむ	the rain stops
* ちがう	違う	to be different; to be wrong （〜と）
なくなる		to be lost; to disappear （〜が）

＊Words that appear in the dialogue

* いなくなる		(someone) is gone; to disappear（〜が）
* おせわになる	お世話になる	to be in someone's care（〜に）
* おなかをこわす		to have a stomachache
きにいる	気に入る	to find something agreeable（〜が/を）
わるぐちをいう	悪口を言う	to talk behind someone's back

Ru-verbs

こたえる	答える	to answer（〜に）
はなれる	離れる	(something/someone) separates; parts from（〜と）

Irregular Verbs

がっかりする		to be disappointed（〜に）
がまんする	我慢する	to be tolerant/patient（〜を）
どうじょうする	同情する	to sympathize（〜に）
* 〜かおをする	〜顔をする	to look . . . (facial expression)
カンニングする		to cheat in an exam
チェックする		to check（〜を）
せわをする	世話をする	to take care of . . .（〜の）
ゆうしょうする	優勝する	to win a championship
* もどってくる	戻ってくる	(something/someone) comes back

Adverbs and Other Expressions

* そんな〜		such . . . ; that kind of . . .
〜ために		for . . . ; for the sake of . . .
* ものすごく		extremely
* そろそろ		it is about time to . . .
さいごに	最後に	finally
* げんきでね	元気でね	Take care of yourself.
* そうそう		You are right.

会
L23

文 法 G r a m m a r
ぶん　ぼう

1 Causative-passive Sentences

"Causative-passive" sentences are the passive version of causative sentences. You can use causative-passive sentences when you want to say that you were made to do, or harassed or talked into doing, something that you did not want to.

（下手だから歌いたくなかったのに）歌を歌わされました。
へた　　　　うた　　　　　　　　　　うた　うた
(I didn't want to sing because I'm not a good singer, but) I was forced to sing.

（きらいだから食べたくないんですが、いつも）野菜を食べさせられます。
た　　　　　　　　　　　　　　や さい　た
(I don't want to eat vegetables because I don't like them, but) I am (always) made to eat vegetables.

You make the causative-passive forms this way:

Causative-passive form

· *ru*-verbs: Drop *-ru* and add *-sase-rare-ru*.

　　食べる　→　食べさせられる
　　た　　　　　た

· *u*-verbs that end with す: Drop *-u* and add *-ase-rare-ru*.

　　話す　→　話させられる
　　はな　　　はな

· all the other *u*-verbs: Drop *-u* and add *-asare-ru*.

行く	→ 行かされる		泳ぐ	→ 泳がされる
待つ	→ 待たされる		遊ぶ	→ 遊ばされる
読む	→ 読まされる		買う	→ 買わされる
取る	→ 取らされる			

· irregular verbs:

　　する　→　させられる　　　　くる　→　こさせられる

In the table above, you must have noticed that the causative-passive morphology in *ru*-verbs, *u*-verbs ending with す, and irregular verbs is indeed the combination of the causative and the passive forms: *-(s)ase-rare*. In *u*-verbs other than those that end with す, however, the causative-passive suffix *-asare* is shorter than the sum of the causative (*-ase*) and the passive (*-rare*) suffixes.[1]

---

[1] The more transparently combinative *aserare* form, such as 書かせられる, is indeed grammatical, but causative-passive verbs of the *asare* form, such as 書かされる, are much more common.

The basic makeup of a causative-passive sentence is like this:

Causative-passive sentence

私は 彼女に 車を洗わされました。
わたし かのじょ くるま あら
(puppet) は (puppet master) に (action)

I was tricked by my girlfriend into washing her car.

· The puppet is forced into performing an action. Marked with は or が.
· The puppet master wields power over, and manipulates, the puppet. The
   particle is に.
· The action forced upon the puppet is described with a causative-passive verb.

If you compare a causative-passive sentence with a causative sentence, you notice that the actors are switched between the two:

Causative-passive:  宿題を手伝わされました。
しゅくだい てつだ

I was forced by my friend into helping him with his homework.

Causative: 友だち は 私 に 宿題を手伝わせました。
とも わたし しゅくだい てつだ

My friend made me help him with his homework.

Compare a causative-passive sentence with a plain (noncausative, nonpassive) sentence. These two types of sentences have the same subject. You add the "puppet master" role to a plain sentence and make the verb longer, and you get a causative-passive sentence.

Causative-passive: まなは お母さんに 勉強させられました。
かあ べんきょう

Mana was ordered by her mother to study.

Plain: まなは ———— 勉強しました。
べんきょう

Mana studied.

2 〜ても

"A ても B" is "B, even if A." That is, B is still true in case of A (so is certainly true if A is not the case). Compare ても sentences with たら sentences, which have a more straightforward "if-then" meaning:[2]

雨が降っても、バーベキューをします。
We will have a barbecue, even if it rains.

雨が降ったら、バーベーキューをしません。
We will not have a barbecue if it rains.

暑くても、エアコンをつけません。
I will not turn on the air conditioner, even if it is hot.

暑かったら、エアコンをつけます。
I will turn on the air conditioner, if it is hot.

子供でも、わかります。
Even a child will get it. (You will be able to understand it, even if you are a child.)

子供だったら、わかりません。
If you are a child, you will not get it.

You can form a ても clause by adding も to the verb or adjective *te*-form. With な-adjectives and nouns, you have でも. Note that verb たら and ても forms look very much like each other, but adjective たら and ても forms look quite distinct.

〜ても (affirmative)				Compare:
· verbs:	買う	→	買っても	買ったら
· い-adjectives:	悲しい	→	悲しくても （×悲しかっても）	悲しかったら
· な-adjectives:	元気（な）	→	元気でも （×元気だっても）	元気だったら
· nouns:	学生	→	学生でも （×学生だっても）	学生だったら

---

[2] You can put a question word like だれ or いつ in a ても clause and have a generalized concessive clause meaning "no matter" or "regardless of" who, when, and so forth.

だれに聞いても、教えてくれませんでした。
No matter who I asked, they didn't tell me.

いつ行っても、東京はにぎやかです。
No matter when you visit, Tokyo is lively.

You can also form a negative て も clause, based on the short form negative.

~ても (negative)			Compare:
・verbs:	買わない	→ 買わなくても	買わなかったら
・い-adjectives:	悲しくない	→ 悲しくなくても	悲しくなかったら
・な-adjectives:	元気じゃない	→ 元気じゃなくても	元気じゃなかったら
・nouns:	学生じゃない	→ 学生じゃなくても	学生じゃなかったら

The て も clause itself does not have tense. It can be followed either by a present tense clause (as in the above examples), or by a past tense clause.

私は、かぜをひいていても、毎日、授業に行きました。
I went to class every day, even when I had a cold.

日本語の授業が難しくても、取ったでしょう。
I would have taken the Japanese class, even if it could have been difficult.

3 〜ことにする

ことにする means "decide to do . . ." It follows the short form present tense of a verb. You can use a negated verb, too.

車を買うことにしました。
We have decided to buy a car.

あの人がかわいそうだから、あまり文句を言わないことにします。
I will not make too many complaints. I am feeling sorry for him already.

会
L23

verb (short, present) ＋ ことにする	*decide to do . . .*

We sometimes use the volitional form of this construction, such as 行くことにしよう, instead of the simple volitional form of a verb, 行こう, in suggesting an activity. ことにしよう has the additional implication that the suggestion is being made after a deliberation.

今年の夏はベトナムに行くことにしよう。
Let's take the plunge. Let's go to Vietnam this summer.

4 〜ことにしている

ことにしている means "do something as a regular practice," that is, you have made up your mind that you should do something and have stuck to that resolution.

毎日十一時までに寝ることにしています。
まいにちじゅういち じ　　　　　ね
I make it a rule to go to bed by eleven every night.

絶対にお酒を飲まないことにしています。
ぜったい　　さけ　の
I have made this firm decision not to drink and have strictly followed it.

verb (short, present) ＋ ことにしている　　　　*do . . . as a regular practice*

5 〜まで

A まで means "till A." The A in "A まで B" is the description of the change that coincides with or causes the end of B. The A, therefore, is usually a verb of the "change" kind (see Lesson 7). The verb in A is always in the present tense and in the affirmative.

晴れるまで、カフェでコーヒーを飲みながら、待ちます。
は　　　　　　　　　　　　　　　の　　　　　　ま
I will wait in the cafe, drinking coffee, till it clears up.

日本語が上手になるまで、国に帰りません。
に ほん ご　じょうず　　　　　　くに　かえ
I will not go back to my country, till I become fluent in Japanese.

verb (short, present, affirmative) ＋ まで　　　　*till A*

When the subject of A is different from the subject of B, the former is marked with the particle が rather than は.

赤ちゃんが寝るまで、（私は）歌を歌ってあげます。
あか　　　　　ね　　　　　わたし　うた　うた
I will sing a lullaby till the baby falls asleep.

You can use "A まで B" in a sentence describing a situation in the past. Note that the verb in A is in the present tense nonetheless.

日本の生活に慣れるまで、大変でした。
に ほん　せいかつ　な　　　　　たいへん
It was tough until I got used to living in Japan.

6 〜方

The noun-forming suffix 方 follows the stem of a verb and means "the way in which the action is performed" or "how to do . . . ."

泳ぐ	→ 泳ぎ方	*how to swim*
考える	→ 考え方	*the way people think*

Nouns that are marked with other particles when they go with a verb are marked with の before 〜方.

漢字を読む	→ 漢字の読み方	*how to read the kanji*
はしを使う	→ はしの使い方	*how to use chopsticks*
空港に行く	→ 空港の行き方 [3]	*how to go to the airport*
お風呂に入る	→ お風呂の入り方	*how to take a bath*

With compound する verbs, such as 勉強する, we have:

日本語を勉強する	→ 日本語の勉強のし方
ホテルを予約する	→ ホテルの予約のし方

〜方 is a noun and is followed by particles like は and を.

この野菜の食べ方はいろいろあります。
There are many ways to eat this vegetable.

すみません。この漢字の書き方を教えていただけませんか。
Excuse me, can you tell me how to write this kanji?

---

[3] The goal of movement, normally marked with に, can be marked with the combination of particles への. Therefore we also say 空港への行き方 (how to get to the airport).

練習 Practice
れん しゅう

I 荷物を持たされます 🖝 Grammar 1
に もつ も

A. Change the following into the causative-passive forms. 🔊 K23-09

Example 寝る → 寝させられる
ね   ね

1. 食べる   4. 取る   7. 習う   10. 迎えに行く
   た   と   なら   むか   い
2. やめる   5. 作る   8. 歌う   11. 世話をする
                     つく   うた   せ わ
3. 受ける   6. 待つ   9. 話す   12. 戻ってくる
   う   ま   はな   もど

B. Kenta and Yui are forced to do the following by each other. Describe the pictures using the causative-passive forms. 🔊 K23-10

Example けんたさんはゆいさんに荷物を持たされます。
に もつ も

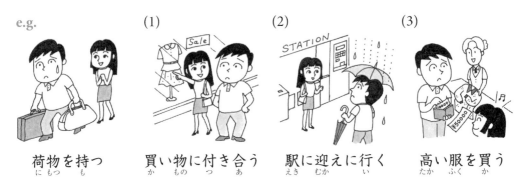

e.g. 荷物を持つ
      に もつ も

(1) 買い物に付き合う
    か もの つ あ

(2) 駅に迎えに行く
    えき むか い

(3) 高い服を買う
    たか ふく か

(4) 犬の世話をする
    いぬ せ わ

(5) お弁当を作る
    べんとう つく

(6) 夕食をおごる
    ゆうしょく

(7) アイロンをかける

(8)

部屋を掃除する
へ や そう じ

(9)

毎晩会社の文句を聞く
まいばんかいしゃ もん く き

(10)

靴を磨く
くつ みが

C. Pair Work—Ask your partner if, as a child, their parents made them do the following things using the causative-passive forms. 🔊 K23-11

(Example) 買い物に行く
か もの い
→ A：子供の時、買い物に行かされましたか。
こ ども とき か もの い
B：はい、行かされました。／いいえ、行かされませんでした。
い い

1. お皿を洗う
さら あら
2. 自分の部屋を掃除する
じ ぶん へ や そう じ
3. ピアノを習う
なら
4. 毎日勉強する
まいにちべんきょう

5. 妹 ／ 弟 の世話をする
いもうと おとうと せ わ
6. きらいな物を食べる
もの た
7. 料理を手伝う
りょう り て つだ
8. 塾に行く
じゅく い

D. Pair Work—First play *janken* (rock paper scissors) and decide who is in charge. Each time you win *janken*, you can give an order, such as dancing, singing a song, drawing a picture, and opening a window. The other person will act out the order. You will then describe the actions, using the causative and causative-passive sentences. Repeat *janken* several times.

(Example) open the window
→ A：窓を開けなさい。
まど あ
B：はい、わかりました。　(B will act out opening the window.)
A：Bさんに窓を開けさせました。
まど あ
B：Aさんに窓を開けさせられました。
まど あ

会
L23

じゃんけん

じゃんけん (rock scissors paper) is a children's game. Players call out "*Jan, ken, pon*" and make one of three forms with one hand: rock, scissors, or paper. "Rock" breaks "scissors," "scissors" cut "paper," and "paper" covers "rock." It is often played to determine who will be "it" in games of tag or who will go first in selecting teams.

E. Group Work—Talk with your classmates about what you were forced to do when you were children. Then discuss whether you would make your children do the same or not. You can use the cues in I-C (p. 261) as topics of your talk.

[Example] 毎日勉強する
まいにちべんきょう
→ A：子供の時、毎日両親に勉強させられた？
こども とき まいにちりょうしん べんきょう
B：うん、させられた。
A：じゃあ、自分の子供にも毎日勉強させる？
じぶん こども まいにちべんきょう
B：もちろん。毎日塾に行かせて、遅くまで勉強させる。
まいにちじゅく い おそ べんきょう
A：それはかわいそうだよ。私だったら、子供がやりたいことを
わたし こども
させたい。好きなスポーツとか楽器とか。
す がっき

Ⅱ 学生がうるさくても、怒りません ☞Grammar 2
がくせい おこ

A. Make sentences using 〜ても. 🔊 K23-12

[Example] 学生がうるさい → 学生がうるさくても、絶対に怒りません。
がくせい がくせい ぜったい おこ

絶対に怒りません。
ぜったい おこ

山下先生
やましたせんせい

e.g. 学生がうるさい
がくせい
1. 学生が授業中に寝ている
がくせい じゅぎょうちゅう ね
2. 学生が質問に答えられない
がくせい しつもん こた
3. 学生に文句を言われる
がくせい もんく い
4. 学生がカンニングする
がくせい

5. サークルの練習が厳しい

6. 先輩がいじわるだ

7. 先輩に荷物を持たされる

8. 友だちと遊ぶ時間がない

9. 十年待つ

10. 親に反対される

11. 今は離れている

12. 言葉や文化が違う

B. Answer the following questions using 〜ても. K23-13

Example Q：いじめられたら、学校を休みますか。

A：いいえ。いじめられても、学校を休みません。

1. 授業がつまらなかったら、先生に文句を言いますか。

2. 先生に怒られたら、泣きますか。

3. 試験の結果が悪かったら、落ち込みますか。

4. 友だちとけんかしたら、自分から謝りますか。

5. 宝くじに当たったら、みんなにおごってあげますか。

6. スーパーで袋がただだったら、もらいますか。

7. 道に迷ったら、だれかに聞きますか。

8. レストランで子供がうるさかったら、注意しますか。

9. 自分が作った料理がまずかったら、捨てますか。

10. 誕生日のプレゼントが靴下だったら、がっかりしますか。

C. Pair Work—Ask your partner the questions in B above.

Example A：いじめられたら、学校を休みますか。

B：はい。いじめられたら、学校を休みます。／

いいえ。いじめられても、学校を休みません。

L23

D. Complete the following sentences using ても or でも.

1. _____、怒りません。
   _{おこ}

2. _____、仕事を続けます。
   _{しごと} _{つづ}

3. _____、幸せです。
   _{しあわ}

4. _____、日本に住みたいです。
   _{にほん} _す

5. _____、同情してあげません。
   _{どうじょう}

Ⅲ 日本語の勉強を続けることにしました ☛Grammar 3
_{に ほん ご}   _{べんきょう}   _{つづ}

A. The semester is over and people are leaving. Say what they have decided to do, using 〜ことにする. 🔊 K23-14

(Example) メアリー：will go back to her country and continue her study of Japanese

→ メアリーさんは国に帰って、日本語の勉強を続けることにしました。
_{くに} _{かえ} _{に ほん ご} _{べんきょう} _{つづ}

1. ヤスミン：will do research about Japanese society
2. カルロス：will take (受ける) an interview at a Japanese company
   _う
3. たけし：will quit the company and look for a new job
4. ゆい：will study abroad
5. 山下先生：will teach Japanese in China
   _{やましたせんせい}
6. メアリーさんのホストファミリー：will go to the U.S. to see Mary
7. けん：will become an elementary school teacher
8. ジョン：will not return to Australia because he will learn karate in Japan

B. Pair Work—You have just found that your class was canceled. Talk with your partner about what you want to do together. Decide at least two activities and report to the class what you have decided to do.

(Example) A：山下先生の授業、休講になったって。
_{やましたせんせい} _{じゅぎょう} _{きゅうこう}
B：本当？じゃあ、うちでアニメを見ない？
_{ほんとう} _み
A：アニメはちょっと……映画を見ない？
_{えい が} _み

→ Report to the class:

私たちは、Bさんのうちで怖い映画を見ることにしました。
_{わたし} _{こわ えいが み}
そして、映画の後、「カレーハウス」に行って、カレーを
_{えい が あと} _い
食べることにしました。
_た

C. Group Work—Congratulations! Your family (your group) won a lottery. Discuss how you will spend your money with your family.

[Example] A ： 湖の近くに別荘 (vacation home) を買うことにしよう。

B ： 別荘より店のほうがいいよ。店を始めることにしよう。

C ： どんな店？……

Ⅳ メッセージをチェックすることにしています ☞ Grammar 4

A. Say what Mary and Takeshi make a habit of doing or not doing, using 〜ことにしている. 🔊 K23-15

[Example] メアリーさんは起きたら、メッセージをチェックすることにしています。

e.g. check messages when she gets up

(1) not talk behind someone's back

(2) study in the library on weekends

(3) take a walk with her dog twice a day

(4) not watch TV and study at the same time

(5) ask a person when she doesn't understand

(6) not cry even if he is sad

(7) buy flowers, cook, etc., on Mother's Day

(8) not drink coffee before going to bed

会
L23

B. Group Work—Talk about what you make a practice of doing or not doing regarding the following topics.

Example ダイエットのために

→　A：ダイエットのために、何をすることにしていますか。

B：体にいい食べ物を食べることにしています。それから夜遅く食べないことにしています。

C：エレベーター (elevator) を使わないで、階段を使うことにしています。

1. 日本語が上手になるために
2. 環境のために
3. お金をためるために
4. 健康のために

Ⅴ　大学を卒業するまで、日本にいるつもりです　☞Grammar 5

A. Describe how long they will stay in Japan or until when they will not get married, using ～まで. 🔊 K23-16

Example ジョンさんは大学を卒業するまで、日本にいるつもりです。

(a) ＿＿＿＿＿＿＿＿＿＿＿まで、日本にいるつもりです。

e.g.	ジョン	till he graduates from college
1.	メアリー	till this semester ends
2.	ソラ	till she becomes fluent in Japanese
3.	ロバート	till money runs out
4.	カルロス	till he dies

(b) ＿＿＿＿＿＿＿＿＿＿＿まで結婚しません。

5.	ジョン	till he finds an ideal partner
6.	けん	till his favorite team wins the championship
7.	ナオミ	till she saves one million yen
8.	ウデイ	till he becomes thirty years old

B. Complete the following sentences.

1. 日本語がぺらぺらになるまで、＿＿＿＿＿＿＿＿＿＿＿＿＿＿＿＿＿＿＿＿。

2. 死ぬまで、＿＿＿＿＿＿＿＿＿＿＿＿＿＿＿＿＿＿＿＿＿＿＿＿＿＿。

3. 雨がやむまで、＿＿＿＿＿＿＿＿＿＿＿＿＿＿＿＿＿＿＿＿＿＿＿。

4. ＿＿＿＿＿＿＿＿＿＿＿＿＿＿＿＿＿＿＿＿まで、仕事を続けます。

5. ＿＿＿＿＿＿＿＿＿＿＿＿＿＿まで、留守番をしなければいけません。

6. ＿＿＿＿＿＿＿＿＿＿＿＿＿＿＿＿＿まで、我慢しました。

C. Pair Work—Suggest the following plans to your partner. (The card for Student B is on p. 270.) When you respond, use 〜まで. Expand the conversation like the example.

Example　Ａ：一緒に遊ぶ／Ｂ：You have a final exam pretty soon.

→　Ａ：一緒に遊ぼうよ。
　　Ｂ：もうすぐ期末試験だから、試験が終わるまで遊べないんだ。
　　Ａ：残念。じゃあ、試験が終わったら一緒に遊ぼうね。

Student A—Suggest 1, 3, and 5 to your partner.
　　　　　　Use 2, 4, and 6 to respond to your partner's suggestions.

1. 出かける

2. You have no money, but you will receive a salary soon.

3. ケーキを食べる

4. You caught a cold and have a sore throat.

5. 海外旅行に行く

6. Your parents are strict and won't let you live away from home.

会
L23

Ⅵ アプリの使い方を教えてくれませんか ☞ Grammar 6
つか　かた　おし

A. You want to know how to do the things below. Ask questions using 〜方. 🔊 K23-17
かた

Example　how to use this app

→　すみませんが、このアプリの使い方を教えてくれませんか。
つか　かた　おし

1. how to make delicious coffee
2. how to iron
3. how to ride a bicycle
4. how to drive
5. how to play the guitar

6. how to do a survey
7. how to make sushi
8. how to make a Shinkansen reservation
9. how to bake a cake
10. how to wear kimono

B. Pair Work—Look at the pictures and explain how.

Example　お金をおろす
かね

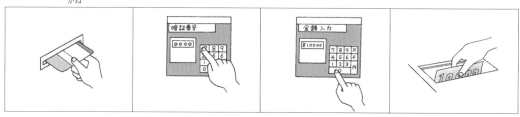

→　お金のおろし方を説明します。まず、カードを入れます。
かね　かた　せつめい　い

それから、暗証番号 (PIN) と金額 (amount) を押します。
あんしょうばんごう　きんがく　お

最後に、お金を取ります。（カードを取るのを忘れないでください！）
さいご　かね　と　と　わす

1. すきやきを作る
つく

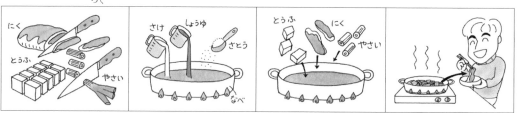

2. 切符を買う
きっぷ　か

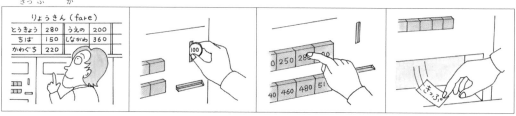

3. お茶をいれる
　　ちゃ

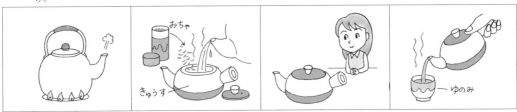

C. Pair Work—Ask your partner how to do the following. When you answer, explain it in detail.

(Example) how to take a Japanese bath

→　Ａ：日本のお風呂の入り方を教えてくれませんか。
　　　　　に ほん　　ふ ろ　　はい　かた　　おし

　　Ｂ：お風呂の入り方ですか。まず、お風呂に入る前に、体を洗い
　　　　　ふ ろ　　はい　かた　　　　　　　　　ふ ろ　　はい　まえ　　からだ　あら
　　　　ます。それから、お風呂に入ってゆっくりします。
　　　　　　　　　　　　　　ふ ろ　　はい

1. how to memorize kanji
2. how to take an inexpensive trip
3. how to find a part-time job
4. how to go to the airport
5. how to ride a bus
6. (your own)

Ⅶ　まとめの練習
　　　　　　　れんしゅう

A. Pair Work—Using Dialogue Ⅰ and Ⅲ as models, make short dialogues with your partner for the following situations.

1. You have lived with a host family in Japan for three months. You are leaving for your country tomorrow.

2. You and your friend had not seen each other for ten years. You have had a chance to meet the friend at a reunion. You have had a good time and now it is time to leave.

B. Pair Work/Group Work—Using Dialogue Ⅱ as a model, talk about good and bad memories in Japan or in Japanese class in a pair/group.

C. State your future plans. Have you decided to continue studying Japanese? What else have you decided to do? State the reasons, too.

(Example) 私は日本語の勉強を続けることにしました。日本文化にとても興味が
　　　　　わたし　に ほん ご　　べんきょう　つづ　　　　　　　　　　　　に ほんぶん か　　　　　きょう み
　　　　あって、それについてもっと勉強したいからです。
　　　　　　　　　　　　　　　　　　べんきょう

会
L23

D. Do you agree with the following statements? Discuss with your classmates.

(Example)

勉強が好きじゃなくても、大学に行ったほうがいい。
→ 　A：私は賛成です。大学を卒業しなかったら、いい会社に就職できません。がんばって勉強したほうがいいと思います。
　　B：私は反対です。自分が好きなことをしたほうがいいと思います。

1. 仕事が楽しくなくても、一年間ぐらい我慢して続けたほうがいい。
2. 授業がつまらなかったら、先生に文句を言ったほうがいい。
3. レストランにうるさい子供がいたら、注意したほうがいい。
4. もらったプレゼントが気に入らなくても、うれしそうな顔をしたほうがいい。
5. 結婚する前に一緒に住んだほうがいい。

Pair Work Ⓥ **C.** (p. 267)

(Example) A：一緒に遊ぶ／B：You have a final exam pretty soon.
→ 　A：一緒に遊ぼうよ。
　　B：もうすぐ期末試験だから、試験が終わるまで遊べないんだ。
　　A：残念。じゃあ、試験が終わったら一緒に遊ぼうね。

Student B—Suggest 2, 4 and 6 to your partner.
　　　　Use 1, 3, and 5 to respond to your partner's suggestions.

1. Your host family is out. You have to stay home.
2. 買い物に行く
3. You are on a diet and have decided to lose ten kilograms (22 lb.).
4. カラオケで歌う
5. You are working on a big project and can't take a vacation.
6. 一緒に住む

Let's Find Out

調べてみよう
しら

クールジャパン

1. Setting

You are an employee at a local travel agency. You are currently working on making a new travel plan called "Cool Japan," which needs to be different from conventional tours such as visiting temples in Kyoto. Find an interesting travel destination and make a creative travel plan.

2. Tasks

(1) Do some research and decide the destination(s).

(2) Your "Cool Japan" travel plan may include the following subtopics:

A) How to get there and how long it takes from Tokyo.

B) The best time (season, month, or specific dates) to visit the places and the reasons.

C) Things to do at the place(s) during the time you mentioned in (B).

D) Famous product(s) at the place(s).

E) Special local food/drinks/events tourists must try.

(3) Your travel plan must be presented visually.

長野のスノーモンキー
なが の

日本のお茶
に ほん　　ちゃ

日本のお酒　　　写真提供：東光の酒蔵
に ほん　　さけ

Culture Notes

ことわざ Japanese Proverbs

Here are some Japanese proverbs and sayings. Do they represent a totally different culture from yours, or are there similar elements?

猫に小判
Giving gold coins to a cat.
(Casting pearls before swine.)

仏の顔も三度
Even Buddha would be upset
if his face were stroked three times.
(To try the patience of a saint.)

郷に入れば郷に従え
When in a village,
follow their customs.
(When in Rome,
do as the Romans do.)

うそつきはどろぼうのはじまり
All thieves started
their careers with a lie.

石の上にも三年
Even the coldest rock
becomes warm if you sit
on it for three years.
(Perseverance prevails.)

猿も木から落ちる
Even monkeys fall from trees.
(Nobody is perfect.)

出る杭は打たれる
The stake that sticks out
gets hammered down.
(Don't be too conspicuous.)

善は急げ
Hasten to do good.

花より団子
A rice dumpling is
better than a flower.
(Substance over show.)

読み書き編
よ　か　へん
R e a d i n g   a n d   W r i t i n g

第13課

日本のおもしろい経験 Interesting Experiences in Japan
けい けん

146	物 (thing)	▶ぶつ ぶっ ▷もの	食べ物 (たべもの) food　飲み物 (のみもの) drink 物 (もの) things　買い物 (かいもの) shopping 動物 (どうぶつ) animal　物価 (ぶっか) commodity prices
			(8) ノ 一 十 牛 牛 牛 物 物
147	鳥 (bird)	▶ちょう ▷とり	鳥 (とり) bird; poultry 焼き鳥 (やきとり) grilled chicken　白鳥 (はくちょう) swan
			(11) ノ ィ 宀 户 户 自 鳥 鳥 鳥 鳥 鳥
148	料 (ingredients; fare)	▶りょう	料理 (りょうり) cooking 料金 (りょうきん) charge　授業料 (じゅぎょうりょう) tuition 給料 (きゅうりょう) salary
			(10) ` ` ` ` ` 半 米 米 米 米 料
149	理 (reason)	▶り	料理 (りょうり) cooking 理由 (りゆう) reason　地理 (ちり) geography 無理な (むりな) impossible
			(11) 一 T 王 王 尹 尹 理 理 理 理 理
150	特 (special)	▶とく とっ	特に (とくに) especially 特別な (とくべつな) special　特徴 (とくちょう) characteristic 特急 (とっきゅう) super express
			(10) ノ 一 牛 牛 牛 牜 特 特 特 特
151	安 (cheap; ease)	▶あん ▷やす	安い (やすい) cheap 安全な (あんぜんな) safe　安心 (あんしん) relief 不安な (ふあんな) anxious; worried
			(6) ` ` 宀 宀 安 安
152	飯 (food; cooked rice)	▶はん	ご飯 (ごはん) rice; meal　朝ご飯 (あさごはん) breakfast 昼ご飯 (ひるごはん) lunch 晩ご飯 (ばんごはん) dinner
			(12) ノ ト ヘ 今 今 今 倉 食 飣 飣 飯 飯
153	肉 (meat)	▶にく	肉 (にく) meat 牛肉 (ぎゅうにく) beef　豚肉 (ぶたにく) pork 肉屋 (にくや) meat shop　筋肉 (きんにく) muscle
			(6) 丨 冂 冂 内 肉 肉

154	悪	▸あく ▷わる (bad; wrong)	悪い (わるい) bad 気分が悪い (きぶんがわるい) to feel sick 最悪 (さいあく) the worst　悪魔 (あくま) devil
			⑾ 一 丆 币 币 审 亜 亜 悪 悪 悪
155	体	▸たい ▷からだ (body)	体 (からだ) body 体重 (たいじゅう) body weight 体操 (たいそう) gymnastics; physical exercises
			⑺ ノ イ 仁 什 休 休 体
156	同	▸どう ▷おな (same)	同じ (おなじ) same 同僚 (どうりょう) coworker 同級生 (どうきゅうせい) classmate　同時 (どうじ) same time
			⑹ 丨 冂 冂 同 同 同
157	着	▸ちゃく ▷つ き ぎ (to reach; to wear)	着く (つく) to arrive　着る (きる) to wear 着物 (きもの) kimono　水着 (みずぎ) swimwear 大阪着 (おおさかちゃく) arriving at Osaka
			⑿ 丶 丷 丷 丷 丷 羊 羊 羊 着 着 着 着
158	空	▸くう ▷そら あ から (sky; empty)	空港 (くうこう) airport　空気 (くうき) air 空 (そら) sky　空く (あく) to be vacant 空手 (からて) karate
			⑻ 丶 宀 宀 灾 灾 空 空 空
159	港	▸こう ▷みなと (port; harbor)	空港 (くうこう) airport 神戸港 (こうべこう) Kobe Port　港 (みなと) port 香港 (ホンコン) Hong Kong
			⑿ 丶 氵 氵 汁 浐 浐 浐 洪 洪 港 港
160	昼	▸ちゅう ▷ひる (noon; daytime)	昼 (ひる) noon; daytime　昼ご飯 (ひるごはん) lunch 昼寝 (ひるね) nap　昼休み (ひるやすみ) lunch break 昼食 (ちゅうしょく) lunch
			⑼ 亅 ヨ 尸 尺 尺 尽 昼 昼
161	海	▸かい ▷うみ (sea)	海 (うみ) sea 日本海 (にほんかい) the Japan Sea　海外 (かいがい) overseas 海岸 (かいがん) coast　北海道 (ほっかいどう) Hokkaido
			⑼ 丶 氵 氵 汇 海 海 海 海

(▸ indicates the *on-yomi* [pronunciation originally borrowed from Chinese] and ▷ indicates the *kun-yomi* [native Japanese reading].)

Ⅰ 漢字の練習

A. 次の漢字の読み方 (reading) を覚えましょう。太字 (bold type) は新しい読み方です。

1. 国 （くに）　　　3. **一生** （いっしょう）　5. **時々** （ときどき）

2. **気分** （きぶん）　4. **先月** （せんげつ）　6. **その時** （そのとき）

（☞　国 (058)　分 (052)　生 (054)　時 (015)　々 (133)）

B. 次の漢字を読みましょう。（答 (answer) は下にあります。）

1. 毎日　　　4. 一度　　　7. 勉強する　　10. 思う

2. ある日　　5. 電車　　　8. 時間　　　11. 近く

3. 高い　　　6. 話す　　　9. 買う

Ⅱ 日本のおもしろい経験

■■■ 単　語 ■■■

経験 （けいけん）　experience	13 すっぽん　snapping turtle; terrapin
3 めずらしい　rare	14 かめ　turtle
6 なんでも　anything; everything	16 一生に一度 （いっしょうにいちど）　once in
7 なべ　pot	a lifetime
8 鳥 （とり）　bird; poultry	18 やっぱり　after all
10 ニヤニヤする　to grin [irr. verb]	18 もう〜ない　not any longer
11 不安な （ふあんな）　anxious; worried	

[Ⅰ-B の答] 1. まいにち　　4. いちど　　　7. べんきょうする　10. おもう
　　　　　2. あるひ　　　5. でんしゃ　　8. じかん　　　　11. ちかく
　　　　　3. たかい　　　6. はなす　　　9. かう

A. 質問に答えてください。(Answer the questions.)

1. (1)–(4) は日本の食べ物です。下の a–d のどの写真だと思いますか。

    (1) （　　　　）うめぼし (pickled plums)

    (2) （　　　　）のり (seaweed)

    (3) （　　　　）天ぷら (deep-fried vegetables/seafood)

    (4) （　　　　）焼き鳥 (grilled chicken)

a.

b.

c.

d.

2. 日本料理の中で何が一番好きですか。

B. 留学生のエイミーさんは日本の食べ物について書きました。読みましょう。　🔊 Y13-1

1　　私は日本料理が大好きです。特に天ぷらや焼き鳥が好きです。国で
は日本料理は安くないから、あまり食べられませんでした。今、毎日
食べられるので、とてもうれしいです。日本にはめずらしい食べ物が
たくさんあります。国では、うめぼし、のりなどを見たことも聞いた
5　こともありませんでした。私はめずらしい物に興味があるので、おい
しそうな食べ物は、なんでも食べてみます。

　　ある日、ホストファミリーと晩ご飯を食べに行きました。なべの中
に野菜や肉がたくさんありました。私は「これは何の肉？鳥の肉？」
と聞きました。お父さんは「食べてみて。おいしいから」と言いました。
10　「どう？おいしい？」「はい、とても。でも、何ですか？」みんなはニ
ヤニヤして、何も言いません。私はちょっと不安になりました。でも、
おなかがすいていたし、おいしかったので、たくさん食べました。「ご
ちそうさま」「エイミーさん、実は、これはすっぽんですよ」「すっぽん？」

「すっぽんはかめです」「えっ！……」私は気分が悪くなりました。お
15 父さんはすっぽんは体によくて、高い食べ物だと言っていました。

　これは一生に一度のとてもおもしろい経験でした。国に帰って、友
だちに「かめを食べたことがある」と言えます。かめはおいしかった
です。でも、やっぱり、もうかめを食べたくないです。

C. 文を読んで ○ (= true) か × (= false) を書いてください。

（　　）1. エイミーさんは日本料理は大好きだが、国ではあまり食べなかった。
（　　）2. エイミーさんは、国でうめぼしを食べたことがある。
（　　）3. エイミーさんは、めずらしい食べ物は何も食べられない。
（　　）4. エイミーさんは、ホストファミリーとなべ料理を食べた。
（　　）5. なべの中には鳥の肉があった。
（　　）6. なべ料理はとてもおいしかった。
（　　）7. エイミーさんは、すっぽんはめずらしいから、たくさん食べた。
（　　）8. エイミーさんは、またすっぽんを食べるつもりだ。

Ⅲ 留学生座談会
りゅうがくせいざだんかい

■■■ 単　語 ■■■
たん　　ご

座談会（ざだんかい）	18 ドア　door
round-table discussion	18 自動（じどう）　automatic
7 遅れる（おくれる）　to be late [*ru*-verb]	19 チップ　tip
8 時間通り（じかんどおり）　on time	21 デザート　desert
9 着く（つく）　to arrive（〜に）[*u*-verb]	23 プリン　pudding
11 アナウンス　announcement	27 水着（みずぎ）　swimwear
14 タクシー　taxi	

A. 質問に答えてください。

1. よく電車に乗りますか。

2. あなたの国にコンビニがありますか。コンビニに何をしに行きますか。

B. 留学生座談会でオリバーさん（イギリス人）、アメリアさん（アメリカ人）、ワティさん（インドネシア人）が日本の経験について話しました。p. 280 の記事 (article) を読みましょう。

🔊 Y13-2

C. 質問に答えてください。

1. どうして電車のアナウンスは「すみません」と言いましたか。

2. アメリアさんはどうしてタクシーにびっくりしましたか。

3. ワティさんはコンビニで何を買いますか。

4. オリバーさんはどうして日本のコンビニは "convenient" だと思いましたか。

Ⅳ 書く練習

A. あなたのおもしろい経験を書きましょう。

B. 日本や他の (other) 国・町に行って、何にびっくりしましたか。経験について書きましょう。その後、グループで話しましょう。

留学生座談会

——今日は留学生に日本の経験について聞きたいと思います。三人は同じ大学で勉強しています。みなさん、日本に来て何にびっくりしましたか。

オリバーさん（イギリス）

オリバー　そうですね。電車にびっくりしましたね。イギリスでは電車はよく遅れますが、日本ではいつも時間通りです。先月、電車が三分遅く着いたんです。その時、「すみません」と電車のアナウンスがありました。すごくびっくりしました。

アメリア　私はタクシーにびっくりしました。初めて日本に来て、空港か

らホテルまでタクシーに乗りました。日本のタクシーはすごいですね。ドアが自動だし、チップもいりません。

アメリアさん（アメリカ）

ワティ　私はコンビニにびっくりしました。日本のコンビニにはいろいろなデザートがあります。時々、昼にコンビニでお弁当とデザートを買います。コンビニのプリンを食べたことがありますか。世界で一番おいしいと思います。

オリバー　コンビニは便利ですね。友だちと海に遊びに行ったんですが、友だちが水着を忘れたんです。でも近くのコンビニで水着が買えました。コンビニは本当に "convenient" だと思いました。

ワティさん（インドネシア）

第14課
悩みの相談 Personal Advice Column
なや　　　そう　だん

162	彼 (he)	▷かれ　かの	彼(かれ) he; boyfriend　彼女(かのじょ) she; girlfriend 彼ら(かれら) they　彼氏(かれし) boyfriend
			(8) ノ ク 彳 勹 犭 彷 彷 彼 彼
163	代 (age; replace)	▶だい ▷か	時代(じだい) age; era　電気代(でんきだい) electricity fee 九十年代(きゅうじゅうねんだい) 90's 十代(じゅうだい) in one's teens　代わりに(かわりに) instead
			(5) ノ イ 仁 代 代
164	留 (to stay; to keep)	▶りゅう　る	留学生(りゅうがくせい) international students 留学する(りゅうがくする) to study abroad 留守(るす) absence; not at home
			(10) ノ ヒ ム 卬 卯 卯 留 留 留 留
165	族 (family; tribe)	▶ぞく	家族(かぞく) family 民族(みんぞく) ethnic group　水族館(すいぞくかん) aquarium 王族(おうぞく) member of royalty
			(11) ' 宀 宀 方 ガ ガ 扩 扩 族 族
166	親 (parent; intimacy)	▶しん ▷おや　した	父親(ちちおや) father　親切な(しんせつな) kind 親友(しんゆう) best friend　両親(りょうしん) parents 親しい(したしい) intimate　母親(ははおや) mother
			(16) ' 宀 宀 宀 立 立 辛 辛 辛 亲 亲 亲 亲 親 親 親
167	切 (to cut)	▶せつ ▷き　きっ	親切な(しんせつな) kind　切る(きる) to cut 切符(きっぷ) ticket　切手(きって) postage stamp 大切な(たいせつな) precious
			(4) 一 七 切 切
168	英 (English; excellent)	▶えい	英語(えいご) English language　英国(えいこく) United Kingdom 英会話(えいかいわ) English conversation 英雄(えいゆう) hero
			(8) 一 十 廾 艹 苎 苎 英 英
169	店 (shop)	▶てん ▷みせ	店(みせ) shop 店員(てんいん) store clerk　売店(ばいてん) stall; kiosk 書店(しょてん) bookstore　店長(てんちょう) store manager
			(8) ' 宀 宀 广 庁 庁 店 店

170	去	▶きょ こ ▷さ (past; to leave)	去年(きょねん) last year 過去(かこ) the past 去る(さる) to leave 消去する(しょうきょする) to erase
			(5) 一 十 土 去 去
171	急	▶きゅう ▷いそ (to hurry; emergency)	急に(きゅうに) suddenly 急ぐ(いそぐ) to hurry 急行(きゅうこう) express train 特急(とっきゅう) super express
			(9) ノ ク ⺈ 刍 刍 刍 急 急 急
172	乗	▶じょう ▷の (to ride)	乗る(のる) to ride 乗り物(のりもの) vehicle 乗車(じょうしゃ) riding a car 乗馬(じょうば) horseback riding
			(9) 一 二 三 千 千 垂 垂 乗 乗
173	当	▶とう ▷あ (to hit)	本当に(ほんとうに) really お弁当(おべんとう) boxed lunch 当時(とうじ) at that time 当たる(あたる) to hit
			(6) �١ ⺌ ⺌ 屶 当 当
174	音	▶おん ▷おと ね (sound)	音楽(おんがく) music 発音(はつおん) pronunciation 音(おと) sound 本音(ほんね) real intention
			(9) ⺊ 一 ナ 立 立 咅 音 音 音
175	楽	▶がく がっ らく ▷たの (pleasure)	音楽(おんがく) music 楽しい(たのしい) fun 楽器(がっき) musical instrument 楽な(らくな) easy; comfortable
			(13) ⺊ ⺊ ⺊ 白 白 泊 泊 泊 洎 逌 楽 楽 楽
176	医	▶い (doctor; medicine)	医者(いしゃ) doctor 歯医者(はいしゃ) dentist 医学(いがく) medical science 医院(いいん) clinic
			(7) 一 一 尸 尸 医 医 医
177	者	▶しゃ じゃ ▷もの (person)	医者(いしゃ) doctor 学者(がくしゃ) scholar 読者(どくしゃ) reader 若者(わかもの) young people 忍者(にんじゃ) ninja
			(8) 一 十 土 耂 者 者 者 者

(▶ indicates the *on-yomi* and ▷ indicates the *kun-yomi*.)

I 漢字の練習

A. 次の漢字の読み方 (reading) を覚えましょう。太字 (bold type) は新しい読み方です。

1. **彼女**（かのじょ）　4. **家族**（かぞく）　6. **北海道**（ほっかいどう）

2. **年上**（としうえ）　5. **上手**（じょうず）　7. **三か月後**（さんかげつご）

3. **六年間**（ろくねんかん）　　（☞　女 (038)　家 (096)　上 (026)　手 (116)

　　　　　　　　　　　　　　　　北 (047)　海 (161)　道 (109)）

B. 次の漢字を読みましょう。（答 (answer) は下にあります。）

1. 会社員　3. 言う　5. 学校　7. 買い物　9. 気分

2. 早く　　4. 住む　6. 使う　8. 病気

II 悩みの相談

■■■ 単　語 ■■■

悩み（なやみ）worry

アドバイス　advice

3 時代（じだい）age; era

3 先輩（せんぱい）senior member of a group

4 ～年間（～ねんかん）for . . . years

4 付き合う（つきあう）to date [*u*-verb]

13 愛す（あいす）to love [*u*-verb]

35 父親（ちちおや）father

39 出張（しゅっちょう）business trip

46 本当に（ほんとうに）really

49 場合（ばあい）case

A. 質問に答えてください。(Answer the questions.)

1. あなたは悩みがありますか。だれに相談しますか。

2. あなたの友だちはどんな悩みがありますか。どんなアドバイスをしましたか。

[I-B の答] 1. かいしゃいん　3. いう　　5. がっこう　7. かいもの　9. きぶん
　　　　　2. はやく　　4. すむ　　6. つかう　8. びょうき

B. 悩みの相談を読みましょう。

1 結婚と仕事 🔊 Y14-1

26歳の会社員です。三歳年上の彼がいます。彼は大学時代の先輩で、六年間付き合っています。このごろ、彼は「早く結婚したい」と言っています。彼はやさしいし、仕事もできるし、私も結婚したいと思っています。でも、彼は東京に住んでいて、私は大阪に住んでいます。彼は今の仕事をやめられないと言っています。私もやめたくありません。私が仕事をやめて東京に行ったほうがいいんでしょうか。彼を愛しています。

2 日本語が上手にならない 🔊 Y14-2

カナダ人の留学生です。日本の大学で勉強しています。私の悩みは日本語です。今、日本人のホストファミリーと住んでいます。家族は親切ですが、みんなは私と英語を話したがっています。だから、私は「英語を話さなきゃ」と思って、英語を話します。学校に日本人の友だちがたくさんいますが、みんなの英語は私の日本語より上手です。だから、たいてい英語を使います。買い物の時も「すみません。あのう、これください」と日本語で言いますが、お店の人は「ツーハンドレッドエンね。サンキュー！」と英語で言います。もう六か月も日本にいますが、ぜんぜん日本語が上手になりません。どうしたらいいでしょうか。

3 飛行機がきらい 🔊 Y14-3

私は子供の時から飛行機がきらいです。去年、父親が急に病気になったので、飛行機で北海道に帰らなければいけませんでした。その時、気分が悪くて大変でした。実は、三か月後に会社の出張でブラジルに行くんですが、日本からサンパウロまで27時間ぐらい飛行機に乗っていなければいけません。どうしたらいいでしょうか。アドバイスをお願いします。

アドバイス 🔊 Y14-4

私も飛行機に乗るのが好きじゃないので、あなたの悩みが本当によくわかります。私はよく飛行機の中で、大好きなモーツァルトの音楽を聞きます。でも、あなたの場合はもっと大変そうなので、お医者さんに行って相談してみたらどうですか。

C. 質問に答えてください。
しつもん　こた

1 結婚と仕事
けっこん

　1. この人の彼はどんな人ですか。

　2. どうしてこの人はすぐ彼と結婚しないのですか。
　　　　　　　　　　　　　　　　けっこん

　3. あなたはこの人が仕事をやめて結婚したほうがいいと思いますか。
　　　どうしてですか。

　4. あなたならどうすると思いますか。
　　　(What would you do if you were in a similar situation?)

2 日本語が上手にならない

　1. この人はホストファミリーと日本語で話しますか。どうしてですか。

　2. 日本人の友だちと日本語で話しますか。どうしてですか。

　3. お店の人はどうですか。

　4. あなたも同じ悩みがありますか。
　　　　　　　　なや

3 飛行機がきらい
ひこうき

　1. この人はいつ飛行機に乗りましたか。飛行機はどうでしたか。
　　　　　　　　ひこうき

　2. どうしてブラジルに行きたくないのですか。

　3. あなたはこの人がブラジルに行くと思いますか。

Ⅲ 書く練習
　　　れんしゅう

A. Ⅱ-Bの **1** と **2** の人にアドバイスを書きましょう。

B. Imagine that you are one of the characters in the list below, and write about their problems.

　　留学生　　　お父さん／お母さん　　　日本語の先生　　　猫　　　その他 (other)
　　　　　　　　　　　　　　　　　　　　　　　　　　　ねこ　　　た

第15課 LESSON 15

私が好きな所 My Favorite Place

178	死	▶し ▷し (death; to die)	死ぬ(しぬ) to die 死(し) death　必死(ひっし) desperate 死者(ししゃ) the dead (6) 一 ナ ア 歹 歹 死
179	意	▶い (mind; meaning)	意味(いみ) meaning 注意する(ちゅういする) to watch out 意見(いけん) opinion　用意する(よういする) to prepare (13) ` 一 ナ ウ 立 产 音 音 音 音 意 意 意
180	味	▶み ▷あじ (flavor; taste)	意味(いみ) meaning 趣味(しゅみ) hobby　興味(きょうみ) interest 味噌(みそ) soybean paste　味(あじ) taste (8) l 口 口 口― 口二 咮 咮 味
181	注	▶ちゅう ▷そそ (to pour; to shed)	注意する(ちゅういする) to watch out 注文する(ちゅうもんする) to order 注ぐ(そそぐ) to pour (8) ` ` ` ` ` ` 汁 注 注
182	夏	▶か ▷なつ (summer)	夏(なつ) summer 夏休み(なつやすみ) summer vacation 初夏(しょか) early summer (10) 一 一 一 厂 币 百 百 百 頁 夏 夏
183	魚	▶ぎょ ▷さかな うお (fish)	魚(さかな) fish 魚屋(さかなや) fish shop　金魚(きんぎょ) goldfish 人魚(にんぎょ) mermaid　魚市場(うおいちば) fish market (11) ノ ク ア 内 内 角 角 缶 魚 魚 魚
184	寺	▶じ ▷てら　でら (temple)	お寺(おてら) temple 東寺(とうじ) Toji (the name of a temple) 寺院(じいん) sacred building　禅寺(ぜんでら) Zen temple (6) 一 十 土 土 寺 寺
185	広	▶こう ▷ひろ (spacious; wide)	広い(ひろい) wide; spacious 広場(ひろば) square; open space 広島(ひろしま) Hiroshima　広告(こうこく) advertisement (5) ` 一 广 広 広

186	足 (foot; leg)	▶そく ▷あし　た	足(あし) foot; leg　足りる(たりる) to be sufficient 一足(いっそく) one pair of shoes 水不足(みずぶそく) lack of water
			(7) ⟋ ⼝ ⼞ ⼞ ⼞ ⼞ 足
187	転 (to roll over)	▶てん ▷ころ	自転車(じてんしゃ) bicycle 運転する(うんてんする) to drive　回転ずし(かいてんずし) conveyor belt sushi　転ぶ(ころぶ) to tumble; to fall down
			(11) ⼀ ⼁ ⻗ ⻗ ⾃ ⾃ 車 軒 軒 転 転
188	借 (to borrow)	▶しゃく 　しゃっ ▷か	借りる(かりる) to borrow 借地(しゃくち) rented land　借金(しゃっきん) debt 借家(しゃくや) rented house
			(10) ⼃ ⼁ ⼂ ⼂ ⼂ ⼂ ⼂ 借 借 借
189	走 (to run)	▶そう ▷はし	走る(はしる) to run 走り書き(はしりがき) hasty writing 脱走(だっそう) escape from a prison
			(7) ⼀ ⼗ ⼟ ⼟ ⼟ ⾛ 走
190	場 (place)	▶じょう ▷ば	場所(ばしょ) place 工場(こうじょう) factory　市場(いちば) market 場合(ばあい) case　駐車場(ちゅうしゃじょう) parking lot
			(12) ⼀ ⼗ ⼟ ⼟ ⼟ ⼟ ⼟ ⼟ ⼟ 場 場 場
191	建 (to build)	▶けん ▷たて　た	建物(たてもの) building 建てる(たてる) to build　建つ(たつ) to be built 建国(けんこく) founding a nation
			(9) ⼅ ⼓ ⼐ ⼐ ⼐ 書 建 建 建
192	地 (ground)	▶ち　じ	地下(ちか) underground 地下鉄(ちかてつ) subway　地図(ちず) map 地球(ちきゅう) the earth　地震(じしん) earthquake
			(6) ⼀ ⼗ ⼟ ⼟ ⼟ 地
193	通 (to pass; to commute)	▶つう ▷とお　かよ	通る(とおる) to go through; to pass 通う(かよう) to commute　通学(つうがく) going to school 通勤(つうきん) going to work
			(10) ⼀ ⼂ ⼇ ⼇ ⾅ ⾅ 甬 甬 通 通

(▶ indicates the *on-yomi* and ▷ indicates the *kun-yomi*.)

Ⅰ 漢字の練習
かん じ れんしゅう

A. 次の漢字の読み方 (reading) を覚えましょう。太字 (bold type) は新しい読み方です。
かん じ かた おぼ ふと じ

1. 生まれる （うまれる）
2. 二十万人 （にじゅうまんにん）
3. 一年中 （いちねんじゅう）
4. 楽しむ （たのしむ）
5. 人気 （にんき）
6. 地下 （ちか）

（☞ 生 (054) 中 (028) 下 (027)）

B. 次の漢字を読みましょう。(答 (answer) は下にあります。)
かん じ こたえ

1. 近く
2. 有名
3. 神社
4. 青い
5. 色
6. 赤い
7. 南
8. 今年
9. 今度
10. 古い
11. 売る

Ⅱ 私が好きな所

■■■ 単 語 ■■■
たん ご

1
1 生まれる （うまれる） to be born [*ru*-verb]
1 原爆 （げんばく） atomic bomb
3 落とされる （おとされる） to be dropped
6 残す （のこす） to leave; to preserve [*u*-verb]
6 平和記念資料館 （へいわきねんしりょうかん） Peace Memorial Museum
8 平和 （へいわ） peace
10 島 （しま） island

11 日 （ひ） day
12 緑 （みどり） green
13 鹿 （しか） deer
2
5 南 （みなみ） south
6 一年中 （いちねんじゅう） all year
6 楽しむ （たのしむ） to enjoy [*u*-verb]
9 くじら whale

[Ⅰ-B の答] 1. ちかく 4. あおい 7. みなみ 10. ふるい
こたえ 2. ゆうめい 5. いろ 8. ことし 11. うる
3. じんじゃ 6. あかい 9. こんど

3

3 自然（しぜん）nature

4 紅葉（こうよう）autumn leaves/colors

4 混む（こむ）to get crowded [*u*-verb]

　　混んでいる（こんでいる）to be crowded

7 竹（たけ）bamboo

9 トロッコ列車（トロッコれっしゃ）small train usually for tourists

10 景色（けしき）scenery

4

1 若者（わかもの）young people

1 ファッション　fashion

1 場所（ばしょ）place

4 待ち合わせをする（まちあわせをする）to meet up [irr. verb]

5 主人（しゅじん）head of a family

9 スクランブル交差点（スクランブルこうさてん）scramble crossing

10 渡る（わたる）to cross [*u*-verb]

12 地下（ちか）underground

12 通る（とおる）to go through; to pass [*u*-verb]

A. 質問に答えてください。(Answer the questions.)

1. あなたはどんな所に行ってみたいですか。どうしてですか。

2. (1)–(4) はどんな所ですか。行ったことがありますか。

　　(1) 広島・宮島　　(2) 沖縄　　(3) 京都　　(4) 東京

3. 上の (1)–(4) は右の地図の a–d のどこですか。

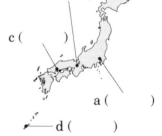

b (　　　)

c (　　　)

a (　　　)

d (　　　)

B. 四人の日本人が好きな所を紹介しています。読みましょう。

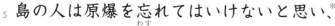

1 **広島と宮島**  Y15-1

　　広島は私が生まれた町です。広島には原爆ドームがあります。1945 年 8 月 6 日、広島に世界で初めて原爆が落とされました。この原爆で二十万人の人が死にました。広

5 島の人は原爆を忘れてはいけないと思い、*原爆ドームを残しました。近くには平和記念資料館があり、原爆につ

---

l. 5　忘れてはいけないと思い

In the written language, sentences can be connected by using either the stem or *te*-form of the verb.

　　原爆を忘れてはいけないと思い、原爆ドームを残しました。

　　＝原爆を忘れてはいけないと思って、原爆ドームを残しました。

宮島
みやじま

いて読んだり、写真を見たりできます。ここに来た人は、平和の意味について考えます。

広島の近くには宮島があります。宮島は小 10 さい島で、有名な神社があります。この神社は海の近くにあるので、天気がいい日は、海の青い色と神社の赤い色、そして山の緑がとてもきれいです。この島には鹿がたくさんいます。鹿はたいていおなかがすいているので、食べ物を持っている人は注意したほうがいいでしょう。

2 沖縄
おきなわ 🔊 Y15-2

1 私は今まで日本のいろいろな所に行きましたが、その中で沖縄が一番好きです。沖縄はエメラルドグリーンの海と白いビーチで有名です。世界のビーチの中で一番きれいだと思 5 います。沖縄は日本の一番南にあって、冬も暖かいです。だから、ゴルフなどのスポーツが一年中楽しめます。

今年の夏、私は沖縄で初めてダイビングをしてみました。海の中にはいろいろな色の魚がたくさん泳いでいて、本当に感動しました。十二月から四月まではくじらが見られるので、今度は冬に行こうと 10 思っています。

3 京都（嵐山・嵯峨野）
きょうと　あらしやま　さがの 🔊 Y15-3

1 京都には古いお寺がたくさんありますが、私がよく行く所は嵐山です。嵐山にはお寺も自然もあります。嵐山は人気があって、紅葉の時は特に混んでいます。

嵐山
あらしやま

5 嵐山の近くに嵯峨野があります。嵯峨野は広いので、足が疲れるかもしれません。歩きたくない人は自転車を

借りたほうがいいでしょう。嵯峨野には竹がたくさんあり、竹で作ったおみやげを売っています。

　嵯峨野からトロッコ列車が走っています。列車から見える山と川の
10 景色はとてもきれいです。

読
L15

④ 東京（渋谷） 🔊 Y15-4

1 　渋谷は若者のファッションで有名な場所で、おしゃれな店やカフェがたくさんあります。私はよく友だちと渋谷に買い物に行きます。駅を出てハチ公の前で友だちと待ち合わせをします。左の写真が犬のハチ公です。ハチ
5 公は死んだ主人を毎日ここで待っていて、有名になりました。ハチ公の話は映画にもなりました。今はたくさんの人がここに来て、ハチ公と写真をとります。

　この建物はSHIBUYA109（イチマルキュー）で、若者に人気がある服を売っています。ハチ公の前からス
10 クランブル交差点を渡ってSHIBUYA109まで歩きます。ここはいつもにぎやかです。雨の日は駅からSHIBUYA109まで地下を通って行けるので便利です。

写真提供：SHIBUYA109エンタテイメント

C. 質問に答えてください。

1. ①を読んで、次の質問に答えましょう。

　　a. 原爆が世界で初めて落とされた所はどこですか。それはいつでしたか。何人の人が死にましたか。

　　b. 平和記念資料館で何ができますか。

　　c. 宮島はどんな所ですか。

　　d. 宮島で食べ物を持っている人は、どうして気をつけなければいけないのですか。

2. ②–④について質問を考えて、となりの人に聞きましょう。
   しつもん かんが

3. あなたは広島・宮島、沖縄、京都、東京の中でどこに一番行ってみたいで
   ひろしま みやじま おきなわ きょうと   いちばん
   すか。そこで何がしてみたいですか。

D. 次の人たちは旅行に行きたがっています。広島・宮島、沖縄、京都、東京の中でどこがい
                              ひろしま みやじま おきなわ きょうと
   いと思いますか。どうしてですか。

自然や動物 (animals) が好きで、人がたくさんいる所がきらいです。
し ぜん どうぶつ

ジョンさん

ハワイで生まれたので、海とスポーツが大好きです。

ケリーさん

日本の若者のファッションに興味があります。
    わかもの   きょう み

ナオミさん

紅葉を見たことがありません。
こうよう

ウデイさん

Ⅲ 書く練習
     れん しゅう

あなたが好きな所を紹介しましょう。
           しょうかい

第16課
まんが「ドラえもん」 The Manga *Doraemon*

194	供	▶きょう ▷ども そな (companion; offer)	子供(こども) child 供える(そなえる) to offer something to a spirit 提供(ていきょう) offer (8) ノ イ 亻 仁 什 世 供 供 供
195	世	▶せ せい ▷よ (world; generation)	世界(せかい) the world　世話(せわ) care 世代(せだい) generation　三世(さんせい) the third generation 世の中(よのなか) society (5) 一 十 卅 廿 世
196	界	▶かい (world)	世界(せかい) the world 視界(しかい) visibility　政界(せいかい) political world 限界(げんかい) limit (9) 丶 口 四 四 甲 尹 昗 界 界
197	全	▶ぜん ▷まった すべ (all)	全部(ぜんぶ) all 安全(あんぜん) safety　全国(ぜんこく) whole country 全く(まったく) entirely　全て(すべて) all (6) ノ 人 合 今 全 全
198	部	▶ぶ へ (part; section)	全部(ぜんぶ) all　部屋(へや) room テニス部(テニスぶ) tennis club 部長(ぶちょう) department manager (11) 丶 亠 亠 立 立 音 音 音 咅 部 部
199	始	▶し ▷はじ (to begin)	始まる(はじまる) (something) begins 始める(はじめる) to begin (something) 始発(しはつ) first train (of the day)　開始(かいし) start (8) く 女 女 女 如 如 始 始
200	週	▶しゅう (week)	毎週(まいしゅう) every week　先週(せんしゅう) last week 一週間(いっしゅうかん) one week 二週目(にしゅうめ) second week　週末(しゅうまつ) weekend (11) 丿 冂 月 冃 円 用 周 周 冂 调 週
201	考	▶こう ▷かんが (to think; idea)	考える(かんがえる) to think 考え(かんがえ) idea　考古学(こうこがく) archaeology 参考(さんこう) reference (6) 一 十 土 耂 考 考

202	開	▶かい / ▷あ ひら / (to open)	開ける（あける）to open (something) 開く（あく）(something) opens　開く（ひらく）to open 開店（かいてん）opening of a store (12) 丨 冂 冂 冂 冂 門 門 門 門 閂 閂 開 開
203	屋	▶おく / ▷や / (shop; house)	部屋（へや）room　本屋（ほんや）bookstore 魚屋（さかなや）fish shop　屋上（おくじょう）rooftop 屋内（おくない）indoor (9) ﾌ 尸 尸 尸 尸 屋 屋 屋 屋
204	方	▶ほう / ▷かた がた / (direction; person)	味方（みかた）ally; person on one's side 読み方（よみかた）way of reading　夕方（ゆうがた）evening 両方（りょうほう）both　方法（ほうほう）method (4) ﾠ 亠 方 方
205	運	▶うん / ▷はこ / (transport; luck)	運動（うんどう）exercise　運転（うんてん）driving 運がいい（うんがいい）lucky　運命（うんめい）fate 運ぶ（はこぶ）to carry (12) 冖 冖 冖 冃 冃 冒 軍 軍 運 運
206	動	▶どう / ▷うご / (to move)	運動（うんどう）exercise 動く（うごく）to move　自動車（じどうしゃ）automobile 動物（どうぶつ）animal　動詞（どうし）verb (11) 冖 冖 冃 冃 冒 車 車 重 動 動
207	教	▶きょう / ▷おし / (to teach)	教える（おしえる）to teach　教室（きょうしつ）classroom 教会（きょうかい）church　キリスト教（キリストきょう）Christianity　教科書（きょうかしょ）textbook (11) 一 十 土 尹 孝 孝 孝 孝 教 教
208	室	▶しつ / (room)	教室（きょうしつ）classroom 研究室（けんきゅうしつ）professor's office　地下室（ちかしつ）basement　待合室（まちあいしつ）waiting room (9) 丷 宀 宀 宊 宊 空 室 室
209	以	▶い / (by means of; compared with)	～以外（～いがい）other than . . . ～以上（～いじょう）. . . or more　～以下（～いか）. . . or less ～以内（～いない）within . . .　以前（いぜん）before; formerly (5) 丨 丬 以 以 以

Ⅰ 漢字の練習
かんじ れんしゅう

A. 次の漢字の読み方を覚えましょう。太字は新しい読み方です。
かんじ おぼ ふとじ

1. 空 （そら）　　2. 小学生 （しょうがくせい）　　3. 出す （だす）

（☞　空 (158)　小 (061)　出 (049)）

B. 次の漢字を読みましょう。（答は下にあります。）
かんじ こたえ

1. 国　　　　　4. 次　　　　　7. 自分

2. 来た　　　　5. 毎週　　　　8. 書く

3. 使う　　　　6. テストの前

Ⅱ まんが「ドラえもん」

■■■ 単　語 ■■■
たん ご

1 空 （そら）　sky

1 飛ぶ （とぶ）　to fly [*u*-verb]

1 違う （ちがう）　to be different [*u*-verb]

3 そんな〜　such . . .

4 未来 （みらい）　future

4 ロボット　robot

5 ひみつ　secret

5 道具 （どうぐ）　tool

5 ポケット　pocket

6 小学生 （しょうがくせい）　elementary
　　school students

7 助ける （たすける）　to help; to rescue [*ru*-verb]

11 〜のようなもの　something like . . .

12 写す （うつす）　to copy [*u*-verb]

17 番組 （ばんぐみ）　broadcast program

17 続く （つづく）　to continue [*u*-verb]

19 例えば （たとえば）　for example

19 どこでも　anywhere

20 すると　. . . Then . . .

24 また　in addition

24 弱い （よわい）　weak

24 味方 （みかた）　person on one's side

29 戻る （もどる）　to return; to go back
　　[*u*-verb]

[Ⅰ-B の答]　1. くに　　　　4. つぎ　　　　　7. じぶん
こたえ　　　2. きた　　　　5. まいしゅう　　8. かく
　　　　　　3. つかう　　　6. テストのまえ

A. 質問に答えてください。
しつもん　こた

　1. あなたはどんなまんがを読んだことがありますか。
　　日本のまんがを知っていますか。

　2. 右の絵は「ドラえもん」です。何だと思いますか。
え
　　「ドラえもん」を見たことがありますか。
　　あなたの国でも「ドラえもん」が見られますか。

© 藤子プロ

B. まんが「ドラえもん」について読みましょう。　🔊 Y16

は人気があるのでしょうか。

　それは、ドラえもんが夢をたくさんくれるからです。例えば、「ど
ゆめ　　　　　　　　　　　　　　　　　　　　　　　たと
こでもドア」。行きたい所を考えて、このドアを開けます。すると、
ドアの向こうにはその場所があるのです。このドアであなたの部屋か
む
らどこでも行きたい所に行けます。あなたもこんな「ひみつ道具」が
どうぐ
あるといいと思いませんか。

　また、ドラえもんは弱い子供の味方です。のび太くんは勉強もあま
よわ　　　　　　　　　　　た
りできないし、けんかも弱いし、運動もできません。でも、ドラえも
んはいつものび太くんを助けてくれます。子供たちはそんなやさしい
た　　たす
ドラえもんが大好きなのです。
だい

　そして、ドラえもんはのび太くんにいろいろなことを教えてくれま
た
す。「アンキパン」の話に戻りましょう。……教室ではテストが始ま
もど
りました。でも、のび太くんは何も覚えていません。のび太くんはテ
おぼ
ストの前に、おなかが痛くなって、トイレに行ったのです。やっぱり
いた
自分で勉強しなければいけないのです。

　ドラえもんのテレビ番組は、シンガポールやベトナムなど、日本以
ばんぐみ
外の国でも見られます。あなたの国にもドラえもんが来るかもしれま
せん。

C. 質問に答えてください。

1. ドラえもんはどこから来ましたか。

2. ドラえもんはポケットの中に何を持っていますか。

3. 「アンキパン」はどんな道具ですか。

4. 「どこでもドア」はどんな道具ですか。

5. のび太くんのテストはどうでしたか。

6. どうして「ドラえもん」は人気がありますか。三つ書いてください。

7. 「ドラえもん」のテレビ番組はどの国で見られますか。

「ドラえもん」

子供の時、「空を飛んでみたい」「違う世界に行ってみたい」と思いませんでしたか。まんが「ドラえもん」の中でそんな夢がかないます。

ドラえもんは未来から来たロボットです。未来のいろいろな便利な「ひみつ道具」をポケットの中に持っていて、小学生ののび太くんが困った時、その道具を使って助けてくれます。

ある日、のび太くんはテストがあるのを忘れて、ぜんぜん勉強しませんでした。困ったのび太くんはドラえもんに言いました。「ドラえもん、助けてよ。次のテストは自分で勉強するから。」ドラえもんはポケットからパンのようなものを出して、のび太くんにあげました。「これは『アンキパン』だよ。覚えられるから。」のび太くんはパンに写して、全部食べました。もうテストは大丈夫です。のび太くんはうれしそうに学校に行きました……。

まんが「ドラえもん」は一九七〇年に雑誌で始まりました。七三年にはテレビ番組になり、今も毎週続いています。どうしてドラえもん

© 藤子プロ

D. In what order did the following events take place? Write a–f in each (   ).

(   ) → (   ) → (   ) → (   ) → (   ) → (   )

a. のび太くんはおなかが痛くなったので、トイレに行った。

b. のび太くんはテストがぜんぜんできなかった。

c. のび太くんは「アンキパン」に覚えたいことを写して、全部食べた。

d. のび太くんはテストがあるのを忘れていた。

e. ドラえもんはポケットから「アンキパン」を出した。

f. のび太くんは困って、ドラえもんに相談した。

E. 次の質問に答えましょう。

1. あなたは「アンキパン」で何を覚えたいですか。

2. あなたはどんな時「どこでもドア」を使いたいですか。

Ⅲ 書く練習

あなたはドラえもんにどんな道具を出してもらいたいですか。それで何をしたいですか。ほしい道具について書きましょう。

第17課

オノ・ヨーコ Yoko Ono

#	漢字	読み	語例	筆順
210	野 (field)	▶や ▷の	分野 (ぶんや) realm; field　小野さん (おのさん) Mr./Ms. Ono　長野 (ながの) Nagano　野球 (やきゅう) baseball　野菜 (やさい) vegetable	(11) 丨 口 日 日 甲 甲 里 野 野 野 野
211	習 (to learn)	▶しゅう ▷なら	習う (ならう) to learn　習字 (しゅうじ) calligraphy　練習 (れんしゅう) practice　習慣 (しゅうかん) habit; custom	(11) 刁 刁 刁 刁 羽 羽 羽 習 習 習 習
212	主 (main; lord)	▶しゅ ▷おも ぬし	主に (おもに) mainly　ご主人 (ごしゅじん) husband　主婦 (しゅふ) housewife　主語 (しゅご) subject of a sentence　持ち主 (もちぬし) owner	(5) 丶 一 十 宇 主
213	歳 (year; age)	▶さい せい	二十五歳 (にじゅうごさい) twenty-five years old　お歳暮 (おせいぼ) year-end gift　二十歳 (はたち) twenty years old	(13) 丿 卜 止 止 产 产 庐 岸 岸 岸 歳 歳 歳
214	集 (to gather)	▶しゅう ▷あつ	集める (あつめる) to collect　特集 (とくしゅう) (magazine) feature　集中する (しゅうちゅうする) to concentrate	(12) 丿 亻 亻 亻 仹 件 隹 隹 隹 集 集 集
215	発 (to start; to reveal)	▶はっ はつ ぱつ	発表する (はっぴょうする) to make public; to give a presentation　発音 (はつおん) pronunciation　出発 (しゅっぱつ) departure　発明 (はつめい) invention	(9) フ ヌ ヌ 癶 癶 癶 癶 癶 発 発
216	表 (to express; surface)	▶ぴょう ひょう ▷あらわ おもて	発表する (はっぴょうする) to make public; to give a presentation　表紙 (ひょうし) cover page　表現 (ひょうげん) expression　表す (あらわす) to express　表 (おもて) the front	(8) 一 十 キ 主 主 表 表 表
217	品 (goods; refinement)	▶ひん ▷じな しな	作品 (さくひん) work (of art, etc.)　上品な (じょうひんな) elegant　手品 (てじな) magic　品物 (しなもの) article of merchandise	(9) 丶 口 口 口 吕 吕 吕 品 品

218	写	▶しゃ ▷うつ (to copy)	写真 (しゃしん) photograph　写す (うつす) to copy 写生 (しゃせい) sketch 描写する (びょうしゃする) to describe
			(5) ⼁ ⼍ ⼍ 写 写
219	真	▶しん ▷ま (true; reality)	写真 (しゃしん) photograph　真ん中 (まんなか) center 〜の真上 (〜のまうえ) right above . . . 真夜中 (まよなか) midnight
			(10) 一 十 ナ 广 市 市 肖 肖 直 真 真
220	字	▶じ (letter; character)	文字 (もじ) letter; character　赤字 (あかじ) deficit 名字 (みょうじ) family name　大文字 (おおもじ) uppercase letters　漢字 (かんじ) Chinese character
			(6) ⼁ ⼍ 宀 宀 字 字
221	活	▶かつ　かっ (lively)	活動 (かつどう) activity　生活 (せいかつ) life; living 活発な (かっぱつな) active　活用 (かつよう) conjugation 活気 (かっき) liveliness
			(9) ⼂ ⼃ 氵 氵 氵 汗 汗 活 活
222	結	▶けっ　けつ ▷むす (to tie; to join)	結婚する (けっこんする) to get married 結果 (けっか) result　結論 (けつろん) conclusion 結ぶ (むすぶ) to tie a knot
			(12) ⼂ ⼂ 纟 纟 纟 糸 糸 紀 紀 結 結 結
223	婚	▶こん (marriage)	結婚する (けっこんする) to get married 離婚 (りこん) divorce　婚約者 (こんやくしゃ) fiancé(e) 新婚 (しんこん) newlywed　未婚 (みこん) unmarried
			(11) 〈 女 女 女 女 妡 妡 妡 婚 婚 婚
224	歩	▶ほ　ぽ ▷ある (to walk)	歩く (あるく) to walk 歩道 (ほどう) sidewalk　散歩する (さんぽする) to stroll 一歩 (いっぽ) one step　進歩 (しんぽ) progress
			(8) ⼁ ⼂ ⼂ 止 止 ⽌ ⽌ 歩

(▶ indicates the *on-yomi* and ▷ indicates the *kun-yomi*.)

Ⅰ 漢字の練習
かんじ　れんしゅう

A. 次の漢字の読み方を覚えましょう。太字は新しい読み方です。
かんじ　　　　　おぼ　　　　　　　ふとじ

1. 作品 （さくひん）　　3. その後 （そのご）　　5. 年代 （ねんだい）

2. 文字 （もじ）　　　4. 二人 （ふたり）　　　6. 何度も （なんども）

（☞　作 (076)　文 (070)　二 (002)　人 (018)）

B. 次の漢字を読みましょう。（答は次のページの下にあります。）
かんじ　　　　　　　　　　　　　こたえ

1. 生まれる　　4. 音楽　　7. 三年後　　10. この年

2. 父親　　　5. 名前　　8. 歌

3. 仕事　　　6. 始める　　9. 作る

Ⅱ オノ・ヨーコ

━■■■ 単　語 ■■■━
　　　　　たん　ご

2 芸術 （げいじゅつ） art

4 主に （おもに） mainly

4 詩 （し） poem

6 俳句 （はいく） haiku

7 数える （かぞえる） to count [*ru*-verb]

8 雲 （くも） cloud

9 名前をつける （なまえをつける） to name [*ru*-verb]

10 完成する （かんせいする） to be completed [irr. verb]

11 展覧会 （てんらんかい） art exhibition

11 作品 （さくひん） work (of art, etc.)

12 天井 （てんじょう） ceiling

12 はしご ladders

12 虫めがね （むしめがね） magnifying glass

16 文字 （もじ） letter; character

19 その後 （そのご） after that

22 1960 年代 （せんきゅうひゃくろくじゅうねんだい） 1960's

23 ～のための for the sake of . . .

26 何度も （なんども） many times

27 影響を受ける （えいきょうをうける） to be affected （～に） [*ru*-verb]

29 主夫 （しゅふ） house husband

31 大ヒット （だいヒット） big hit

32 しかし however

33 銃で撃たれる （じゅうでうたれる） to be shot

35 分野 （ぶんや） field; realm

A. 質問に答えてください。
　　しつもん　　こた

　1. 左の英語は右のカタカナのどれですか。

　　　　a.　Vietnam　　・　　　　　・(1) メンバー

　　　　b.　member　　・　　　　　・(2) ニューヨーク

　　　　c.　grapefruit　・　　　　　・(3) イギリス

　　　　d.　rock band　・　　　　　・(4) ベトナム

　　　　e.　Britain　　　・　　　　　・(5) アルバム

　　　　f.　album　　　・　　　　　・(6) グレープフルーツ

　　　　g.　New York　・　　　　　・(7) ロックバンド

　2. ビートルズを知っていますか。どんなビートルズの歌を知っていますか。

　3. この人はオノ・ヨーコ（小野洋子）です。
　　　　　　　　　　　　　　　ようこ
　　　どんな人だと思いますか。

写真提供：共同通信社

B. オノ・ヨーコ（小野洋子）の伝記 (biography) を読みましょう。 🔊 Y17

1　オノ・ヨーコ（小野洋子）は 1933 年に東京で生まれました。ヨーコの両親は芸術が好きで、ヨーコも子供の時、ピアノを習っていました。ヨーコは 1953 年、父親の仕事で家族とアメリカに行き、ニューヨークの大学に入りました。大学では主に音楽と詩を勉強しました。

5　1964 年、31 歳の時、ヨーコは自分の詩を集めて『グレープフルーツ』を発表します。ヨーコの詩は短くて、俳句みたいです。

数えなさい*
雲を数えて
名前をつけなさい

10　この詩は、読んだ人が雲を数えて名前をつけた時に完成します。

1966 年、イギリスでヨーコの展覧会がありました。その中の作品の一つが「天井の絵」（写真）でした。見に来た人は、はしごの上で虫めがねを使って天井にある絵を見るのです。ある日、一人の髪が長い男が来て、虫めがねで天井の絵を見てみました。そこには小さい "yes" の

15　文字がありました。"yes"――この言葉に、男はとても感動しました。彼の名前はジョン・レノン。有名なロックバンド、ビートルズのメンバーでした。その後、二人はいっしょに音楽活動や芸

20　術活動を始めます。そして、三年後、二人は結婚しました。

「YES オノ・ヨーコ」2003 年 水戸芸術館現代美術ギャラリーでの展示風景
© YOKO ONO
写真提供・協力：朝日新聞社／水戸芸術館現代美術センター／ジャパン・ソサエティ

---

l.7　数えなさい　　*l.9*　名前をつけなさい

The verb stem ＋なさい is a command that has a strong implication. See Lesson 22 for details.

勉強しなさい。　*Study.*　　起きなさい。　*Get up.*

1960 年代、世界はベトナム戦争の中にありました。ヨーコとジョンはいろいろな平和活動をしました。1971 年に、二人は平和のための歌、「ハッピー・クリスマス（戦争は終わった）」を作りました。同じ年、ジョ

25 ンは「イマジン」を発表しました。ヨーコは『グレープフルーツ』の中である言葉を何度も使っています。それが "imagine" です。ジョンはヨーコの詩に影響を受けて、この歌を作ったそうです。1975 年、ヨーコとジョンの間には男の子ショーンが生まれ、ジョンは音楽活動をやめて、主夫になります。

30 1980 年、ジョンはまた音楽活動を始め、ヨーコと一枚のアルバムを発表しました。この中の歌、「スターティング・オーバー」は大ヒットになりました。しかし、この年の 12 月 8 日、ヨーコとジョンがニューヨークの家の前で車を降りて歩いていた時、ジョンは銃で撃たれました。

35 ジョンが死んでからも、オノ・ヨーコは芸術の分野でいろいろな作品を発表し、平和のための活動をしています。

C. オノ・ヨーコ（小野洋子）の年表 (chronology) を作りましょう。

1933 年	オノ・ヨーコ（小野洋子）＿＿＿＿＿＿＿＿＿
＿＿＿＿年	アメリカに行く
1964 年	＿＿＿＿＿＿＿＿＿＿＿＿＿＿＿＿＿
＿＿＿＿年	イギリスで展覧会をする
＿＿＿＿年	ジョン・レノンと結婚する
1971 年	＿＿＿＿＿＿＿＿＿＿＿＿＿＿＿＿＿
1975 年	＿＿＿＿＿＿＿＿＿＿＿＿＿＿＿＿＿
＿＿＿＿年	ジョンとアルバムを発表する
	＿＿＿＿＿＿＿＿＿＿＿＿＿＿＿＿＿

Ⅲ 書く練習

A. 下は「イマジン」の歌詞 (lyrics) です。日本語に訳してみましょう。

Imagine

by John Lennon and Yoko Ono

Imagine there's no heaven
It's easy if you try
No hell below us
Above us only sky
Imagine all the people
Living for today

Words and Music by John Lennon and Yoko Ono
© by LENONO MUSIC
Permission granted by FUJIPACIFIC MUSIC INC.
Authorized for sale in Japan only.

読
L17

B. Imagine that you're 64 years old. Write an essay reflecting on your life so far.

C. 有名人、あなたの家族、友だちについて調べて書きましょう。

第18課　L E S S O N　18
大学生活 College Life

225	目	▶もく ▷め (eye)	目的(もくてき) purpose　　目(め) eyes 目薬(めぐすり) eye drops　　二番目(にばんめ) the second 目上の人(めうえのひと) one's superiors
			(5) 丨　冂　冃　目　目
226	的	▶てき ▷まと (target; -ish)	目的(もくてき) purpose 現代的(げんだいてき) modern　　社会的(しゃかいてき) social 的(まと) target
			(8) ′　亻　亣　自　白　白′　的　的
227	洋	▶よう (ocean; overseas)	洋服(ようふく) (Western) clothes 東洋(とうよう) the East　　洋食(ようしょく) Western food 大西洋(たいせいよう) the Atlantic
			(9) 丶　冫　氵　汀　汫　浐　浐　浐　洋
228	服	▶ふく (clothes)	服(ふく) clothes　　洋服(ようふく) (Western) clothes 制服(せいふく) uniform　　和服(わふく) Japanese clothes
			(8) 刀　刀　月　月　肝　服　服
229	堂	▶どう (hall)	食堂(しょくどう) cafeteria 公会堂(こうかいどう) public hall 堂々とした(どうどうとした) dignified; imposing
			(11) ′　丷　ヅ　ヅ　严　严　严　営　営　堂　堂
230	力	▶りょく　りき ▷ちから (power)	力仕事(ちからしごと) physical labor (such as construction) 協力(きょうりょく) cooperation　　努力(どりょく) endeavor 力士(りきし) sumo wrestler
			(2) フ　力
231	授	▶じゅ ▷さず (to instruct)	授業(じゅぎょう) class 教授(きょうじゅ) professor　　授かる(さずかる) to be given
			(11) ﹁　扌　扌　扌′　扌″　扌″　扌″　扌″　护　抒　授
232	業	▶ぎょう (business; vocation)	授業(じゅぎょう) class 職業(しょくぎょう) occupation　　産業(さんぎょう) industry サービス業(サービスぎょう) service industry
			(13) ′　″　″″　″″　丱　丱　业　业　业　菐　業　業

233	試	▶し ▷こころ (test; to try)	試験(しけん) exam 試合(しあい) game; match　入試(にゅうし) entrance exam 試みる(こころみる) to try ⑬ ` ゛ ⼆ ⼆ ⾔ ⾔ ⾔ ⾔ 訂 訂 訂 試 試
234	験	▶けん (to examine)	試験(しけん) exam 実験(じっけん) experiment　経験(けいけん) experience 受験(じゅけん) taking an examination ⑱ 丨 厂 厂 斤 斤 馬 馬 馬 馬 馭 馭 験 験 験 験 験 験
235	貸	▶たい ▷か (to lend; loan)	貸す(かす) to lend 貸し出し(かしだし) lending 賃貸マンション(ちんたいマンション) rental condo ⑫ ノ イ イ 代 代 代 伐 伐 貸 貸 貸 貸
236	図	▶と　ず ▷はか (drawing; to devise)	図書館(としょかん) library　地図(ちず) map 図(ず) figure　合図(あいず) signal　図る(はかる) to attempt ⑺ 丨 冂 冂 冈 図 図 図
237	館	▶かん (building; hall)	図書館(としょかん) library　旅館(りょかん) Japanese inn 映画館(えいがかん) movie theater 大使館(たいしかん) embassy ⑯ ノ 人 今 今 今 食 食 食 食 館 館 館 館 館 館
238	終	▶しゅう ▷お (end)	終わる(おわる) to come to an end 終わり(おわり) end　終点(しゅうてん) last stop 最終〜(さいしゅう〜) the last . . . ⑪ く 幺 幺 幺 糸 糸 紵 終 終 終
239	宿	▶しゅく ▷やど (inn; to lodge in)	宿題(しゅくだい) homework 下宿(げしゅく) boardinghouse　宿泊(しゅくはく) lodging 宿(やど) inn ⑪ ' ' ⼧ ⼧ 宀 宀 宿 宿 宿 宿 宿
240	題	▶だい (title; topic)	宿題(しゅくだい) homework 問題(もんだい) problem; question 話題(わだい) topic of conversation　題(だい) title ⑱ ⼀ 冂 日 日 旦 早 早 是 是 是 是 題 題 題 題 題 題

読
L18

(▶ indicates the *on-yomi* and ▷ indicates the *kun-yomi*.)

Ⅰ 漢字の練習

A. 次の漢字の読み方を覚えましょう。太字は新しい読み方です。

1. 以上（いじょう）　　5. 入れる（いれる）　　9. 空手（からて）

2. 女子（じょし）　　　6. 毎月（まいつき）　　10. 親しい（したしい）

3. 男子（だんし）　　　7. 食堂（しょくどう）　11. 来週（らいしゅう）

4. 電気代（でんきだい）　8. 三日（みっか）　　　12. 図書館（としょかん）

（☞　子 (060)　男 (039)　入 (072)　月 (019)　食 (042)

三 (003)　日 (016)　空 (158)　親 (166)　書 (093)）

B. 次の漢字を読みましょう。(答は下にあります。)

1. 人気　　　3. 一か月　　　5. 一週間　　　7. 同じ

2. 旅行　　　4. 生活　　　　6. 始まる　　　8. 楽しみ

Ⅱ 大学生のアルバイト

━ ■ ■ ■ 単　語 ■ ■ ■ ━

目的（もくてき）object; purpose
収入（しゅうにゅう）income
〜未満（〜みまん）less than . . .
〜以上（〜いじょう）. . . or more
女子学生（じょしがくせい）female
　　student
男子学生（だんしがくせい）male student

生活のゆとり（せいかつのゆとり）extra
　　money to spare for the cost of living
生活費（せいかつひ）the cost of living
洋服（ようふく）clothes
貯金する（ちょきんする）to deposit
　　money (in a bank) [irr. verb]

[Ⅰ-B の答] 1. にんき　　　3. いっかげつ　　　5. いっしゅうかん　　7. おなじ
　　　　　　2. りょこう　　　4. せいかつ　　　　6. はじまる　　　　8. たのしみ

A. 質問に答えてください。
しつもん　こた

1. あなたはアルバイトをしたことがありますか。
   どんなアルバイトをしましたか／していますか。

2. あなたのアルバイトの目的は何ですか。

3. あなたの国で人気があるアルバイトは何ですか。

B. 日本の大学生のアルバイトについて調べました。下のグラフ (graph) を見て、質問に答え
   しら　　　　　　　　　　　　　　　　　　　　　　　　　　　　　　しつもん　こた
てください。

読
L18

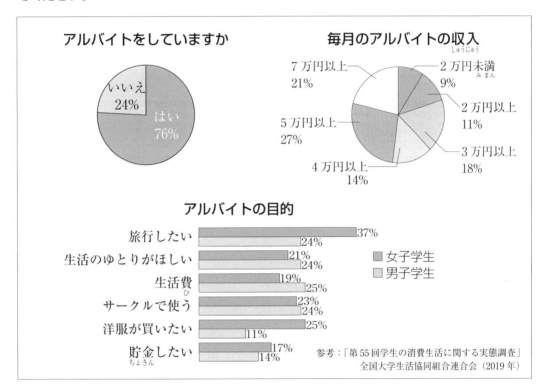

参考：「第55回学生の消費生活に関する実態調査」
全国大学生活協同組合連合会（2019年）

1. アルバイトをしている人としていない人と、どちらのほうが多いですか。
   　　　　　　　　　　　　　　　　　　　　　　　　　　　　　　おお

2. 毎月、アルバイトで5万円以上収入がある人は何パーセントですか。
   　　　　　　　　　　　　　しゅうにゅう

3. 女子学生のアルバイトの目的で一番多いのは何ですか。
   　　　　　　　　　　　　　　　　いちばん

4. 男子学生のアルバイトの目的で一番少ないのは何ですか。

Ⅲ 橋本くんの大学生活
（はし もと）

■■■ 単 語 ■■■
（たん　ご）

2 ワンルームマンション
　studio apartment
4 食費（しょくひ）　cost of food
7 毎月（まいつき）　every month
9 家庭教師（かていきょうし）　tutor

13 引っ越し（ひっこし）　moving
13 力仕事（ちからしごと）　physical labor
　（such as construction）
23 初めは（はじめは）　at first
25 親しい（したしい）　close; intimate

A. ある新聞が大学生の橋本くんの生活を紹介しています。* 🔊 Y18
（はしもと）　　　　　　　（しょうかい）

橋本くんは大学三年生だ。大学の近くのワンルームマンションに住んでいる。家賃は一か月五万円だ。食費、電気代などを入れて、一か月の生活費は、十万円ぐらいだ。毎月、両親が七万円送ってくれる。

今、家庭教師をしたり、大学の食堂でアルバイトをしたりしている。家庭教師は一週間に一回、食堂は三日だ。時々、引っ越しなどの力仕事もする。アルバイトをしながら勉強するのは大変だ。時々遅刻したり、授業をサボったりしてしまう。

橋本くんは空手のサークルに入っている。一週間に三日、練習をする。また、時々サークルのみんなと飲みに行く。

「お酒は好きじゃないから、初めはあまり行きたくなかったんです。でも、そのおかげで、先輩たちと親しくなれたし、今の彼女にも会えたんですよ。」

来週から試験が始まる。同じクラスの友だちにノートを貸してもらって、図書館で勉強するつもりだ。「もっと早く勉強を始めればよかった」と思っている。橋本くんは今、試験が終わってから、サークルのみんなと旅行に行くのを楽しみにしている。

B. 質問に答えてください。
しつもん こた

1. 橋本くんはどんな所に住んでいますか。
はしもと

2. 橋本くんはどんなアルバイトをしていますか。

3. 橋本くんはいい学生だと思いますか。どうしてですか。

4. 橋本くんはサークルの友だちと飲みに行って、どんないいことがありましたか。

5. 橋本くんは今、何をしなければいけませんか。

6. 橋本くんは今、何を楽しみにしていますか。

C. 下は一人で生活している大学生の生活費です。あなたはいくらぐらい使いますか。
ひ
生活費を書きましょう。

	日本の大学生の生活費 ひ	あなたの生活費
食費 しょく ひ	26,390 円	円
家賃・電気代など や ちん	53,930 円	円
本代	1,860 円	円
電車・バス代など	4,070 円	円
電話代	3,550 円	円
その他 (other) た	39,290 円	円
計 (total) けい	129,090 円	円

参考:「第55回学生の消費生活に関する実態調査」
全国大学生活協同組合連合会（2019 年）

---

* Note that this passage is written in short form, which expresses formality rather than casualness, as expected in journalistic and scholarly articles.

D. 次の文を読んで、あなたがすること／そう思うことに○、しないこと／そう思わないことに×を書いてください。

(　) 1. 授業を聞きながら、時々寝てしまう。

(　) 2. 今年、五回以上授業をサボってしまった。

(　) 3. よく朝寝坊をする。

(　) 4. よく友だちに宿題を見せてもらう。

(　) 5. 授業中によく携帯を見てしまう。

(　) 6. よく授業に遅刻する。

(　) 7. やさしい先生のほうがきびしい先生より好きだ。

(　) 8. 試験の後、「もっと勉強すればよかった」とよく思う。

いくつ○がありましたか。

7～8	……とても悪い学生
5～6	……悪い学生
3～4	……普通の (average) 学生
1～2	……いい学生
0	……とてもいい学生

Ⅳ 書く練習

A. Write a newspaper article on the lifestyle of a student, presenting yourself as an example. Refer to yourself in the third person. Use the short forms.

B. 興味があることについてアンケートを作って聞きましょう。
アンケートの後で、わかったことを書きましょう。

第19課 LESSON 19

手紙とメール Letters and E-mails

241	春 (spring)	▶しゅん ▷はる	春(はる) spring 春巻(はるまき) spring roll　春分(しゅんぶん) vernal equinox 青春(せいしゅん) youth
			(9) 一 二 三 声 夫 表 表 春 春
242	秋 (autumn)	▶しゅう ▷あき	秋(あき) autumn 秋学期(あきがっき) fall semester 秋分(しゅうぶん) autumnal equinox
			(9) 一 二 千 千 禾 禾 秒 秒 秋
243	冬 (winter)	▶とう ▷ふゆ	冬(ふゆ) winter　冬休み(ふゆやすみ) winter vacation 暖冬(だんとう) warm winter 春夏秋冬(しゅんかしゅうとう) four seasons
			(5) ノ ク 冬 冬 冬
244	花 (flower)	▶か ▷はな　ばな	花(はな) flower　花見(はなみ) flower viewing 花火(はなび) fireworks　花粉症(かふんしょう) hay fever 生け花(いけばな) flower arrangement
			(7) 一 艹 艹 艹 花 花 花
245	様 (Mr.; Ms.; condition)	▶よう ▷さま	～様(～さま) Mr./Ms. . . . お客様(おきゃくさま) customer (respectful) 皆様(みなさま) everyone　様子(ようす) manner
			(14) 一 十 オ 才 术 栏 栏 栏 栏 様 様 様 様 様
246	不 (negative; non-)	▶ふ　ぶ	不安な(ふあんな) anxious; worried 不景気(ふけいき) recession　不便(ふべん) inconvenience 水不足(みずぶそく) lack of water
			(4) 一 ア オ 不
247	姉 (older sister)	▶し ▷あね　ねえ	姉(あね) older sister　お姉さん(おねえさん) older sister 姉妹(しまい) sisters　姉妹都市(しまいとし) sister city
			(8) く 女 女 女' 女" 娇 姉 姉
248	兄 (older brother)	▶きょう ▷あに　にい	兄(あに) older brother お兄さん(おにいさん) older brother 兄弟(きょうだい) brothers
			(5) 丨 ロ ロ 尸 兄

249 漢	▶かん (China)	漢字(かんじ) Chinese character 漢方薬(かんぽうやく) Chinese herbal medicine 漢和辞典(かんわじてん) kanji dictionary	
		(13) 丶 氵 氵 浐 浐 浐 淓 淓 淓 漢 漢	
250 卒	▶そつ (to graduate)	卒業する(そつぎょうする) to graduate 卒業式(そつぎょうしき) graduation ceremony 大卒(だいそつ) university graduate	
		(8) 丶 亠 广 犬 � 卒 卒 卒	
251 工	▶こう く (craft; construction)	工学(こうがく) engineering 工事(こうじ) construction　工場(こうじょう) factory 大工(だいく) carpenter	
		(3) 一 T 工	
252 研	▶けん ▷と (to polish; study)	研究(けんきゅう) research 研究者(けんきゅうしゃ) researcher　研修(けんしゅう) training 研ぐ(とぐ) to sharpen	
		(9) 一 丆 厂 石 石 石 硏 硏 研	
253 究	▶きゅう ▷きわ (research)	研究(けんきゅう) research 探究(たんきゅう) inquiry 究める(きわめる) to investigate thoroughly	
		(7) 丶 宀 宀 宄 空 究 究	
254 質	▶しつ しち (quality; matter)	質問(しつもん) question 質がいい(しつがいい) good quality　素質(そしつ) aptitude 質屋(しちや) pawn shop	
		(15) 丿 丿 斤 斤 斤 斤 斦 所 所 所 質 質 質 質 質	
255 問	▶もん ▷と (question)	質問(しつもん) question 問題(もんだい) problem; question　訪問(ほうもん) visit 問う(とう) to question	
		(11) 丨 冂 冂 門 門 門 門 門 門 問 問	
256 多	▶た ▷おお (many; much)	多い(おおい) many 多分(たぶん) probably　多くの〜(おおくの〜) many 多数決(たすうけつ) decision by majority	
		(6) 丿 夕 夕 多 多 多	

(▶ indicates the *on-yomi* and ▷ indicates the *kun-yomi*.)

Ⅰ 漢字の練習
れんしゅう

A. 次の漢字の読み方を覚えましょう。太字は新しい読み方です。
おぼ　　　　　　　　　　　ふとじ

1. 世話 （せわ）

2. 不安 （ふあん）

3. 思い出す （おもいだす）

4. 大切 （たいせつ）

5. 友人 （ゆうじん）

6. 大学院 （だいがくいん）

（☞　安 (151)　大 (055)　友 (094)）

B. 次の漢字を読みましょう。（答は下にあります。）
こたえ

1. 手紙	4. 上手	7. 来年	10. 特に
2. さむい日	5. 教える	8. その時	11. 試験
3. 出る	6. 本当に	9. 十日	

[Ⅰ-B の答] 1. てがみ 　 4. じょうず 　 7. らいねん 　 10. とくに
こたえ　　　2. さむいひ 　 5. おしえる 　 8. そのとき 　 11. しけん
　　　　　　3. でる 　　　 6. ほんとうに 　9. とおか

Ⅱ お礼の手紙
れい

━━━ 単　語 ━━━
たん　ご

2 いかが　how (polite expression of どう)	10 思い出す（おもいだす）　to recall [*u*-verb]
4 たつ　(time) pass [*u*-verb]	11 なつかしい　to miss; to long for
5 ～中（～ちゅう）　while . . .	15 それでは　well then
5 たいへん　greatly	15 みな様（みなさま）　everyone (polite
5 お世話になる（おせわになる）　to be in	expression of みなさん)
someone's care（～に）[*u*-verb]	16 大切にする（たいせつにする）　to take
9 しょうぎ　Japanese chess	good care of [irr. verb]

A. 質問に答えてください。
こた

1. あなたはよく手紙やカード (greeting card) を書きますか。どんな時に書きますか。

2. 日本語の手紙はたいてい季節のあいさつ (greeting) で始まります。次の文はど
　 きせつ
の季節ですか。

春　　夏　　秋　　冬

a. 暑い日が続きます。　　　　　　　　　　　　　　（　　　　）
　 あつ　　　つづ
b. 桜 (cherry tree) の花がきれいな季節になりました。（　　　　）
　 さくら　　　　　　　　　　　　　　 きせつ
c. 今年初めて雪が降りました。　　　　　　　　　　（　　　　）
　 　　 はじ　　 ふ
d. 山の紅葉がとてもきれいです。　　　　　　　　　（　　　　）
　 　 こうよう

B. フランス人のジャンさんはホームステイの家族へお礼の手紙を書きました。次のページの
れい
手紙を読みましょう。　🔊 Y19-1

C. 質問に答えてください。
こた

1. ジャンさんはどうしてもっと早く手紙を書かなかったのですか。

2. ジャンさんは何がなつかしいですか。

3. ジャンさんは冬休みに何をしますか。

4. ジャンさんはいつ日本にもどるつもりですか。

小野様

パリではさむい日がつづいていますが、東京はいかがですか。
もっと早く手紙を書こうと思っていたのですが、大学の授業で
いそがしくて、日本を出てから三か月もたってしまいました。
留学中はたいへんお世話になりました。はじめは日本語がわ
からなくて、不安でした。でもお母さんのおかげで、日本語が
上手になりました。日本語や日本の生活についていろいろ教
えてくださってどうもありがとうございました。
お姉さんといっしょにテニスをしたり、お兄さんとしょうぎをした
りしたことを今も思い出します。お父さんが作ってくれたカレーも
なつかしいです。日本に行って本当によかったと思います。
私はこの冬休みに自分で漢字を勉強しようと思っています。
来年大学を卒業したら、もう一度日本にもどるつもりです。その
時、会えるのを楽しみにしています。

それでは、みな様によろしくおったえください。
お体を大切になさってください。

十二月十日

ジャン・ベルナール

Ⅲ マリアさんのメール

■■■ 単 語 ■■■

2 突然（とつぜん）suddenly
3 友人（ゆうじん）friend
3 〜の紹介で（〜のしょうかいで）through the introduction of
5 国際（こくさい）international
7 電気工学（でんきこうがく）electrical engineering
10 受ける（うける）to take (an examination) [ru-verb]

11 〜のために for . . .
13 申し込み（もうしこみ）application
15 もし〜たら if . . .
17 質問（しつもん）question
17 申し訳ありません（もうしわけありません）You have my apologies.
18 どうぞよろしくお願いします（どうぞよろしくおねがいします）Thank you in advance.

A. マリアさんは日本に留学しているパクさんにメールを書きました。次のページのメールを読みましょう。 🔊 Y19-2

B. 下の文を完成してください。

マリアさんは今カリフォルニア大学で＿＿＿＿＿＿＿＿を勉強しています。卒業したら、＿＿＿＿＿＿＿＿＿＿＿＿＿たいと思っています。パクさんは＿＿＿＿＿＿＿＿＿＿＿＿ています。マリアさんは日本の大学院について聞きたいので、パクさんにメールを書きました。メールで質問を三つしました。

1) ＿＿＿＿＿＿＿＿＿＿＿＿＿＿＿＿＿＿＿＿

2) ＿＿＿＿＿＿＿＿＿＿＿＿＿＿＿＿＿＿＿＿

3) ＿＿＿＿＿＿＿＿＿＿＿＿＿＿＿＿＿＿＿＿

From:	Maria Lopez <marial@cali-u.edu>
To:	parks@sakura-u.ac.jp
Subject:	はじめまして

パク・スーマン様

突然のメールで失礼します。私はマリア・ロペスと言います。
友人のモハメッドさんの紹介でメールを書いています。

私は今、カリフォルニア大学の四年生です。
卒業したら、日本の大学院で国際政治を勉強しようと思っています。
私の専攻は政治で、大学では特にアメリカと日本の関係について
勉強しました。パクさんは日本の大学院で電気工学を研究して
いらっしゃると聞きました。
日本の大学院について教えていただけないでしょうか。

大学院に入る前に、日本語の試験を受けなければいけないと
聞きましたが、パクさんは試験のためにどんな勉強を
なさいましたか。

また、日本は生活費が高いそうなので、奨学金の申し込みを
したいのですが、どうしたらいいでしょうか。
もし奨学金がもらえなかったら、アルバイトを探そうと思っています。
留学生がアルバイトを見つけるのはむずかしいでしょうか。

質問が多くなってしまって、申し訳ありません。
お忙しいと思いますが、どうぞよろしくお願いします。

マリア・ロペス
marial@cali-u.edu

読
L19

Ⅳ 書く練習
<ruby>練習<rt>れんしゅう</rt></ruby>

A. お世話になった人にお礼の手紙を書きましょう。
<rt>れい</rt>

B. 好きな日本の有名人にメールを書いて、知りたいことを聞きましょう。

カード / はがきの表現
<rt>ひょうげん</rt>
Useful Expressions for Greeting Cards

1. New Year's Greetings

あけましておめでとうございます。
(Happy New Year)

謹賀新年 (Happy New Year)
きんがしんねん

昨年は大変お世話になりました。
さくねん　たいへん　せわ
(Thank you for all your kind help
during the past year.)

本年もどうぞよろしくお願いいたします。
ほんねん　　　　　　　ねが
(I hope for your continued goodwill
this year.)

2. Summer Greetings

暑中お見舞い申し上げます。 (I hope you are keeping well during the hot weather.)
しょちゅう　みま　もう　あ

3. Sending Congratulations

ご卒業おめでとうございます。 (Congratulations on your graduation.)

ご結婚おめでとうございます。 (Congratulations on your marriage.)

誕生日おめでとう。 (Happy Birthday)
たんじょうび

4. Sending Get-well Cards

早くよくなってください。 (Get well soon.)

第20課 LESSON 20

猫の皿 A Cat's Plate
ねこ

257 皿 (plate)	▷さら　ざら	皿(さら) plate; dish 紙皿(かみざら) paper plate　灰皿(はいざら) ashtray
		(5) 丨 冂 冋 皿 皿
258 声 (voice)	▶せい ▷こえ	声(こえ) voice 音声学(おんせいがく) phonetics 擬声語(ぎせいご) onomatopoeia　声優(せいゆう) voice actor
		(7) 一 十 士 声 声 声 声
259 茶 (tea)	▶ちゃ　さ	お茶(おちゃ) Japanese tea　茶店(ちゃみせ) teahouse 紅茶(こうちゃ) black tea　茶色(ちゃいろ) brown 喫茶店(きっさてん) cafe
		(9) 一 十 艹 ヴ 苁 苶 苶 苶 茶
260 止 (to stop)	▶し ▷と	止まる(とまる) (something) stops 中止する(ちゅうしする) to cancel 禁止する(きんしする) to prohibit
		(4) 丨 ト 止 止
261 枚 (sheet of . . .)	▶まい	一枚(いちまい) one sheet 枚数(まいすう) number of flat things
		(8) 一 十 才 木 朾 朾 枚 枚
262 両 (both)	▶りょう	三両(さんりょう) three *ryoo*　両親(りょうしん) parents 両手(りょうて) both hands　両替(りょうがえ) exchange 両方(りょうほう) both
		(6) 一 厂 冂 両 両 両
263 無 (none)	▶む　ぶ ▷な	無理な(むりな) impossible 無駄な(むだな) wasteful　無料(むりょう) free of charge 無礼な(ぶれいな) rude　無い(ない) there is no . . .
		(12) ノ 上 二 午 午 無 無 無 無 無 無 無
264 払 (to pay)	▷はら　ばら	払う(はらう) to pay 支払い(しはらい) payment　払い戻し(はらいもどし) refund 分割払い(ぶんかつばらい) payment in installments
		(5) 一 寸 才 扗 払

265 心	▶しん ▷こころ (heart; mind)	心(こころ) heart; mind　心配する(しんぱいする) to worry 熱心な(ねっしんな) enthusiastic　安心な(あんしんな) safe 好奇心(こうきしん) curiosity	
		⑷ 丶 心 心 心	
266 笑	▶しょう ▷わら え (to laugh)	笑う(わらう) to laugh 笑顔(えがお) smiling face　微笑む(ほほえむ) to smile 爆笑する(ばくしょうする) to burst into laughter	
		⑽ 丿 ⺮ ⺮ ⺮ ⺮ ⺮ 竺 竺 笑 笑	
267 絶	▶ぜっ ぜつ ▷た (to discontinue)	絶対に(ぜったいに) definitely 絶える(たえる) to die out　絶滅(ぜつめつ) extinction 気絶する(きぜつする) to faint　絶望(ぜつぼう) despair	
		⑿ 乚 幺 幺 糸 糸 糸 糸 紆 紹 絅 絶	
268 対	▶たい つい (opposite)	絶対に(ぜったいに) definitely 反対する(はんたいする) to oppose　日本対中国(にほんたいちゅうごく) Japan versus China　一対(いっつい) a pair	
		⑺ 丶 亠 ナ 文 文 対 対	
269 痛	▶つう ▷いた (pain)	痛い(いたい) painful 痛み止め(いたみどめ) painkiller　頭痛(ずつう) headache 腹痛(ふくつう) stomachache　腰痛(ようつう) lower back pain	
		⑿ 丶 亠 广 广 疒 疒 疒 疒 病 病 痛 痛	
270 最	▶さい ▷もっと (utmost)	最悪(さいあく) the worst　最近(さいきん) recently 最高(さいこう) the best　最新(さいしん) the latest 最後に(さいごに) lastly　最も(もっとも) most	
		⑿ 丶 冂 曰 曰 旦 旱 旱 昻 昂 最 最	
271 続	▶ぞく ▷つづ (to continue)	続ける(つづける) to continue　手続き(てつづき) procedure 相続する(そうぞくする) to inherit 連続ドラマ(れんぞくドラマ) serial TV drama	
		⒀ 乚 幺 幺 糸 糸 糸 紆 紆 紵 紵 続 続	

(▶ indicates the *on-yomi* and ▷ indicates the *kun-yomi*.)

Ⅰ 漢字の練習
れんしゅう

A. 次の漢字の読み方を覚えましょう。太字は新しい読み方です。
おぼ ふとじ

1. 外 （そと）   2. 最悪 （さいあく）   (☞ 外 (057)　悪 (154))

B. 次の漢字を読みましょう。(答は下にあります。)
こたえ

1. 時代	4. 所	7. 歩く	10. 家族
2. 話	5. 物	8. 主人	11. 売れる
3. 一人	6. 入る	9. 知らない	12. 仕事

Ⅱ 猫の皿
ねこ

■ ■ ■ 単　語 ■ ■ ■
たん　ご

落語 （らくご） comic monologue
1 江戸時代 （えどじだい） Edo period
　 (1603−1867)
3 落語家 （らくごか） comic storyteller
4 身ぶり （みぶり） gesture
7 いなか countryside
8 江戸 （えど） former name of Tokyo
8 値段 （ねだん） price
9 茶店 （ちゃみせ） teahouse
10 えさ feed
11 止まる （とまる） to stop [u-verb]
12 両 （りょう） a unit of currency used in the
　　Edo period
12 する to cost [irr. verb]

14 あんなに so; such
15 そうだ！ I have an idea!
15 だます to deceive [u-verb]
17 抱く （だく） to hold something in one's
　　　arm [u-verb]
17 にこにこする to smile [irr. verb]
28 やった！ I did it!
29 心 （こころ） mind; heart
33 絶対に （ぜったいに） definitely; no matter what
33 渡す （わたす） to give; to hand [u-verb]
34 がっかりする to be disappointed [irr. verb]
34 ひっかく to scratch [u-verb]
42 売れる （うれる） to be sold [ru-verb]

[Ⅰ-B の答] 　1. じだい　　　4. ところ　　　7. あるく　　　10. かぞく
こたえ　　　2. はなし　　　5. もの　　　　8. しゅじん　　11. うれる
　　　　　3. ひとり　　　6. はいる　　　9. しらない　　12. しごと

A. 質問に答えてください。

1. これは日本です。何年ぐらい前だと思いますか。

広重／東都大伝馬街繁栄之図（東京都立中央図書館特別文庫室所蔵）

2. この人は何をしていると思いますか。

写真提供：アフロ

B. 落語「猫の皿」を読みましょう。 🔊 Y20

1　落語は今から三百年以上前の江戸時代に始まりました。この時代に
たくさんの人の前でおもしろい話をして、お金をもらう人がいました。
このおもしろい話を落語と言い、落語をする人を落語家と言います。
落語家は一人でいろいろな声や身ぶりを使って、おもしろい話をしま
5　す。今でも落語はとても人気があります。
　　江戸時代の落語の一つ、「猫の皿」を読んでみましょう。

　　ある所に、一人の男がいました。男はいなかに行って古い物を買い、
江戸でそれを高い値段で売っていました。
　　ある日、男は川の近くにある茶店に入りました。男は茶店でお茶を
10　飲みながら、外を見ていました。その時、猫が歩いてきて、えさが入っ
た皿の前で止まりました。男はびっくりしました。その皿はとてもめ
ずらしい物で、一枚三百両もする皿だったのです。
　　男は思いました。
　　「茶店の主人はあの皿がいくらか知らないんだ。だからあんなに高い
15　物を猫の皿に使っているんだ。そうだ！　主人をだまして、あの皿をい
ただこう！」
　　男は猫を抱き、にこにこしながら主人に言いました。
　　「かわいい猫だね。私は猫が大好きなんだ。前に猫を飼っていたけど、
どこかに行っちゃって……。ご主人、この猫くれないか。」
20　「無理でございます。この猫は私の家
族みたいで、とてもかわいいんです。」
と主人は言いました。
　　「じゃあ、三両払うから、どうだ？」
　　三両というお金はとても大きいお金
25　です。

「わかりました。猫をさしあげましょう。」茶店の主人はうれしそうに言いました。

「やった！」

男は心の中で笑いました。そして主人に三両払って、言いました。

30　「この猫の皿もいっしょに持っていくよ。」

「それはさしあげられません。」主人は言いました。

「どうして。こんなきたない皿。いいだろう。」

男は何度も頼みましたが、主人は絶対に皿を渡しませんでした。

男はがっかりしました。その時、猫が男をひっかきました。

35　「痛い！ 何だ、この猫！ こんな猫、いらないよ！」

皿はもらえないし、猫はひっかくし、最悪です。男は主人に聞いてみました。

「どうしてその皿を渡したくないんだ。」

「これはとてもめずらしい皿で、一枚三百両もいたします。家に置く

40 とあぶないので、こちらに持ってきたんです。」

主人は話を続けました。

「それに、ここに皿を置いておくと、時々猫が三両で売れるんですよ。」

C. 質問に答えてください。

1. 男はどんな仕事をしていましたか。

2. 茶店にあった皿の値段はいくらですか。

3. どうして男は猫をほしがったのですか。

4. 男はいくらで猫を買いましたか。

5. 男は皿を持って帰りましたか。

6. どうして主人は皿を茶店に置いておくのですか。

7. 茶店の主人と、男と、どちらがかしこい (clever) ですか。

Ⅲ 書く練習
れんしゅう

A. 下のまんがを見て、話を考えて書きましょう。

(1)   (2)   (3)

B. あなたが知っているおもしろい話や楽しい話を書きましょう。

読
L20

第21課

LESSON 21

厄年 Unlucky Ages
やく どし

272	信 (to trust; to believe)	▶しん	信じる(しんじる) to believe 自信(じしん) confidence　信号(しんごう) traffic signal 迷信(めいしん) superstition
			(9) ノ イ イ 伫 伫 信 信 信 信
273	経 (to pass through)	▶けい	経験(けいけん) experience　経済(けいざい) economy 神経質(しんけいしつ) oversensitive　経営学(けいえいがく) management studies　パリ経由(パリけいゆ) via Paris
			(11) く 幺 幺 糸 糸 糸 紀 叙 叙 経 経 経
274	台 (stand)	▶たい　だい	台風(たいふう) typhoon 二台(にだい) two vehicles/machines/etc. 舞台(ぶたい) stage　台所(だいどころ) kitchen
			(5) ム ム 台 台 台
275	風 (wind)	▶ふう　ふ ▷かぜ	台風(たいふう) typhoon お風呂(おふろ) bath　和風(わふう) Japanese style 風(かぜ) wind　風邪をひく(かぜをひく) to catch a cold
			(9) ノ 几 凡 凡 凡 凨 風 風 風
276	犬 (dog)	▶けん ▷いぬ	犬(いぬ) dog 子犬(こいぬ) puppy　番犬(ばんけん) watchdog 盲導犬(もうどうけん) seeing-eye dog
			(4) 一 ナ 大 犬
277	重 (heavy; to pile up)	▶じゅう ちょう ▷おも　かさ	重い(おもい) heavy; serious (illness) 重ねる(かさねる) to pile up　体重(たいじゅう) body weight 貴重品(きちょうひん) valuables
			(9) ノ 一 千 斤 斤 盲 重 重 重
278	初 (first)	▶しょ ▷はじ　はつ	初めは(はじめは) at first　初めて(はじめて) first time 最初(さいしょ) first　初雪(はつゆき) first snow 初恋(はつこい) first love
			(7) ` ラ ネ ネ ネ 初 初
279	若 (young)	▷わか	若い(わかい) young 若者(わかもの) young people 若々しい(わかわかしい) youthful
			(8) 一 十 サ サ 芋 芋 若 若

280	送 (to send)	▶そう ▷おく	送る(おくる) to send　送金(そうきん) sending money 送料(そうりょう) postage　放送(ほうそう) broadcast 回送電車(かいそうでんしゃ) out-of-service train
			(9)　丶　丷　屮　ユ　关　关　送　送
281	幸 (happiness)	▶こう ▷しあわ 　さいわ	幸せな(しあわせな) happy 幸福な(こうふくな) happy　幸運(こううん) good fortune 不幸(ふこう) misfortune　幸い(さいわい) fortunately
			(8)　一　十　土　士　幸　幸　幸　幸
282	計 (to measure)	▶けい ▷はか	時計(とけい) watch; clock 計画(けいかく) plan　合計(ごうけい) sum 計る(はかる) to measure
			(9)　丶　二　亠　言　言　言　計
283	遅 (late)	▶ち ▷おく　おそ	遅れる(おくれる) to be late　乗り遅れる(のりおくれる) to miss (transportation)　遅い(おそい) late 遅刻する(ちこくする) to be late
			(12)　フ　コ　尸　尸　尸　戸　屖　屖　犀　犀　遅　遅
284	配 (to deliver)	▶ぱい　はい ▷くば	心配な(しんぱいな) worried about 配る(くばる) to distribute　配達(はいたつ) delivery 宅配便(たくはいびん) home delivery service
			(10)　一　冂　冂　西　西　酉　酉　配′　配
285	弟 (younger brother)	▶だい　で ▷おとうと	弟(おとうと) younger brother　兄弟(きょうだい) brothers 弟子(でし) apprentice
			(7)　丶　丷　丷　弟　弟　弟
286	妹 (younger sister)	▶まい ▷いもうと	妹(いもうと) younger sister 姉妹(しまい) sisters　姉妹校(しまいこう) sister school
			(8)　く　タ　女　女　好　妹　妹　妹

(▶ indicates the *on-yomi* and ▷ indicates the *kun-yomi*.)

読
L21

Ⅰ 漢字の練習
れんしゅう

A. 次の漢字の読み方を覚えましょう。太字は新しい読み方です。
　　　　　　　　　　　おぼ　　　　　　　　ふとじ

1. 入院（にゅういん）　　3. 時計（とけい）　　5. 心配（しんぱい）

2. 食事（しょくじ）　　　4. 通う（かよう）

（☞　入 (072)　事 (078)　時 (015)　通 (193)　心 (265)）

B. 次の漢字を読みましょう。（答は下にあります。）
　　　　　　　　　　　　　　　　こたえ

1. 悪い　　　　4. 二十五歳　　　7. 去年　　　10. 部屋

2. 起こる　　　5. 病気　　　　　8. 親　　　　11. 自転車

3. 昔　　　　　6. 長い間　　　　9. 乗る　　　12. 写真

Ⅱ 厄　年
やく　どし

── ■·■ 単　語 ■·■ ──
　　　　　　　　　たん　ご

迷信（めいしん）　superstition

起こる（おこる）　to occur; to happen
　　[*u*-verb]

1 多くの〜（おおくの〜）　many . . .

4 ただの〜　nothing more than . . .

7 入院する（にゅういんする）　to be
　　hospitalized [irr. verb]

9 占い（うらない）　fortune-telling

9 気にする（きにする）　to worry [irr. verb]

11 長い間（ながいあいだ）　long time

12 一生懸命（いっしょうけんめい）　very hard

16 ぜいたくをする　to indulge in luxury
　　[irr. verb]

17 めったに〜ない　seldom

17 食事（しょくじ）　meal

21 ところが　however; on the contrary

27 楽しみ（たのしみ）　pleasure

28 通う（かよう）　to commute to（〜に）
　　[*u*-verb]

30 不便な（ふべんな）　inconvenient

35 心配な（しんぱいな）　worried about

36 お守り（おまもり）　charm (against evils);
　　amulet

A. 質問に答えてください。

1. あなたの国にはどんな迷信がありますか。

   例 (example)：黒い猫を見ると、悪いことが起こります。

2. 今までに悪いことがたくさん起こった時がありましたか。

   その時どうしましたか。

B. 厄年の話を読みましょう。 🔊 Y21

> 厄年(やくどし) Critical or unlucky ages. According to Japanese folk belief, at certain ages an individual is most likely to experience calamities or misfortunes. It is customary in these unlucky years to visit temples and shrines to pray for better fortune.

1　「厄年」という言葉を聞いたことがありますか。昔から多くの日本人は、厄年に悪いことがよく起こると信じています。男の人の厄年は二十五歳と四十二歳と六十一歳、女の人の厄年は十九歳と三十三歳と三十七歳です。これはただの迷信だと言う人もいますが、厄年に大変なことを経験する人も多いそうです。ある友だちは台風で家が壊れて
5　しまいました。ある友だちは飼っていた犬に死なれました。また、ある友だちは急に重い病気になって入院しなければいけませんでした。

　私は今年が厄年です。友だちは気をつけたほうがいいと言いましたが、私は占いや迷信が大きらいなので、初めはぜんぜん気にしていま
10　せんでした。でも……

　私は今、オーストラリアで勉強しています。外国で勉強するのは長い間の夢でした。日本で大学を卒業してから、一生懸命仕事をしてお金をためました。そして、去年ここに来ました。

　ここには若い日本人の留学生がたくさんいます。みんな親にお金を
15　送ってもらって、いいアパートに住んで、いい車に乗っています。休

読
L21

みには、いろいろな所に旅行に行ったりしています。私はそんなぜい
たくができません。安いアパートに住んで、めったに外で食事をした
り、旅行に行ったりしません。でも、夢がかなったので、毎日がとて
も幸せでした。ほかの日本人をうらやましいと思ったことはありませ
20 んでした。

　ところが、きのう大変なことがありました。アパートに帰った時、
ドアのかぎが壊され、部屋がめちゃくちゃになっていたのです。びっ
くりして何が起こったのかわかりませんでした。でも、すぐ「どろぼ
うに入られた。」と気がつきました。

25　いろいろな物を取られました。パソコン、カメラ、時計、そして自
転車も。ネットで日本の家族と話したり、ビデオを見たりするのは、
私の楽しみでした。カメラにはオーストラリアで初めて行った旅行の
写真が入っていました。自転車は、学校に通う時使っていました。今
日からバスで通わなければいけません。バスはよく遅れるし、一時間
30 に一台しか来ないから、とても不便です。

　「どうしてどろぼうは私のアパートに入ったんだろう。どうしてお
金持ちの日本人のアパートに入らなかったんだろう。」と思ってしま
いました。日本人の友だちに話したら、「厄年だから、やっぱり悪い
ことが起こったんだよ。」と言われました。

35　今、とても心配です。また悪いことが起こるかもしれません。今度、
弟か妹にお守りを送ってもらおうと思います。みなさんは厄年を信じ
ますか。

C. 質問に答えてください。
こた

1. 厄年にこの人の友だちはどんなことを経験しましたか。
   やくどし

   (1) _____

   (2) _____

   (3) _____

2. この人はオーストラリアに行く前、厄年を信じていましたか。

3. この人の夢は何でしたか。
   ゆめ

4. この人と若い日本人の留学生は、どんなところが違いますか。
   ちが

5. きのう何がありましたか。

6. 何を取られましたか。
   と

7. 今日からどうやって学校に通いますか。

8. 友だちはどうして悪いことが起こったと思っていますか。

9. この人は今、厄年を信じていますか。

Ⅲ 書く練習
れんしゅう

あなたの悪い経験について書きましょう。

第22課

桜さんの日記 Sakura's Diary
さくら

287	記	▶き (to write down)	日記 (にっき) diary 記入する (きにゅうする) to fill in　記事 (きじ) (news) article 暗記する (あんきする) to memorize
			(10) ` ⼀ ⼆ ⼆ ⾔ ⾔ ⾔ 訂 訂 記
288	銀	▶ぎん (silver)	銀行 (ぎんこう) bank 銀メダル (ぎんメダル) silver medal 銀世界 (ぎんせかい) land covered with snow
			(14) ノ ⼈ ⼂ ⼆ ⾦ ⾦ ⾦ 釒 釘 釘 釦 鋃 銀
289	回	▶かい ▷まわ (. . . times; to turn)	一回 (いっかい) one time 回送バス (かいそうバス) out-of-service bus　最終回 (さいしゅうかい) last inning; last episode　回す (まわす) to turn
			(6) ⼁ ⼞ ⼞ ⼞ 回 回
290	夕	▷ゆう (evening)	夕方 (ゆうがた) evening 夕食 (ゆうしょく) dinner　七夕 (たなばた) Tanabata 夕日 (ゆうひ) setting sun　夕刊 (ゆうかん) evening newspaper
			(3) ノ ⼣ 夕
291	黒	▶こく ▷くろ (black)	黒木さん (くろきさん) Mr./Ms. Kuroki　黒い (くろい) black 白黒写真 (しろくろしゃしん) black and white photograph 黒板 (こくばん) blackboard
			(11) ⼂ ⼞ ⽥ ⽇ 甲 甲 里 黒 黒 黒 黒
292	用	▶よう (task; to use)	用事 (ようじ) a thing to take care of 用意する (よういする) to prepare 子供用 (こどもよう) for children　費用 (ひよう) cost
			(5) ノ ⼏ ⽉ ⽉ 用
293	末	▶まつ ▷すえ (the end of)	週末 (しゅうまつ) weekend 月末 (げつまつ) end of the month　年末 (ねんまつ) year-end 期末試験 (きまつしけん) final examination　末 (すえ) the end
			(5) ⼀ ⼆ キ 末 末
294	待	▶たい ▷ま　まち (to wait)	待つ (まつ) to wait 待合室 (まちあいしつ) waiting room 期待する (きたいする) to expect　招待 (しょうたい) invitation
			(9) ノ ⼣ ⼻ ⼻ 待 待 待 待 待

295	残	▶ざん ▷のこ (to remain)	残業(ざんぎょう) overtime work　残す(のこす) to leave 残念(ざんねん) regrettable　心残り(こころのこり) regret 残高(ざんだか) account balance
			(10) 一 フ 万 歹 歹 歺 歼 残 残 残
296	駅	▶えき (station)	駅(えき) station　東京駅(とうきょうえき) Tokyo Station 駅員(えきいん) station attendant 駅前(えきまえ) near/in front of the station
			(14) ｜ 厂 厂 丌 г г 馬 馬 馬 馬 馬 馰 馿 駅
297	番	▶ばん (order; number)	一番(いちばん) the first 番号(ばんごう) number　番組(ばんぐみ) TV program 交番(こうばん) police box　順番(じゅんばん) turn; order
			(12) ノ ^ ^ 厂 平 平 平 来 乑 番 番 番
298	説	▶せつ　せっ (theory; to explain)	説明する(せつめいする) to explain　小説(しょうせつ) novel 小説家(しょうせつか) novelist 説教する(せっきょうする) to preach
			(14) ` ^ 宀 言 言 言 言 訂 訂 訪 説 訪 説
299	案	▶あん (idea; proposal)	案内する(あんないする) to guide 案内所(あんないじょ) information desk 案(あん) idea; proposal　提案(ていあん) proposal
			(10) ` ' '' 宀 它 安 安 安 案 案
300	内	▶ない ▷うち (inside; inner)	案内する(あんないする) to guide 家内(かない) my wife　国内(こくない) domestic 内科(ないか) internal medicine　内側(うちがわ) inside
			(4) ｜ 冂 内 内
301	忘	▶ぼう ▷わす (to forget)	忘れる(わすれる) to forget 忘れ物(わすれもの) lost article 忘年会(ぼうねんかい) year-end party
			(7) ` 亠 亡 忘 忘 忘 忘
302	守	▶す　しゅ ▷まも (to keep; to protect)	守る(まもる) to keep (a promise) 留守(るす) absence; not at home　お守り(おまもり) charm 守衛(しゅえい) security guard
			(6) ` ' '' 宀 宁 守 守

読
L22

(▶ indicates the *on-yomi* and ▷ indicates the *kun-yomi*.)

Ⅰ 漢字の練習
れんしゅう

A. 次の漢字の読み方を覚えましょう。太字は新しい読み方です。
おぼ　　　　　　　　　　　　　ふとじ

1. 日記 （にっき）

4. 説明 （せつめい）

2. 夕方 （ゆうがた）

5. 代わりに （かわりに）

3. 親友 （しんゆう）

6. 二日間 （ふつかかん）

（☞　日 (016)　方 (204)　明 (120)　代 (163)　二 (002)）

B. 次の漢字を読みましょう。（答は下にあります。）
こたえ

1. 彼女　　　3. 一か月　　　5. 後は　　　7. 本当に

2. 東京　　　4. 急に　　　6. 夜　　　8. 先週

Ⅱ 桜さんの日記
さくら

■■■ 単　語 ■■■
たん　ご

5 うらやましがる　(somebody is) envious

8 相変わらず （あいかわらず）　as usual

11 タイプ　type

13 うまく　well; successfully; skillfully
　　うまくいく　to go well [u-verb]

17 メッセージ　message

20 待ち遠しい （まちどおしい）　to wait
　　eagerly for . . . （～が）

23 なんだか　somehow

24 しかたがない　cannot be helped

25 ホーム　platform

25 楽しそうに （たのしそうに）　joyfully

27 親友 （しんゆう）　best friend

33 勇気 （ゆうき）　courage

33 逃げる （にげる）　to run away; to escape
　　　　　　　　　[ru-verb]

35 代わりに （かわりに）　instead

35 二日間 （ふつかかん）　for two days

[Ⅰ-B の答]　1. かのじょ　　　3. いっかげつ　　　5. あとは　　　7. ほんとうに
こたえ
　　　　　　2. とうきょう　　　4. きゅうに　　　6. よる　　　8. せんしゅう

A. 質問に答えてください。
_{こた}

1. あなたは日記を書きますか。日記にどんなことを書きますか。

2. 彼や彼女がいない時、友だちにだれか紹介してもらったことがありますか。
_{しょうかい}

B. 桜さんの日記を読みましょう。 🔊 Y22
_{さくら}

1 <u>三月二十一日（日）</u>

　涼に会いに東京に行った。彼が東京の銀行に就職してからもう二
_{りょう}　　　　　　　　　　　　　　　　　　　　　　_{しゅうしょく}
年がたつ。大学の時は毎日会っていたのに、今は私が東京に行ったり、
彼が大阪に来たりして、一か月に一回ぐらいしか会えない。夏菜はい
_{おおさか}　　　　　　　　　　　　　　　　　　　　　　　　　　_{か な}
5 つも私たちのことをうらやましがっているけど、東京まで会いに行く
のは大変。早く大阪に帰ってきてほしい。
_{たいへん}

<u>四月二十三日（金）</u>

　今日は涼が大阪に来て、夕方お酒を飲みに行った。涼は相変わらず
_{りょう}　_{おおさか}　　　　　_{さけ}　　　　　　　　　　_{あい か}
仕事が忙しそうだ。涼の同僚の黒木さんが彼女を探していると聞い
_{いそが}　　　　　_{どうりょう}　　　　　　　　　　_{さが}
10 た。東京に行った時、涼に紹介してもらったけど、すごくおもしろく
_{しょうかい}
ていい人だ。黒木さんは夏菜のように静かな人がタイプかもしれない。
_{か な}　　_{しず}
今度二人を会わせようと思う。夏菜が東京に行った時、涼が黒木さん
を紹介する予定。うまくいくといいけど。
_{よ てい}

<u>五月十二日（水）</u>

15 　今日の夏菜はちょっと変だった。東京のことを聞いてみたが、あま
_{か な}　　　　　　_{へん}
り話してくれなかった。黒木さんに急に用事ができて、会えなかった
と言っただけで、後は話したくなさそうだった。夜、涼にメッセージ
_{りょう}
を送ったけど、返事がなかった。涼ならいろいろ教えてくれると思っ
_{へん じ}
たのに、残念。仕事が忙しいんだろう。でも、週末は大阪で会える。
_{ざんねん}　　_{いそが}　　　　　　　　　　　　_{おおさか}
20 今から待ち遠しい。
_{どお}

読
L22

五月十四日(金)

　今日も残業で疲れた。それに「急に出張が入って大阪に行けなくなった」という涼のメッセージが携帯に入っていた。なんだか落ち込んでしまった。仕事だからしかたがないけど。

25　　帰る時、駅のホームで夏菜を見た。男の人と一緒に楽しそうに話していた。顔は見えなかったけど、背が高い男の人だった。彼氏ができたのかな。どうして私に言ってくれないんだろう。一番の親友なのに。

五月二十二日(土)

　今日涼から手紙が来た。……

30　桜へ
　　桜に手紙を書くのは本当にひさしぶりだね。ぼくは桜にうそをついていた。ずっと言わなきゃいけないと思っていたんだけど、勇気がなくて今まで逃げていた。うまく説明できるといいんだけど……。夏菜さんが東京に来た時、黒木は急に用事ができて、来られなくなってしまった。それで、ぼくが代わりに二
35　日間東京を案内してあげたんだ。美術館に行ったり、東京ディズニーランドに行ったりして、楽しかった。彼女が大阪に帰った後も、彼女のことが忘れられなかった。先週の週末、「出張で大阪に行けない」と言ったけど、本当は大阪で夏菜さんに
40　会っていたんだ。約束を守れなくてごめん。

C. 正しいものに○をつけてください。

（　　　　）1. 涼は今、東京に住んでいる。

（　　　　）2. いつも涼と桜は東京で会っていた。

（　　　　）3. 涼と黒木は同じ銀行で働いている。

（　　　　）4. 夏菜は東京で黒木に会った。

（　　　　）5. 涼は出張に行っていたから、桜に会えなかった。

D. 質問に答えてください。

1. 桜が夏菜に東京のことを聞いた時、夏菜はどうしてあまり話したがらなかったのですか。

2. 涼は桜にどんなうそをつきましたか。どうしてうそをついたのですか。

3. あなたが涼／桜／夏菜だったら、どうしますか。

Ⅲ 書く練習

読
L22

A. 二か月後の桜さんの日記を書きましょう。

B. 自分の日記を書きましょう。

第23課

顔文字と絵文字 Emoticons and Emoji
え

303	顔 (face)	▶がん ▷かお　がお	顔(かお) face　顔文字(かおもじ) emoticon 顔色(かおいろ) complexion　笑顔(えがお) smiling face 洗顔(せんがん) washing one's face
			⒅ ` 一 十 立 立 产 产 彦 彦 彦 彦 彦 節 節 顔 顔 顔 顔 顔
304	悲 (sad)	▶ひ ▷かな	悲しい(かなしい) sad 悲劇(ひげき) tragedy　悲惨な(ひさんな) miserable 悲しむ(かなしむ) to grieve
			⑿)] ヲ ヲ 非 非 非 非 非 悲 悲 悲
305	怒 (to get angry)	▶ど ▷おこ　いか	怒る(おこる) to get angry 怒り(いかり) anger; rage 喜怒哀楽(きどあいらく) human emotions
			⑼ く タ タ 女 奴 奴 怒 怒 怒
306	違 (to differ)	▶い ▷ちが	違う(ちがう) different　違い(ちがい) difference 間違える(まちがえる) to make a mistake 違法(いほう) illegal　違反(いはん) violation
			⒀ ` ヰ 五 产 告 告 肯 章 章 韋 韋 違 違
307	変 (change; abnormal)	▶へん ▷か	変な(へんな) strange　大変な(たいへんな) tough 変化(へんか) change　変人(へんじん) eccentric person 変える(かえる) to change (something)
			⑼ ` 一 亠 方 亦 亦 亦 変 変
308	比 (to compare)	▶ひ ▷くら	比べる(くらべる) to compare 比較(ひかく) comparison　比例(ひれい) proportion 対比(たいひ) contrast　比喩(ひゆ) figure of speech
			⑷ 一 上 比 比
309	情 (emotion; condition)	▶じょう ▷なさ	表情(ひょうじょう) expression　同情する(どうじょうする) to sympathize　友情(ゆうじょう) friendship 情報(じょうほう) information　情け(なさけ) mercy
			⑾ ` ` 忄 忄 忄 忰 忰 情 情 情 情
310	感 (to sense; to feel)	▶かん	感情(かんじょう) emotion　感動する(かんどうする) to be moved 感じる(かんじる) to feel　感謝(かんしゃ) gratitude 感想(かんそう) impression
			⒀) 厂 厂 厂 厄 咸 咸 咸 咸 咸 感 感 感

311	調	▶ちょう ▷しら (to investigate)	調査(ちょうさ) survey; research　調べる(しらべる) to look into 調子(ちょうし) condition 強調する(きょうちょうする) to emphasize
			⒂ ` ⸁ ⸑ ⸒ ⸓ 言 言 訁 訇 訊 調 調 調 調

312	査	▶さ (to inspect)	調査(ちょうさ) survey; research 検査(けんさ) inspection　審査(しんさ) screening 捜査(そうさ) criminal investigation
			⑼ 一 十 オ 木 木 杳 杳 杳 査

313	果	▶か ▷は (fruit; result)	結果(けっか) result　果物(くだもの) fruit 果汁(かじゅう) fruit juice　効果(こうか) effect 使い果たす(つかいはたす) to use up
			⑻ 丶 口 日 日 旦 甲 甲 果

314	化	▶か　け ▷ば (to change into)	文化(ぶんか) culture 化学(かがく) chemistry　同化(どうか) assimilation お化け(おばけ) goblin; ghost　化粧(けしょう) makeup
			⑷ ノ イ イ 化

315	横	▶おう ▷よこ (sideways)	横(よこ) side　横書き(よこがき) horizontal writing 横綱(よこづな) grand champion of sumo 横断する(おうだんする) to traverse
			⒂ 一 十 オ 木 杧 杧 栌 槛 槛 槠 横 横 横 横

316	相	▶しょう　そう ▷あい (mutual)	相手(あいて) partner 首相(しゅしょう) prime minister　相談(そうだん) consultation 相互の(そうごの) mutual
			⑼ 一 十 オ 木 机 机 相 相 相

317	答	▶とう ▷こた　こたえ (answer)	答える(こたえる) to answer　答え/答(こたえ) answer 回答(かいとう) reply; answer 正答(せいとう) correct answer
			⑿ ノ ⺮ ⺮ ⺮ 竺 竺 竺 答 答 答 答 答

読
L23

(▶ indicates the *on-yomi* and ▷ indicates the *kun-yomi*.)

Ⅰ 漢字の練習
<ruby>れんしゅう</ruby>

A. 次の漢字の読み方を覚えましょう。太字は新しい読み方です。
<ruby>おぼ</ruby> <ruby>ふとじ</ruby>

1. 表す（あらわす）　　3. 世界中（せかいじゅう）　　5. 口（くち）

2. 一方（いっぽう）　　4. 使い方（つかいかた）

（☞　表 (216)　方 (204)　口 (048)）

B. 次の漢字を読みましょう。（答は下にあります。）

1. 文字	4. 自分	7. 以外	10. 生まれる
2. 多くの	5. 以上	8. 意味	11. 家族
3. 気持ち	6. 生活	9. 考える	12. 今度

Ⅱ 顔文字と絵文字
<ruby>え</ruby>

■■■単　語■■■
<ruby>たん</ruby> <ruby>ご</ruby>

1 顔文字（かおもじ）　emoticon	23 世界中（せかいじゅう）　all over the world
1 絵文字（えもじ）　emoji	31 縦（たて）　vertical
2 SNS（エスエヌエス）　social media	31 横（よこ）　side; horizontal
11 表す（あらわす）　to express; to show [*u*-verb]	34 ことわざ　proverb
11 このように　like this; this way	34 ～は…という意味（いみ）だ　～ means that . . .
15 記号（きごう）　symbol	41 答え（こたえ）　answer
18 一方（いっぽう）　on the otherhand	47 あいさつ　greetings
18 表情（ひょうじょう）　expression	47 キスをする　to kiss [irr. verb]
19 感情（かんじょう）　feeling; emotion	

[Ⅰ-Bの答]
<ruby>こたえ</ruby>

1. もじ	4. じぶん	7. いがい	10. うまれる
2. おおくの	5. いじょう	8. いみ	11. かぞく
3. きもち	6. せいかつ	9. かんがえる	12. こんど

A. 質問に答えてください。

1. 下のものを見たことがありますか。どこで見ましたか。

(1) から (4) はどんな意味ですか。

(1) 😃　　　(2) 😷　　　(3) (>_<)　　　(4) ¯_(ツ)_/¯

2. あなたも使いますか。どうして使いますか。だれに使いますか。

B. 次の話を読みましょう。　🔊 Y23

「顔文字と絵文字」

今、多くの人がメールやSNSなどのメッセージで顔文字と絵文字を使っています。みなさんも顔文字や絵文字があるメールをもらったり、使ったりしたことがあるでしょう。下のメッセージを見てみましょう。

> (1) クラスが休講！ ＼(^o^)／
> (2) クラスが休講！ (@_@)
> (3) クラスが休講！😢
> (4) クラスが休講！😠

(1)と(2)は顔文字、(3)と(4)は絵文字です。(1)はクラスが休講になって「うれしい」、(2)は「びっくりした」、(3)は「悲しい」、そして(4)は「怒っている」という気持ちを表しています。このように顔文字と絵文字を使えば、自分の気持ちを簡単に伝えられます。では、顔文字と絵文字はどんな違いがあるのでしょうか。

顔文字は、1万以上あると言われています。顔文字を使って、いろいろな気持ちが伝えられます。でも、顔文字は文字や記号で作られているので、変なものもたくさんあり、もらった人は意味がわからない時もあります。例えば、「ヾ(*ΦωΦ)ノ」はどんな意味かわかりますか。

読
L23

一方、絵文字は顔文字と比べて表情はとてもわかりやすいです。例えば、😂という絵文字を見たら、「うれしくて泣いている」という感情がすぐわかります。また、絵文字には、食べ物やスポーツなど生活を表すものがたくさんあります。感情以外にいろいろなことが表せて便利です。

ところで、絵文字は、日本で作られたものです。知っていましたか。今、「emoji」という言葉は、「Karaoke」のように世界中で使われています。最近の調査の結果によると、絵文字のほうが顔文字より多く使われているそうです。

このように顔文字と絵文字は違いますが、言葉や文化によって使い方や意味の違いも見られます。まず、日本語と英語の顔文字を比べてみましょう。

| （日本語） | (^_^) | (>_<) | (@_@) |
| （英語） | :-D | :-< | :-O |

日本語の顔文字は顔が縦になっていますが、英語の顔文字は横になっています。また、日本語では目で表情を表すものが多いですが、英語では口で表情を表すものが多いです。日本には「目は口ほどに物を言う」ということわざがあります。これは「何も言わなくても、相手の目を見れば、何を考えているかわかる」という意味です。だから、日本ではこのような顔文字が生まれたのかもしれません。

次に絵文字を見てみましょう。下の二つの絵文字🙏の意味は同じでしょうか。

遅くなる。🙏
Hope you get better. 🙏

答えがわかりますか。日本語の文では、🙏は「お願いします」「ごめんなさい」という意味ですが、英語の文では「お祈りします」という意味で使われています。このように同じ絵文字でも文化によって意味が変わる場合があります。

45　また、キスを表す絵文字😗は、フランスやスペインなどでは、自分の家族や友だちに「さようなら」の意味でよく使うそうです。フランスやスペインではあいさつにキスをするからです。でも、日本ではあいさつにキスをしません。日本人が、外国人から「It was nice meeting you again. 😗」のようなメッセージをもらったら、「この人は私が好き？」と思うか
50　もしれません。

　今度、SNS で顔文字や絵文字を見たら、考えてみましょう。「これを使った人はどんな人？」「どんな気持ちを伝えたい？」文字だけでは表せない気持ちがもっとわかるかもしれません。

C. 質問に答えてください。

1. どうして顔文字や絵文字を使いますか。

2. 調査によると、顔文字と絵文字とどちらのほうがよく使われますか。

3. 絵文字はどこで生まれましたか。

4. 日本語と英語の顔文字の違いは何ですか。二つ書いてください。

5. 🙏という絵文字は、日本ではどんな意味ですか。

D. 下の顔文字／絵文字はどんな文に使いますか。文を書いてみましょう。

[Example] 彼女にふられちゃった (T＿T)

1. _____ ＼(^^)／

2. _____ m(＿)m

3. _____ (-_-;)

4. _____ 😱

5. _____ 🙏

6. _____ 💪

Ⅲ 書く練習

日本人の友だち／日本語のクラスメイト (classmate) に、メッセージを書いて送りましょう。
メッセージに三つ以上の顔文字か絵文字を使ってください。
メッセージをもらったら、返事を書きましょう。

みなさん『げんき』で日本語を勉強してくれて
ありがとう。m(＿)m 🙏 😂

これからも日本語の勉強、がんばってください。(^_^)/~~ 👋 😘

げんき著者

巻末
かん まつ
Appendix

文法さくいん Grammar Index
ぶんぽう

単語さくいん1 Vocabulary Index (J-E)

会……会話・文法編
　　　（Conversation and Grammar section）
読……読み書き編
　　　（Reading and Writing section）
G……あいさつ（Greetings）
(e)……Useful Expressions
Ⅰ・Ⅱ・Ⅲ……問題番号（読み書き編）
　　　　（number of exercise in the
　　　　Reading and Writing section）
[u] u-verb　[ru] ru-verb　[irr.] irregular verb

あ

あいかわらず　相変わらず　as usual
　　　読L22-II
あいさつ　greetings　読L23-II
あいす　愛す　to love [u]　読L14-II
アイスクリーム　ice cream　会L3
あいだ　間　between　会L4
あいて　相手　partner; the other person
　　　会L22
アイロンをかける　to iron (clothes) [ru]
　　　会L16
あう　会う　to meet; to see (a person) [u]
　　　会L4
アウトドア　outdoor activities　読L11-II
あおい　青い　blue　会L9, 会L9(e)
あおしんごう　青信号　green light
　　　会L9(e)
あかい　赤い　red　会L9, 会L9(e)
あかちゃん　赤ちゃん　baby　会L17
あかるい　明るい　bright　会L18
あかるい　明るい　cheerful　読L11-II
あき　秋　fall　会L10
あきらめる　to give up [ru]　会L14
あく　開く　(something) opens [u]　会L18
あける　開ける　to open (something) [ru]
　　　会L6
あげる　to give (to others) [ru]　会L14
あさ　朝　morning　会L3
あさごはん　朝ご飯　breakfast　会L3
あさって　the day after tomorrow
　　　会L4(e), 会L8
あさねぼうする　朝寝坊する　to
　　　oversleep [irr.]　会L16
あし　足　leg; foot　会L7(e), 会L12
アジアけんきゅう　アジア研究　Asian
　　　studies　会L1
あした　明日　tomorrow　会L3, 会L4(e)
あずけいれ　預け入れ　deposit
　　　会L13(e)
あそこ　over there　会L2

あそぶ　遊ぶ　to play; to spend time
　　　pleasantly [u]　会L6
あたたかい　暖かい　warm　会L10
あたま　頭　head　会L7(e)
あたまがいい　頭がいい　bright; smart;
　　　clever　会L7
あたらしい　新しい　new　会L5
あちら　that way (polite)　会L20
あつい　熱い　hot (thing)　会L5
あつい　暑い　hot (weather)　会L5
あつめる　集める　to collect [ru]　会L16
あと　後　the rest　会L18
（〜の）あと　後　after (an event)
　　　読L8-II, 会L11
あとで　後で　later on　会L6
アドバイス　advice　読L14-II
アナウンス　announcement　読L13-III
あなた　you　会L4
あに　兄　(my) older brother　会L7
アニメ　animation　会L20
あね　姉　(my) older sister　会L7
あの　that . . . (over there)　会L2
あのう　um . . .　会L1
アパート　apartment; smaller apartment
　　　building　会L13
あぶない　危ない　dangerous　会L17
アプリ　application　会L13
アボカド　avocado　会L8(e)
あまい　甘い　sweet　会L12
あまのがわ　天の川　the Milky Way
　　　読L12-II
あまり + negative　not much　会L3
あむ　編む　to knit [u]　会L13
あめ　雨　rain　会L8
あめがやむ　雨がやむ　the rain stops [u]
　　　会L23
アメリカ　U.S.A.　会L1
あやまる　謝る　to apologize [u]　会L18
あらう　洗う　to wash [u]　会L8
あらわす　表す　to express; to show [u]
　　　読L23-II
ありがとう　Thank you.　会G
ありがとうございます　Thank you.
　　　(polite)　会G
ある　there is . . . [u]　会L4
ある〜　one . . .　読L12-II
あるいて　歩いて　on foot　会L10
あるく　歩く　to walk [u]　会L12
アルバイト　part-time job　会L4
あれ　that one (over there)　会L2
アレルギー　allergy　会L8(e), 会L12
アンケート　questionnaire　読L8-II

あんしょうばんごう　暗証番号
　　　personal identification number　会L13(e)
あんぜん (な)　安全　safe　会L21
あんないする　案内する　to show
　　　(someone) around [irr.]　読L9-II, 会L16
あんなに　so; such　読L20-II

い

いい　good　会L3
いいえ　No.; Not at all.　会G
いいこ　いい子　good child　会L9
いいこと　good deed　読L10-II
いう　言う　to say [u]　会L8
いう (もんくを)　言う (文句を)　to
　　　complain [u]　会L8
いう (わるぐちを)　言う (悪口を)　to
　　　talk behind someone's back [u]　会L23
いえ　家　home; house　会L3
〜いがい　〜以外　other than . . .　会L16
いかが　how (polite expression of どう)
　　　読L19-II
〜いき　〜行き　bound for . . .　会L10(e)
イギリス　Britain　会L1, 会L2
いく　行く　to go [u]　会L3
いくら　how much　会L2
いじめる　to bully [ru]　会L21
いしゃ　医者　doctor　会L1, 会L10
〜いじょう　〜以上　. . . or more
　　　読L18-II
いじわる (な)　意地悪　mean-spirited
　　　会L9
いす　chair　会L2(e), 会L4
いそがしい　忙しい　busy (people/days)
　　　会L5
いそぐ　急ぐ　to hurry [u]　会L6
いたい　痛い　hurt; painful　会L12
いたす　致す　extra-modest expression
　　　for する [u]　会L20
いただきます　Thank you for the meal.
　　　(before eating)　会G
いただく　頂く　extra-modest expression
　　　for たべる and のむ [u]　会L20
いただく　頂く　humble expression for
　　　もらう [u]　会L20
いたみどめ　痛み止め　painkiller
　　　会L12(e)
イタリア　Italy　読L6-III
いちがつ　一月　January　会L4(e)
いちご　strawberry　会L8(e)
いちごうしゃ　一号車　Car No. 1
　　　会L10(e)
いちじ　一時　one o'clock　会L1, 会L1(e)

おくる　送る　to send [u]　会L14

おくる　送る　to walk/drive (someone) [u]　会L19

おくれる　遅れる　to become late [ru]　読L13-III, 会L19

おこさん　お子さん　(your/someone's) child (polite)　会L19

おこす　起こす　to wake (someone) up [u]　会L16

おこる　起こる　to occur; to happen [u]　読L21-II

おこる　怒る　to get angry [u]　読L12-II, 会L19

おごる　to treat (someone) to a meal [u]　会L16

おさきにしつれいします　お先に失礼します　See you. (lit., I'm leaving ahead of you.)　会L18

おさけ　お酒　sake; alcoholic drink　会L3

おさら　お皿　plate; dish　会L14

おじいさん　grandfather; old man　会L7

おしえる　教える　to teach; to instruct [ru]　会L6

おじさん　uncle; middle-aged man　会L14

おじぞうさん　guardian deity of children　読L10-II

おしゃれ（な）　fashionable; stylish　会L14

おしょうがつ　お正月　New Year's　読L10-II, 会L11

おじょうさん　お嬢さん　(someone's) daughter (polite)　会L22

おしり　お尻　buttocks　会L7(e)

おしろ　お城　castle　読L5-II

おす　押す　to press; to push [u]　会L18

おせわになる　お世話になる　to be in someone's care [u]　読L19-II, 会L23

おそい　遅い　slow; late　会L10

おそく　遅く　(do something) late　読L4-III, 会L8

おそくなる　遅くなる　to be late [u]　会L8

おだいじに　お大事に　Get well soon.　会L12

おたく　お宅　(someone's) home/house　会L20

おちこむ　落ち込む　to get depressed [u]　会L16

おちゃ　お茶　green tea　会L3

おちる　落ちる　(something) drops [ru]　会L18

おつかれさま（でした）　お疲れ様（でした）　You must be tired after working so hard. (greeting between friends and coworkers)　会L18

おっしゃる　honorific expression for いう [u]　会L19

おてあらい　お手洗い　restroom　会L12

おてら　お寺　temple　会L4

おと　音　sound　会L20

おとうさん　お父さん　father　会L1, 会L2

おとうと　弟　younger brother　会L1, 会L7

おとこのひと　男の人　man　読L5-II, 会L7

おとされる　落とされる　to be dropped　読L15-II

おとす　落とす　to drop (something) [u]　会L18

おととい　the day before yesterday　会L4(e), 会L19

おととし　the year before last　会L4(e)

おとな　大人　adult　読L12-II, 会L13

おどる　踊る　to dance [u]　会L9

おなか　stomach　会L7(e), 会L12

おなかがすく　to become hungry [u]　会L11

おなかをこわす　to have a stomachache [u]　会L23

おなじ　同じ　same　会L12

おにいさん　お兄さん　older brother　会L1, 会L7

おにぎり　rice ball　会L20

おねえさん　お姉さん　older sister　会L1, 会L7

おねがいします（～を）　. . . , please.　会L2

おねがいする　お願いする　to request help [irr.]　会L22

おばあさん　grandmother; old woman　会L7

おばさん　aunt; middle-aged woman　会L14

おはよう　Good morning.　会G

おはようございます　Good morning. (polite)　会G

おひきだし　お引き出し　withdrawal　会L13(e)

おふりこみ　お振込　bank transfer　会L13(e)

おふろ　お風呂　bath　会L8

おふろにはいる　お風呂に入る　to take a bath [u]　会L8

おへんじ　お返事　reply　読L11-II

おべんとう　お弁当　boxed lunch　会L9

おぼえる　覚える　to memorize [ru]　会L9

おまつり　お祭り　festival　会L11

おまもり　お守り　charm (against evils); amulet　読L21-II

おまんじゅう　sweet bun　読L4-III

おみやげ　お土産　souvenir　会L5

おめでとうございます　Congratulations!　会L17

おもい　重い　heavy; serious (illness)　会L20

おもいだす　思い出す　to recall [u]　読L19-II

おもいで　思い出　memory　会L23

おもう　思う　to think [u]　会L8

おもしろい　面白い　interesting; funny　会L5

おもち　rice cake　読L10-II

おもちゃ　toy　会L11

おもに　主に　mainly　読L17-II

おや　親　parent　会L16

おやすみ（なさい）　Good night.　会G

おやすみになる　お休みになる　honorific expression for ねる [u]　会L19

おゆ　お湯　hot water　会L17

おゆがわく　お湯が沸く　water boils [u]　会L18

おゆをわかす　お湯を沸かす　to boil water [u]　会L17

およぐ　泳ぐ　to swim [u]　会L5

おりる　降りる　to get off [ru]　会L6

おる　extra-modest expression for いる [u]　会L20

おれい　お礼　expression of gratitude　会L19

オレンジ　orange　会L9(e)

おろす　下ろす　to withdraw (money) [u]　会L15

おわる　終わる　(something) ends [u]　会L9

おんがく　音楽　music　会L3

おんせん　温泉　spa; hot spring　会L11

おんなのひと　女の人　woman　読L5-II, 会L7

か

か　蚊　mosquito　会L21

～か～　or　会L10

～が　. . . , but　読L5-II, 会L7

カーテン　curtain　会L2(e), 会L18

～かい　～回　. . . times　会L13

～かい　～階　. . . th floor　会L20

かいがいりょこう　海外旅行　trip to a foreign country　会L23

かいぎ　会議　business meeting; conference　会L21

がいこく　外国　foreign country　会L11

がいこくご　外国語　foreign language　会L13

がいこくじん　外国人　foreigner　会L15

かいさつ　改札　gate　会L10(e)

かいしゃ　会社　company　会L7

かいしゃいん　会社員　office worker　会L1, 会L8

かいだん　階段　stairs　会L10(e), 会L23
かいもの　買い物　shopping　会L4
かう　買う　to buy [u]　会L4
かう　飼う　to own (a pet) [u]　会L11
かえす　返す　to return (a thing) [u]　会L6
かえる　帰る　to go back; to return [u]
　　会L3
かお　顔　face　会L7(e), 会L10
かおがあおい　顔が青い　to look pale
　　会L9(e)
かおもじ　顔文字　emoticon　読L23-II
～かおをする　～顔をする　to look . . .
　(facial expression) [irr.]　会L23
かかりのもの　係の者　our person in
　charge　会L20
かかる　to take (amount of time/money)
　[u]　会L10
かぎ　鍵　lock; key　会L17
かぎをかける　鍵をかける　to lock [ru]
　　会L17
かく　書く　to write [u]　会L4
かく　描く　to draw; to paint [u]　会L15
かぐ　家具　furniture　会L15
がくせい　学生　student　会L1
がくわり　学割　student discount　会L10(e)
～かげつ　～か月　for . . . months　会L10
かける　to sit down [ru]　会L19
かける（アイロンを）　to iron (clothes)
　[ru]　会L16
かける（かぎを）　かける（鍵を）　to lock
　[ru]　会L17
かける（パーマを）　to have one's hair
　permed [ru]　会L17(e)
かける（めがねを）　かける（眼鏡を）　to
　put on (glasses) [ru]　会L7
かさ　bamboo hat　読L10-II
かさ　傘　umbrella　会L2
かし　菓子　snack; sweets　会L11
かじ　火事　fire　会L17
かじ　家事　housework　会L22
かしこまりました　Certainly.　会L20
かしゅ　歌手　singer　会L11
かす　貸す　to lend [u]　会L16
かぜ　風　wind　会L22
かぜ　風邪　cold　会L12
かぜがふく　風が吹く　the wind blows
　[u]　会L22
かぜをひく　風邪をひく　to catch a cold
　[u]　会L12
かぞえる　数える　to count [ru]　読L17-II
かぞく　家族　family　会L7
ガソリン　gasoline　会L21
かた　肩　shoulder　会L7(e)
かたいいいかた　かたい言い方
　bookish expression　会L11(e)

かたづける　片付ける　to tidy up [ru]
　　会L18
かたみち　片道　one way　会L10(e)
かつ　勝つ　to win [u]　会L22
がっかりする　to be disappointed [irr.]
　　読L20-II, 会L23
がっき　楽器　musical instrument　会L13
かっこ　parenthesis　会L11(e)
かっこいい　good-looking　会L5
がっこう　学校　school　会L3
カット　cut　会L17(e)
かつどう　活動　activity　会L15
かていきょうし　家庭教師　tutor
　　読L18-III
かど　角　corner　会L6(e), 会L20
～かな（あ）　I wonder . . . (casual)　会L17
かなう　to be realized [u]　読L12-II
かなしい　悲しい　sad　読L10-II, 会L13
カナダ　Canada　会L1
かね　金　money　会L6
かねもち　金持ち　rich person　会L10
かのじょ　彼女　she; girlfriend　会L12
かばん　bag　会L2
カフェ　cafe　会L3
かぶき　歌舞伎　Kabuki; traditional
　Japanese theatrical art　会L9
かぶせる　to put (a hat) on a person's head
　[ru]　読L10-II
かぶる　to put on (a hat) [u]　会L7
かふんしょう　花粉症　hay fever
　　会L12(e)
がまんする　我慢する　to be tolerant/
　patient [irr.]　会L23
かみ　髪　hair　会L7, 会L7(e)
かみ　紙　paper　会L17
かみがた　髪形　hairstyle　会L17(e)
かみさま　神様　God　読L12-II, 会L22
かみをとかす　髪をとかす　to comb
　one's hair [u]　会L17
かめ　turtle　読L13-II
カメラ　camera　会L8
かよう　通う　to commute to [u]
　　読L21-II
かようび　火曜日　Tuesday　会L4, 会L4(e)
～から　from . . .　読L7-II, 会L9
カラー　hair coloring　会L17(e)
からい　辛い　hot and spicy; salty　会L13
カラオケ　karaoke　会L8
からだ　体　body　会L13
からだにきをつける　体に気をつける
　to take care of oneself [ru]　読L7-II
からて　空手　karate　会L13
かりる　借りる　to borrow [ru]　会L6
かる　刈る　to crop [u]　会L17(e)
かるい　軽い　light　会L20

かれ　彼　he; boyfriend　会L12
カレー　curry　会L13
かれし　彼氏　boyfriend　会L12
かわ　川　river　会L11
かわいい　cute　会L7
かわいそう（な）　pitiful; feel sorry for;
　poor thing　読L12-II, 会L23
かわりに　代わりに　instead　読L22-II
がんか　眼科　ophthalmologist　会L12(e)
かんがえる　考える　to think (about); to
　consider [ru]　会L18
かんきょう　環境　environment　会L21
かんこうする　観光する　to do
　sightseeing [irr.]　会L15
かんこく　韓国　Korea　会L1, 会L2
かんごし　看護師　nurse　会L1, 会L11
かんじ　漢字　kanji; Chinese character
　　会L6
かんじょう　感情　feeling; emotion
　　読L23-II
かんせいする　完成する　to be
　completed [irr.]　読L17-II
かんたん（な）　簡単　easy; simple　会L10
かんどうする　感動する　to be moved/
　touched (by . . .) [irr.]　会L13
カンニングする　to cheat in an exam [irr.]
　　会L23
かんぱい　乾杯　Cheers! (a toast)　会L8
がんばる　頑張る　to do one's best; to try
　hard [u]　会L13

き　木　tree　会L22
きいろい　黄色い　yellow　会L9(e)
きえる　消える　(something) goes off [ru]
　　会L18
きおん　気温　temperature (weather)
　　会L8
きがえる　着替える　to change clothes
　[ru]　会L21
きがつく　気が付く　to notice [u]　会L21
きく　聞く　to ask [u]　会L5
きく　聞く　to listen; to hear [u]　会L3
きごう　記号　symbol　読L23-II
きこえる　聞こえる　to be audible [ru]
　　会L20
キスをする　to kiss [irr.]　読L23-II
きせつ　季節　season　会L10
きた　北　north　会L6(e)
ギター　guitar　会L9
きたない　汚い　dirty　会L16
きつえん　喫煙　smoking　会L15(e)
きっぷ　切符　(train) ticket　会L12
きっぷうりば　切符売り場　ticket
　vending area　会L10(e)

あいうえお　かきくけこ　さしすせそ　たちつてと　なにぬねの　はひふへほ　まみむめも　やゆよ　らりるれろ　わをん

こうせいぶっしつ　抗生物質　antibiotic 会L12(e)

こうちゃ　紅茶　black tea　会L13

こうつうけいアイシーカード　交通系 IC カード　rechargeable card such as Suica, Icoca, Pasmo, etc.　会L10(e)

こうはい　後輩　junior member of a group　会L22

こうよう　紅葉　autumn leaves/colors 読L15-II

こえ　声　voice　読L10-II

コーヒー　coffee　会L3

ゴールド　gold　会L9(e)

ごがつ　五月　May　会L4(e)

こくさい　国際　international　読L19-III

こくさいかんけい　国際関係 international relations　会L1

こくばん　黒板　blackboard　会L2(e)

ここ　here　会L2

ごご　午後　P.M.　会L1

ここのか　九日　nine days　会L13

ここのか　九日　the ninth day of a month 会L4(e)

ここのつ　九つ　nine　会L9

こころ　心　mind; heart　読L20-II

ござる　extra-modest expression for ある [u]　会L20

ごじ　五時　five o'clock　会L1(e)

ごしゅじん　ご主人　(your/someone's) husband　会L14

ごぜん　午前　A.M.　会L1

ごぜんちゅう　午前中　in the morning 読L9-II, 会L21

こたえ　答／答え　answer 会L11(e), 読L23-II

こたえる　答える　to answer [ru] 読L8-II, 会L23

ごちそう　excellent food　読L9-II

ごちそうさま（でした）　Thank you for the meal. (after eating)　会G

ごちそうする　to treat/invite (someone) to a meal [irr.]　会L19

こちら　this person (polite)　会L11

こちら　this way (polite)　会L19

こっせつする　骨折する　to break (a bone)　会L12(e)

こと　things; matters　読L11-II, 会L21

ことし　今年　this year　会L4(e), 会L10

ことば　言葉　language　会L13

こども　子供　child　会L4

ことわざ　proverb　読L23-II

この　this . . .　会L2

このあいだ　この間　the other day 読L8-II, 会L16

このぐらい　about this much　会L16

このごろ　these days　会L10

このように　like this; this way　読L23-II

ごはん　ご飯　rice; meal　会L4

コピーをとる　コピーを取る　to make a photocopy [u]　会L22

ごふん　五分　five minutes　会L1(e)

こまる　困る　to have difficulty [u] 会L16

ごみ　garbage　会L16

こむ　混む　to get crowded [u] 読L15-II, 会L17

ごめん　I'm sorry. (casual)　会L16

ごめんなさい　I'm sorry.　会L4

ごらんになる　ご覧になる　honorific expression for みる [u]　会L19

ゴルフ　golf　会L13

これ　this one　会L2

これから　from now on　読L11-II, 会L16

～ころ　time of . . . ; when . . .　会L21

～ごろ　at about . . .　会L3

ごろごろする　to chill out at home; to stay home do nothing [irr.]　会L10

ころぶ　転ぶ　to fall down [u]　会L18

こわい　怖い　frightening　会L5

こわす　壊す　to break (something) [u] 会L18

こわれる　壊れる　(something) breaks [ru]　会L18

こんいろ　紺色　navy　会L9(e)

こんがっき　今学期　this semester　会L11

こんげつ　今月　this month 会L4(e), 会L8

コンサート　concert　会L9

こんしゅう　今週　this week 会L4(e), 会L6

コンタクト（レンズ）　contact lenses 会L17

こんでいる　混んでいる　to be crowded 読L15-II

こんど　今度　near future　会L9

こんな～　. . . like this; this kind of . . . 会L14

こんなふう　like this　会L22

こんにちは　Good afternoon.　会G

こんばん　今晩　tonight　会L3

こんばんは　Good evening.　会G

コンビニ　convenience store　会L2

コンピューター　computer　会L1, 会L2

さ

さあ　I am not sure . . .　会L14

サークル　club activity　会L7

サーフィン　surfing　会L5

～さい　～歳　. . . years old　会L1

さいあく（な）　最悪　the worst　会L17

さいきん　最近　recently　会L15

さいごに　最後に　finally; lastly 読L8-II, 会L23

さいふ　財布　wallet　会L2

さがす　探す　to look for [u]　会L15

さかな　魚　fish　会L2

さく　咲く　to bloom [u]　会L18

さくひん　作品　work (of art, etc.) 読L17-II

さくぶん　作文　essay; composition　会L9

さくら　桜　cherry blossom　会L18

さけ　酒　sake; alcohol　会L3

さしあげる　差し上げる　humble expression for あげる [ru]　会L20

さす　刺す　to bite [u]　会L21

さそう　誘う　to invite [u]　会L15

ざだんかい　座談会　round-table discussion　読L13-III

～さつ　～冊　[counter for bound volumes]　会L14, 会L14(e)

さっか　作家　writer　会L11

サッカー　soccer　会L10

ざっし　雑誌　magazine　会L3

さとう　砂糖　sugar　会L16

さびしい　寂しい　lonely　会L9

サボる　to cut (classes) [u]　会L11

～さま　～様　Mr./Ms. . . .　読L5-II

さむい　寒い　cold (weather)　会L5

さようなら　Good-bye.　会G

さら　皿　plate; dish　会L14

さらいげつ　再来月　the month after next　会L4(e)

さらいしゅう　再来週　the week after next　会L4(e)

さらいねん　再来年　the year after next 会L4(e)

サラリーマン　salaryman; office worker 会L17

さる　猿　monkey　会L22

さわる　触る　to touch [u]　会L21

～さん　Mr./Ms. . . .　会L1

さんかする　参加する　to participate [irr.]　会L15

さんがつ　三月　March　会L4(e)

ざんぎょう　残業　overtime work 読L8-II, 会L17

さんじ　三時　three o'clock　会L1(e)

さんじっぷん／さんじゅっぷん　三十分 thirty minutes　会L1(e)

さんせいする　賛成する　to agree [irr.] 会L22

ざんだかしょうかい　残高照会　balance inquiry　会L13(e)

ざんねん（ですね）　残念（ですね） That's too bad.　会L8

さんふじんか　産婦人科　obstetrician and gynecologist　会L12(e)
さんぷん　三分　three minutes　会L1(e)
さんぽする　散歩する　to take a walk [irr.]　会L9

し

し　詩　poem　読L17-II
じ　字　letter; character　会L20
〜じ　〜時　o'clock　会L1
しあい　試合　match; game　会L12
しあわせ (な)　幸せ　happy (lasting happiness)　読L10-II, 会L13
ジーンズ　jeans　会L2
シェフ　chef　読L6-III, 会L11
しか　鹿　deer　読L15-II
しか　歯科　dentist　会L12(e)
しかし　however　読L17-II
しかたがない　cannot be helped　会L22-II
しがつ　四月　April　会L4(e)
じかん　時間　time　会L10
〜じかん　〜時間　...hours　会L4
じかんどおり　時間通り　on time　読L13-III
しけん　試験　exam　会L9
しごと　仕事　job; work; occupation　会L8
じしょ　辞書　dictionary　会L2(e), 会L15
じしん　地震　earthquake　会L15
しずか (な)　静か　quiet　会L5
しぜん　自然　nature　読L15-II
じぞう　guardian deity of children　読L10-II
した　下　under　会L4
じだい　時代　age; era　読L14-II
したしい　親しい　close; intimate　読L18-III
しちがつ　七月　July　会L4(e)
しちじ　七時　seven o'clock　会L1(e)
しっています　知っています　I know　会L7
じつは　実は　actually; in fact　会L16
しっぱいする　失敗する　to fail; to be unsuccessful [irr.]　会L22
じっぷん　十分　ten minutes　会L1(e)
しつもん　質問　question　会L11(e), 読L19-III
しつれいしました　失礼しました　I'm very sorry.　会L20
しつれいします　失礼します　Excuse me.; Sorry to interrupt you.　会L16
していせき　指定席　reserved seat　会L10(e)
してん　支店　branch office　会L20
じてんしゃ　自転車　bicycle　会L2
じどう　自動　automatic　読L13-III

しぬ　死ぬ　to die [u]　会L6
じはつ　次発　departing second　会L10(e)
じびか　耳鼻科　otorhinolaryngologist; ENT doctor　会L12(e)
じぶん　自分　oneself　読L10-II, 会L17
じぶんで　自分で　(do something) by oneself　会L16
しま　島　island　読L15-II
しまる　閉まる　(something) closes [u]　会L18
しめきり　締め切り　deadline　会L11(e), 会L15
しめる　閉める　to close (something) [ru]　会L6
じゃあ　then . . . ; if that is the case, . . .　会L2
ジャーナリスト　journalist　会L11
しゃかい　社会　society　会L23
じゃがいも　potato　会L8(e)
ジャケット　jacket　会L15
しゃしん　写真　picture; photograph　会L4
しゃちょう　社長　president of a company　会L11
シャツ　shirt　会L14
しゃべる　to chat [u]　会L15
シャワー　shower　会L6
シャワーをあびる　シャワーを浴びる　to take a shower [ru]　会L6
シャンプー　shampoo　会L17(e), 会L18
じゆう　自由　freedom　会L22
じゅういちがつ　十一月　November　会L4(e)
じゅういちじ　十一時　eleven o'clock　会L1(e)
じゅういちにち　十一日　the eleventh day of a month　会L4(e)
じゅういっぷん　十一分　eleven minutes　会L1(e)
じゅうがつ　十月　October　会L4(e)
しゅうかん　習慣　custom　会L15
〜しゅうかん　〜週間　for . . . weeks　会L10
じゅうきゅうふん　十九分　nineteen minutes　会L1(e)
じゅうごふん　十五分　fifteen minutes　会L1(e)
じゅうさんぷん　十三分　thirteen minutes　会L1(e)
じゅうじ　十時　ten o'clock　会L1(e)
しゅうしょくする　就職する　to get a full-time job (at . . .) [irr.]　会L17
ジュース　juice　会L12
じゆうせき　自由席　general admission seat　会L10(e)
じゅうでうたれる　銃で撃たれる　to be shot　読L17-II

しゅうでん　終電　last train (of the day)　会L10(e), 会L21
じゅうななふん　十七分　seventeen minutes　会L1(e)
じゆうに　自由に　freely　会L22
じゅうにがつ　十二月　December　会L4(e)
じゅうにじ　十二時　twelve o'clock　会L1(e)
じゅうにふん　十二分　twelve minutes　会L1(e)
しゅうにゅう　収入　income　読L18-II
じゅうはちふん / じゅうはっぷん　十八分　eighteen minutes　会L1(e)
しゅうまつ　週末　weekend　会L3
じゅうよっか　十四日　the fourteenth day of a month　会L4(e)
じゅうよんぷん　十四分　fourteen minutes　会L1(e)
じゅうろっぷん　十六分　sixteen minutes　会L1(e)
じゅぎょう　授業　class　会L11
じゅぎょうちゅうに　授業中に　in class; during the class　会L16
じゅぎょうりょう　授業料　tuition　会L21
じゅく　塾　cram school　読L7-II, 会L22
しゅくだい　宿題　homework　会L5
しゅじゅつ　手術　operation　会L12(e)
しゅしょう　首相　prime minister　会L17
しゅじん　主人　head of a familiy　読L15-II
しゅっしん　出身　coming from　会L11
しゅっちょう　出張　business trip　読L14-II, 会L19
じゅっぷん　十分　ten minutes　会L1(e)
しゅふ　主婦　housewife　会L1
しゅふ　主夫　house husband　読L17-II
しゅみ　趣味　hobby; pastime　会L20
しゅるい　種類　a kind; a sort　会L19
じゅんび　準備　preparation　会L17
しょうかいする　紹介する　to introduce [irr.]　会L11
しょうがくきん　奨学金　scholarship　会L16
しょうがくせい　小学生　elementary school students　読L16-II
しょうがつ　正月　New Year's　読L10-II, 会L11
しょうがっこう　小学校　elementary school　会L23
しょうぎ　Japanese chess　読L19-II
じょうしゃけん　乗車券　(boarding) ticket　会L10(e)

そうだんする　相談する　to consult [irr.]　会L14

そうです　That's right.　会L1

そうですか　I see.; Is that so?　会L1

そうですね　That's right.; Let me see.　会L3

そこ　there　会L2

そして　and then　読L9-II, 会L11

そだてる　育てる　to raise; to bring up [ru]　会L22

そつぎょうしき　卒業式　graduation ceremony　会L15

そつぎょうする　卒業する　to graduate (from . . .) [irr.]　会L15

そと　外　outside　会L18

その　that . . .　会L2

そのご　その後　after that　読L17-II

そば　soba; Japanese buckwheat noodles　会L15

ソファ　sofa　会L18

そめる　to dye [ru]　会L17(e)

そら　空　sky　読L16-II

そる　to shave [u]　会L17(e)

それ　that one　会L2

それから　and then　会L4

それで　then; therefore　会L19

それでは　well then　読L19-II

それに　moreover,. . .　会L12

そろえる　to make hair even; to trim [ru]　会L17(e)

そろそろ　it is about time to . . .　会L23

そんな〜　such . . .; that kind of . . .　読L16-II, 会L23

そんなこと (は) ない　I don't think so.　会L22

〜だい　〜代　charge; fee　会L12

〜だい　〜台　[counter for equipment]　会L14, 会L14(e)

ダイエットする　to go on a diet [irr.]　会L11

たいおんけい　体温計　thermometer　会L12(e)

だいがく　大学　college; university　会L1

だいがくいん　大学院　graduate school　会L16

だいがくいんせい　大学院生　graduate student　会L1

だいがくせい　大学生　college student　会L1

だいきらい (な)　大嫌い　to hate　会L5

だいじょうぶ　大丈夫　It's okay.; Not to worry.; Everything is under control.　会L5

だいすき (な)　大好き　very fond of; to love　会L5

たいせつ (な)　大切　precious; important　会L18

たいせつにする　大切にする　to take good care of [irr.]　読L19-II

たいてい　usually　会L3

だいとうりょう　大統領　president of a country　会L11

だいヒット　大ヒット　big hit　読L17-II

タイプ　type　読L22-II

たいふう　台風　typhoon　会L16

たいへん　greatly　読L19-II

たいへん (な)　大変　tough (situation)　読L5-II, 会L6

だいよくじょう　大浴場　large spa　会L15(e)

タオル　towel　会L18

たかい　高い　expensive; high　会L2

だから　so; therefore　会L4

たからくじ　宝くじ　lottery　会L17

たからくじにあたる　宝くじに当たる　to win a lottery [u]　会L17

だく　抱く　to hold something in one's arm [u]　読L20-II

たくさん　many; a lot　会L4

タクシー　taxi　読L13-III

たけ　竹　bamboo　読L15-II

〜だけ　just . . .; only . . .　会L11

だす　出す　to take (something) out; to hand in (something) [u]　会L16

たすかる　助かる　to be saved; to be helped [u]　会L18

たすける　助ける　to help; to rescue [ru]　読L16-II, 会L22

ただ　free of charge　会L23

ただいま　I'm home.　会G

ただの〜　nothing more than . . .　読L21-II

〜たち　[makes a noun plural]　会L14

たつ　(time) pass [u]　読L19-II

たつ　立つ　to stand up [u]　会L6

たて　縦　vertical　読L23-II

たてもの　建物　building　会L15

たとえば　例えば　for example　会L11(e), 読L16-II, 会L17

たのしい　楽しい　fun　会L5

たのしそうに　楽しそうに　joyfully　読L22-II

たのしみ　楽しみ　pleasure　読L21-II

たのしみです　楽しみです　cannot wait; to look forward to it　会L15

たのしみにする (〜を)　楽しみにする　to look forward (to) [irr.]　読L7-II

たのしむ　楽しむ　to enjoy [u]　読L15-II

たのむ　頼む　to ask (a favor) [u]　会L18

たばこをすう　たばこを吸う　to smoke [u]　会L6

ダブル　double room　会L15(e)

たぶん　多分　probably; maybe　会L12

たべもの　食べ物　food　会L5

たべる　食べる　to eat [ru]　会L3

たまご　卵　egg　会L12

だます　to deceive [u]　読L20-II

たまねぎ　onion　会L8(e)

だめ (な)　no good　会L13

〜ために　for . . .; for the sake of . . .　会L23

ためる　to save money [ru]　会L21

たりる　足りる　to be sufficient; to be enough [ru]　会L17

だれ　who　会L2

〜(ん) だろう　short form of 〜(ん) でしょう　会L18

たんご　単語　word; vocabulary　会L9

たんざく　strip of fancy paper　読L12-II

だんしがくせい　男子学生　male student　読L18-II

たんじょうび　誕生日　birthday　会L5

ちいさい　小さい　small　会L5

チェックアウト (する)　checking out　会L15(e)

チェックイン (する)　checking in　会L15(e)

チェックする　to check [irr.]　会L23

ちか　地下　underground　読L15-II

ちかい　近い　close; near　会L13

ちがい　違い　difference　会L17

ちがう　違う　to be different; to be wrong [u]　読L16-II, 会L23

ちかく　近く　near; nearby　会L4

ちかてつ　地下鉄　subway　会L10

ちからしごと　力仕事　physical labor (such as construction)　読L18-III

ちかん　groper; pervert　会L21

チケット　ticket　会L9

ちこくする　遅刻する　to be late (for an appointment) [irr.]　会L11

ちず　地図　map　会L15

ちち　父　(my) father　会L7

ちちおや　父親　father　読L14-II

チップ　tip　読L13-III

ちゃ　茶　green tea　会L3

ちゃいろい　茶色い　brown　会L9(e)

ちゃみせ　茶店　teahouse　読L20-II

〜ちゃん　suffix for names of children　会L22

〜ちゅう　〜中　while . . .　読L19-II

ちゅういする　注意する　to give warning; to watch out [irr.]　会L14

ちゅうがくせい　中学生　junior high school student　会L19

ちゅうごく　中国　China　会L1, 会L2

ちゅうしゃ　注射　injection　会L12(e)

ちゅうもんする　注文する　to place an order [irr.]　会L18

ちょうさ　調査　survey　会L23

ちょうしょくつき　朝食付き　with breakfast　会L15(e)

ちょうど　exactly　会L14

ちょきんする　貯金する　to deposit money (in a bank) [irr.]　読L18-II

チョコレート　chocolate　会L14

ちょっと　a little　会L3

ツアー　tour　会L10

ついたち　一日　the first day of a month　会L4(e)

ツイン　twin room　会L15(e)

つうちょう　通帳　passbook　会L13(e)

つうちょうきにゅう　通帳記入　passbook update　会L13(e)

つかう　使う　to use [u]　会L6

つかまる　捕まる　to be arrested; to be caught [u]　会L21

つかれている　疲れている　to be tired　読L8-II

つかれる　疲れる　to get tired [ru]　会L11

つき　月　moon　会L20

つぎ　次　next　会L6

つきあう　付き合う　to date (someone); to keep company [u]　読L14-II, 会L15

つぎに　次に　secondly　読L8-II

つぎは〜　次は〜　next (stop), . . .　会L10(e)

つく　着く　to arrive [u]　読L13-III, 会L15

つく　(something) turns on [u]　会L18

つくえ　机　desk　会L2(e), 会L4

つくる　作る　to make [u]　会L8

つける　to turn on [ru]　会L6

つごうがわるい　都合が悪い　inconvenient; to have a scheduling conflict　会L17

つたえる　伝える　to convey message [ru]　会L20

つづく　続く　to continue [u]　読L16-II

つづける　続ける　to continue [ru]　会L20

つつむ　包む　to wrap; to cover [u]　会L21

つまらない　boring　会L5

つめたい　冷たい　cold (things/people)　会L10

つよい　強い　strong　会L17

つり　fishing　会L11

つれていく　連れていく　to take (someone) to (a place) [u]　会L16

つれてかえる　連れて帰る　to bring (a person) back [u]　読L12-II

つれてくる　連れてくる　to bring (a person) [irr.]　会L6

て　手　hand; arm　会L7(e)

〜で　by (means of transportation); with (a tool)　会L10

ティーシャツ　Tシャツ　T-shirt　会L2

ていきけん　定期券　commuter's pass　会L10(e)

ていねいないいかた　ていねいな言い方　polite expression　会L11(e)

〜ていらっしゃる　honorific expression for 〜ている [u]　会L19

デート　date (romantic, not calendar)　会L3

〜ておる　extra-modest expression for 〜ている [u]　会L20

でかける　出かける　to go out [ru]　会L5

てがみ　手紙　letter　会L9

できる　to come into existence; to be made [ru]　会L14

できるだけ　as much as possible　会L12

できれば　if possible　会L20

でぐち　出口　exit　会L10(e)

〜でござる　extra-modest expression for です [u]　会L20

デザート　desert　読L13-III

〜です　I am . . . .　会G

てすうりょう　手数料　commission　会L13(e)

テスト　test　会L5

てつだう　手伝う　to help [u]　会L6

てつやする　徹夜する　to stay up all night [irr.]　会L22

テニス　tennis　会L3

では　well then (polite)　会L20

では、おげんきで　では、お元気で　Take care.　読L5-II

デパート　department store　会L7

てぶくろ　手袋　gloves　会L10

でも　but　会L3

てら　寺　temple　会L4

でる　出る　to appear; to attend; to exit [ru]　読L6-I, 会L9

テレビ　TV　会L3

てん　天　the heavens; the sky　読L12-II

〜てん　〜点　. . . points　会L11

てんき　天気　weather　会L5

でんき　電気　electricity; light　会L2(e), 会L6

でんきこうがく　電気工学　electrical engineering　読L19-III

てんきよほう　天気予報　weather forecast　会L8

でんしゃ　電車　train　会L6

てんじょう　天井　ceiling　読L17-II

でんしレンジ　電子レンジ　microwave oven　会L17

でんち　電池　battery　会L15

てんてき　点滴　intravenous feeding　会L12(e)

てんぷら　天ぷら　tempura　会L10

てんらんかい　展覧会　art exhibition　読L17-II

でんわ　電話　telephone　会L1

でんわする　電話する　to call [irr.]　会L6

と　戸　door　読L10-II

〜と　together with (a person); and　会L4

〜ど　〜度　. . . degrees (temperature)　会L8

ドア　door　会L2(e), 読L13-III

(〜は)…といういみだ　(〜は)…という意味だ　〜 means that . . .　読L23-II

ドイツ　Germany　会L20

トイレ　toilet; restroom　会L2

どう　how　会L8

どうぐ　道具　tool　読L16-II

どうしたらいい　what should one do　会L14

どうして　why　会L4

どうしよう　What should I/we do?　会L18

どうじょうする　同情する　to sympathize [irr.]　会L23

どうぞ　Please.; Here it is.　会L2

どうぞよろしくおねがいします　どうぞよろしくお願いします　Thank you in advance.　読L19-III

どうですか　How about . . . ?; How is . . . ?　会L3

どうぶつ　動物　animal　会L20

どうぶつえん　動物園　zoo　会L10

どうも　Thank you.　会L2

どうやって　how; by what means　会L10

どうりょう　同僚　colleague　会L21

とお　十　ten　会L9

とおい　遠い　far (away)　会L21

とおか　十日　ten days　会L13

とおか　十日　the tenth day of a month　会L4(e)

とおる　通る　to go through; to pass [u]　読L15-II

〜とか　... for example　会L22

とき　時　when ...; at the time of ...　会L4

ときどき　時々　sometimes　会L3

とくに　特に　especially　会L13

とけい　時計　watch; clock　会L2

どこ　where　会L2

どこでも　anywhere　読L16-II

ところ　所　place　会L8

ところが　however; on the contrary　読L21-II

ところで　by the way　会L9

とし　年　year　読L10-II

としうえ　年上　someone older　会L10

としょかん　図書館　library　会L2

どちら　where (polite)　会L19

どちら　which　会L10

とっきゅう　特急　super express　会L10(e)

とつぜん　突然　suddenly　読L19-III

どっち　which　会L10

とても　very　会L5

となり　隣　next　会L4

とにかく　anyhow; anyway　会L21

どの　which ...　会L2

どのぐらい　how much; how long　会L10

とぶ　飛ぶ　to fly [u]　読L16-II

トマト　tomato　会L8

とまる　泊まる　to stay (at a hotel, etc.) [u]　会L10

とまる　止まる　to stop [u]　読L20-II

〜ともうします　〜と申します　my name is ...　会L13

ともだち　友だち　friend　会L1

どようび　土曜日　Saturday　会L3, 会L4(e)

ドライブ　drive　会L11

とり　鳥　bird; poultry　読L13-II

とりにく　鶏肉　chicken　会L8(e)

とる　取る　to take (a class); to get (a grade) [u]　読L7-II, 会L11

とる　撮る　to take (a picture) [u]　会L4

とる　to take off [u]　読L10-II

どれ　which one　会L2

トレーナー　sweatshirt　会L14

トロッコれっしゃ　トロッコ列車　small train usually for tourists　読L15-II

どろぼう　泥棒　thief; burglar　会L21

とんかつ　pork cutlet　会L2

どんな　what kind of ...　会L5

な

ないか　内科　physician　会L12(e)

なおす　直す　to correct; to fix [u]　会L16

なか　中　inside　会L4

ながい　長い　long　会L7

ながいあいだ　長い間　long time　読L21-II

なかがいい　仲がいい　be on good/close terms; to get along well　会L19

なく　泣く　to cry [u]　読L12-II, 会L13

なくす　to lose [u]　会L12

なくなる　to be lost; to disappear [u]　会L23

なぐる　殴る　to strike; to hit; to punch [u]　会L21

なさる　honorific expression for する [u]　会L19

なす　eggplant　会L8(e)

なぜ　why　会L19

なつ　夏　summer　会L8

なつかしい　to miss; to long for　読L19-II

〜など　and so forth　読L12-II

ななつ　七つ　seven　会L9

ななふん　七分　seven minutes　会L1(e)

なに / なん　何　what　会L1

なにか　何か　something　会L8

なにも + negative　何も　not ... anything　会L7

なのか　七日　seven days　会L13

なのか　七日　the seventh day of a month　会L4(e)

なべ　pot　読L13-II

なまえ　名前　name　会L1

なまえをつける　名前をつける　to name [ru]　読L17-II

なまけもの　怠け者　lazy person　会L19

なやみ　悩み　worry　読L14-II, 会L19

ならう　習う　to learn [u]　会L11

なる　to become [u]　会L10

なれる　慣れる　to get used to ... [ru]　会L17

なん / なに　何　what　会L1

なんだか　somehow　読L22-II

なんでも　anything; everything　読L13-II

なんども　何度も　many times　読L17-II, 会L22

に

にあう　似合う　to look good (on somebody) [u]　会L14

にかげつまえ　二か月前　two months ago　会L4(e)

にがつ　二月　February　会L4(e)

にぎやか (な)　lively　会L5

にく　肉　meat　会L2

〜にくらべて　〜に比べて　compared with ...　会L17

にげる　逃げる　to run away; to escape [ru]　読L22-II

にこにこする　to smile [irr.]　読L20-II

にさんにち　二三日　for two to three days　会L12

にし　西　west　会L6(e)

にじ　二時　two o'clock　会L1(e)

にじっぷん　二十分　twenty minutes　会L1(e)

にじはん　二時半　half past two　会L1

にしゅうかんまえ　二週間前　two weeks ago　会L4(e)

にじゅうよっか　二十四日　the twenty-fourth day of a month　会L4(e)

にじゅっぷん　二十分　twenty minutes　会L1(e)

にちようび　日曜日　Sunday　会L3, 会L4(e)

〜について　about ...; concerning ...　会L8

にっき　日記　diary　読L9-II, 会L18

にふん　二分　two minutes　会L1(e)

にほん　日本　Japan　会L1

にほんご　日本語　Japanese language　会L1

にほんじん　日本人　Japanese people　会L1

にもつ　荷物　baggage　会L6

ニヤニヤする　to grin [irr.]　読L13-II

にゅういんする　入院する　to be hospitalized [irr.]　読L21-II

ニュース　news　会L17

〜によると　according to ...　会L17

にわ　庭　garden　会L15

〜にん　〜人　[counter for people]　会L7

にんきがある　人気がある　to be popular [u]　会L9

にんじん　carrot　会L8(e)

ぬ

ぬいぐるみ　stuffed animal (e.g., teddy bear)　会L14

ぬぐ　脱ぐ　to take off (clothes) [u]　会L17

ぬすむ　盗む　to steal; to rob [u]　会L21

ね

ねがい　願い　wish　読L12-II

ネクタイ　necktie　会L14

ねこ　猫　cat　会L4

ねだん　値段　price　読L20-II

ねつがある　熱がある　to have a fever [u]　会L12

ねむい　眠い　sleepy　会L10

ねる　寝る　to sleep; to go to sleep [ru]　会L3

〜ねん　〜年　... years　会L10

~ねんかん　~年間　for . . . years
　　　　読L14-II

~ねんせい　~年生　. . . year student
　　　　会L1

の

ノート　notebook　会L2
のこす　残す　to leave; to preserve [u]
　　　　読L15-II
~のしょうかいで　~の紹介で
　　through the introduction of　読L19-III
~のために　for . . .　読L19-III
~のための　for the sake of . . .　読L17-II
のど　喉　throat　会L12
のどがかわく　喉が渇く　to become
　　thirsty [u]　会L12
のぼる　登る　to climb [u]　会L11
のみもの　飲み物　drink　会L5
のむ　飲む　to drink [u]　会L3
~のようなもの　something like . . .
　　　　読L16-II
のりおくれる　乗り遅れる　to miss (a
　　train, bus, etc.) [ru]　会L16
のりかえ　乗り換え　transfer　会L10(e)
のる　乗る　to ride; to board [u]　会L5

は

は　歯　tooth　会L7(e), 会L12
~は…といういみだ　~は…という意味
　　だ　~ means that . . .　読L23-II
ばあい　場合　case　読L14-II
パーティー　party　会L8
パートナー　partner　会L14
バーベキュー　barbecue　会L8
パーマ　perm　会L17(e)
パーマをかける　to have one's hair
　　permed [ru]　会L17(e)
はい　yes　会L1
はいいろ　灰色　gray　会L9(e)
はいく　俳句　haiku　読L17-II
バイク　motorcycle　会L13
ばいてん　売店　shop; stand　会L10(e)
はいゆう　俳優　actor; actress　会L11
はいる　入る　to enter [u]　会L6
ばかにする　to insult; to make a fool of . . .
　　[irr.]　会L21
はく　to put on (items below your waist) [u]
　　　　会L7
はく　吐く　to throw up [u]　会L12(e)
~はく　~泊　. . . nights　会L15(e)
はこぶ　運ぶ　to carry [u]　会L22
はし　chopsticks　会L8
はしご　ladders　読L17-II
はじまる　始まる　(something) begins
　　[u]　会L9

はじめて　初めて　for the first time
　　　　会L12
はじめは　初めは　at first　読L18-III
はじめまして　How do you do ?　会G
はじめる　始める　to begin [ru]　会L8
ばしょ　場所　place　読L15-II, 会L23
はしる　走る　to run [u]　会L11
バス　bus　会L5
はずかしい　恥ずかしい　embarrassing;
　　to feel embarrassed　会L18
はずかしがりや　恥ずかしがり屋　shy
　　person　会L19
バスてい　バス停　bus stop　会L4
パソコン　personal computer　会L6
はたけ　畑　farm　読L12-II
はたらく　働く　to work [u]　会L7
はたをおる　はたを織る　to weave [u]
　　　　読L12-II
はちがつ　八月　August　会L4(e)
はちじ　八時　eight o'clock　会L1(e)
はちふん　八分　eight minutes　会L1(e)
ばつ　×(wrong)　会L11(e)
はつおん　発音　pronunciation　会L11(e)
はつか　二十日　the twentieth day of a
　　month　会L4(e)
はっしん　発疹　rash　会L12(e)
はっぴょうする　発表する　to make
　　a presentation; to make public [irr.]
　　　　会L15
はっぷん　八分　eight minutes　会L1(e)
はな　花　flower　会L4
はな　鼻　nose　会L7(e)
はなし　話　story; talk　読L8-II, 会L19
はなしをする　話をする　to have a talk
　　[irr.]　読L9-II, 会L19
はなす　話す　to speak; to talk [u]　会L3
バナナ　banana　会L18
はなみず　鼻水　runny nose　会L12(e)
はなれる　離れる　(something/someone)
　　separates; parts from [ru]　会L23
はは　母　(my) mother　会L7
はやい　早い　early　会L3
はやい　速い　fast　会L7
はやく　早く / 速く　(do something)
　　early; fast　会L10
はらう　払う　to pay [u]　会L12
ハラルフード　halal　会L8(e)
はる　春　spring　会L10
はる　貼る　to post; to stick [u]　会L21
はれ　晴れ　sunny weather　会L8
はれる　晴れる　to become sunny [ru]
　　　　会L19
バレンタインデー　Valentine's Day
　　　　会L14
はん　半　half　会L1

パン　bread　会L4
~ばん　~番　number . . .　会L1, 会L11(e)
ばんぐみ　番組　broadcast program
　　　　読L16-II
ばんごう　番号　number　会L1
ばんごはん　晩ご飯　dinner　会L3
~ばんせん　~番線　track number . . .
　　　　会L10(e)
パンダ　panda　会L17
はんたいする　反対する　to oppose; to
　　object to [irr.]　会L22
バンド　band　会L11-II
はんにん　犯人　criminal　会L21
ハンバーガー　hamburger　会L3

ひ

ひ　日　day　読L15-II, 会L16
ピアノ　piano　会L9
ヒーター　heater　会L17
ピーナッツ　peanut　会L8(e)
ビール　beer　会L11
ひがし　東　east　会L6(e)
~ひき　~匹　[counter for smaller
　　animals]　会L14, 会L14(e)
ひきだし　引き出し　withdrawal
　　　　会L13(e)
ひく　弾く　to play (a string instrument or
　　piano) [u]　会L9
ひげ　beard　会L17
ひげをそる　to shave one's beard [u]
　　　　会L17
ひこうき　飛行機　airplane　会L10
ピザ　pizza　読L6-III, 会L9
ひさしぶり　久しぶり　it has been a long
　　time　会L11
ビジネス　business　会L1, 会L2
びじゅつかん　美術館　art museum
　　　　会L11
ひだり　左　left　会L4
ひだりがわ　左側　left side　会L6(e)
ひっかく　to scratch [u]　読L20-II
びっくりする　to be surprised [irr.]
　　　　読L10-II, 会L21
ひっこし　引っ越し　moving　読L18-III
ひっこす　引っ越す　to move (to another
　　place to live) [u]　会L19
ひと　人　person　会L4
ひどい　awful　会L21
ひとつ　一つ　one　会L9
ひとつめ　一つ目　first　会L6(e)
ひとびと　人々　people　読L12-II
ひとり　一人　one person　会L7
ひとりぐらし　一人暮らし　living alone
　　　　会L22
ひとりで　一人で　alone　会L4

ひふか　皮膚科　dermatologist　会L12(e)

ひま (な)　暇　not busy; free (time)　会L5

ひみつ　秘密　secret　読L16-II, 会L17

びよういん　美容院　beauty parlor　会L10

びょういん　病院　hospital　会L4

びょうき　病気　illness; sickness
　　　　　　　　　　会L9, 会L12(e)

ひょうじょう　表情　expression
　　　　　　　　　　読L23-II

ひる　昼　noon　読L9-II

ひるごはん　昼ご飯　lunch　会L3

ひるねをする　昼寝をする　to take a
　nap [irr.]　会L21

ひろい　広い　wide; spacious　会L12

ひろう　拾う　to pick up (something) [u]
　　　　　　　　　　会L22

ピンク　pink　会L9(e)

びんぼう (な)　貧乏　poor　会L22

ファイル　(file) folder; portfolio; file　会L16

ファッション　fashion　読L15-II

ふあん (な)　不安　anxious; worried
　　　　　　　　読L13-II, 会L18

フィリピン　Philippines　会L1

ブーツ　boots　会L17

プール　swimming pool　会L15

ぶか　部下　subordinate　会L22

ふく　服　clothes　会L12

ふくしゅう　復習　review of a lesson
　　　　　　　　　　会L22

ふくろ　袋　bag; sack; plastic/paper bag
　会L8(e), 会L23

ふしぎ (な)　不思議　mysterious　会L20

ふたつ　二つ　two　会L9

ふたつめ　二つ目　second　会L6(e)

ぶたにく　豚肉　pork　会L8(e)

ふたり　二人　two people　会L7

ふたりずつ　二人ずつ　two people each
　　　　　　　　　　会L11(e)

ぶちょう　部長　department manager
　　　　　　　　　　会L19

ふつう　普通　local (train)　会L10(e)

ふつか　二日　the second day of a month
　　　　　　　　　　会L4(e)

ふつか　二日　two days　会L13

ぶっか　物価　consumer prices　会L13

ふつかかん　二日間　for two days
　　　　　　　　　　読L22-II

ふつかよい　二日酔い　hangover　会L12

ぶどう　grape　会L8(e)

ふとっています　太っています　to be
　on the heavy side　会L7

ふとる　太る　to gain weight; overweight
　[u]　会L7

ふね　船　ship; boat　会L10

ふべん (な)　不便　inconvenient
　　　　　　　　　　読L21-II

ふむ　踏む　to step on [u]　会L21

ふゆ　冬　winter　会L8

ふりこみ　振込　bank transfer　会L13(e)

プリン　pudding　読L13-III

ふる　to turn down (somebody); to reject;
　to jilt [u]　会L21

ふる (あめ / ゆきが)　降る (雨 / 雪が)
　(rain/snow) falls [u]　会L8

ふるい　古い　old (thing)　会L5

プレゼント　present　会L12

ふろ　風呂　bath　会L8

ブロー　blow-dry　会L17(e)

プロジェクト　project　会L22

ふろにはいる　風呂に入る　to take a
　bath [u]　会L8

プロポーズする　to propose marriage
　[irr.]　会L14

フロント　receptionist; front desk
　　　　　　　　　　会L15(e)

ぶんか　文化　culture　読L11-II, 会L16

ぶんがく　文学　literature　会L1, 読L7-II

ぶんぽう　文法　grammar
　　　　　　　　会L11(e), 会L13

ぶんや　分野　field; realm　読L17-II

へいじつ　平日　weekday　読L11-II

へいわ　平和　peace　読L15-II

へいわきねんしりょうかん　平和記
　念資料館　Peace Memorial Museum
　　　　　　　　　　読L15-II

ページ　page　会L6

ベージュ　beige　会L9(e)

へた (な)　下手　clumsy; poor at . . .
　　　　　　　　　　会L8

ペット　pet　会L15

ヘッドホン　headphones　会L20

べつに ＋ negative　別に　nothing in
　particular　会L7

へや　部屋　room　会L5

ぺらぺら (な)　fluent　会L22

ペン　pen　会L2

へん (な)　変　strange; unusual　会L21

べんきょうする　勉強する　to study
　[irr.]　会L3

べんごし　弁護士　lawyer　会L1, 会L13

へんじ　返事　reply　読L11-II, 会L16

べんとう　弁当　boxed lunch　会L9

べんぴ　便秘　constipation　会L12(e)

へんぴんする　返品する　to return
　(merchandise) [irr.]　会L20

べんり (な)　便利　convenient　会L7

ほうげん　方言　dialect　会L11(e)

ぼうし　帽子　hat; cap　会L2

ほ (う)っておく　放っておく　to leave
　(someone/something) alone; to neglect
　[u]　会L22

～ほうめん　～方面　serving . . . areas
　　　　　　　　　　会L10(e)

ホーム　platform　会L10(e), 読L22-II

ホームシック　homesickness　会L12

ホームステイ　homestay; living with a
　local family　会L8

ボール　ball　会L22

ほかに　anything else　会L11(e)

ほかの　他の　other　会L16

ぼく　僕　I (used by men)　会L5

ポケット　pocket　読L16-II

ほけん　保険　insurance　会L15

ほけんしょう　保険証　health insurance
　certificate　会L12(e)

ほけんにはいる　保険に入る　to buy
　insurance [u]　会L15

ほしい　欲しい　to want　会L14

ぼしゅう　募集　recruitment　会L13

～ぼしゅう　～募集　looking for . . .
　　　　　　　　　　読L11-II

ポスター　poster　会L21

ホストファミリー　host family
　　　　　　　　読L9-II, 会L11

ポップコーン　popcorn　会L18

ホテル　hotel　会L4

ほめる　to praise; to say nice things [ru]
　　　　　　　　　　会L21

ホラー　horror　読L11-II

ボランティア　volunteer　読L11-II, 会L15

ホワイトデー　"White Day" (yet another
　gift-giving day)　会L14

ほん　本　book　会L2, 会L2(e)

～ほん　～本　[counter for long objects]
　　　　　　　　会L14, 会L14(e)

ぼんおどり　盆踊り　Bon dance
　(Japanese traditional dance)　会L23

ほんとうですか　本当ですか　Really?
　　　　　　　　　　会L6

ほんとうに　本当に　really
　　　　　　　　読L14-II, 会L18

ほんとうは　本当は　in fact; originally
　　　　　　　　　　会L19

ほんや　本屋　bookstore　会L4

ほんやくする　翻訳する　to translate
　[irr.]　会L22

まあまあ　okay; so-so　会L11

~まい　~枚　[counter for flat objects]
会L5, 会L14(e)

まいあさ　毎朝　every morning　会L19

まいしゅう　毎週　every week　会L8

まいつき　毎月　every month　読L18-III

まいにち　毎日　every day　会L3

まいばん　毎晩　every night　会L3

まいる　参る　extra-modest expression
for いく and くる [u]　会L20

まえ　前　before . . .　会L17

まえ　前　front　会L4

まがる　曲がる　to turn (right/left) [u]
会L6(e), 会L20

まける　負ける　to lose (a match) [ru]
会L22

まことに　誠に　really (very polite)　会L20

まじめ (な)　serious; sober; diligent
読L12-II, 会L19

まず　first of all　読L8-II, 会L18

まずい　(food is) terrible　会L23

また　again　会L20

また　in addition　読L16-II

まだ　still　会L19

まだ + negative　not . . . yet　会L8

またせる　待たせる　to keep (someone)
waiting [ru]　会L20

まち　町　town; city　会L4

まちあわせをする　待ち合わせをする
to meet up [irr.]　読L15-II

まちがい　間違い　mistake　会L19

まちがえる　間違える　to make a
mistake [ru]　会L21

まちどおしい　待ち遠しい　to wait
eagerly for . . .　読L22-II

まつ　待つ　to wait [u]　会L4

まっすぐ　straight　会L6(e), 読L6-I

まつり　祭り　festival　会L11

~まで　to (a place/a time)　会L9

~までに　by (time/date)　読L12-II, 会L18

まど　窓　window　会L2(e), 会L6

まにあう　間に合う　to be in time [u]
会L22

マフラー　winter scarf　会L14

まゆげ　眉毛　eyebrow　会L7(e)

まる　○ (correct)　会L11(e)

まんが　漫画　comic book　会L14

まんがか　漫画家　cartoonist　会L11

まんじゅう　sweet bun　読L4-III

マンション　larger apartment building;
condominium　会L13

み

みえる　見える　to be visible [ru]　会L15

みがく　磨く　to brush (teeth); to polish
[u]　会L13

みかた　味方　person on one's side
読L16-II

みかん　mandarin orange　会L8(e), 会L14

みぎ　右　right　会L4

みぎがわ　右側　right side　会L6(e)

みじかい　短い　short (length)　会L7

みず　水　water　会L3

みずいろ　水色　light blue　会L9(e)

みずうみ　湖　lake　会L11

みずぎ　水着　swimwear　読L13-III

みせ　店　shop; store　読L4-III, 会L13

みせる　見せる　to show [ru]　会L16

~みたいなX　X like . . .　会L20

みち　道　way; road; directions　会L16

みちにまよう　道に迷う　to become lost;
to lose one's way [u]　会L16

みっか　三日　the third day of a month
会L4(e)

みっか　三日　three days　会L13

みつかる　見つかる　to be found [u]
会L16

みつける　見つける　to find [ru]　会L21

みっつ　三つ　three　会L9

みっつめ　三つ目　third　会L6(e)

みどり　緑　green　会L9(e), 読L15-II

みなさま　みな様　everyone (polite
expression of みなさん)　読L19-II

みなさん　皆さん　everyone; all of you
読L6-III, 会L14

みなみ　南　south　会L6(e), 読L15-II

みぶり　身ぶり　gesture　読L20-II

~みまん　~未満　less than . . .　読L18-II

みみ　耳　ear　会L7(e)

みやげ　土産　souvenir　会L5

みらい　未来　future　読L16-II

みる　見る　to see; to look at; to watch [ru]
会L3

みんな　all　読L7-II, 会L9

みんなで　all (of the people) together　会L8

む

むいか　六日　six days　会L13

むいか　六日　the sixth day of a month
会L4(e)

むかえにいく　迎えに行く　to go to pick
up [u]　会L16

むかえにくる　迎えに来る　to come to
pick up [irr.]　会L16

むかし　昔　old days; past　会L21

むかしむかし　昔々　once upon a time
読L10-II

むこう　向こう　the other side; over there
読L12-II

むし　虫　insect　会L18

むしば　虫歯　bad tooth　会L12(e)

むしめがね　虫めがね　magnifying glass
読L17-II

むずかしい　難しい　difficult　会L5

むすめ　娘　daughter　読L12-II

むだづかい　無駄遣い　waste (money)
会L22

むっつ　六つ　six　会L9

むね　胸　breast　会L7(e)

むらさき　紫　purple　会L9(e)

むり (な)　無理　impossible　会L18

め

め　目　eye　会L7, 会L7(e)

~め　~目　-th　会L15

~めい　~名　. . . person(s)　会L15(e)

~めいさま　~名様　party of . . . people
会L19

めいしん　迷信　superstition　読L21-II

メール　e-mail　会L9

めがね　眼鏡　glasses　会L7

メキシコ　Mexico　読L5-II

めしあがる　召し上がる　honorific
expression for たべる and のむ [u]
会L19

めずらしい　rare　読L13-II

めちゃくちゃ (な)　messy; disorganized
会L21

メッセージ　message; text
読L22-II, 会L23

めったに~ない　seldom　読L21-II

メニュー　menu　会L2

めまいがする　to feel dizzy　会L12(e)

めんきょ　免許　license　会L22

めんせつ　面接　interview　会L23

も

もう　already　会L9

もういちど　もう一度　one more time
会L15

もうしこみ　申し込み　application
読L19-III

もうしわけありません　申し訳ありま
せん　You have my apologies.
読L19-III, 会L20

もうす　申す　extra-modest expression
for いう [u]　会L20

もうすぐ　very soon; in a few moments/
days　会L12

もうすこし　もう少し　a little more
会L22

もう~ない　not any longer　読L13-II

もくてき　目的　object; purpose
読L18-II

もくようび　木曜日　Thursday
会L4, 会L4(e)

もじ　文字　letter; character　読L17-II
もし〜たら　if . . .　読L19-III
もしもし　Hello? (used on the phone)　会L4
もち　rice cake　読L10-II
もちろん　of course　会L7
もつ　持つ　to carry; to hold [u]　会L6
もっていく　持っていく　to take (a thing) [u]　会L8
もってくる　持ってくる　to bring (a thing) [irr.]　会L6
もっと　more　会L11
もてる　to be popular (in terms of romantic interest) [ru]　会L19
もどってくる　戻ってくる　(something/someone) comes back [irr.]　会L23
もどる　戻る　to return; to come/go back [u]　読L16-II, 会L20
もの　物　thing (concrete object)　会L12
ものすごく　extremely　会L23
もも　peach　会L8(e)
もらう　to get (from somebody) [u]　会L9
もんく　文句　complaint　会L21
もんくをいう　文句を言う　to complain [u]　会L21

〜や　〜屋　. . . shop　会L20
やきゅう　野球　baseball　会L10
やく　焼く　to bake; to burn; to grill [u]　会L21
やくす　訳す　to translate [u]　会L16
やくそく　約束　promise; appointment　会L13
やくそくをまもる　約束を守る　to keep a promise [u]　会L13
やけどをする　to burn oneself　会L12(e)
やさい　野菜　vegetable　会L2
やさしい　easy (problem); kind (person)　会L5
やすい　安い　inexpensive; cheap (thing)　会L5
やすみ　休み　holiday; day off; absence　会L5
やすむ　休む　to be absent (from); to rest [u]　会L6
やせています　to be thin　会L7
やせる　to lose weight [ru]　会L7
やちん　家賃　rent　会L18
やった！　I did it!　読L20-II
やっつ　八つ　eight　会L9
やっぱり　after all　読L13-II, 会L17
やま　山　mountain　読L5-II, 会L11
やまみち　山道　mountain road　読L10-II
やめる　to quit [ru]　会L11
やる　to do; to perform [u]　会L5

やる　to give (to pets, plants, younger siblings, etc.) [u]　会L21

ゆ　湯　hot water　会L17
ゆうがた　夕方　evening　会L18
ゆうき　勇気　courage　読L22-II
ゆうしょうする　優勝する　to win a championship [irr.]　会L23
ゆうしょく　夕食　dinner　会L23
ゆうじん　友人　friend　読L19-III
ゆうびんきょく　郵便局　post office　会L2
ゆうめい（な）　有名　famous　会L8
ゆうめいじん　有名人　celebrity　会L10
ゆき　雪　snow　読L10-II, 会L10
ゆっくり　slowly; leisurely; unhurriedly　会L6
ゆび　指　finger　会L7(e)
ゆびわ　指輪　ring　会L14
ゆめ　夢　dream　会L11

よ

ようか　八日　eight days　会L13
ようか　八日　the eighth day of a month　会L4(e)
ようこそ　Welcome.　会L19
ようじ　用事　business to take care of　会L12
ようふく　洋服　clothes　読L18-II
ヨーロッパ　Europe　会L22
よかったら　if you like　会L7
よきん　預金　savings　会L13(e)
よく　often; much　会L3
よく　well　会L14
よこ　横　side; horizontal　読L23-II
よごす　汚す　to make dirty [u]　会L18
よごれる　汚れる　to become dirty [ru]　会L18
よじ　四時　four o'clock　会L1(e)
よしゅう　予習　preparation of a lesson　会L22
よっか　四日　four days　会L13
よっか　四日　the fourth day of a month　会L4(e)
よっつ　四つ　four　会L9
よてい　予定　schedule; plan　会L15
よぶ　呼ぶ　to call (one's name); to invite [u]　会L19
よむ　読む　to read [u]　会L3
よやく　予約　reservation　会L10
よやくする　予約する　to reserve [irr.]　会L15
よる　夜　night　読L5-II, 会L6
よる　寄る　to stop by [u]　会L19

よろしかったら　if it is okay (polite)　会L20
よろしくおつたえください　よろしくお伝えください　Please give my best regards (to . . .).　会L19
よろしくおねがいします　よろしくお願いします　Nice to meet you.　会G
よわい　弱い　weak　読L16-II
よんぷん　四分　four minutes　会L1(e)

ら

らいがっき　来学期　next semester　会L11
らいげつ　来月　next month　会L4(e), 会L8
らいしゅう　来週　next week　会L4(e), 会L6
らいねん　来年　next year　会L4(e), 会L6
らく（な）　楽　easy; comfortable　会L22
らくご　落語　comic monologue　読L20-II
らくごか　落語家　comic storyteller　読L20-II
ラジオ　radio　会L14

り

りこんする　離婚する　to get a divorce [irr.]　会L17
りそう　理想　ideal　会L23
りゅうがくする　留学する　to study abroad [irr.]　会L11
りゅうがくせい　留学生　international student　会L1
りょう　両　a unit of currency used in the Edo period　読L20-II
りょう　寮　dormitory　読L9-II, 会L17
りょうがえ　両替　money exchange　会L13(e)
りょうしん　両親　parents　会L14
りょうり　料理　cooking; dish　読L6-III, 会L10
りょうりする　料理する　to cook [irr.]　会L8
りょかん　旅館　Japanese inn　会L15
りょこう　旅行　travel　会L5
りょこうがいしゃ　旅行会社　travel agency　会L17
りょこうする　旅行する　to travel [irr.]　会L10
りれきしょ　履歴書　résumé　会L14
りんご　apple　会L8(e), 会L10

ルームメイト　roommate　会L11
るす　留守　absence; not at home　会L21
るすばん　留守番　looking after a house during someone's absence　会L23

あいうえお　かきくけこ　さしすせそ　たちつてと　なにぬねの　はひふへほ　まみむめも　やゆよ　らりる**れろ**　わをん

れい　例　example　会L11(e)
れいぞうこ　冷蔵庫　refrigerator　会L18
れきし　歴史　history　会L1, 会L2
レストラン　restaurant　会L4
レポート　(term) paper　会L4
れんしゅう　練習　exercise　会L11(e)
れんしゅうする　練習する　to practice
　　[irr.]　会L10
レントゲン　X-ray　会L12(e)
れんらくする　連絡する　to contact [irr.]
　　　　　　　　会L21

ろうそく　candle　会L18

ろくがつ　六月　June　会L4(e)
ろくじ　六時　six o'clock　会L1(e)
ろっぷん　六分　six minutes　会L1(e)
ロボット　robot　読L16-II

ワイン　wine　読L6-III
わかい　若い　young　会L9
わかもの　若者　young people　読L15-II
わかる　to understand [u]　会L4
わかれる　別れる　to break up; to
　　separate [ru]　会L12
わすれる　忘れる　to forget; to leave
　　behind [ru]　会L6
わたくし　私　I (formal)　会L13
わたし　私　I　会L1

わたしたち　私たち　we　読L12-II, 会L14
わたす　渡す　to give; to hand [u]
　　　　　　　　読L20-II
わたる　渡る　to cross [u]
　　　　　　会L6(e), 読L15-II
わらう　笑う　to laugh [u]　会L16
わりびきけん　割引券　discount coupon
　　　　　　　　会L15
わるい　悪い　bad　会L12
わるぐちをいう　悪口を言う　to talk
　　behind someone's back [u]　会L23
ワンルームマンション　studio apartment
　　　　　　　　読L18-III

単語さくいん2 Vocabulary Index (E-J)
たんご

会……会話・文法編
　　（Conversation and Grammar section）
読……読み書き編
　　（Reading and Writing section）
G……あいさつ（Greetings）
(e)……Useful Expressions
Ⅰ・Ⅱ・Ⅲ……問題番号（読み書き編）
　　（number of exercise in the
　　Reading and Writing section）
[u] u-verb　[ru] ru-verb　[irr.] irregular verb

A

about (approximate measurement)
　〜ぐらい　会L4
about...　〜について　会L8
about this much　このぐらい　会L16
absence　やすみ　休み　会L5
absence　るす　留守　会L21
absent (from)　やすむ　休む [u]　会L6
according to...　〜によると　会L17
account　こうざ　口座　会L13(e)
activity　かつどう　活動　会L15
actor　はいゆう　俳優　会L11
actress　はいゆう　俳優　会L11
actually　じつは　実は　会L16
adult　おとな　大人　読L12-II, 会L13
advertisement　こうこく　広告　会L13
advice　アドバイス　読L14-II
(be) affected　えいきょうをうける　影
　響を受ける [ru]　読L17-II
after...　〜ご　〜後　会L10
after (an event)　（〜の）あと　（〜の）
　後　読L8-II, 会L11
after all　やっぱり　読L13-II, 会L17
after meals　しょくご　食後　会L12(e)
after that　そのご　その後　読L17-II
again　また　会L20
age　じだい　時代　読L14-II
agree　さんせいする　賛成する [irr.]
　　　　　　　　　　　　　　会L22
air conditioner　エアコン　会L6
airplane　ひこうき　飛行機　会L10
airport　くうこう　空港　会L13
alcoholic drink　（お）さけ　（お）酒　会L3
all　ぜんぶ　全部　会L13
all　みんな　読L7-II, 会L9
all day long　いちにちじゅう　一日中
　　　　　　　　　　　　　　会L15
all of you　みなさん　皆さん　会L14
all over the world　せかいじゅう　世界
　中　読L23-II
all the time　ずっと　会L22
all (of the people) together　みんなで
　　　　　　　　　　　　　　会L8

all year　いちねんじゅう　一年中
　　　　　　　　　　　　読L15-II
allergy　アレルギー　会L8(e), 会L12
alone　ひとりで　一人で　会L4
already　もう　会L9
always　いつも　読L6-III, 会L8
A.M.　ごぜん　午前　会L1
amount　きんがく　金額　会L13(e)
amulet　おまもり　お守り　読L21-II
and　〜と　会L4
and so forth　〜など　読L12-II
and then　そして　読L9-II, 会L11
and then　それから　会L4
(get) angry　おこる　怒る [u]　読L12-II
animal　どうぶつ　動物　会L20
animation　アニメ　会L20
announcement　アナウンス　読L13-III
annoying　うるさい　会L22
answer　こたえ　答/ 答え
　　　　　　　　会L11(e), 読L23-II
answer　こたえる　答える [ru]
　　　　　　　　読L8-II, 会L23
antibiotic　こうせいぶっしつ　抗生物
　質　会L12(e)
anxious　ふあん（な）　不安
　　　　　　　　読L13-II, 会L18
anyhow　とにかく　会L21
anything　なんでも　読L13-II
anything else　ほかに　会L11(e)
anyway　とにかく　会L21
anywhere　どこでも　読L16-II
apartment　アパート　会L13
apologize　あやまる　謝る [u]　会L18
appear　でる　出る [ru]　会L9
apple　りんご　会L8(e), 会L10
application　アプリ　会L13
application　もうしこみ　申し込み
　　　　　　　　　　　　読L19-III
appointment　やくそく　約束　会L13
April　しがつ　四月　会L4(e)
arm　て　手　会L7(e)
(be) arrested　つかまる　捕まる [u]
　　　　　　　　　　　　　　会L21
arrive　つく　着く [u]　読L13-III, 会L15
art　げいじゅつ　芸術　読L17-II
art exhibition　てんらんかい　展覧会
　　　　　　　　　　　　読L17-II
art museum　びじゅつかん　美術館
　　　　　　　　　　　　　　会L11
as far as (a place)　〜まで　会L5
as much as possible　できるだけ　会L12
as usual　あいかわらず　相変わらず
　　　　　　　　　　　　読L22-II
Asian studies　アジアけんきゅう　アジ
　ア研究　会L1
ask　きく　聞く [u]　会L5

ask (a favor)　たのむ　頼む [u]　会L18
astronaut　うちゅうひこうし　宇宙飛
　行士　会L11
at about...　〜ごろ　会L3
at first　はじめは　初めは　読L18-III
at the time of...　とき　時　会L4
athlete　スポーツせんしゅ　スポーツ
　選手　会L11
atomic bomb　げんばく　原爆
　　　　　　　　　　　　読L15-II
attend　でる　出る [ru]　会L9
audible　きこえる　聞こえる [ru]　会L20
August　はちがつ　八月　会L4(e)
aunt　おばさん　会L14
Australia　オーストラリア　会L1, 会L11
automatic　じどう　自動　読L13-III
autumn colors/leaves　こうよう　紅葉
　　　　　　　　　　　　読L15-II
avocado　アボカド　会L8(e)
awesome　すごい　会L13
awful　ひどい　会L21

B

baby　あかちゃん　赤ちゃん　会L17
back　うしろ　後ろ　会L4
back (body)　せなか　背中　会L7(e)
bad　わるい　悪い　会L12
bad tooth　むしば　虫歯　会L12(e)
bag　かばん　会L2
bag　ふくろ　袋　会L8(e)
baggage　にもつ　荷物　会L6
bake　やく　焼く [u]　会L21
balance inquiry　ざんだかしょうかい
　残高照会　会L13(e)
ball　ボール　会L22
bamboo　たけ　竹　読L15-II
bamboo hat　かさ　読L10-II
banana　バナナ　会L18
band　バンド　読L11-II
bank　ぎんこう　銀行　会L2
bank card　キャッシュカード　会L13(e)
bank transfer　（お）ふりこみ　（お）振込
　　　　　　　　　　　　　　会L13(e)
barbecue　バーベキュー　会L8
baseball　やきゅう　野球　会L10
bath　（お）ふろ　（お）風呂　会L8
battery　でんち　電池　会L15
beard　ひげ　会L17
beautiful　きれい（な）　会L5
beauty parlor　びよういん　美容院
　　　　　　　　　　　　　　会L10
become　なる [u]　会L10
become dirty　よごれる　汚れる [ru]
　　　　　　　　　　　　　　会L18
become late　おくれる　遅れる [ru]
　　　　　　　　　読L13-III, 会L19

become lost　みちにまよう　道に迷う
　[u]　会L16

become sunny　はれる　晴れる [ru]
　　　　　　　　　　　　　　会L19

beef　ぎゅうにく　牛肉　会L8(e)

beer　ビール　会L11

before . . .　まえ　前　会L17

begin　はじめる　始める [ru]　会L8

(something) begins　はじまる　始まる
　[u]　会L9

beige　ベージュ　会L9(e)

believe　しんじる　信じる [ru]　会L21

best　いちばん　一番　会L10

best friend　しんゆう　親友　読L22-II

between　あいだ　間　会L4

big hit　だいヒット　大ヒット　読L17-II

bicycle　じてんしゃ　自転車　会L2

biology　せいぶつがく　生物学　会L1

bird　とり　鳥　読L13-II

birthday　たんじょうび　誕生日　会L5

bite　さす　刺す [u]　会L21

black　くろい　黒い　会L9, 会L9(e)

black and white　しろくろ　白黒　会L9(e)

black tea　こうちゃ　紅茶　会L13

blackboard　こくばん　黒板　会L2(e)

bloom　さく　咲く [u]　会L18

blow-dry　ブロー　会L17(e)

blue　あおい　青い　会L9, 会L9(e)

board　のる　乗る [u]　会L5

boarding ticket　じょうしゃけん　乗車
　券　会L10(e)

boat　ふね　船　会L10

body　からだ　体　会L13

boil water　おゆをわかす　お湯を沸か
　す [u]　会L17

Bon dance (Japanese traditional dance)
　ぼんおどり　盆踊り　会L23

book　ほん　本　会L2, 会L2(e)

bookish expression　かたいいいかた
　かたい言い方　会L11(e)

bookstore　ほんや　本屋　会L4

boots　ブーツ　会L17

boring　つまらない　会L5

(be) born　うまれる　生まれる [ru]
　　　　　　　　　読L15-II, 会L17

borrow　かりる　借りる [ru]　会L6

bound for . . .　～いき　～行き　会L10(e)

boxed lunch　（お）べんとう　（お）弁当
　　　　　　　　　　　　　　会L9

boyfriend　かれ / かれし　彼 / 彼氏
　　　　　　　　　　　　　　会L12

branch office　してん　支店　会L20

bread　パン　会L4

break (a bone)　こっせつする　骨折す
　る　会L12(e)

break (something)　こわす　壊す [u]
　　　　　　　　　　　　　　会L18

(something) breaks　こわれる　壊れる
　[ru]　会L18

break up　わかれる　別れる [ru]　会L12

breakfast　あさごはん　朝ご飯　会L3

breast　むね　胸　会L7(e)

bright　あかるい　明るい　会L18

bright　あたまがいい　頭がいい　会L7

bring (a person)　つれてくる　連れて
　くる [irr.]　会L6

bring (a person) back　つれてかえる
　連れて帰る [u]　読L12-II

bring (a thing)　もってくる　持ってく
　る [irr.]　会L6

bring up　そだてる　育てる [ru]　会L22

Britain　イギリス　会L1, 会L2

broadcast program　ばんぐみ　番組
　　　　　　　　　　　　　読L16-II

brothers and sisters　きょうだい　兄弟
　　　　　　　　　　　　　　会L7

brown　ちゃいろい　茶色い　会L9(e)

brush (teeth)　みがく　磨く [u]　会L13

building　たてもの　建物　会L15

Bullet Train　しんかんせん　新幹線
　　　　　　　　　　　　　　会L10

bully　いじめる [ru]　会L21

burglar　どろぼう　泥棒　会L21

burn　やく　焼く [u]　会L21

burn oneself　やけどをする　会L12(e)

bus　バス　会L5

bus stop　バスてい　バス停　会L4

business　ビジネス　会L1, 会L2

business meeting　かいぎ　会議　会L21

business to take care of　ようじ　用事
　　　　　　　　　　　　　　会L12

business trip　しゅっちょう　出張
　　　　　　　　　　　読L14-II, 会L19

busy (people/days)　いそがしい　忙し
　い　会L5

but　でも　会L3

. . ., but　～が　読L5-II, 会L7

. . ., but　～けど　会L15

buttocks　（お）しり　（お）尻　会L7(e)

buy　かう　買う [u]　会L4

buy insurance　ほけんにはいる　保険
　に入る [u]　会L15

by (means of transportation)　～で
　　　　　　　　　　　　　　会L10

by (time/date)　～までに
　　　　　　　　　読L12-II, 会L18

by all means　ぜひ　是非　会L9

(do something) by oneself　じぶんで
　自分で　会L16

by the end of today　きょうじゅうに
　今日中に　会L16

by the way　ところで　会L9

by what means　どうやって　会L10

──────── C ────────

cabbage　キャベツ　会L8(e)

cafe　カフェ　会L3

cafeteria　しょくどう　食堂　会L7

cake　ケーキ　会L10

call　でんわする　電話する [irr.]　会L6

call (one's name)　よぶ　呼ぶ [u]
　　　　　　　　　　　　　　会L19

camera　カメラ　会L8

camp　キャンプ　会L11

Canada　カナダ　会L1

candle　ろうそく　会L18

cannot be helped　しかたがない
　　　　　　　　　　　　　読L22-II

cannot wait　たのしみです　楽しみで
　す　会L15

cap　ぼうし　帽子　会L2

car　くるま　車　会L7

Car No. 1　いちごうしゃ　一号車　会L10(e)

careful　きをつける　気をつける [ru]
　　　　　　　　　　　　　　会L15

carrot　にんじん　会L8(e)

carry　はこぶ　運ぶ [u]　会L22

carry　もつ　持つ [u]　会L6

cartoonist　まんがか　漫画家　会L11

case　ばあい　場合　読L14-II

cash　げんきん　現金　会L13(e)

castle　（お）しろ　（お）城　読L5-II

cat　ねこ　猫　会L4

catch a cold　かぜをひく　風邪をひく
　[u]　会L12

(be) caught　つかまる　捕まる [u]
　　　　　　　　　　　　　　会L21

cautious　きをつける　気をつける [ru]
　　　　　　　　　　　　　　会L15

ceiling　てんじょう　天井　読L17-II

celebrity　ゆうめいじん　有名人　会L10

cell phone　けいたい（でんわ）　携帯
　（電話）　会L18

Certainly.　かしこまりました　会L20

chair　いす　会L2(e), 会L4

change clothes　きがえる　着替える
　[ru]　会L21

character　じ　字　会L20

character　もじ　文字　読L17-II

charge　～だい　～代　会L12

charm (against evils)　おまもり　お守
　り　読L21-II

chat　しゃべる [u]　会L15

cheap　けち（な）　会L14

cheap (thing)　やすい　安い　会L5

cheat in an exam　カンニングする
　[irr.]　会L23

check　チェックする [irr.]　会L23

checking in　チェックイン（する）
　　　　　　　　　　　　　　会L15(e)

checking out　チェックアウト（する）
　　　　　　　　　　　　　　会L15(e)

cheerful　あかるい　明るい　読L11-II

Cheers! (a toast)　かんぱい　乾杯　会L8

chef　シェフ　会L11, 読L6-III

cherry blossom　さくら　桜　会L18

chicken　とりにく　鶏肉　会L8(e)

(your/someone's) child (polite)　おこさん　お子さん　会L19

child　こども　子供　会L4

chill out at home　ごろごろする [irr.]　会L10

China　ちゅうごく　中国　会L1, 会L2

Chinese character　かんじ　漢字　会L6

chocolate　チョコレート　会L14

choose　えらぶ　選ぶ [u]　会L17

chopsticks　はし　会L8

Christmas　クリスマス　会L14

city　まち　町　会L4

class　クラス　会L4

class　じゅぎょう　授業　会L11

class cancellation　きゅうこう　休講　会L23

classroom　きょうしつ　教室　会L15

clean　きれい（な）　会L5

clean　そうじする　掃除する [irr.]　会L8

clever　あたまがいい　頭がいい　会L7

client　おきゃくさん　お客さん　会L17

climb　のぼる　登る [u]　会L11

clock　とけい　時計　会L2

close　したしい　親しい　読L18-III

close　ちかい　近い　会L13

close (something)　しめる　閉める [ru]　会L6

(something) closes　しまる　閉まる [u]　会L18

clothes　ふく　服　会L12

clothes　ようふく　洋服　読L18-II

cloud　くも　雲　読L17-II

cloudy weather　くもり　曇り　会L8

club activity　サークル　会L7

clumsy　へた（な）　下手　会L8

coffee　コーヒー　会L3

cold　かぜ　風邪　会L12

cold (things/people)　つめたい　冷たい　会L10

cold (weather)　さむい　寒い　会L5

colleague　どうりょう　同僚　会L21

collect　あつめる　集める [ru]　会L16

college　だいがく　大学　会L1

college student　だいがくせい　大学生　会L1

colloquial expression　くだけたいいかた　くだけた言い方　会L11(e)

color　いろ　色　会L9

comb one's hair　かみをとかす　髪をとかす [u]　会L16

come　くる　来る [irr.]　会L3

come back　もどる　戻る [u]　会L20

come into existence　できる [ru]　会L14

come to pick up　むかえにくる　迎えに来る [irr.]　会L16

(something/someone) comes back　もどってくる　戻ってくる [irr.]　会L23

comfortable　らく（な）　楽　会L22

comic book　まんが　漫画　会L14

comic monologue　らくご　落語　読L20-II

comic storyteller　らくごか　落語家　読L20-II

coming from　しゅっしん　出身　会L11

commission　てすうりょう　手数料　会L13(e)

common language　きょうつうご　共通語　会L11(e)

commute to　かよう　通う [u]　読L21-II

commuter's pass　ていきけん　定期券　会L10(e)

company　かいしゃ　会社　会L7

compare　くらべる　比べる [ru]　会L21

compared with . . .　〜にくらべて　〜に比べて　会L17

complain　もんくをいう　文句を言う [u]　会L21

complaint　もんく　文句　会L21

(be) completed　かんせいする　完成する [irr.]　読L17-II

composition　さくぶん　作文　会L9

computer　コンピューター　会L1, 会L2

concerning . . .　〜について　会L8

concert　コンサート　会L9

condominium　マンション　会L13

conference　かいぎ　会議　会L21

Congratulations!　おめでとうございます　会L17

consider　かんがえる　考える [ru]　会L18

constipation　べんぴ　便秘　会L12(e)

consult　そうだんする　相談する [irr.]　会L14

consumer prices　ぶっか　物価　会L13

contact　れんらくする　連絡する [irr.]　会L21

contact lenses　コンタクト（レンズ）　会L17

continue　つづける　続ける [ru]　会L20

continue　つづく　続く [u]　読L16-II

convenience store　コンビニ　会L2

convenient　べんり（な）　便利　会L7

convey message　つたえる　伝える [ru]　会L20

cook　りょうりする　料理する [irr.]　会L8

cooking　りょうり　料理　読L6-III

cool (weather)　すずしい　涼しい　会L10

copy　うつす　写す [u]　読L16-II

corner　かど　角　会L6(e), 会L20

correct　なおす　直す [u]　会L16

correct（○）　まる　会L11(e)

cosmetics　けしょうひん　化粧品　会L14

cost　する [irr.]　読L20-II

cost of food　しょくひ　食費　読L18-III

cost of living, the　せいかつひ　生活費　読L18-II

cough　せき　会L12

cough　せきがでる　せきが出る [ru]　会L12

count　かぞえる　数える [ru]　読L17-II

(counter for bound volumes)　〜さつ　〜冊　会L14, 会L14(e)

(counter for equipment)　〜だい　〜台　会L14, 会L14(e)

(counter for flat objects)　〜まい　〜枚　会L5, 会L14(e)

(counter for long objects)　〜ほん　〜本　会L14, 会L14(e)

(counter for people)　〜にん　〜人　会L7

(counter for smaller animals)　〜ひき　〜匹　会L14, 会L14(e)

country　くに　国　会L6

countryside　いなか　読L20-II

courage　ゆうき　勇気　読L22-II

cover　つつむ　包む [u]　会L21

cow　うし　牛　読L12-II

cram school　じゅく　塾　読L7-II, 会L22

credit card　クレジットカード　会L13(e)

criminal　はんにん　犯人　会L21

crop　かる　刈る [u]　会L17(e)

cross　わたる　渡る [u]　会L6(e), 読L15-II

(be) crowded　こんでいる　混んでいる　読L15-II

cry　なく　泣く [u]　読L12-II, 会L13

cucumber　きゅうり　会L8(e)

cuisine　りょうり　料理　会L10

culture　ぶんか　文化　読L11-II, 会L16

curry　カレー　会L13

curtain　カーテン　会L2(e), 会L18

custom　しゅうかん　習慣　会L15

customer　おきゃくさん　お客さん　会L17

cut　カット　会L17(e)

cut　きる　切る [u]　会L8, 会L17(e)

cut (classes)　サボる [u]　会L11

cute　かわいい　会L7

D

dance　おどる　踊る [u]　会L9

dangerous　あぶない　危ない　会L17

dark　くらい　暗い　会L18

date (romantic)　デート　会L3

date (someone)　つきあう　付き合う [u]　読L14-II, 会L15

daughter　むすめ　娘　読L12-II

(someone's) daughter (polite)　おじょうさん　お嬢さん　会L22

day　ひ　日　読L15-II, 会L16

day after tomorrow, the　あさって　会L4(e), 会L8

day before yesterday, the　おととい
　　　　　会L4(e), 会L19
day off　やすみ　休み　会L5
deadline　しめきり　締め切り
　　　　　会L11(e), 会L15
deceive　だます [u]　読L20-II
December　じゅうにがつ　十二月
　　　　　会L4(e)
decide　きめる　決める [ru]　会L10
decide on (an item)　する [irr.]　会L15
(be) decided　きまる　決まる [u]
　　　　　会L19
deer　しか　鹿　読L15-II
definitely　ぜったいに　絶対に
　　　　　読L20-II, 会L22
. . . degrees (temperature)　～ど　～度
　　　　　会L8
delicious　おいしい　会L2
dentist　しか　歯科　会L12(e)
departing first　せんぱつ　先発
　　　　　会L10(e)
departing second　じはつ　次発
　　　　　会L10(e)
department manager　ぶちょう　部長
　　　　　会L19
department store　デパート　会L7
deposit　(お)あずけいれ　(お)預け入れ
　　　　　会L13(e)
deposit money (in a bank)　ちょきんす
　る　貯金する [irr.]　読L18-II
dermatologist　ひふか　皮膚科
　　　　　会L12(e)
desert　デザート　読L13-III
desk　つくえ　机　会L2(e), 会L4
dialect　ほうげん　方言　会L11(e)
diarrhea　げり　下痢　会L12(e)
diary　にっき　日記　読L9-II, 会L18
dictionary　じしょ　辞書　会L2(e), 会L15
die　しぬ　死ぬ [u]　会L6
difference　ちがい　違い　会L17
different　ちがう　違う [u]
　　　　　読L16-II, 会L23
different kinds of　いろいろ (な)　会L13
difficult　むずかしい　難しい　会L5
diligent　まじめ (な)　読L12-II, 会L19
dining commons　しょくどう　食堂
　　　　　会L7
dinner　ばんごはん　晩ご飯　会L3
dinner　ゆうしょく　夕食　会L23
directions　みち　道　会L16
dirty　きたない　汚い　会L16
disappear　いなくなる [u]　会L23
disappear　なくなる [u]　会L23
(be) disappointed　がっかりする [irr.]
　　　　　読L20-II, 会L23
discount coupon　わりびきけん　割引
　券　会L15
disgusted with　きらい (な)　嫌い　会L5
dish　(お)さら　(お)皿　会L14

dish　りょうり　料理　読L6-III
dislike　きらい (な)　嫌い　会L5
disorganized　めちゃくちゃ (な)　会L21
do　する [irr.]　会L3
do　やる [u]　会L5
do laundry　せんたくする　洗濯する
　[irr.]　会L8
do one's best　がんばる　頑張る [u]
　　　　　会L13
do sightseeing　かんこうする　観光す
　る [irr.]　会L15
doctor　いしゃ　医者　会L1, 会L10
document　しょるい　書類　会L22
dog　いぬ　犬　会L4
don't look well　げんきがない　元気が
　ない　会L12
door　と　戸　読L10-II, 読L13-III
door　ドア　会L2(e)
dormitory　りょう　寮　読L9-II, 会L17
double room　ダブル　会L15(e)
draw　かく　描く [u]　会L15
drawing　え　絵　会L15
dream　ゆめ　夢　会L11
drink　のみもの　飲み物　会L5
drink　のむ　飲む [u]　会L3
drive　うんてんする　運転する [irr.]
　　　　　会L8
drive　ドライブ　会L11
drive (someone)　おくる　送る [u]
　　　　　会L19
drop (something)　おとす　落とす [u]
　　　　　会L18
(be) dropped　おとされる　落とされる
　　　　　読L15-II
(something) drops　おちる　落ちる
　[ru]　会L18
during the class　じゅぎょうちゅうに
　授業中に　会L16
dye　そめる [ru]　会L17(e)

Ⓔ

ear　みみ　耳　会L7(e)
early　はやい　早い　会L3
(do something) early　はやく　早く /
　速く　会L10
earthquake　じしん　地震　会L15
east　ひがし　東　会L6(e)
easy　かんたん (な)　簡単　会L10
easy　らく (な)　楽　会L22
easy (problem)　やさしい　易しい　会L5
eat　たべる　食べる [ru]　会L3
economics　けいざい　経済　会L1, 会L2
Edo period　えどじだい　江戸時代
　　　　　読L20-II
egg　たまご　卵　会L12
eggplant　なす　会L8(e)
Egypt　エジプト　会L1
eight　やっつ　八つ　会L9
eight days　ようか　八日　会L13

eight minutes　はっぷん / はちふん
　八分　会L1(e)
eight o'clock　はちじ　八時　会L1(e)
eighteen minutes　じゅうはっぷん /
　じゅうはちふん　十八分　会L1(e)
eighth day of a month, the　ようか　八
　日　会L4(e)
electrical engineering　でんきこうがく
　電気工学　読L19-III
electricity　でんき　電気　会L2(e), 会L6
elementary school　しょうがっこう
　小学校　会L23
elementary school students　しょうが
　くせい　小学生　読L16-II
elephant　ぞう　象　会L13
eleven minutes　じゅういっぷん　十一
　分　会L1(e)
eleven o'clock　じゅういちじ　十一時
　　　　　会L1(e)
eleventh day of a month, the　じゅうい
　ちにち　十一日　会L4(e)
e-mail　メール　会L9
embarrassing　はずかしい　恥ずかし
　い　会L18
emoji　えもじ　絵文字　読L23-II
emoticon　かおもじ　顔文字　読L23-II
emotion　かんじょう　感情　読L23-II
(something) ends　おわる　終わる [u]
　　　　　会L9
energetic　げんき (な)　元気　会L5
English (language)　えいご　英語　会L2
English conversation　えいかいわ　英
　会話　会L22
enjoy　たのしむ　楽しむ [u]　読L15-II
enough　たりる　足りる [ru]　会L17
ENT doctor　じびか　耳鼻科　会L12(e)
enter　はいる　入る [u]　会L6
entrance　いりぐち　入口　会L10(e)
envious　うらやましい　会L17
(somebody is) envious　うらやましがる
　　　　　読L22-II
environment　かんきょう　環境　会L21
era　じだい　時代　読L14-II
erase　けす　消す [u]　会L6
eraser　けしゴム　消しゴム　会L2(e)
escape　にげる　逃げる [ru]　読L22-II
especially　とくに　特に　会L13
essay　さくぶん　作文　会L9
Europe　ヨーロッパ　会L22
evening　ゆうがた　夕方　会L18
every day　まいにち　毎日　会L3
every month　まいつき　毎月　読L18-III
every morning　まいあさ　毎朝　会L19
every night　まいばん　毎晩　会L3
every week　まいしゅう　毎週　会L8
everyone　みなさん　皆さん
　　　　　読L6-III, 会L14
everyone (polite expression of みなさ
　ん)　みなさま　みな様　読L19-II

everything　なんでも　読L13-II
Everything is under control.　だいじょうぶ　大丈夫　会L5
exactly　ちょうど　会L14
exam　しけん　試験　会L9
example　れい　例　会L11(e)
excellent food　ごちそう　読L9-II
exchange　こうかんする　交換する [irr.]　会L20
Excuse me.　しつれいします　失礼します　会L16
Excuse me.　すみません　会G
exercise　うんどうする　運動する [irr.]　会L9
exercise　れんしゅう　練習　会L11(e)
exit　でぐち　出口　会L10(e)
exit　でる　出る [ru]　読L6-I, 会L9
expensive　たかい　高い　会L2
experience　けいけん　経験　読L13-II, 会L15
explain　せつめいする　説明する [irr.]　会L16
express　あらわす　表す [u]　読L23-II
express　きゅうこう　急行　会L10(e)
expression　ひょうじょう　表情　読L23-II
expression of gratitude　おれい　お礼　会L19
extra money to spare for the cost of living　せいかつのゆとり　生活のゆとり　読L18-II
extra-modest expression for ～ている　～ておる [u]　会L20
extra-modest expression for ある　ござる [u]　会L20
extra-modest expression for いう　もうす　申す [u]　会L20
extra-modest expression for いく and くる　まいる　参る [u]　会L20
extra-modest expression for いる　おる [u]　会L20
extra-modest expression for する　いたす　致す [u]　会L20
extra-modest expression for たべる and のむ　いただく　頂く [u]　会L20
extra-modest expression for です　～でござる [u]　会L20
extremely　すごく　会L5
extremely　ものすごく　会L23
eye　め　目　会L7, 会L7(e)
eyebrow　まゆげ　眉毛　会L7(e)

F

face　かお　顔　会L7(e), 会L10
factory　こうじょう　工場　会L21
fail　しっぱいする　失敗する [irr.]　会L22
fall　あき　秋　会L10
fall down　ころぶ　転ぶ [u]　会L18

(rain/snow) falls　（あめ / ゆきが）ふる　（雨 / 雪が）降る [u]　会L8
family　かぞく　家族　会L7
famous　ゆうめい（な）　有名　会L8
(hand) fan　せんす　扇子　会L20
far (away)　とおい　遠い　会L21
farm　はたけ　畑　読L12-II
fashion　ファッション　読L15-II
fashionable　おしゃれ（な）　会L14
fast　はやい　速い　会L7
(do something) fast　はやく　早く / 速く　会L10
father　おとうさん　お父さん　会L1, 会L2
father　ちちおや　父親　読L14-II
(my) father　ちち　父　会L7
February　にがつ　二月　会L4(e)
fee　～だい　～代　会L12
feed　えさ　読L20-II
feel dizzy　めまいがする　会L12(e)
feel embarrassed　はずかしい　恥ずかしい　会L18
feel sick　きぶんがわるい　気分が悪い　会L13
feel sorry for　かわいそう（な）　会L23
feeling　かんじょう　感情　読L23-II
female student　じょしがくせい　女子学生　読L18-II
festival　（お）まつり　（お）祭り　会L11
few, a　すくない　少ない　会L17
few seconds, a　しょうしょう　少々　会L19
field　ぶんや　分野　読L17-II
fifteen minutes　じゅうごふん　十五分　会L1(e)
fifth day of a month, the　いつか　五日　会L4(e)
file　ファイル　会L16
final examination　きまつしけん　期末試験　会L16
finally　さいごに　最後に　会L23
find　みつける　見つける [ru]　会L21
find something agreeable　きにいる　気に入る [u]　会L23
finger　ゆび　指　会L7(e)
fire　かじ　火事　会L17
firefighter　しょうぼうし　消防士　会L11
first　ひとつめ　一つ目　会L6(e)
first day　いちにちめ　一日目　会L15
first day of a month, the　ついたち　一日　会L4(e)
first floor　いっかい　一階　会L20
first of all　まず　読L8-II, 会L18
first-year student　いちねんせい　一年生　会L1
fish　さかな　魚　会L2
fishing　つり　会L11
five　いつつ　五つ　会L9

five days　いつか　五日　会L13
five minutes　ごふん　五分　会L1(e)
five o'clock　ごじ　五時　会L1(e)
fix　なおす　直す [u]　会L16
flower　はな　花　会L4
fluent　ぺらぺら（な）　会L22
fly　とぶ　飛ぶ [u]　読L16-II
(file) folder　ファイル　会L16
fond of　すき（な）　好き　会L5
food　たべもの　食べ物　会L5
foot　あし　足　会L7(e), 会L12
for . . .　～（の）ために　読L19-III, 会L23
for a long time　ずっと　会L22
for example　たとえば　例えば　会L11(e), 会L16-II, 会L17
. . . for example　～とか　会L22
for . . . months　～かげつ　～か月　会L10
for the first time　はじめて　初めて　会L12
for the sake of . . .　～のための　読L17-II
for the sake of . . .　～ために　会L23
for two days　ふつかかん　二日間　読L22-II
for two to three days　にさんにち　二三日　会L12
for . . . years　～ねんかん　～年間　読L14-II
for . . . weeks　～しゅうかん　～週間　会L10
foreign country　がいこく　外国　会L11
foreign language　がいこくご　外国語　会L13
foreigner　がいこくじん　外国人　会L15
forget　わすれる　忘れる [ru]　会L6
former name of Tokyo　えど　江戸　読L20-II
fortune-telling　うらない　占い　読L21-II
(be) found　みつかる　見つかる [u]　会L16
four　よっつ　四つ　会L9
four days　よっか　四日　会L13
four minutes　よんぷん　四分　会L1(e)
four o'clock　よじ　四時　会L1(e)
fourteen minutes　じゅうよんぷん　十四分　会L1(e)
fourteenth day of a month, the　じゅうよっか　十四日　会L4(e)
fourth day of a month, the　よっか　四日　会L4(e)
free (time)　ひま（な）　暇　会L5
free of charge　ただ　会L23
freedom　じゆう　自由　会L22
freely　じゆうに　自由に　会L22
Friday　きんようび　金曜日　会L4, 会L4(e)
friend　ともだち　友だち　会L1

A B C D E **F** **G** **H** I J K L M N O P Q R S T U V W X Y Z

friend　ゆうじん　友人　読L19-III
frightening　こわい　怖い　会L5
from . . .　〜から　読L7-II, 会L9
from now on　これから　読L11-II, 会L16
front　まえ　前　会L4
front desk　フロント　会L15(e)
fruit　くだもの　果物　会L5
fun　たのしい　楽しい　会L5
funny　おもしろい　面白い　会L5
furniture　かぐ　家具　会L15
future　しょうらい　将来　会L11
future　みらい　未来　読L16-II

G

gain weight　ふとる　太る [u]　会L7
game　ゲーム　会L4
game　しあい　試合　会L12
garbage　ごみ　会L16
garden　にわ　庭　会L15
gasoline　ガソリン　会L21
gate　かいさつ　改札　会L10(e)
general admission seat　じゆうせき　自由席　会L10(e)
(generic counter for smaller items)　〜こ　〜個　会L14, 会L14(e)
Germany　ドイツ　会L20
gesture　みぶり　身ぶり　読L20-II
get (a grade)　とる　取る [u]　会L11
get (from somebody)　もらう [u]　会L9
get a divorce　りこんする　離婚する [irr.]　会L17
get a full-time job (at . . .)　しゅうしょくする　就職する [irr.]　会L17
get acquainted with　しりあう　知り合う [u]　会L19
get along well　なかがいい　仲がいい　会L19
get angry　おこる　怒る [u]　読L12-II, 会L19
get crowded　こむ　混む [u]　読L15-II, 会L17
get depressed　おちこむ　落ち込む [u]　会L16
get off　おりる　降りる [ru]　会L6
get to know　しる　知る [u]　会L7
get up　おきる　起きる [ru]　会L3
get used to . . .　なれる　慣れる [ru]　会L17
Get well soon.　おだいじに　お大事に　会L12
girlfriend　かのじょ　彼女　会L12
give　わたす　渡す [u]　読L20-II
give (me)　くれる [ru]　会L14
give (pets, plants, younger siblings, etc.)　やる [u]　会L21
give (to others)　あげる [ru]　会L14
give up　あきらめる [ru]　会L14
give warning　ちゅういする　注意する [irr.]　会L14

glad　うれしい　会L13
glasses　めがね　眼鏡　会L7
gloves　てぶくろ　手袋　会L10
go　いく　行く [u]　会L3
go back　かえる　帰る [u]　会L3
go back　もどる　戻る [u]　読L16-II
go on a diet　ダイエットする [irr.]　会L11
go out　でかける　出かける [ru]　会L5
go through　とおる　通る [u]　読L15-II
go to pick up　むかえにいく　迎えに行く [u]　会L16
go to sleep　ねる　寝る [ru]　会L3
go well　うまくいく [u]　読L22-II
God　かみさま　神様　読L12-II, 会L22
(something) goes off　きえる　消える [ru]　会L18
gold　きんいろ　金色　会L9(e)
gold　ゴールド　会L9(e)
golf　ゴルフ　会L13
good　いい　会L3
Good afternoon.　こんにちは　会G
good at . . .　じょうず（な）　上手　会L8
good child　いいこ　いい子　会L9
good deed　いいこと　読L10-II
Good evening.　こんばんは　会G
Good morning.　おはよう / おはようございます　会G
Good night.　おやすみ（なさい）　会G
Good-bye.　さようなら　会G
good-looking　かっこいい　会L5
government　せいふ　政府　会L21
grade (on a test, etc.)　せいせき　成績　会L12
graduate (from . . .)　そつぎょうする　卒業する [irr.]　会L15
graduate school　だいがくいん　大学院　会L16
graduate student　だいがくいんせい　大学院生　会L1
graduation ceremony　そつぎょうしき　卒業式　会L15
grammar　ぶんぽう　文法　会L11(e), 会L13
grandfather　おじいさん　会L7
grandmother　おばあさん　会L7
grape　ぶどう　会L8(e)
gray　グレー　会L9(e)
gray　はいいろ　灰色　会L9(e)
greatly　たいへん　読L19-II
green　グリーン　会L9(e)
green　みどり　緑　会L9(e), 読L15-II
green light　あおしんごう　青信号　会L9(e)
green tea　（お）ちゃ　（お）茶　会L3
greetings　あいさつ　読L23-II
grill　やく　焼く [u]　会L21
grin　ニヤニヤする [irr.]　読L13-II
groper　ちかん　会L21

guardian deity of children　じぞう / おじぞうさん　読L10-II
guest　おきゃくさん　お客さん　会L17
guitar　ギター　会L9

H

haiku　はいく　俳句　読L17-II
hair　かみ　髪　会L7, 会L7(e)
hair coloring　カラー　会L17(e)
hairstyle　かみがた　髪形　会L17(e)
halal　ハラルフード　会L8(e)
half　はん　半　会L1
half past two　にじはん　二時半　会L1
hamburger　ハンバーガー　会L3
hand　て　手　会L7(e)
hand　わたす　渡す [u]　読L20-II
hand in (something)　だす　出す [u]　会L16
hangover　ふつかよい　二日酔い　会L12
happen　おこる　起こる [u]　読L21-II
happy (lasting happiness)　しあわせ（な）　幸せ　読L10-II, 会L13
hat　ぼうし　帽子　会L2
hate　だいきらい（な）　大嫌い　会L5
have a fever　ねつがある　熱がある [u]　会L12
have a fight　けんかする [irr.]　会L11
have a scheduling conflict　つごうがわるい　都合が悪い　会L17
have a stomachache　おなかをこわす [u]　会L23
have a talk　はなしをする　話をする [irr.]　読L9-II, 会L19
have difficulty　こまる　困る [u]　会L16
have one's hair permed　パーマをかける [ru]　会L17(e)
hay fever　かふんしょう　花粉症　会L12(e)
he　かれ　彼　会L12
head　あたま　頭　会L7(e)
head of a familiy　しゅじん　主人　読L15-II
headphones　ヘッドホン　会L20
health　けんこう　健康　会L23
health insurance certificate　ほけんしょう　保険証　会L12(e)
healthy　げんき（な）　元気　会L5
hear　きく　聞く [u]　会L3
heart　こころ　心　読L20-II
heater　ヒーター　会L17
heavens, the　てん　天　読L12-II
heavy　おもい　重い　会L20
Hello? (used on the phone)　もしもし　会L4
help　たすける　助ける [ru]　読L16-II, 会L22
help　てつだう　手伝う [u]　会L6
(be) helped　たすかる　助かる [u]　会L18

here　ここ　会L2
Here it is.　どうぞ　会L2
high　たかい　高い　会L2
high school　こうこう　高校　会L1
high school student　こうこうせい　高校生　会L1
history　れきし　歴史　会L1, 会L2
hit　なぐる　殴る [u]　会L21
hobby　しゅみ　趣味　会L20
hold　もつ　持つ [u]　会L6
hold back for the time being　えんりょする　遠慮する [irr.]　会L19
hold something in one's arm　だく　抱く [u]　読L20-II
holiday　やすみ　休み　会L5
home　いえ　家　会L3
home　うち　会L3
(someone's) home　おたく　お宅　会L20
homesickness　ホームシック　会L12
homestay　ホームステイ　会L8
homework　しゅくだい　宿題　会L5, 会L11(e)
honorific expression for 〜ている　〜ていらっしゃる [u]　会L19
honorific expression for いう　おっしゃる [u]　会L19
honorific expression for いく, くる, and いる　いらっしゃる [u]　会L19
honorific expression for くれる　くださる　下さる [u]　会L19
honorific expression for する　なさる [u]　会L19
honorific expression for たべる and のむ　めしあがる　召し上がる [u]　会L19
honorific expression for ねる　おやすみになる　お休みになる [u]　会L19
honorific expression for みる　ごらんになる　ご覧になる [u]　会L19
honorific language　けいご　敬語　会L19
horizontal　よこ　横　読L23-II
horror　ホラー　読L11-II
hospital　びょういん　病院　会L4
(be) hospitalized　にゅういんする　入院する [irr.]　読L21-II
host family　ホストファミリー　読L9-II, 会L11
hot (thing)　あつい　熱い　会L5
hot (weather)　あつい　暑い　会L5
hot and spicy　からい　辛い　会L13
hot spring　おんせん　温泉　会L11
hot water　おゆ　お湯　会L17
hotel　ホテル　会L4
...hours　〜じかん　〜時間　会L4
house　いえ　家　会L3
house　うち　会L3
(someone's) house　おたく　お宅　会L20

house husband　しゅふ　主夫　読L17-II
housewife　しゅふ　主婦　会L1
housework　かじ　家事　会L22
how　どう　会L8
how　どうやって　会L10
how (polite expression of どう)　いかが　読L19-II
How about ...?　どうですか　会L3
How do you do?　はじめまして　会G
How is ...?　どうですか　会L3
how long　どのぐらい　会L10
how much　いくら　会L2
how much　どのぐらい　会L10
however　しかし　読L17-II
however　ところが　会L21-II
humble expression for あげる　さしあげる　差し上げる [ru]　会L20
humble expression for もらう　いただく　頂く [u]　会L20
humbly ask　うかがう　伺う [u]　会L20
humbly visit　うかがう　伺う [u]　会L20
(become) hungry　おなかがすく [u]　会L11
hurry　いそぐ　急ぐ [u]　会L6
hurt　いたい　痛い　会L12
(your/someone's) husband　ごしゅじん　ご主人　会L14

I　わたし　私　会L1
I (formal)　わたくし　私　会L13
I (used by men)　ぼく　僕　会L5
I am ....　〜です　会G
I am not sure ...　さあ　会L14
I did it!　やった！　読L20-II
I do not know　しりません　知りません　会L7
I don't think so.　そんなこと（は）ない　会L22
I have an idea!　そうだ！　読L20-II
I know　しっています　知っています　会L7
I see. (casual)　そうか　会L17
I see.　そうですか　会L1
I wonder ... (casual)　〜かな（あ）　会L17
ice cream　アイスクリーム　会L3
ideal　りそう　理想　会L23
if ...　もし〜たら　読L19-III
if it is okay (polite)　よろしかったら　会L20
if possible　できれば　会L20
if that is the case, ...　じゃあ　会L2
if you like　よかったら　会L7
I'll go and come back.　いってきます　会G
illness　びょうき　病気　会L9, 会L12(e)
I'm home.　ただいま　会G
I'm sorry.　ごめんなさい　会L4

I'm sorry.　すみません　会G
I'm sorry. (casual)　ごめん　会L16
I'm very sorry.　しつれいしました　失礼しました　会L20
important　たいせつ（な）　大切　会L18
impossible　むり（な）　無理　会L18
in a few moments/days　もうすぐ　会L12
in addition　また　読L16-II
in class　じゅぎょうちゅうに　授業中に　会L16
in fact　じつは　実は　会L16
in fact　ほんとうは　本当は　会L19
(be) in someone's care　おせわになる　お世話になる [u]　読L19-II, 会L23
in the morning　ごぜんちゅう　午前中　読L9-II, 会L21
(be) in time　まにあう　間に合う [u]　会L22
in ... time　〜ご　〜後　会L10
income　しゅうにゅう　収入　読L18-II
inconvenient　つごうがわるい　都合が悪い　会L17
inconvenient　ふべん（な）　不便　読L21-II
incredible　すごい　会L13
India　インド　会L1
indulge in luxury　ぜいたくをする [irr.]　読L21-II
inexpensive　やすい　安い　会L5
influenza　インフルエンザ　会L12
injection　ちゅうしゃ　注射　会L12(e)
injury　けが　会L12(e)
insect　むし　虫　会L18
inside　なか　中　会L4
instead　かわりに　代わりに　読L22-II
instruct　おしえる　教える [ru]　会L6
insult　ばかにする [irr.]　会L21
insurance　ほけん　保険　会L15
interested (in)　きょうみがある　興味がある [u]　会L12
interesting　おもしろい　面白い　会L5
international　こくさい　国際　読L19-III
international relations　こくさいかんけい　国際関係　会L1
international student　りゅうがくせい　留学生　会L1
internet　インターネット　会L15
interview　めんせつ　面接　会L23
intimate　したしい　親しい　読L18-III
intravenous feeding　てんてき　点滴　会L12(e)
introduce　しょうかいする　紹介する [irr.]　会L11
invite　さそう　誘う [u]　会L15
invite　よぶ　呼ぶ [u]　会L19
invite someone (to an event/a place)　しょうたいする　招待する [irr.]　会L19

A B C D E F G H I J K L M N O P Q R S T U V W X Y Z

invite (someone) to a meal　ごちそうする [irr.]　会L19

iron (clothes)　アイロンをかける [ru]　会L16

(someone) is gone　いなくなる [u]　会L23

(a person) is in . . .　いる [ru]　会L4

Is that so?　そうですか　会L1

island　しま　島　読L15-II

it has been a long time　ひさしぶり　久しぶり　会L11

it is about time to . . .　そろそろ　会L23

Italy　イタリア　読L6-III

It's okay.　だいじょうぶ　大丈夫　会L5

J

jacket　ジャケット　会L15

January　いちがつ　一月　会L4(e)

Japan　にほん　日本　会L1

Japanese buckwheat noodles　そば　会L15

Japanese chess　しょうぎ　読L19-II

Japanese inn　りょかん　旅館　会L15

Japanese language　にほんご　日本語　会L1

Japanese people　にほんじん　日本人　会L1

Japanese traditional dress　きもの　着物　読L9-II, 会L13

jeans　ジーンズ　会L2

jilt　ふる [u]　会L21

job　しごと　仕事　会L8

journalist　ジャーナリスト　会L11

joyfully　たのしそうに　楽しそうに　読L22-II

juice　ジュース　会L12

July　しちがつ　七月　会L4(e)

June　ろくがつ　六月　会L4(e)

junior high school student　ちゅうがくせい　中学生　会L19

junior member of a group　こうはい　後輩　会L22

just . . .　〜だけ　会L11

K

Kabuki　かぶき　歌舞伎　会L9

kanji　かんじ　漢字　会L6

karaoke　カラオケ　会L8

karate　からて　空手　会L13

keep a promise　やくそくをまもる　約束を守る [u]　会L13

keep company　つきあう　付き合う [u]　会L15

keep (someone) waiting　またせる　待たせる [ru]　会L20

key　かぎ　鍵　会L17

kick　ける [u]　会L21

. . . kilograms　〜キロ　会L13

. . . kilometers　〜キロ　会L13

kimono　きもの　着物　読L9-II, 会L13

kind　しんせつ（な）　親切　会L7

kind (person)　やさしい　会L5

kind, a　しゅるい　種類　会L19

kiss　キスをする [irr.]　会L23-II

knit　あむ　編む [u]　会L13

(get to) know　しる　知る [u]　会L7

Korea　かんこく　韓国　会L1, 会L2

L

ladders　はしご　読L17-II

lake　みずうみ　湖　会L11

landlady　おおやさん　大家さん　会L14

landlord　おおやさん　大家さん　会L14

. . . language　〜ご　〜語　会L1

language　ことば　言葉　会L13

large　おおきい　大きい　会L5

large spa　だいよくじょう　大浴場　会L15(e)

larger apartment building　マンション　会L13

last month　せんげつ　先月　会L4(e), 会L9

last train　しゅうでん　終電　会L10(e)

last train (of the day)　しゅうでん　終電　会L21

last week　せんしゅう　先週　会L4, 会L4(e)

last year　きょねん　去年　会L4(e), 会L9

lastly　さいごに　最後に　読L8-II

late　おそい　遅い　会L10

(do something) late　おそく　遅く　読L4-III, 会L8

late (for)　おそくなる　遅くなる [u]　会L8

late (for an appointment)　ちこくする　遅刻する [irr.]　会L11

later on　あとで　後で　会L6

laugh　わらう　笑う [u]　会L16

lawyer　べんごし　弁護士　会L1, 会L13

lay　おく　置く [u]　会L21

lazy person　なまけもの　怠け者　会L19

lead a life　せいかつする　生活する [irr.]　会L20

learn　ならう　習う [u]　会L11

leave　のこす　残す [u]　読L15-II

leave (someone/something) alone　ほ（う）っておく　放っておく [u]　会L22

leave behind　わすれる　忘れる [ru]　会L6

left　ひだり　左　会L4

left side　ひだりがわ　左側　会L6(e)

leg　あし　足　会L7(e), 会L12

leisurely　ゆっくり　会L6

lend　かす　貸す [u]　会L16

less than . . .　〜みまん　〜未満　読L18-II

let me see . . .　ええと　会L16

Let me see.　そうですね　会L3

letter　じ　字　会L20

letter　てがみ　手紙　会L9

letter　もじ　文字　読L17-II

letter of recommendation　すいせんじょう　推薦状　会L16

library　としょかん　図書館　会L2

license　めんきょ　免許　会L22

life　せいかつ　生活　会L10

light　かるい　軽い　会L20

light　でんき　電気　会L6

light blue　みずいろ　水色　会L9(e)

like　すき（な）　好き　会L5

(X) like . . .　〜みたいなX　会L20

like this　このように　読L23-II

like this　こんなふう　会L22

. . . like this　こんな〜　会L14

line number . . .　〜ぎょうめ　〜行目　会L11(e)

listen　きく　聞く [u]　会L3

literature　ぶんがく　文学　会L1, 読L7-II

little, a　すくない　少ない　会L17

little, a　すこし　少し　読L7-II, 会L21

little, a　ちょっと　会L3

little more, a　もうすこし　もう少し　会L22

live　すむ　住む [u]　会L7

lively　にぎやか（な）　会L5

living　せいかつ　生活　会L10

living alone　ひとりぐらし　一人暮らし　会L22

living with a local family　ホームステイ　会L8

local (train)　ふつう　普通　会L10(e)

lock　かぎ　鍵　会L17

lock　かぎをかける　鍵をかける [ru]　会L17

lonely　さびしい　寂しい　会L9

long　ながい　長い　会L7

long for　なつかしい　読L19-II

long time　ながいあいだ　長い間　読L21-II

look . . . (facial expression)　〜かおをする　〜顔をする [irr.]　会L23

look at　みる　見る [ru]　会L3

look for　さがす　探す [u]　会L15

look forward (to)　（〜を）たのしみにする　楽しみにする [irr.]　読L7-II

look forward to it　たのしみです　楽しみです　会L15

look good (on somebody)　にあう　似合う [u]　会L14

look into (a matter)　しらべる　調べる [ru]　会L15

look pale　かおがあおい　顔が青い　会L9(e)

looking after a house during someone's absence　るすばん　留守番　会L23

looking for . . .　〜ぼしゅう　〜募集　読L11-II

nine o'clock　くじ　九時　会L1(e)

nineteen minutes　じゅうきゅうふん
　十九分　会L1(e)

1960's　せんきゅうひゃくろくじゅうね
　んだい　1960年代　読L17-II

ninth day of a month, the　ここのか
　九日　会L4(e)

no　ううん　会L8

No.　いいえ　会G

no good　だめ(な)　会L13

no matter what　ぜったいに　絶対に
　読L20-II

noisy　うるさい　会L22

non-smoking　きんえん　禁煙
　会L15(e)

noon　ひる　昼　読L9-II

north　きた　北　会L6(e)

nose　はな　鼻　会L7(e)

not ... anything　なにも ＋ negative
　何も　会L7

not any longer　もう〜ない　読L13-II

not at all　ぜんぜん ＋ negative　全然
　会L3

Not at all.　いいえ　会G

not at home　るす　留守　会L21

not busy　ひま(な)　暇　会L5

not much　あまり ＋ negative　会L3

not spacious　せまい　狭い　会L12

not to feel well　きぶんがわるい　気分
　が悪い　会L12(e)

Not to worry.　だいじょうぶ　大丈夫
　会L5

not ... yet　まだ ＋ negative　会L8

notebook　ノート　会L2

nothing in particular　べつに ＋
　negative　別に　会L7

nothing more than ...　ただの〜
　読L21-II

notice　きがつく　気が付く [u]　会L21

novel　しょうせつ　小説　会L20

November　じゅういちがつ　十一月
　会L4(e)

now　いま　今　会L1

number　ばんごう　番号　会L1

number ...　〜ばん　〜番
　会L1, 会L11(e)

nurse　かんごし　看護師　会L1

O

object　もくてき　目的　読L18-II

object to　はんたいする　反対する [irr.]
　会L22

obstetrician and gynecologist　さんふ
　じんか　産婦人科　会L12(e)

occupation　しごと　仕事　会L1

occur　おこる　起こる [u]　読L21-II

o'clock　〜じ　〜時　会L1

October　じゅうがつ　十月　会L4(e)

of course　もちろん　会L7

office worker　かいしゃいん　会社員
　会L1, 会L8

office worker　サラリーマン　会L17

often　よく　会L3

okay　まあまあ　会L11

old (thing)　ふるい　古い　会L5

old days　むかし　昔　会L21

old man　おじいさん　会L7

old woman　おばあさん　会L7

older brother　おにいさん　お兄さん
　会L1, 会L7

(my) older brother　あに　兄　会L7

older sister　おねえさん　お姉さん
　会L1, 会L7

(my) older sister　あね　姉　会L7

on　うえ　上　会L4

(be) on close terms　なかがいい　仲が
　いい　会L19

on foot　あるいて　歩いて　会L10

(be) on good terms　なかがいい　仲が
　いい　会L19

on the contrary　ところが　読L21-II

(be) on the heavy side　ふとっています
　太っています　会L7

on the other hand　いっぽう　一方
　読L23-II

on time　じかんどおり　時間通り
　読L13-III

once a year　いちねんにいちど　一年に
　一度　読L12-II

once in a lifetime　いっしょうにいちど
　一生に一度　読L13-II

once upon a time　むかしむかし　昔々
　読L10-II

one　ひとつ　一つ　会L9

one ...　ある〜　読L12-II

one day　いちにち　一日　会L13

one hour　いちじかん　一時間　会L4

one minute　いっぷん　一分　会L1(e)

one more time　もういちど　もう一度
　会L15

one night with two meals　いっぱくに
　しょくつき　一泊二食付き　会L15(e)

one o'clock　いちじ　一時　会L1, 会L1(e)

one person　ひとり　一人　会L7

one way　かたみち　片道　会L10(e)

oneself　じぶん　自分　読L10-II, 会L17

onion　たまねぎ　会L8(e)

only ...　〜だけ　会L11

open (something)　あける　開ける [ru]
　会L6

(something) opens　あく　開く [u]
　会L18

operation　しゅじゅつ　手術　会L12(e)

ophthalmologist　がんか　眼科
　会L12(e)

oppose　はんたいする　反対する [irr.]
　会L22

or　〜か〜　会L10

... or more　〜いじょう　〜以上
　読L18-II

orange　オレンジ　会L9(e)

originally　ほんとうは　本当は　会L19

orthopedic surgeon　せいけいげか　整
　形外科　会L12(e)

other　ほかの　他の　会L16

other day, the　このあいだ　この間
　読L8-II, 会L16

other person, the　あいて　相手　会L22

other side, the　むこう　向こう
　読L12-II

other than ...　〜いがい　〜以外　会L16

otorhinolaryngologist　じびか　耳鼻科
　会L12(e)

our person in charge　かかりのもの
　係の者　会L20

outdoor activities　アウトドア　読L11-II

outside　そと　外　会L18

over there　あそこ　会L2

over there　むこう　向こう　読L12-II

oversleep　あさねぼうする　朝寝坊す
　る [irr.]　会L16

overtime work　ざんぎょう　残業
　読L8-II, 会L17

overweight　ふとる　太る [u]　会L7

own (a pet)　かう　飼う [u]　会L11

P

page　ページ　会L6

page number ...　〜ページ　会L11(e)

painful　いたい　痛い　会L12

painkiller　いたみどめ　痛み止め
　会L12(e)

paint　かく　描く [u]　会L15

painting　え　絵　会L15

panda　パンダ　会L17

paper　かみ　紙　会L17

(term) paper　レポート　会L4

paper bag　ふくろ　袋　会L23

parent　おや　親　会L16

parenthesis　かっこ　会L11(e)

parents　りょうしん　両親　会L14

park　こうえん　公園　会L4

participate　さんかする　参加する [irr.]
　会L15

partner　あいて　相手　会L22

partner　パートナー　会L14

(something/someone) parts from　は
　なれる　離れる [ru]　会L23

part-time job　アルバイト　会L4

party　パーティー　会L8

party of ... people　〜めいさま　〜名
　様　会L19

pass　とおる　通る [u]　読L15-II

(time) pass　たつ　[u]　読L19-II

passbook　つうちょう　通帳　会L13(e)

passbook update　つうちょうきにゅう
　通帳記入　会L13(e)

past むかし 昔 会L21
pastime しゅみ 趣味 会L20
patient がまんする 我慢する [irr.] 会L23
pay はらう 払う [u] 会L12
peace へいわ 平和 読L15-II
Peace Memorial Museum へいわき ねんしりょうかん 平和記念資料館 読L15-II
peach もも 会L8(e)
peanut ピーナッツ 会L8(e)
pen ペン 会L2
pencil えんぴつ 鉛筆 L2(e), 会L14
people ひとびと 人々 読L12-II
...people 〜じん 〜人 会L1
perform やる [u] 会L5
period せいり 生理 会L12(e)
perm パーマ 会L17(e)
person ひと 人 会L4
...person(s) 〜めい 〜名 会L15(e)
person on one's side みかた 味方 読L16-II
personal computer パソコン 会L6
personal identification number あんしょうばんごう 暗証番号 会L13(e)
personality せいかく 性格 会L19
pervert ちかん 会L21
pet ペット 会L15
Philippines フィリピン 会L1
photograph しゃしん 写真 会L4
physical labor (such as construction) ちからしごと 力仕事 読L18-III
physician ないか 内科 会L12(e)
piano ピアノ 会L9
pick up (something) ひろう 拾う [u] 会L22
picture え 絵 会L15
picture しゃしん 写真 会L4
pink ピンク 会L9(e)
pitiful かわいそう(な) 読L12-II, 会L23
pizza ピザ 読L6-III, 会L9
place おく 置く [u] 会L21
place ところ 所 会L8
place ばしょ 場所 読L15-II, 会L23
place an order ちゅうもんする 注文する [irr.] 会L18
place of origin くに 国 会L6
plan よてい 予定 会L15
plastic bag ふくろ 袋 会L23
plate (お)さら (お)皿 会L14
platform ホーム 会L10(e), 読L22-II
play あそぶ 遊ぶ [u] 会L6
play (a string instrument or piano) ひく 弾く [u] 会L9
Please. どうぞ 会L2
..., please. (〜を)おねがいします 会L2
Please give me... (〜を)ください 会L2

Please give my best regards (to...). よろしくおつたえください よろしくお伝えください 会L19
Please go and come back. いってらっしゃい 会G
pleasure たのしみ 楽しみ 読L21-II
P.M. ごご 午後 会L1
pocket ポケット 読L16-II
poem し 詩 読L17-II
...points 〜てん 〜点 会L11
police けいさつ 警察 会L21
police officer けいさつかん 警察官 会L11
police station けいさつ 警察 会L21
polish みがく 磨く [u] 会L13
polite expression ていねいないいかた ていねいな言い方 会L11(e)
politics せいじ 政治 会L1, 会L12
poor びんぼう(な) 貧乏 会L22
poor at... へた(な) 下手 会L8
poor thing かわいそう(な) 会L23
popcorn ポップコーン 会L18
popular にんきがある 人気がある [u] 会L9
popular (in terms of romantic interest) もてる [ru] 会L19
pork ぶたにく 豚肉 会L8(e)
pork cutlet とんかつ 会L2
portfolio ファイル 会L16
post はる 貼る [u] 会L21
post office ゆうびんきょく 郵便局 会L2
poster ポスター 会L21
pot なべ 読L13-II
potato じゃがいも 会L8(e)
poultry とり 鳥 読L13-II
practice れんしゅうする 練習する [irr.] 会L10
praise ほめる [ru] 会L21
pray おいのりする お祈りする [irr.] 会L17
precious たいせつ(な) 大切 会L18
preparation じゅんび 準備 会L17
preparation of a lesson よしゅう 予習 会L22
present プレゼント 会L12
preserve のこす 残す [u] 読L15-II
president of a company しゃちょう 社長 会L11
president of a country だいとうりょう 大統領 会L11
press おす 押す [u] 会L18
price ねだん 値段 読L20-II
prime minister しゅしょう 首相 会L17
probably たぶん 多分 会L12
Professor... せんせい 先生 会L1
project プロジェクト 会L22
promise やくそく 約束 会L13

pronunciation はつおん 発音 会L11(e)
propose marriage プロポーズする [irr.] 会L14
proverb ことわざ 読L23-II
pudding プリン 読L13-III
punch なぐる 殴る [u] 会L21
purple むらさき 紫 会L9(e)
purpose もくてき 目的 読L18-II
push おす 押す [u] 会L18
put おく 置く [u] 会L21
put (something) in いれる 入れる [ru] 会L16
put makeup on けしょうする 化粧する [irr.] 会L17
put on (a hat) かぶる [u] 会L7
put on (clothes above your waist) きる 着る [ru] 会L7
put on (glasses) (めがねを)かける (眼鏡を)かける [ru] 会L7
put on (items below your waist) はく [u] 会L7
put (a hat) on a person's head かぶせる [ru] 読L10-II

Q

quarrel けんかする [irr.] 会L11
question しつもん 質問 会L11(e), 読L19-III
questionnaire アンケート 読L8-II
quiet しずか(な) 静か 会L5
quit やめる [ru] 会L11

R

radio ラジオ 会L14
rain あめ 雨 会L8
rain stops, the あめがやむ 雨がやむ [u] 会L23
raise そだてる 育てる [ru] 会L22
rare めずらしい 読L13-II
rash はっしん 発疹 会L12(e)
read よむ 読む [u] 会L3
(be) realized かなう [u] 読L12-II
really ほんとうに 本当に 読L14-II, 会L18
really (very polite) まことに 誠に 会L20
Really? ほんとうですか 本当ですか 会L6
realm ぶんや 分野 読L17-II
recall おもいだす 思い出す [u] 読L19-II
recently さいきん 最近 会L15
reception desk うけつけ 受付 会L22
receptionist フロント 会L15(e)
rechargeable card such as Suica, Icoca, Pasmo, etc. こうつうけいアイシーカード 交通系ICカード 会L10(e)
recruitment ぼしゅう 募集 会L13

red　あかい　赤い　会L9, 会L9(e)

refrain from　えんりょする　遠慮する　[irr.]　会L19

refrigerator　れいぞうこ　冷蔵庫　会L18

reject　ふる　[u]　会L21

relatives　しんせき　親せき　会L16

rent　やちん　家賃　会L18

reply　(お)へんじ　(お)返事　読L11-II, 会L16

request help　おねがいする　お願いする　[irr.]　会L22

rescue　たすける　助ける　[ru]　読L16-II, 会L22

research　けんきゅう　研究　会L16

researcher　けんきゅうしゃ　研究者　会L11

reservation　よやく　予約　会L10

reserve　よやくする　予約する　[irr.]　会L15

reserved seat　していせき　指定席　会L10(e)

rest　やすむ　休む　[u]　会L6

rest, the　あと　後　会L18

restaurant　レストラン　会L4

restroom　おてあらい　お手洗い　会L12

restroom　トイレ　会L2

result　けっか　結果　会L23

résumé　りれきしょ　履歴書　会L14

return　かえる　帰る　[u]　会L3

return　もどる　戻る　[u]　読L16-II, 会L20

return (a thing)　かえす　返す　[u]　会L6

return (as a token of gratitude)　おかえし　お返し　会L14

return (merchandise)　へんぴんする　返品する　[irr.]　会L20

review of a lesson　ふくしゅう　復習　会L22

rice　ごはん　ご飯　会L4

rice ball　おにぎり　会L20

rice cake　(お)もち　読L10-II

rich person　(お)かねもち　(お)金持ち　会L10

ride　のる　乗る　[u]　会L5

right　みぎ　右　会L4

right away　いますぐ　今すぐ　会L18

right away　すぐ　会L6

right side　みぎがわ　右側　会L6(e)

ring　ゆびわ　指輪　会L14

river　かわ　川　会L11

road　みち　道　会L16

rob　ぬすむ　盗む　[u]　会L21

robot　ロボット　読L16-II

room　へや　部屋　会L5

roommate　ルームメイト　会L11

round trip　おうふく　往復　会L10(e)

round-table discussion　ざだんかい　座談会　読L13-III

run　はしる　走る　[u]　会L11

run away　にげる　逃げる　[ru]　読L22-II

runny nose　はなみず　鼻水　会L12(e)

S

sack　ふくろ　袋　会L23

sad　かなしい　悲しい　読L10-II, 会L13

safe　あんぜん(な)　安全　会L21

sake　(お)さけ　(お)酒　会L3

salary　きゅうりょう　給料　会L17

salaryman　サラリーマン　会L17

salty　からい　辛い　会L13

same　おなじ　同じ　会L12

Saturday　どようび　土曜日　会L3, 会L4(e)

save money　ためる　[ru]　会L21

(be) saved　たすかる　助かる　[u]　会L18

savings　よきん　預金　会L13(e)

say　いう　言う　[u]　会L8

say nice things　ほめる　[ru]　会L21

scenery　けしき　景色　読L15-II

schedule　よてい　予定　会L15

scholarship　しょうがくきん　奨学金　会L16

school　がっこう　学校　会L3

schoolteacher　きょうし　教師　会L11

scramble crossing　スクランブルこうさてん　スクランブル交差点　読L15-II

scratch　ひっかく　[u]　読L20-II

sea　うみ　海　会L5

season　きせつ　季節　会L10

second　ふたつめ　二つ目　会L6(e)

second day of a month, the　ふつか　二日　会L4(e)

secondly　つぎに　次に　読L8-II

secret　ひみつ　秘密　読L16-II, 会L17

see　みる　見る　[ru]　会L3

see (a person)　あう　会う　[u]　会L4

See you. (lit., I'm leaving ahead of you.)　おさきにしつれいします　お先に失礼します　会L18

seldom　めったに〜ない　読L21-II

select　えらぶ　選ぶ　[u]　会L17

sell　うる　売る　[u]　読L10-II, 会L15

send　おくる　送る　[u]　会L14

senior member of a group　せんぱい　先輩　読L14-II, 会L22

separate　わかれる　別れる　[ru]　会L12

(something/someone) separates　はなれる　離れる　[ru]　会L12

September　くがつ　九月　会L4(e)

serious　まじめ(な)　読L12-II, 会L19

serious (illness)　おもい　重い　会L20

serving . . . areas　〜ほうめん　〜方面　会L10(e)

set　セット　会L17(e)

seven　ななつ　七つ　会L9

seven days　なのか　七日　会L13

seven minutes　ななふん　七分　会L1(e)

seven o'clock　しちじ　七時　会L1(e)

seventeen minutes　じゅうななふん　十七分　会L1(e)

seventh day of a month, the　なのか　七日　会L4(e)

shampoo　シャンプー　会L17(e), 会L18

shave　そる　[u]　会L17(e)

shave one's beard　ひげをそる　[u]　会L17

she　かのじょ　彼女　会L12

Shinkansen　しんかんせん　新幹線　会L10

ship　ふね　船　会L10

shirt　シャツ　会L14

shoes　くつ　靴　会L2

shop　ばいてん　売店　会L10(e)

shop　みせ　店　読L4-III, 会L13

. . . shop　〜や　〜屋　会L20

shopping　かいもの　買い物　会L4

shopping mall　ショッピングモール　会L17

short (length)　みじかい　短い　会L7

short (stature)　せがひくい　背が低い　会L7

short form of 〜(ん)でしょう　〜(ん)だろう　会L18

(be) shot　じゅうでうたれる　銃で撃たれる　読L17-II

shoulder　かた　肩　会L7(e)

show　あらわす　表す　[u]　読L23-II

show　みせる　見せる　[ru]　会L16

show (someone) around　あんないする　案内する　[irr.]　会L9-II, 会L16

shower　シャワー　会L6

shrine　じんじゃ　神社　会L11

shy person　はずかしがりや　恥ずかしがり屋　会L19

sickness　びょうき　病気　会L9, 会L12(e)

side　よこ　横　読L23-II

silver　ぎんいろ　銀色　会L9(e)

silver　シルバー　会L9(e)

simple　かんたん(な)　簡単　会L10

sing　うたう　歌う　[u]　会L7

singer　かしゅ　歌手　会L11

single room　シングル　会L15(e)

sit down　かける　[ru]　会L19

sit down　すわる　座る　[u]　会L6

six　むっつ　六つ　会L9

six days　むいか　六日　会L13

six minutes　ろっぷん　六分　会L1(e)

six o'clock　ろくじ　六時　会L1(e)

sixteen minutes　じゅうろっぷん　十六分　会L1(e)

sixth day of a month, the　むいか　六日　会L4(e)

size　おおきさ　大きさ　会L16

size L　エルサイズ　Lサイズ　会L5
ski　スキー　会L9
skillful　じょうず（な）　上手　会L8
skillfully　うまく　読L22-II
skirt　スカート　会L18
sky　そら　空　読L16-II
sky, the　てん　天　読L12-II
sleep　ねる　寝る [ru]　会L3
sleepy　ねむい　眠い　会L10
slow　おそい　遅い　会L10
slowly　ゆっくり　会L6
small　ちいさい　小さい　会L5
small train usually for tourists　トロッコれっしゃ　トロッコ列車　読L15-II
smaller apartment building　アパート　会L13
smart　あたまがいい　頭がいい　会L7
smartphone　スマホ　会L2
smile　にこにこする [irr.]　読L20-II
smoke　たばこをすう　たばこを吸う [u]　会L6
smoking　きつえん　喫煙　会L15(e)
snack　（お）かし　（お）菓子　会L11
snapping turtle　すっぽん　読L13-II
sneakers　スニーカー　会L20
sneeze　くしゃみ　会L12(e)
snow　ゆき　雪　読L10-II, 会L8
so　あんなに　読L20-II
..., so　〜けど　会L15
(I think) so　そう　会L9
so　だから　会L4
soba　そば　会L15
sober　まじめ（な）　読L12-II, 会L19
soccer　サッカー　会L10
social media　エスエヌエス　SNS　読L23-II
society　しゃかい　社会　会L23
socks　くつした　靴下　会L23
sofa　ソファ　会L18
(be) sold　うれる　売れる [ru]　読L20-II
somehow　なんだか　読L22-II
someone older　としうえ　年上　会L10
something　なにか　何か　会L8
something like ...　〜のようなもの　読L16-II
sometimes　ときどき　時々　会L3
song　うた　歌　会L7
Sorry to interrupt you.　しつれいします　失礼します　会L16
sort, a　しゅるい　種類　会L19
so-so　まあまあ　会L11
sound　おと　音　会L20
soup　スープ　会L18
south　みなみ　南　会L6(e), 読L15-II
souvenir　（お）みやげ　（お）土産　会L5
soy sauce　しょうゆ　しょう油　会L18
spa　おんせん　温泉　会L11
space alien　うちゅうじん　宇宙人　会L20

spacious　ひろい　広い　会L12
Spain　スペイン　会L8
speak　はなす　話す [u]　会L3
speech　スピーチ　会L21
spend time pleasantly　あそぶ　遊ぶ [u]　会L6
spoon　スプーン　会L17
sports　スポーツ　会L3
spring　はる　春　会L10
stairs　かいだん　階段　会L10(e), 会L23
stand　ばいてん　売店　会L10(e)
stand up　たつ　立つ [u]　会L6
station　えき　駅　読L6-I, 会L10
station attendant　えきいん（さん）　駅員（さん）　会L16
stay (at a hotel, etc.)　とまる　泊まる [u]　会L10
stay home do nothing　ごろごろする [irr.]　会L10
stay up all night　てつやする　徹夜する [irr.]　会L22
stays at ...　いる [ru]　会L4
steal　ぬすむ　盗む [u]　会L21
step on　ふむ　踏む [u]　会L21
stick　はる　貼る [u]　会L21
still　まだ　会L19
stingy　けち（な）　会L14
stomach　おなか　会L7(e), 会L12
stop　とまる　止まる [u]　読L20-II
stop by　よる　寄る [u]　会L19
store　みせ　店　読L4-III, 会L13
story　はなし　話　読L8-II, 会L19
straight　まっすぐ　読L6(e), 読L6-I
strange　へん（な）　変　会L21
strawberry　いちご　会L8(e)
stress　ストレス　読L8-II
strict　きびしい　厳しい　会L13
strike　なぐる　殴る [u]　会L21
strip of fancy paper　たんざく　読L12-II
strong　つよい　強い　会L17
student　がくせい　学生　会L1
student discount　がくわり　学割　会L10(e)
studio apartment　ワンルームマンション　読L18-III
study　べんきょうする　勉強する [irr.]　会L3
study abroad　りゅうがくする　留学する [irr.]　会L11
stuffed animal (e.g., teddy bear)　ぬいぐるみ　会L14
stylish　おしゃれ（な）　会L14
subordinate　ぶか　部下　会L22
subway　ちかてつ　地下鉄　会L10
successfully　うまく　読L22-II
such　あんなに　読L20-II
such ...　そんな〜　読L16-II, 会L23
suddenly　きゅうに　急に　会L14
suddenly　とつぜん　突然　読L19-III

sufficient　たりる　足りる [ru]　会L17
(suffix for names of children)　〜ちゃん　会L22
sugar　さとう　砂糖　会L16
summer　なつ　夏　会L8
Sunday　にちようび　日曜日　会L3, 会L4(e)
sunny weather　はれ　晴れ　会L8
super express　とっきゅう　特急　会L10(e)
supermarket　スーパー　会L4
superstition　めいしん　迷信　読L21-II
surfing　サーフィン　会L5
surgeon　げか　外科　会L12(e)
(be) surprised　びっくりする [irr.]　読L10-II, 会L21
survey　ちょうさ　調査　会L23
sushi　すし　会L10
sweater　セーター　会L13
sweatshirt　トレーナー　会L14
sweet　あまい　甘い　会L12
sweet bun　（お）まんじゅう　読L4-III
sweets　（お）かし　（お）菓子　会L11
swim　およぐ　泳ぐ [u]　会L5
swimming pool　プール　会L15
swimwear　みずぎ　水着　読L13-III
switch　スイッチ　会L18
symbol　きごう　記号　読L23-II
sympathize　どうじょうする　同情する [irr.]　会L23

take (a class)　とる　取る [u]　読L7-II, 会L11
take (a picture)　とる　撮る [u]　会L4
take (a thing)　もっていく　持っていく [u]　会L8
take (amount of time/money)　かかる [u]　会L10
take (an examination)　うける　受ける [ru]　読L19-III, 会L22
take a bath　（お）ふろにはいる　（お）風呂に入る [u]　会L8
take a nap　ひるねをする　昼寝をする [irr.]　会L21
take a shower　シャワーをあびる　シャワーを浴びる [ru]　会L6
take a walk　さんぽする　散歩する [irr.]　会L9
Take care.　では、おげんきで　では、お元気で　読L5-II
take care of ...　せわをする　世話をする [irr.]　会L23
take care of oneself　からだにきをつける　体に気をつける [ru]　読L7-II
Take care of yourself.　げんきでね　元気でね　会L23
take good care of　たいせつにする　大切にする [irr.]　読L19-II

take medicine　くすりをのむ　薬を飲む [u]　会L9

take off　とる [u]　読L10-II

take off (clothes)　ぬぐ　脱ぐ [u]　会L17

take (something) out　だす　出す [u]　会L16

take (someone) to (a place)　つれていく　連れていく [u]　会L16

talk　はなし　話　読L8-II, 会L19

talk　はなす　話す [u]　会L3

talk behind someone's back　わるぐちをいう　悪口を言う [u]　会L23

tall (stature)　せがたかい　背が高い　会L7

tax　ぜいきん　税金　会L15

taxi　タクシー　読L13-III

teach　おしえる　教える [ru]　会L6

teacher　せんせい　先生　会L1

teahouse　ちゃみせ　茶店　読L20-II

telephone　でんわ　電話　会L1

tell a lie　うそをつく [u]　会L11

temperature (weather)　きおん　気温　会L8

temple　（お）てら　（お）寺　会L4

tempura　てんぷら　天ぷら　会L10

ten　とお　十　会L9

ten days　とおか　十日　会L13

ten minutes　じゅっぷん / じっぷん　十分　会L1(e)

ten o'clock　じゅうじ　十時　会L1(e)

tennis　テニス　会L3

tenth day of a month, the　とおか　十日　会L4(e)

terrapin　すっぽん　読L13-II

(food is) terrible　まずい　会L23

test　テスト　会L5

text　メッセージ　会L23

textbook　きょうかしょ　教科書　会L6

-th　～め　～目　会L15

...th floor　～かい　～階　会L20

Thank you.　ありがとう / ありがとうございます　会G

Thank you.　どうも　会L2

Thank you for the meal. (after eating)　ごちそうさま（でした）　会G

Thank you for the meal. (before eating)　いただきます　会G

Thank you in advance.　どうぞよろしくおねがいします　どうぞよろしくお願いします　読L19-III

thanks to ...　おかげで　会L18

that ...　その　会L2

that ... (over there)　あの　会L2

that kind of ...　そんな～　会L23

that one　それ　会L2

that one (over there)　あれ　会L2

that way (polite)　あちら　会L20

That would be fine.　けっこうです　結構です　会L6

That wouldn't be necessary.　けっこうです　結構です　会L6

That's right.　そうです　会L1

That's right.　そうですね　会L3

That's too bad.　ざんねん（ですね）　残念（ですね）　会L8

then　それで　会L19

then ...　じゃあ　会L2

...Then ...　すると　読L16-II

there　そこ　会L2

there are many ...　おおい　多い　会L12

there is ...　ある [u]　会L4

therefore　それで　会L19

therefore　だから　会L4

thermometer　たいおんけい　体温計　会L12(e)

these days　このごろ　会L10

thief　どろぼう　泥棒　会L21

thin　やせています　会L7

thin out (hair)　すく [u]　会L17(e)

thing (concrete object)　もの　物　会L12

things　こと　読L11-II, 会L21

think　おもう　思う [u]　会L8

think (about)　かんがえる　考える [ru]　会L18

third　みっつめ　三つ目　会L6(e)

third day of a month, the　みっか　三日　会L4(e)

(become) thirsty　のどがかわく　喉が渇く [u]　会L12

thirteen minutes　じゅうさんぷん　十三分　会L1(e)

thirty minutes　さんじゅっぷん / さんじっぷん　三十分　会L1(e)

this ...　この　会L2

this kind of ...　こんな～　会L14

this month　こんげつ　今月　会L4(e), 会L8

this morning　けさ　今朝　会L8

this one　これ　会L2

this person (polite)　こちら　会L11

this semester　こんがっき　今学期　会L11

this way　このように　読L23-II

this way (polite)　こちら　会L19

this week　こんしゅう　今週　会L4(e), 会L6

this year　ことし　今年　会L4(e), 会L10

three　みっつ　三つ　会L9

three days　みっか　三日　会L13

three minutes　さんぷん　三分　会L1(e)

three o'clock　さんじ　三時　会L1(e)

throat　のど　喉　会L12

through the introduction of　～のしょうかいで　～の紹介で　読L19-III

throw away　すてる　捨てる [ru]　会L8

throw up　はく　吐く　会L12(e)

Thursday　もくようび　木曜日　会L4, 会L4(e)

ticket　チケット　会L9

(train) ticket　きっぷ　切符　会L12

(boarding) ticket　じょうしゃけん　乗車券　会L10(e)

ticket vending area　きっぷうりば　切符売り場　会L10(e)

tidy up　かたづける　片付ける [ru]　会L18

till (a time)　～まで　会L5

time　じかん　時間　会L10

time of ...　～ころ　会L21

...times　～かい　～回　会L13

tip　チップ　読L13-III

(be) tired　つかれている　疲れている　読L8-II

(get) tired　つかれる　疲れる [ru]　会L11

to (a place/a time)　～まで　会L9

today　きょう　今日　会L3, 会L4(e)

together　いっしょに　一緒に　会L5

together with (a person)　～と　会L4

toilet　トイレ　会L2

tolerant　がまんする　我慢する [irr.]　会L23

tomato　トマト　会L8

tomorrow　あした　明日　会L3, 会L4(e)

tonight　こんばん　今晩　会L3

tool　どうぐ　道具　読L16-II

tooth　は　歯　会L7(e), 会L12

touch　さわる　触る [u]　会L21

(be) touched (by ...)　かんどうする　感動する [irr.]　会L13

tough (situation)　たいへん（な）　大変　読L5-II, 会L6

tour　ツアー　会L10

towel　タオル　会L18

town　まち　町　会L4

toy　おもちゃ　会L11

track number ...　～ばんせん　～番線　会L10(e)

traditional Japanese theatrical art　かぶき　歌舞伎　会L9

traffic light　しんごう　信号　会L6(e), 会L20

train　でんしゃ　電車　会L6

transfer　のりかえ　乗り換え　会L10(e)

translate　ほんやくする　翻訳する [irr.]　会L22

translate　やくす　訳す [u]　会L16

travel　りょこう　旅行　会L5

travel　りょこうする　旅行する [irr.]　会L10

travel agency　りょこうがいしゃ　旅行会社　会L17

treat (someone) to a meal　おごる [u]　会L16

treat (someone) to a meal　ごちそうする [irr.]　会L19

tree　き　木　会L22

trim　そろえる [ru]　会L17(e)

trip to a foreign country　かいがいりょ
こう　海外旅行　会L23
try hard　がんばる　頑張る [u]　会L13
T-shirt　ティーシャツ　Tシャツ　会L2
Tuesday　かようび　火曜日
会L4, 会L4(e)
tuition　じゅぎょうりょう　授業料
会L21
turn (right/left)　まがる　曲がる [u]
会L6(e), 会L20
turn off　けす　消す [u]　会L6
turn on　つける [ru]　会L6
(something) turns on　つく [u]　会L18
turtle　かめ　読L13-II
tutor　かていきょうし　家庭教師
読L18-III

TV　テレビ　会L3
twelve minutes　じゅうにふん　十二分
会L1(e)
twelve o'clock　じゅうにじ　十二時
会L1(e)
twentieth day of a month, the　はつか
二十日　会L4(e)
twenty minutes　にじゅっぷん / にじっ
ぷん　二十分　会L1(e)
twenty-fourth day of a month, the　に
じゅうよっか　二十四日　会L4(e)
twin room　ツイン　会L15(e)
two　ふたつ　二つ　会L9
two days　ふつか　二日　会L13
two minutes　にふん　二分　会L1(e)
two months ago　にかげつまえ　二か
月前　会L4(e)
two o'clock　にじ　二時　会L1(e)
two people　ふたり　二人　会L7
two people each　ふたりずつ　二人ず
つ　会L11(e)
two weeks ago　にしゅうかんまえ　二
週間前　会L4(e)
type　タイプ　読L22-II
typhoon　たいふう　台風　会L16

uh-huh　うん　会L8
uh-uh　ううん　会L8
um . . .　あのう　会L1
umbrella　かさ　傘　会L2
uncle　おじさん　会L14
under　した　下　会L4
underground　ちか　地下　読L15-II
understand　わかる [u]　会L4
unhurriedly　ゆっくり　会L6
(unit of currency used in the Edo
period, a)　りょう　両　読L20-II
university　だいがく　大学　会L1
unsuccessful　しっぱいする　失敗する
[irr.]　会L22
unusual　へん (な)　変　会L21
U.S.A.　アメリカ　会L1

use　つかう　使う [u]　会L6
usually　たいてい　会L3

Valentine's Day　バレンタインデー
会L14
various　いろいろ (な)　読L9-II, 会L13
vegetable　やさい　野菜　会L2
vertical　たて　縦　読L23-II
very　ずいぶん　会L17
very　とても　会L5
very fond of　だいすき (な)　大好き
会L5
very hard　いっしょうけんめい　一生懸
命　読L21-II
very soon　もうすぐ　会L12
visible　みえる　見える [ru]　会L15
visitor　おきゃくさん　お客さん　会L17
vocabulary　たんご　単語　会L9
voice　こえ　声　読L10-II
volunteer　ボランティア
読L11-II, 会L15

wait　まつ　待つ [u]　会L4
wait eagerly for . . .　まちどおしい　待
ち遠しい　読L22-II
wake (someone) up　おこす　起こす
[u]　会L16
walk　あるく　歩く [u]　会L12
walk (someone)　おくる　送る [u]
会L19
wallet　さいふ　財布　会L2
want　ほしい　欲しい　会L14
warm　あたたかい　暖かい　会L10
wash　あらう　洗う [u]　会L8
waste (money)　むだづかい　無駄遣い
会L22
watch　とけい　時計　会L2
watch　みる　見る [ru]　会L3
watch out　ちゅういする　注意する
[irr.]　会L14
water　みず　水　会L3
water boils　おゆがわく　お湯が沸く
[u]　会L18
watermelon　すいか　会L8(e)
way　みち　道　会L16
we　わたしたち　私たち　読L12-II, 会L14
weak　よわい　弱い　読L16-II
wear small items (necktie, watch, etc.)
する　[irr.]　会L17
weather　てんき　天気　会L5
weather forecast　てんきよほう　天気
予報　会L8
weave　はたをおる　はたを織る [u]
読L12-II
wedding　けっこんしき　結婚式　会L15
Wednesday　すいようび　水曜日
会L4, 会L4(e)

week after next, the　さらいしゅう　再
来週　会L4(e)
weekday　へいじつ　平日　読L11-II
weekend　しゅうまつ　週末　会L3
Welcome.　ようこそ　会L19
Welcome (to our store).　いらっしゃい
ませ　会L2
Welcome home.　おかえり (なさい)　会G
well　うまく　読L22-II
well　よく　会L14
well . . .　ええと　会L16
well then　それでは　読L19-II
well then (polite)　では　会L20
west　にし　西　会L6(e)
whale　くじら　読L15-II
what　なん / なに　何　会L1
what kind of . . .　どんな　会L5
What should I/we do?　どうしよう
会L18
what should one do　どうしたらいい
会L14
when　いつ　会L3
when . . .　〜ころ　会L21
when . . .　とき　時　会L4
where　どこ　会L2
where (polite)　どちら　会L19
which　どちら / どっち　会L10
which . . .　どの　会L2
which one　どれ　会L2
while . . .　〜ちゅう　〜中　読L19-II
white　しろい　白い　会L9, 会L9(e)
"White Day" (yet another gift-giving
day)　ホワイトデー　会L14
who　だれ　会L2
why　どうして　会L4
why　なぜ　会L4
wide　ひろい　広い　会L12
(your/someone's) wife　おくさん　奥さ
ん　会L14
(your/someone's) wife (polite)　おくさ
ま　奥様　会L19
win　かつ　勝つ [u]　会L22
win a championship　ゆうしょうする
優勝する [irr.]　会L23
win a lottery　たからくじにあたる　宝
くじに当たる [u]　会L17
wind　かぜ　風　会L22
wind blows, the　かぜがふく　風が吹
く [u]　会L22
window　まど　窓　会L2(e), 会L6
wine　ワイン　読L6-III
winter　ふゆ　冬　会L8
winter scarf　マフラー　会L14
wish　ねがい　願い　読L12-II
with (a tool)　〜で　会L10
with breakfast　ちょうしょくつき　朝
食付き　会L15(e)
withdraw (money)　おろす　下ろす [u]
会L15

withdrawal　（お）ひきだし　（お）引き
　出し　会L13(e)
woman　おんなのひと　女の人
　　　　　　　　　　　読L5-II, 会L7
word　たんご　単語　会L9
work　しごと　仕事　会L8
work　はたらく　働く [u]　会L7
work (of art, etc.)　さくひん　作品
　　　　　　　　　　　読L17-II
world　せかい　世界　会L10
worried　ふあん（な）　不安
　　　　　　　　読L13-II, 会L18
worried about　しんぱい（な）　心配
　　　　　　　　読L21-II, 会L22
worry　きにする　気にする [irr.]
　　　　　　　　　　　読L21-II
worry　しんぱいする　心配する [irr.]
　　　　　　　　　　　会L12
worry　なやみ　悩み　読L14-II, 会L19
worst, the　さいあく（な）　最悪　会L17
wrap　つつむ　包む [u]　会L21

write　かく　書く [u]　会L4
writer　さっか　作家　会L11
wrong　ちがう　違う [u]　会L23
wrong (×)　ばつ　会L11(e)

X

X-ray　レントゲン　会L12(e)

Y

year　とし　年　読L10-II
year after next, the　さらいねん　再来
　年　会L4(e)
year before last, the　おととし　会L4(e)
...year student　〜ねんせい　〜年生
　　　　　　　　　　　会L1
...years　〜ねん　〜年　会L10
...years old　〜さい　〜歳　会L1
yellow　きいろい　黄色い　会L9(e)
...yen　〜えん　〜円　会L2
yes　うん　会L8
yes　ええ　会L3

yes　はい　会L1
yesterday　きのう　昨日　会L4, 会L4(e)
you　あなた　会L4
You are right.　そうそう　会L23
You have my apologies.　もうしわけ
　ありません　申し訳ありません
　　　　　　　　読L19-III, 会L20
You must be tired after working so
　hard. (greeting between friends and
　coworkers)　おつかれさま（でした）
　お疲れ様（でした）　会L18
young　わかい　若い　会L9
young people　わかもの　若者
　　　　　　　　　　　読L15-II
younger brother　おとうと　弟
　　　　　　　　　　　会L1, 会L7
younger sister　いもうと　妹
　　　　　　　　　　　会L1, 会L7

Z

zoo　どうぶつえん　動物園　会L10

日本地図 Map of Japan
にほんちず

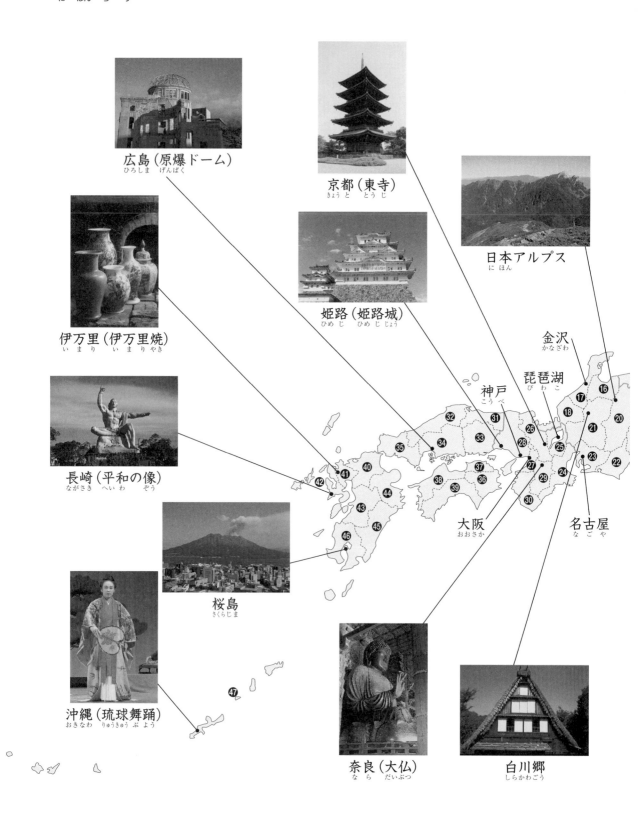

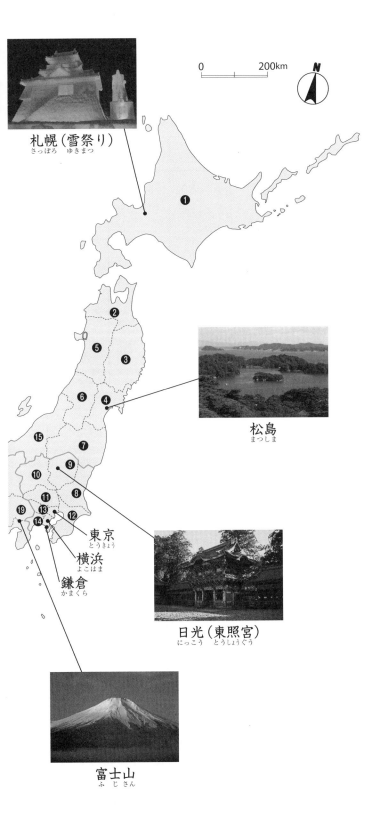

0 ──── 200km

N

札幌(雪祭り)
さっぽろ　ゆきまつ

松島
まつしま

日光(東照宮)
にっこう　とうしょうぐう

東京
とうきょう

横浜
よこはま

鎌倉
かまくら

富士山
ふじさん

北海道地方
ほっかいどう ち ほう
❶ 北海道
ほっかいどう

東北地方
とうほく ち ほう
❷ 青森県
あおもりけん
❸ 岩手県
いわ て けん
❹ 宮城県
みや ぎ けん
❺ 秋田県
あき た けん
❻ 山形県
やまがたけん
❼ 福島県
ふくしまけん

関東地方
かんとう ち ほう
❽ 茨城県
いばら き けん
❾ 栃木県
とち ぎ けん
❿ 群馬県
ぐん ま けん
⓫ 埼玉県
さいたまけん
⓬ 千葉県
ち ば けん
⓭ 東京都
とうきょうと
⓮ 神奈川県
か な がわけん

中部地方
ちゅうぶ ち ほう
⓯ 新潟県
にいがたけん
⓰ 富山県
と やまけん
⓱ 石川県
いしかわけん
⓲ 福井県
ふく い けん
⓳ 山梨県
やまなしけん
⓴ 長野県
なが の けん
㉑ 岐阜県
ぎ ふ けん
㉒ 静岡県
しずおかけん
㉓ 愛知県
あい ち けん

近畿地方
きん き ち ほう
㉔ 三重県
み え けん
㉕ 滋賀県
し が けん
㉖ 京都府
きょう と ふ
㉗ 大阪府
おおさか ふ
㉘ 兵庫県
ひょう ご けん
㉙ 奈良県
な ら けん
㉚ 和歌山県
わ か やまけん

中国地方
ちゅうごく ち ほう
㉛ 鳥取県
とっとりけん
㉜ 島根県
しま ね けん
㉝ 岡山県
おかやまけん
㉞ 広島県
ひろしまけん
㉟ 山口県
やまぐちけん

四国地方
し こく ち ほう
㊱ 徳島県
とくしまけん
㊲ 香川県
か がわけん
㊳ 愛媛県
え ひめけん
㊴ 高知県
こう ちけん

九州地方
きゅうしゅう ち ほう
㊵ 福岡県
ふくおかけん
㊶ 佐賀県
さ が けん
㊷ 長崎県
ながさきけん
㊸ 熊本県
くまもとけん
㊹ 大分県
おおいたけん
㊺ 宮崎県
みやざきけん
㊻ 鹿児島県
か ご しまけん
㊼ 沖縄県
おきなわけん

写真提供・協力:東寺／東大寺(撮影:矢野建彦)／奈良市観光協会／姫路市／伊万里市観光戦略課

数 かず N u m b e r s

	regular				h→p	h→p/b	p	k
1	いち				いっ p	いっ p	(いっ)	いっ
2	に							
3	さん				p	b		
4	よん	し	よ	よ	p			
5	ご							
6	ろく				ろっ p	ろっ p	(ろっ)	ろっ
7	なな	しち	しち					
8	はち				(はっ p)	はっ p	(はっ)	はっ
9	きゅう	く	く					
10	じゅう				じゅっ p じっ p	じゅっ p じっ p	じゅっ じっ	じゅっ じっ
how many	なん				p	b		
	～ドル dollars ～枚 (まい) sheets ～度 (ど) degrees ～十 (じゅう) ten ～万 (まん) ten thousand	～月 (がつ) month	～時 (じ) o'clock ～時間 (じ かん) hours	～年 (ねん) year ～年間 (ねんかん) years ～人 (にん) people ～円 (えん) yen	～分 (ふん) minute ～分間 (ふんかん) minutes	～本 (ほん) sticks ～杯 (はい) cups ～匹 (ひき) animals ～百 (ひゃく) hundred	～ページ page ～ポンド pounds	～か月 (げつ) months ～課 (か) lesson ～回 (かい) times ～個 (こ) small items

This chart shows how sounds in numbers (1-10) and counters change
according to their combination.
1. *Hiragana* indicate the sound changes in numbers, and letters
   show the changes in the initial consonant of counters.
2. ( ) means that the change is optional.
3. An empty box means no sound change occurs.

k→g	s	s→z	t	special vocabulary for numbers			
いっ	いっ	いっ	いっ	ひとつ	ついたち	ひとり	1
				ふたつ	ふつか	ふたり	2
g		z		みっつ	みっか		3
				よっつ	よっか		4
				いつつ	いつか		5
ろっ				むっつ	むいか		6
				ななつ	なのか		7
はっ	はっ	はっ	はっ	やっつ	ようか		8
				ここのつ	ここのか		9
じゅっ じっ	じゅっ じっ	じゅっ じっ	じゅっ じっ	とお	とおか		10
g		z		いくつ			how many
～階 floor ～軒 houses	～セント cents ～週間 weeks ～冊 books ～歳 years of age	～足 shoes ～千 thousand	～通 letters ～丁目 street address	small items years of age cf. はたち (20 years old)	date cf. じゅうよっか (14) はつか (20) にじゅうよっか (24) なんにち (how many)	people cf. ～人 (three or more people)	

活用表 Conjugation Chart
かつ よう ひょう

verb types	dictionary forms	long forms (*masu*) (L3)	*te*-forms (L6)	short past (L9)	short present neg. (L8)	short past neg. (L9)
irr.	する	します	して	した	しない	しなかった
irr.	くる	きます	きて	きた	こない	こなかった
ru	たべる	～ます	～て	～た	～ない	～なかった
u	かう	～います	～って	～った	～わない	～わなかった
u	まつ	～ちます	～って	～った	～たない	～たなかった
u	とる	～ります	～って	～った	～らない	～らなかった
u	ある	～ります	～って	～った	*ない	*なかった
u	よむ	～みます	～んで	～んだ	～まない	～まなかった
u	あそぶ	～びます	～んで	～んだ	～ばない	～ばなかった
u	しぬ	～にます	～んで	～んだ	～なない	～ななかった
u	かく	～きます	～いて	～いた	～かない	～かなかった
u	いく	～きます	*～って	*～った	～かない	～かなかった
u	いそぐ	～ぎます	～いで	～いだ	～がない	～がなかった
u	はなす	～します	～して	～した	～さない	～さなかった

The forms with * are exceptions.

potential (L13)	volitional (L15)	ば-forms (L18)	passive (L21)	causative (L22)	causative-passive (L23)
できる	しよう	すれば	される	させる	させられる
こられる	こよう	くれば	こられる	こさせる	こさせられる
〜られる	〜よう	〜れば	〜られる	〜させる	〜させられる
〜える	〜おう	〜えば	〜われる	〜わせる	〜わされる
〜てる	〜とう	〜てば	〜たれる	〜たせる	〜たされる
〜れる	〜ろう	〜れば	〜られる	〜らせる	〜らされる
		〜れば			
〜める	〜もう	〜めば	〜まれる	〜ませる	〜まされる
〜べる	〜ぼう	〜べば	〜ばれる	〜ばせる	〜ばされる
〜ねる	〜のう	〜ねば	〜なれる	〜なせる	〜なされる
〜ける	〜こう	〜けば	〜かれる	〜かせる	〜かされる
〜ける	〜こう	〜けば	〜かれる	〜かせる	〜かされる
〜げる	〜ごう	〜げば	〜がれる	〜がせる	〜がされる
〜せる	〜そう	〜せば	〜される	〜させる	〜させられる

著者紹介

•••••••••••••••••••••••••••••••••••

坂野 永理（ばんの えり）

テンプル大学で教育学博士号取得。南山大学、関西外国語大学を経て、岡山大学名誉教授。著書に『日本語コミュニケーションゲーム 80』『Kanji Look and Learn』（共著／ジャパンタイムズ出版）がある。

池田 庸子（いけだ ようこ）

ペンシルベニア州立大学で比較文学修士号取得。イースタン・ニュー・メキシコ大学、ペンシルベニア州立大学、関西外国語大学を経て、現在、茨城大学教授。著書に『Kanji Look and Learn』（共著／ジャパンタイムズ出版）がある。

大野 裕（おおの ゆたか）

上智大学で言語学修士号を取得後、マサチューセッツ大学アマースト校で博士コースに在籍。同校および関西外国語大学、名古屋大学留学生センターを経て、現在、立命館大学大学院言語教育情報研究科教授。

品川 恭子（しながわ ちかこ）

ウィスコンシン大学マジソン校で日本語学修士号取得。カリフォルニア大学アーバイン校、関西外国語大学、およびカリフォルニア大学サンタバーバラ校にて日本語教育に従事。著書に『Kanji Look and Learn』（共著／ジャパンタイムズ出版）がある。

渡嘉敷 恭子（とかしき きょうこ）

オハイオ州立大学で日本語言語学修士号取得。コネチカット・カレッジ、オハイオ州立大学を経て、現在、関西外国語大学教授。著書に『Kanji Look and Learn』（共著／ジャパンタイムズ出版）がある。

About the Authors

•••••••••••••••••••••••••••••••••••

Eri Banno is a professor emerita at Okayama University, and has previously taught Japanese at Nanzan University and Kansai Gaidai University. She earned her Ed.D. in education at Temple University. Her publications include the co-authored works *80 Communication Games for Japanese Language Teachers* and *Kanji Look and Learn* (both published by The Japan Times Publishing).

Yoko Ikeda is a professor at Ibaraki University, and has previously taught Japanese at Eastern New Mexico University, Pennsylvania State University, and Kansai Gaidai University. She earned her M.A. in comparative literature at Pennsylvania State University. Her publications include the co-authored *Kanji Look and Learn* (The Japan Times Publishing).

Yutaka Ohno is a professor at Ritsumeikan University's Graduate School of Language Education and Information Science (LEIS), and has previously taught Japanese at the University of Massachusetts Amherst, Kansai Gaidai University, and Nagoya University. He earned his M.A. in linguistics at Sophia University, and enrolled in a doctoral program at the University of Massachusetts-Amherst.

Chikako Shinagawa previously taught Japanese at the University of California (Irvine and Santa Barbara) and Kansai Gaidai University. She earned her M.A. in Japanese at the University of Wisconsin, Madison. Her publications include the co-authored *Kanji Look and Learn* (The Japan Times Publishing).

Kyoko Tokashiki is a professor at Kansai Gaidai University, and has previously taught Japanese at Connecticut College and Ohio State University. She earned her M.A. in Japanese linguistics at Ohio State University. Her publications include the co-authored *Kanji Look and Learn* (The Japan Times Publishing).

Apps for GENKI Users ——『げんき』関連アプリのご案内

GENKI Vocab for 3rd Ed.
1200 Essential Japanese Words
『げんき第3版』単語アプリ

By repeating a process of memorization and self-checking, you can efficiently master all words learned in GENKI.

「暗記学習」と「定着確認」を繰り返しながら「げんき」の全単語を効率よく学習。

▼iOS　　　▼Android

OTO Navi — Sound Navigator
Audio Player for The Japan Times Publishing's books
ジャパンタイムズ出版の音声アプリ

The audio material for GENKI is available through **OTO Navi— Sound Navigator**, an app for listening to audio material provided with books published by The Japan Times Publishing.

1. Scan the QR code below and download OTO Navi from App Store or Google Play.
2. Search for **GENKI Vol. 2 [3rd Ed.]** within the app.
3. Download the audio material and play it at your choice of five playback speeds!

『げんき』の音声は、ジャパンタイムズ出版の音声再生アプリ「**OTO Navi**」でお聞きください。

1. 下のQRコードで、App Store または Google Play から「OTO Navi」をダウンロード。
2. アプリ内で『**初級日本語げんき2** [第3版]』を検索。
3. 音声をダウンロードして、再生してください。5段階の速度変更機能付き。

▼iOS　　　▼Android

Kanji Introduced in the Reading and Writing Section
「読み書き編」学習漢字一覧
（よ）（か）（へん）（がくしゅうかんじ）（いちらん）

第3課	一 001	二 002	三 003	四 004	五 005	六 006	七 007	八 008	九 009	十 010	百 011	千 012	万 013	円 014	時 015	
第4課	日 016	本 017	人 018	月 019	火 020	水 021	木 022	金 023	土 024	曜 025	上 026	下 027	中 028	半 029		
第5課	山 030	川 031	元 032	気 033	天 034	私 035	今 036	田 037	女 038	男 039	見 040	行 041	食 042	飲 043		
第6課	東 044	西 045	南 046	北 047	口 048	出 049	右 050	左 051	分 052	先 053	生 054	大 055	学 056	外 057	国 058	
第7課	京 059	子 060	小 061	会 062	社 063	父 064	母 065	高 066	校 067	毎 068	語 069	文 070	帰 071	入 072		
第8課	員 073	新 074	聞 075	作 076	仕 077	事 078	電 079	車 080	休 081	言 082	読 083	思 084	次 085	何 086		
第9課	午 087	後 088	前 089	名 090	白 091	雨 092	書 093	友 094	間 095	家 096	話 097	少 098	古 099	知 100	来 101	
第10課	住 102	正 103	年 104	売 105	買 106	町 107	長 108	道 109	雪 110	立 111	自 112	夜 113	朝 114	持 115		
第11課	手 116	紙 117	好 118	近 119	明 120	病 121	院 122	映 123	画 124	歌 125	市 126	所 127	勉 128	強 129	有 130	旅 131
第12課	昔 132	々 133	神 134	早 135	起 136	牛 137	使 138	働 139	連 140	別 141	度 142	赤 143	青 144	色 145		
第13課	物 146	鳥 147	料 148	理 149	特 150	安 151	飯 152	肉 153	悪 154	体 155	同 156	着 157	空 158	港 159	昼 160	海 161
第14課	彼 162	代 163	留 164	族 165	親 166	切 167	英 168	店 169	去 170	急 171	乗 172	当 173	音 174	楽 175	医 176	者 177
第15課	死 178	意 179	味 180	注 181	夏 182	魚 183	寺 184	広 185	足 186	転 187	借 188	走 189	場 190	建 191	地 192	通 193
第16課	供 194	世 195	界 196	全 197	部 198	始 199	週 200	考 201	開 202	屋 203	方 204	運 205	動 206	教 207	室 208	以 209
第17課	野 210	習 211	主 212	歳 213	集 214	発 215	表 216	品 217	写 218	真 219	字 220	活 221	結 222	婚 223	歩 224	
第18課	目 225	的 226	洋 227	服 228	堂 229	力 230	授 231	業 232	試 233	験 234	貸 235	図 236	館 237	終 238	宿 239	題 240
第19課	春 241	秋 242	冬 243	花 244	様 245	不 246	姉 247	兄 248	漢 249	卒 250	工 251	研 252	究 253	質 254	問 255	多 256
第20課	皿 257	声 258	茶 259	止 260	枚 261	両 262	無 263	払 264	心 265	笑 266	絶 267	対 268	痛 269	最 270	続 271	
第21課	信 272	経 273	台 274	風 275	犬 276	重 277	初 278	若 279	送 280	幸 281	計 282	遅 283	配 284	弟 285	妹 286	
第22課	記 287	銀 288	回 289	夕 290	黒 291	用 292	末 293	待 294	残 295	駅 296	番 297	説 298	案 299	内 300	忘 301	守 302
第23課	顔 303	悲 304	怒 305	違 306	変 307	比 308	情 309	感 310	調 311	査 312	果 313	化 314	横 315	相 316	答 317	